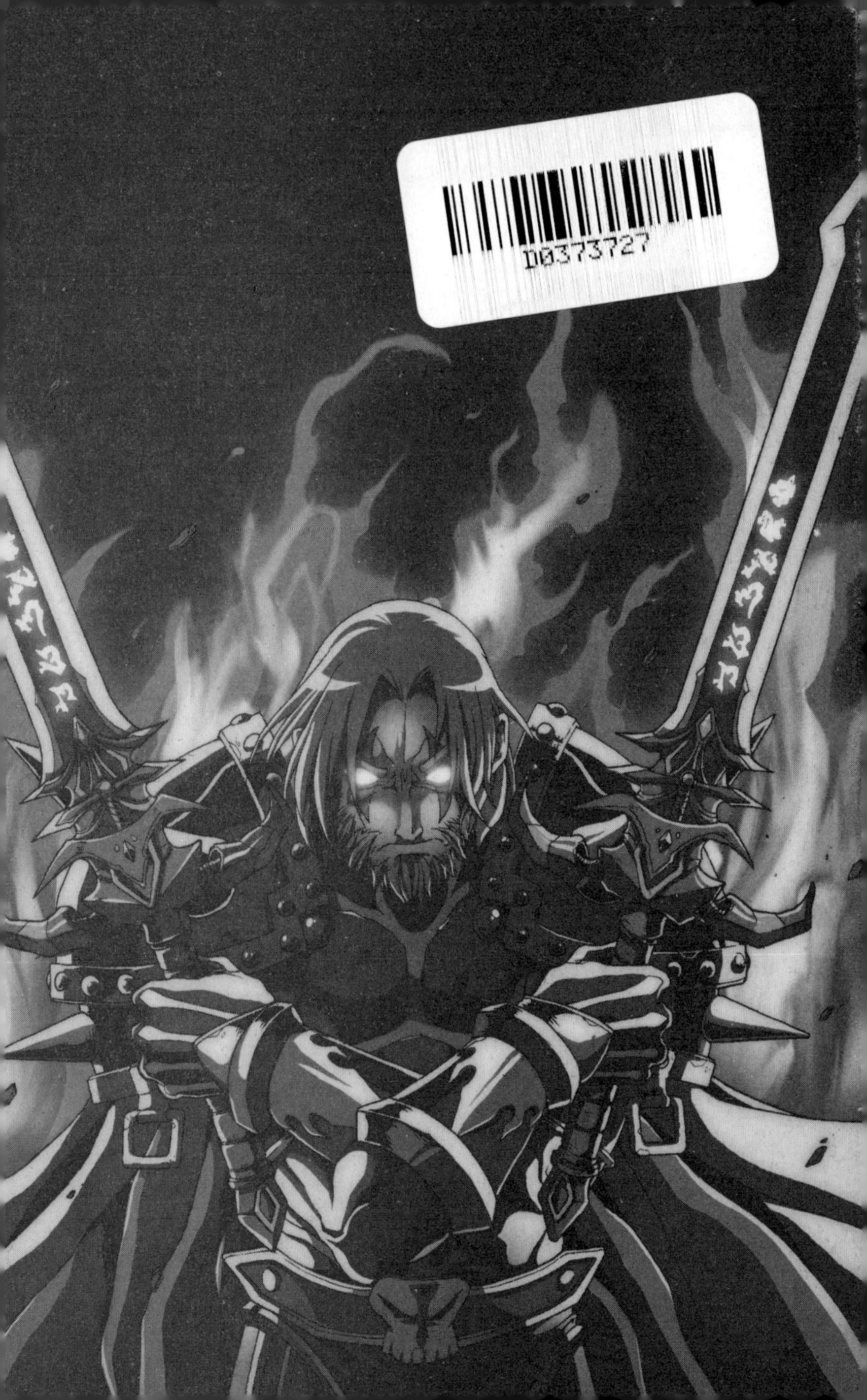

World Of Warcraft: Death Knight

Story by: Dan Jolley
Art by: Rocio Zucchi with Altercomics

Interior Designs, Retouch & Lettering - Michael Paolilli
Creative Consultant - Michael Paolilli
Cover Designer - Louis Csontos
Cover Artist - Rocio Zucchi

Editors - Troy Lewter & Paul Morrissey
Print Production Manager - Lucas Rivera
Managing Editor - Vy Nguyen
Senior Designer - Louis Csontos
Art Director - Al-Insan Lashley
Director of Sales and Manufacturing - Allyson De Simone
Associate Publisher - Marco F. Pavia
President and C.O.O. - John Parker
C.E.O. and Chief Creative Officer - Stu Levy

BLIZZARD ENTERTAINMENT
Senior Vice President, Creative Development - Chris Metzen
Director, Creative Development - Jeff Donais
Lead Developer, Licensed Products - Mike Hummel
Publishing Lead, Creative Development - Rob Tokar
Senior Story Developer - Micky Neilson
Story Developer - James Waugh
Art Director - Glenn Rane
Director, Global Business
Development and Licensing - Cory Jones
Associate Licensing Manager - Jason Bischoff
Historian - Evelyn Fredericksen
Additional Development - Samwise Didier and Tommy Newcomer

A **TOKYOPOP**® Manga

TOKYOPOP Inc.
5900 Wilshire Blvd. Suite 2000
Los Angeles, CA 90036

E-mail: info@TOKYOPOP.com
Come visit us online at www.TOKYOPOP.com

ISBN: 978-1-4278-1496-8

First TOKYOPOP printing: December 2009
10 9 8 7 6 5 4 3 2 1
Printed in the USA

WORLD OF WARCRAFT

DEATH KNIGHT

STORY BY
DAN JOLLEY

ART BY
ROCIO ZUCCHI

TOKYOPOP®

HAMBURG // LONDON // LOS ANGELES // TOKYO

WORLD OF WARCRAFT®

DEATH KNIGHT

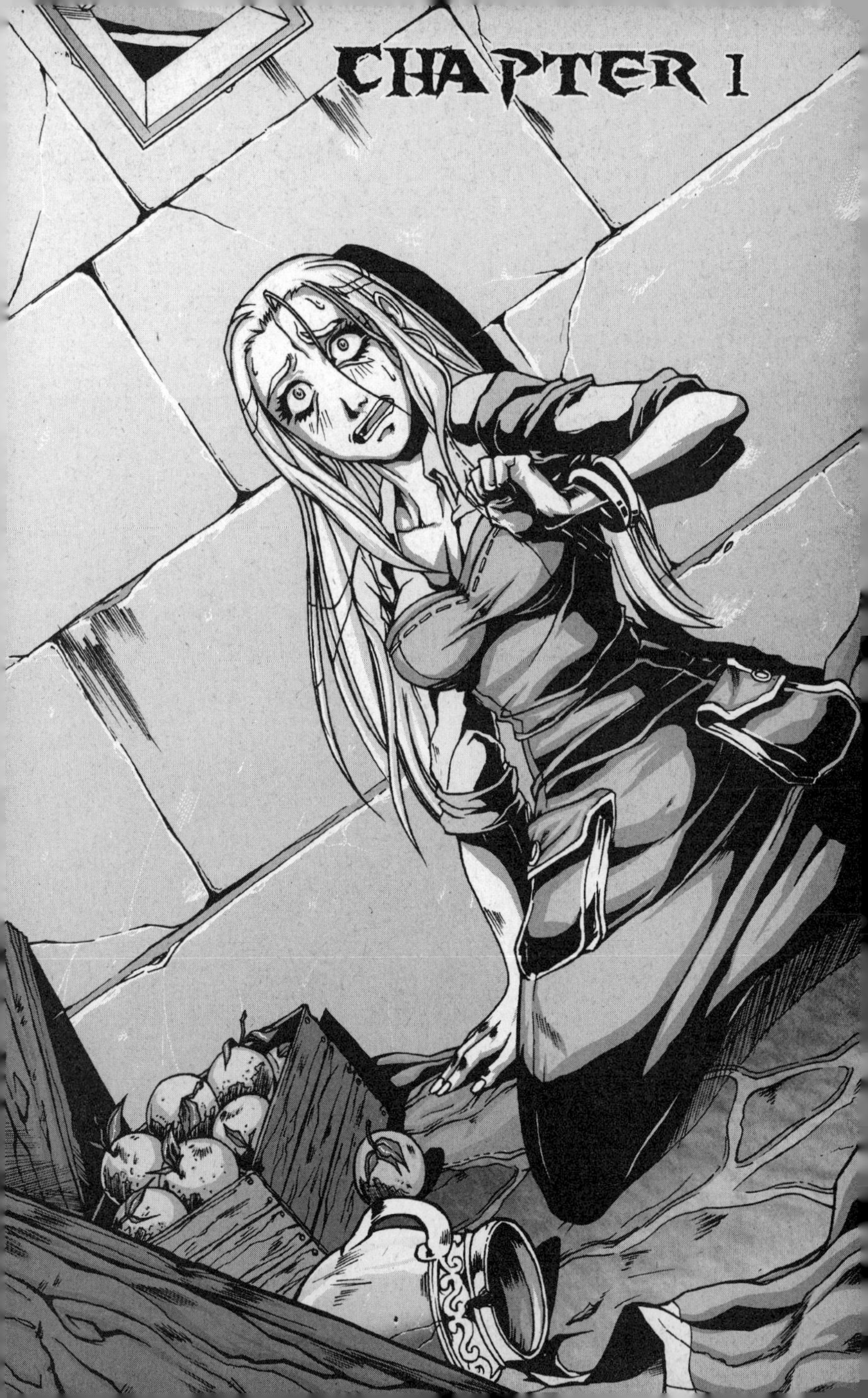
CHAPTER 1

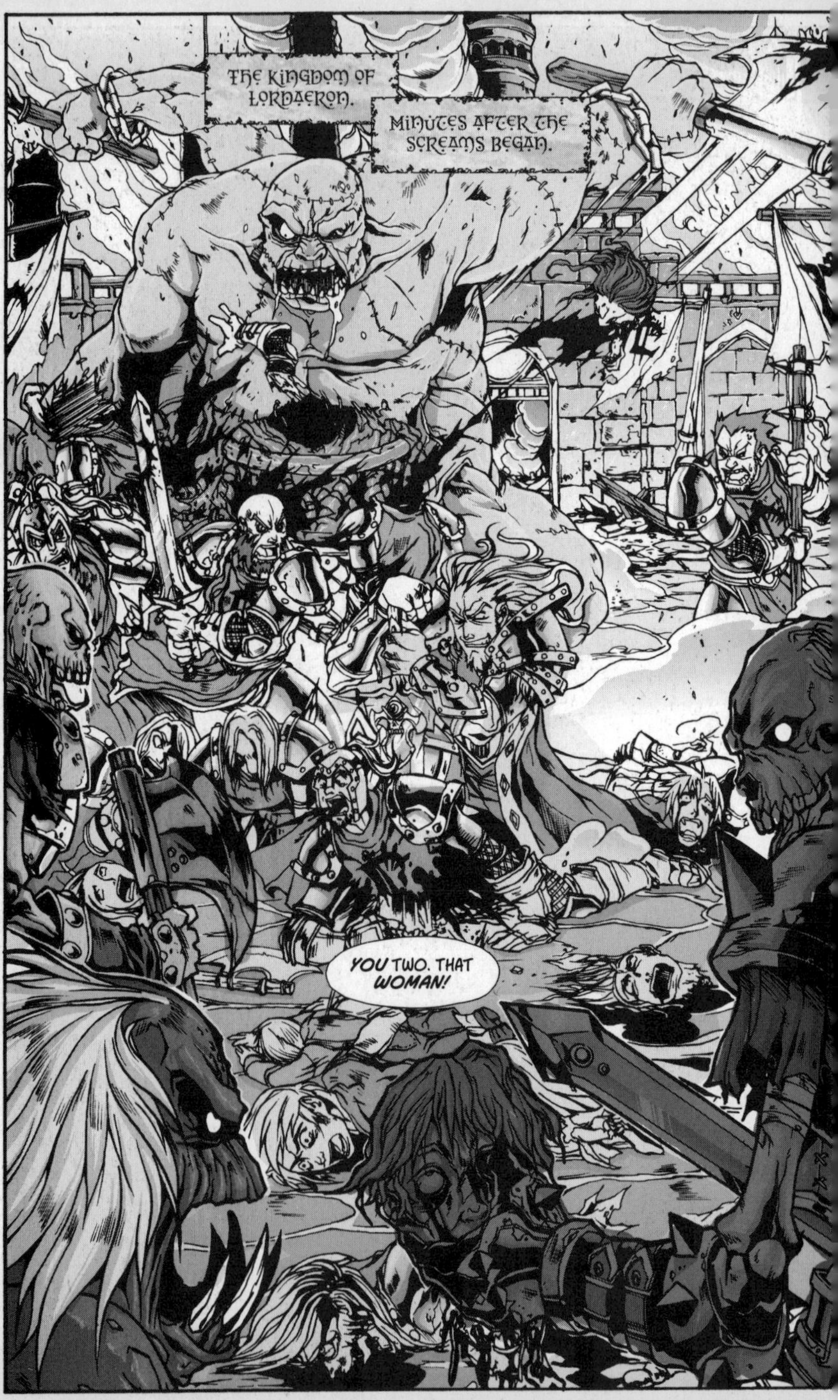
THE KINGDOM OF LORDAERON.
MINUTES AFTER THE SCREAMS BEGAN.
YOU TWO. THAT WOMAN!

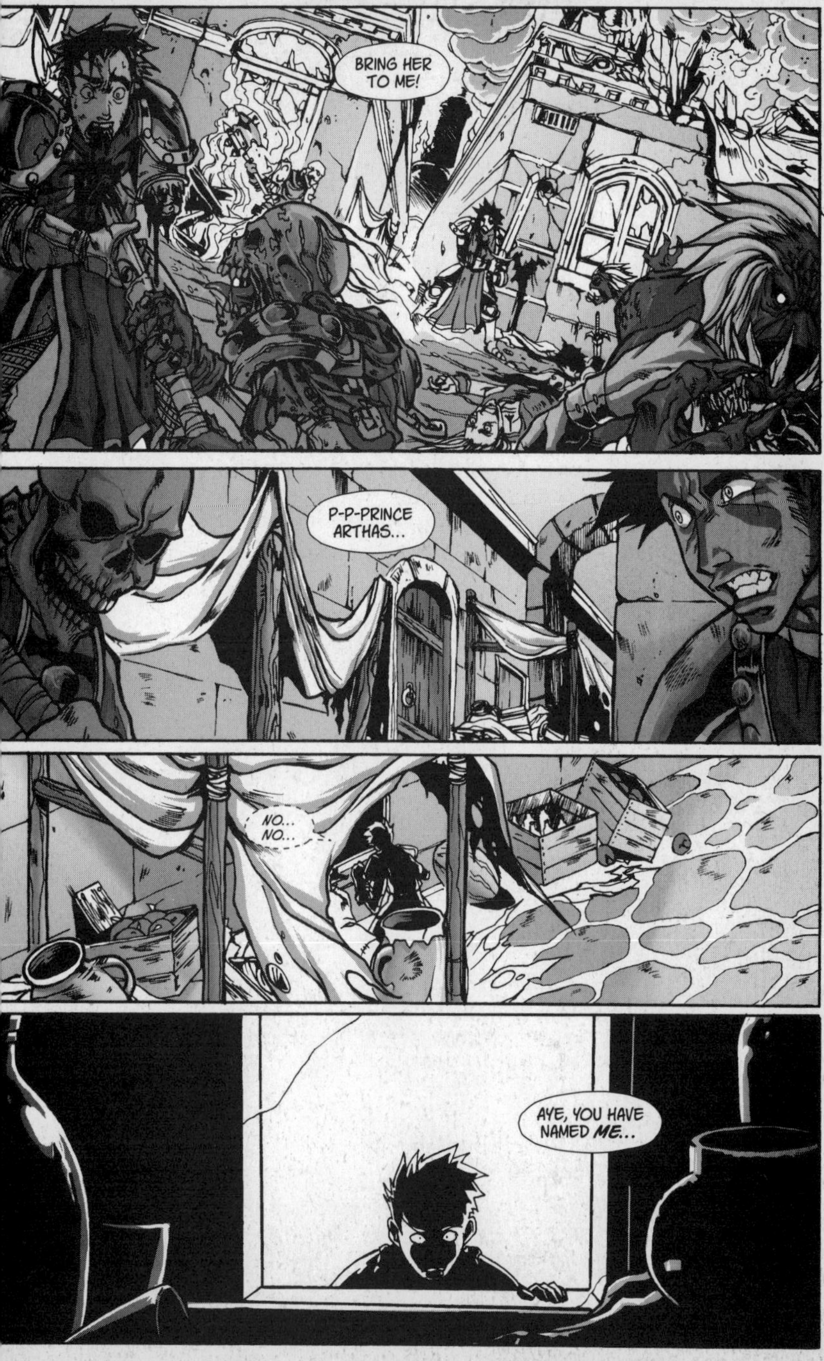
BRING HER TO ME!
P-P-PRINCE ARTHAS...
NO... NO...
AYE, YOU HAVE NAMED *ME*...

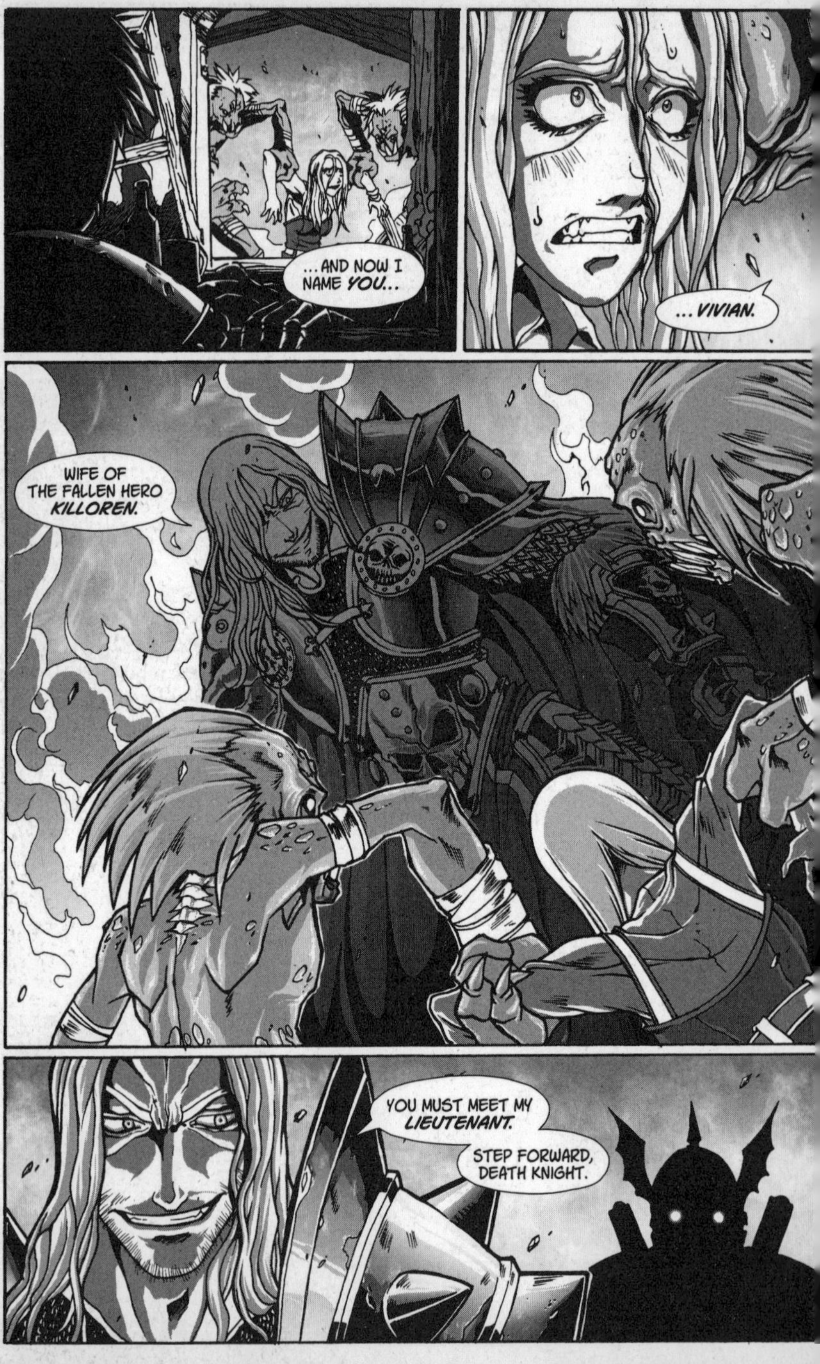
...AND NOW I NAME *YOU*...
...*VIVIAN.*
WIFE OF THE FALLEN HERO *KILLOREN.*
YOU MUST MEET MY *LIEUTENANT.*
STEP FORWARD, DEATH KNIGHT.

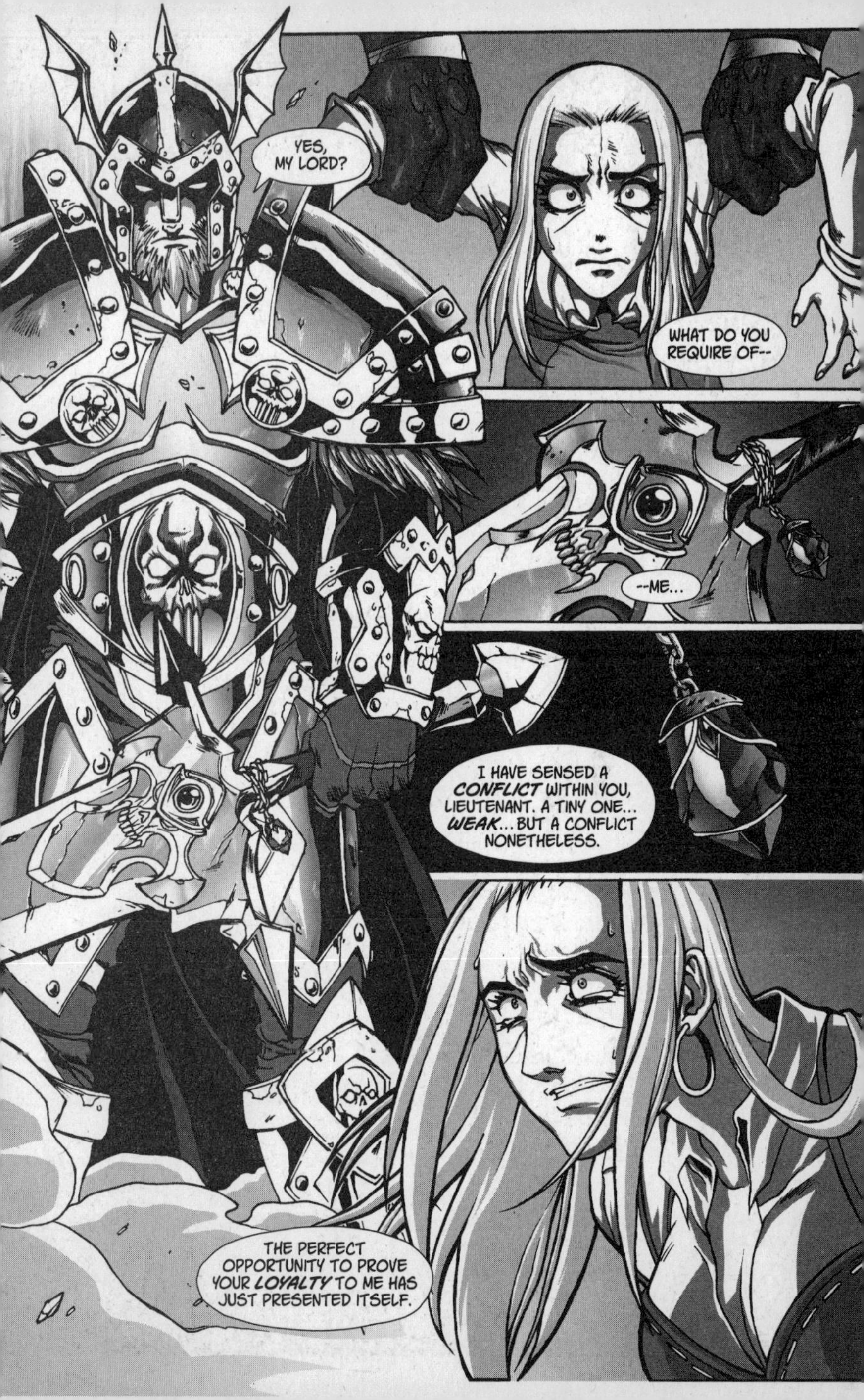
YES, MY LORD?
WHAT DO YOU REQUIRE OF--
--ME...
I HAVE SENSED A *CONFLICT* WITHIN YOU, LIEUTENANT. A TINY ONE... *WEAK*... BUT A CONFLICT NONETHELESS.
THE PERFECT OPPORTUNITY TO PROVE YOUR *LOYALTY* TO ME HAS JUST PRESENTED ITSELF.

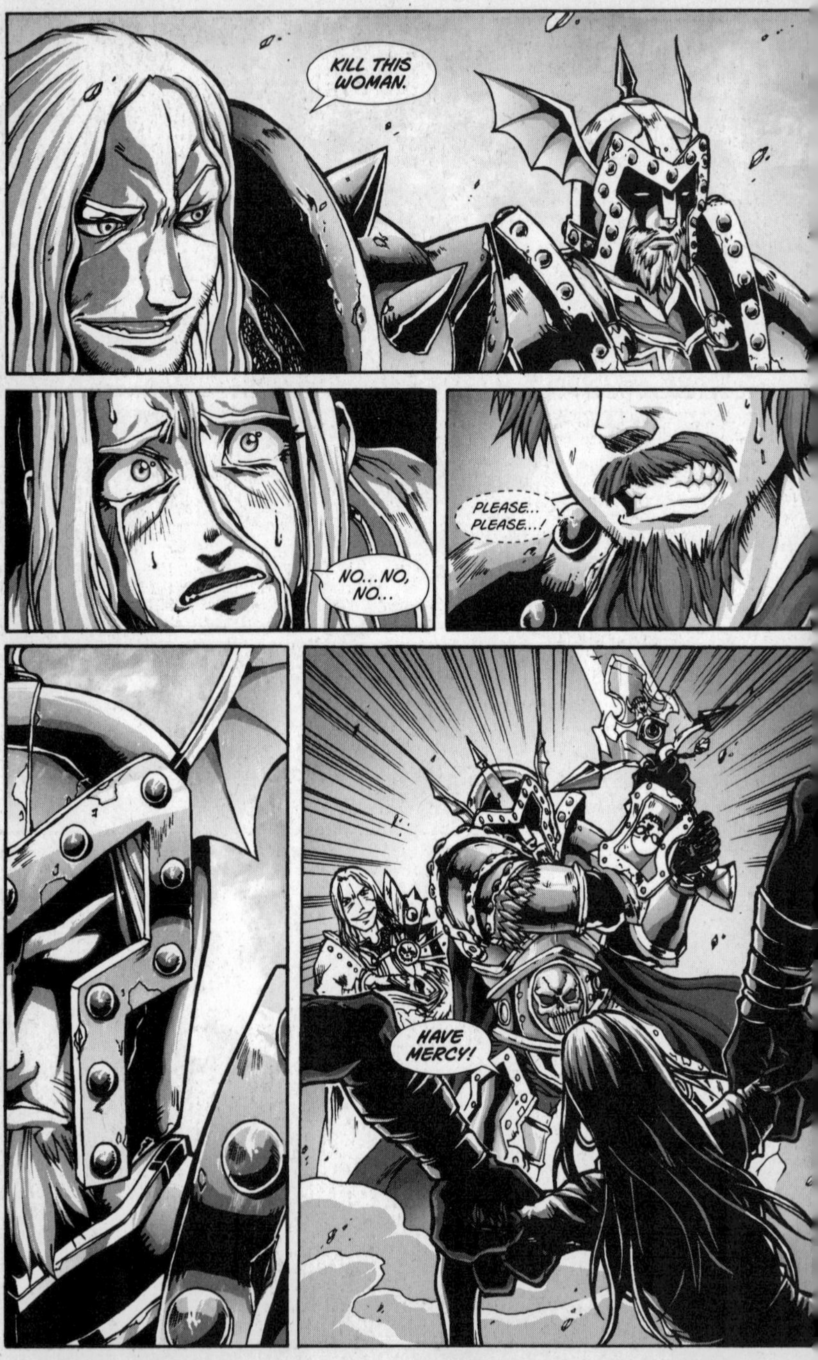
KILL THIS WOMAN.
NO... NO, NO...
PLEASE... PLEASE...!
HAVE MERCY!

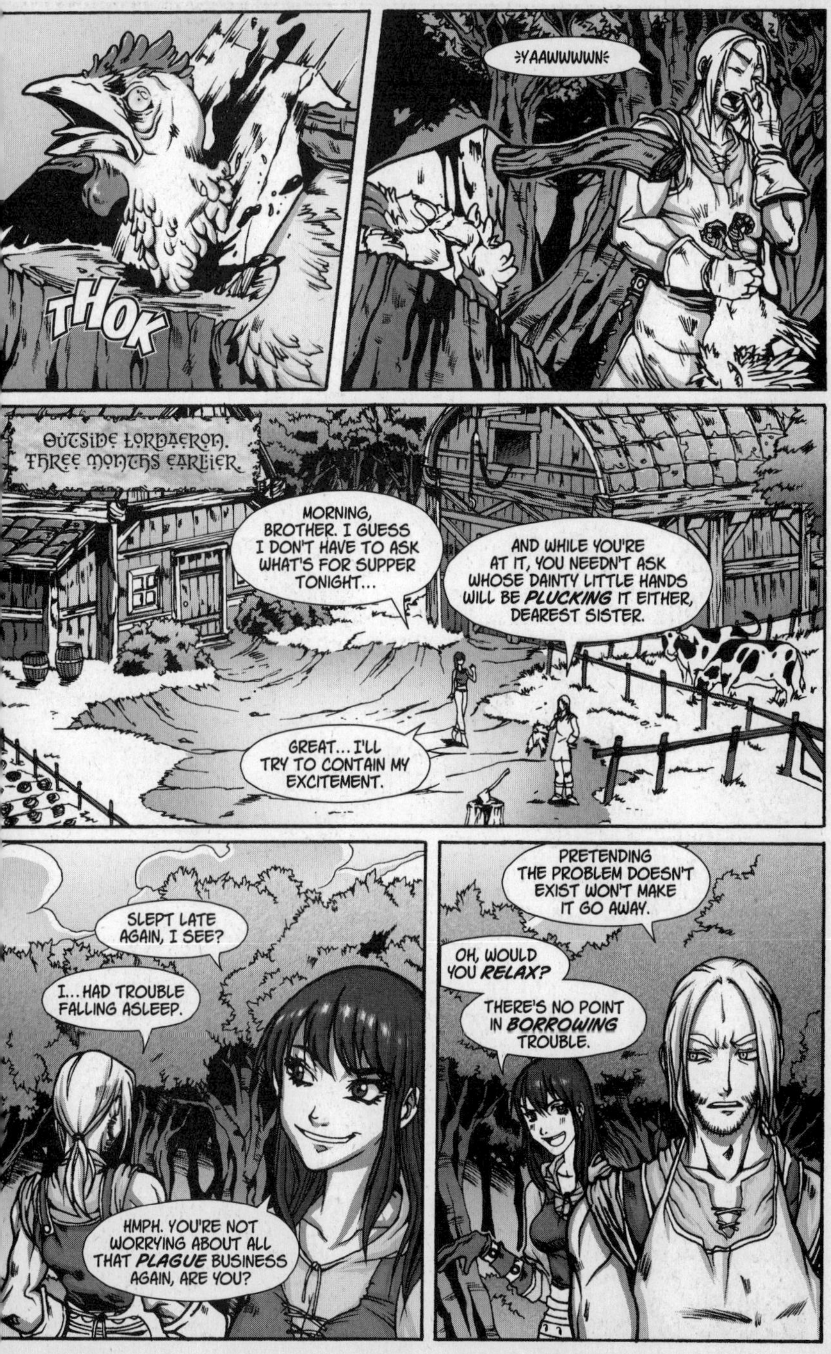
THOK
≶YAAWWWWN≷
OUTSIDE LORDAERON. THREE MONTHS EARLIER.
MORNING, BROTHER. I GUESS I DON'T HAVE TO ASK WHAT'S FOR SUPPER TONIGHT...
AND WHILE YOU'RE AT IT, YOU NEEDN'T ASK WHOSE DAINTY LITTLE HANDS WILL BE PLUCKING IT EITHER, DEAREST SISTER.
GREAT... I'LL TRY TO CONTAIN MY EXCITEMENT.
SLEPT LATE AGAIN, I SEE?
I... HAD TROUBLE FALLING ASLEEP.
HMPH. YOU'RE NOT WORRYING ABOUT ALL THAT PLAGUE BUSINESS AGAIN, ARE YOU?
PRETENDING THE PROBLEM DOESN'T EXIST WON'T MAKE IT GO AWAY.
OH, WOULD YOU RELAX?
THERE'S NO POINT IN BORROWING TROUBLE.

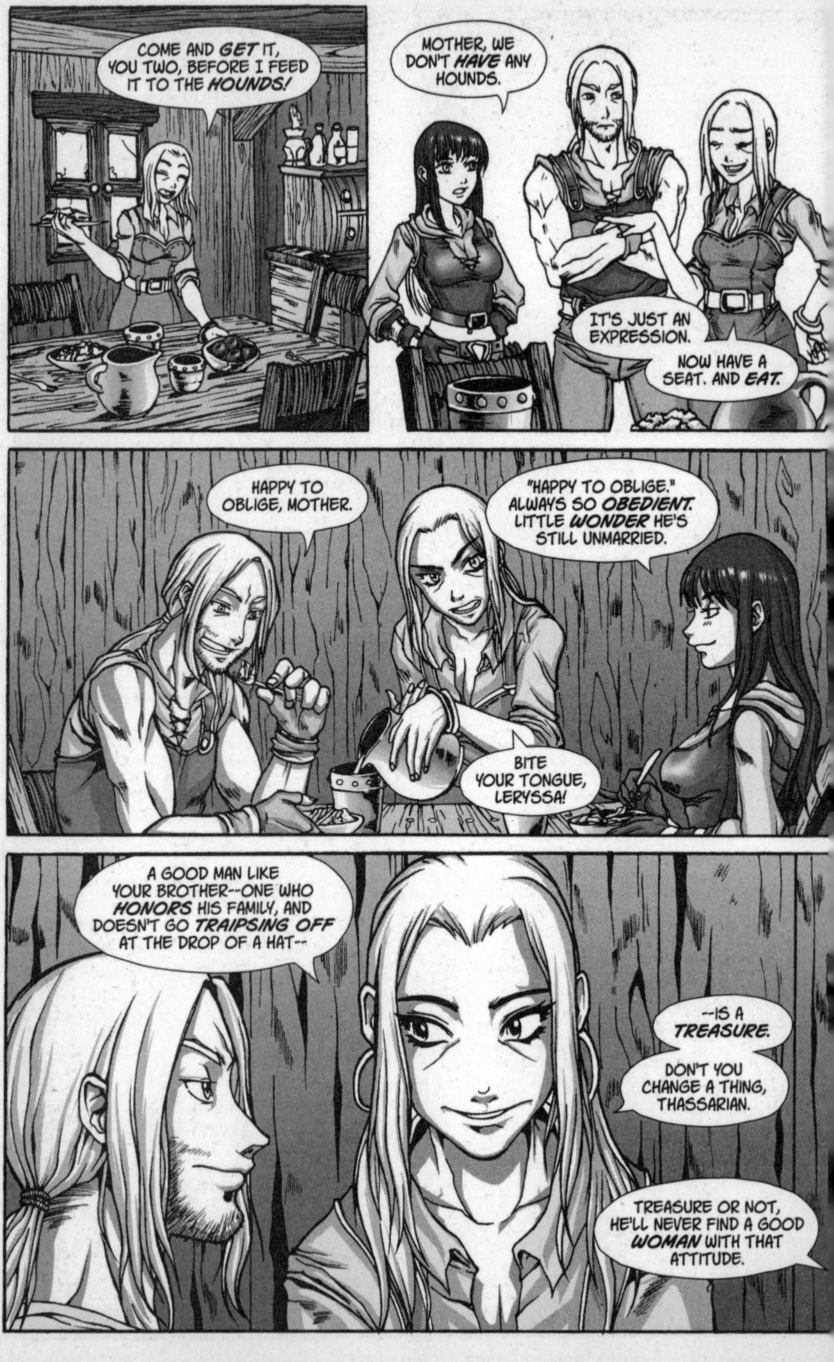
COME AND *GET* IT, YOU TWO, BEFORE I FEED IT TO THE *HOUNDS!*
MOTHER, WE DON'T *HAVE* ANY HOUNDS.
IT'S JUST AN EXPRESSION.
NOW HAVE A SEAT. AND *EAT.*
HAPPY TO OBLIGE, MOTHER.
"HAPPY TO OBLIGE." ALWAYS SO *OBEDIENT.* LITTLE *WONDER* HE'S STILL UNMARRIED.
BITE YOUR TONGUE, LERYSSA!
A GOOD MAN LIKE YOUR BROTHER--ONE WHO *HONORS* HIS FAMILY, AND DOESN'T GO *TRAIPSING OFF* AT THE DROP OF A HAT--
--IS A *TREASURE.*
DON'T YOU CHANGE A THING, THASSARIAN.
TREASURE OR NOT, HE'LL NEVER FIND A GOOD *WOMAN* WITH THAT ATTITUDE.

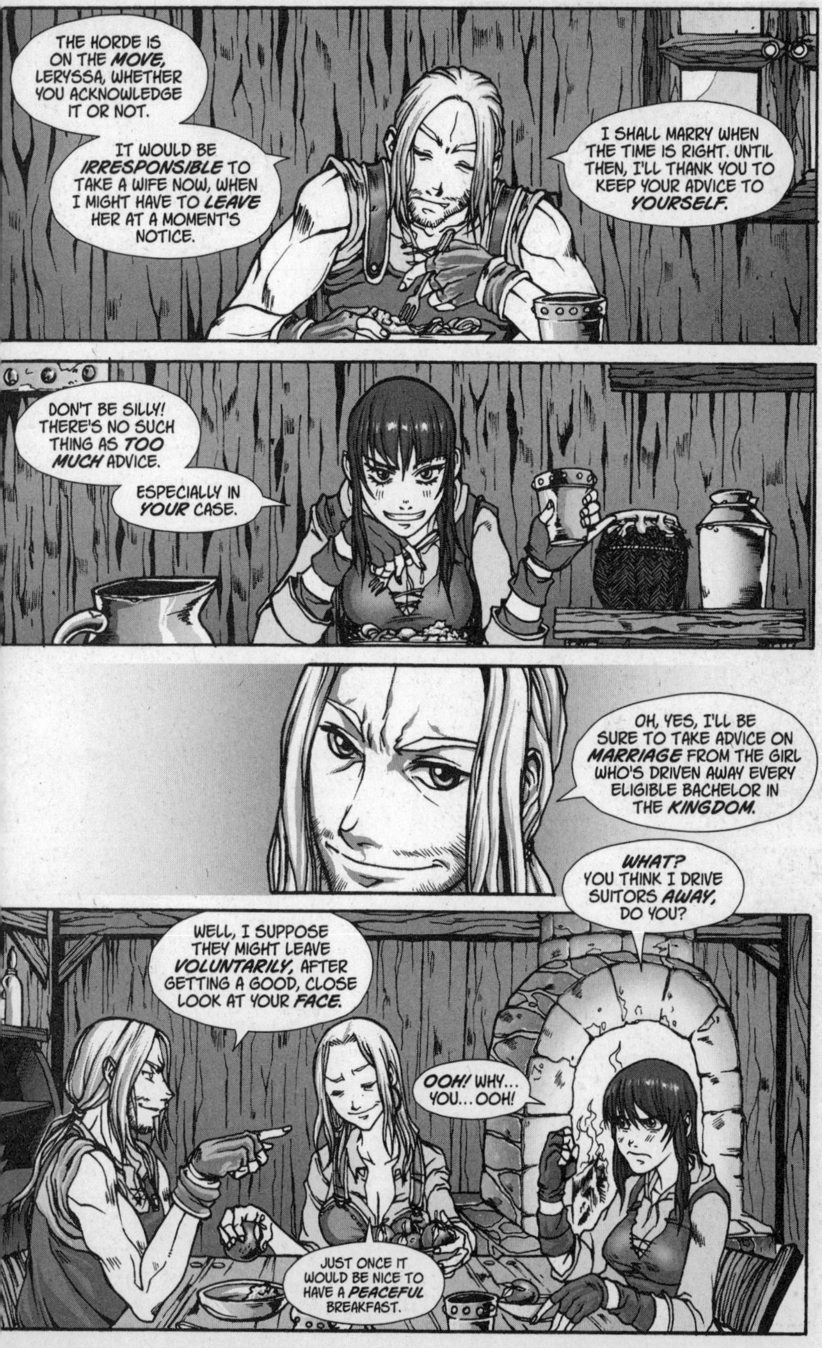
THE HORDE IS ON THE MOVE, LERYSSA, WHETHER YOU ACKNOWLEDGE IT OR NOT.
IT WOULD BE IRRESPONSIBLE TO TAKE A WIFE NOW, WHEN I MIGHT HAVE TO LEAVE HER AT A MOMENT'S NOTICE.
I SHALL MARRY WHEN THE TIME IS RIGHT. UNTIL THEN, I'LL THANK YOU TO KEEP YOUR ADVICE TO YOURSELF.
DON'T BE SILLY! THERE'S NO SUCH THING AS TOO MUCH ADVICE.
ESPECIALLY IN YOUR CASE.
OH, YES, I'LL BE SURE TO TAKE ADVICE ON MARRIAGE FROM THE GIRL WHO'S DRIVEN AWAY EVERY ELIGIBLE BACHELOR IN THE KINGDOM.
WHAT? YOU THINK I DRIVE SUITORS AWAY, DO YOU?
WELL, I SUPPOSE THEY MIGHT LEAVE VOLUNTARILY, AFTER GETTING A GOOD, CLOSE LOOK AT YOUR FACE.
OOH! WHY... YOU... OOH!
JUST ONCE IT WOULD BE NICE TO HAVE A PEACEFUL BREAKFAST.

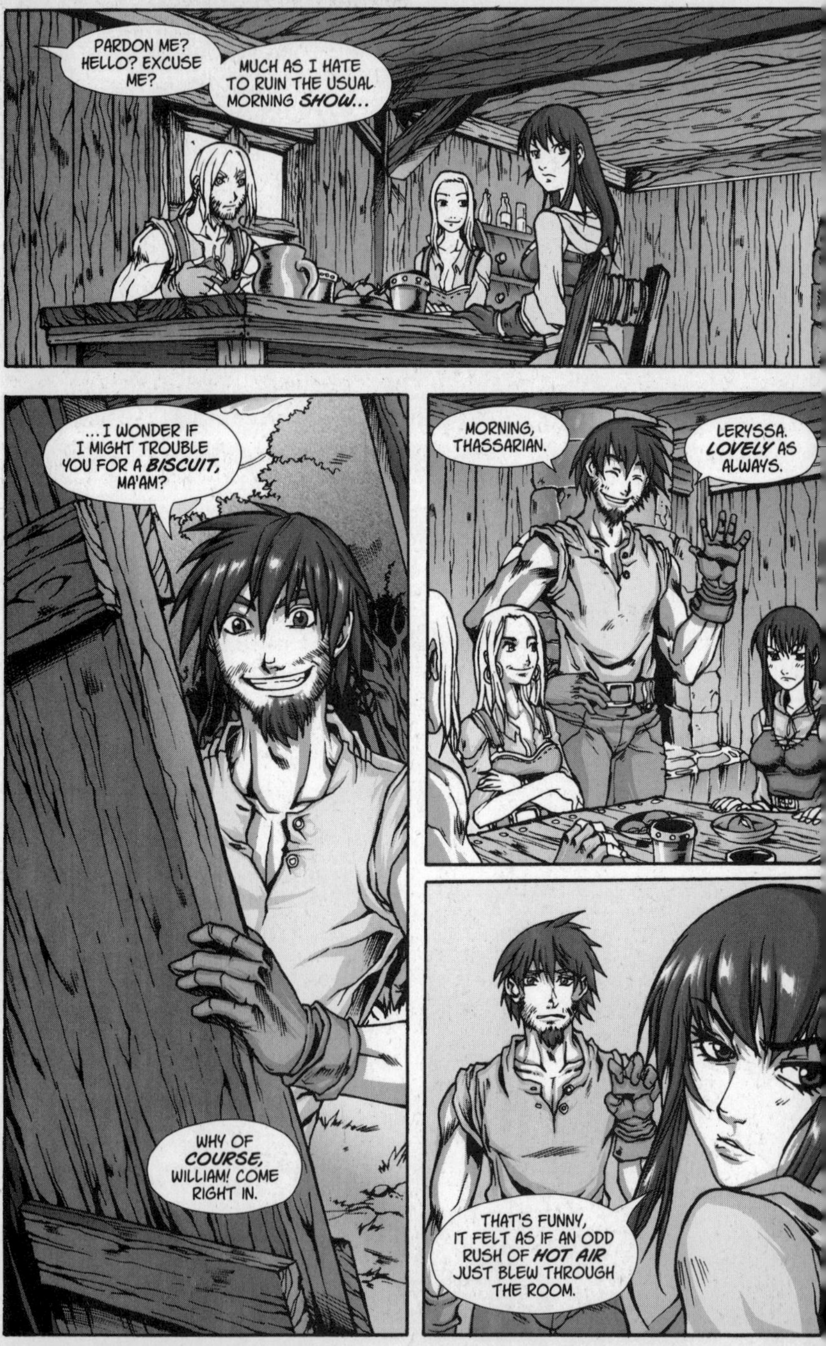
PARDON ME? HELLO? EXCUSE ME?
MUCH AS I HATE TO RUIN THE USUAL MORNING SHOW...
...I WONDER IF I MIGHT TROUBLE YOU FOR A BISCUIT, MA'AM?
WHY OF COURSE, WILLIAM! COME RIGHT IN.
MORNING, THASSARIAN.
LERYSSA. LOVELY AS ALWAYS.
THAT'S FUNNY, IT FELT AS IF AN ODD RUSH OF HOT AIR JUST BLEW THROUGH THE ROOM.

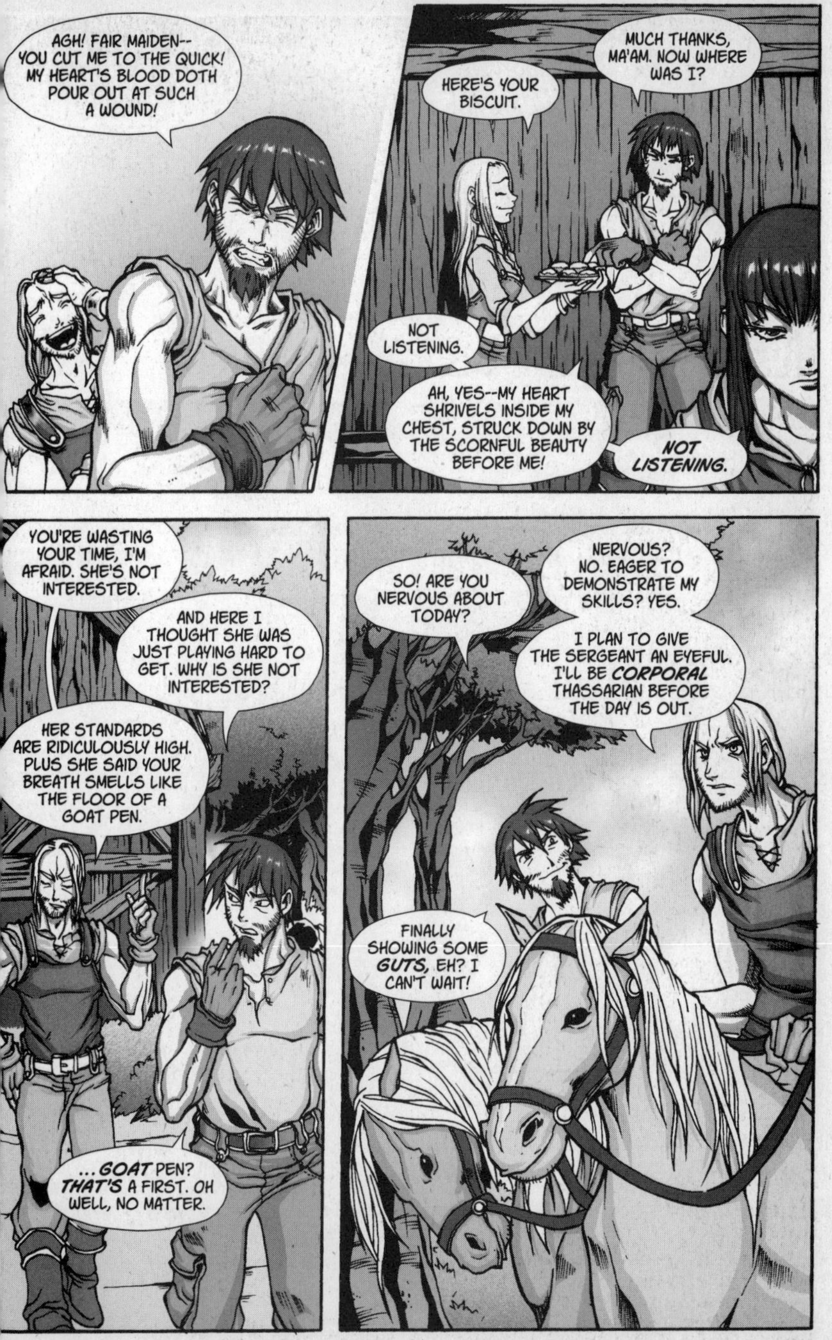

AGH! FAIR MAIDEN-- YOU CUT ME TO THE QUICK! MY HEART'S BLOOD DOTH POUR OUT AT SUCH A WOUND!
HERE'S YOUR BISCUIT.
MUCH THANKS, MA'AM. NOW WHERE WAS I?
NOT LISTENING.
AH, YES--MY HEART SHRIVELS INSIDE MY CHEST, STRUCK DOWN BY THE SCORNFUL BEAUTY BEFORE ME!
NOT LISTENING.
YOU'RE WASTING YOUR TIME, I'M AFRAID. SHE'S NOT INTERESTED.
AND HERE I THOUGHT SHE WAS JUST PLAYING HARD TO GET. WHY IS SHE NOT INTERESTED?
HER STANDARDS ARE RIDICULOUSLY HIGH. PLUS SHE SAID YOUR BREATH SMELLS LIKE THE FLOOR OF A GOAT PEN.
...GOAT PEN? THAT'S A FIRST. OH WELL, NO MATTER.
SO! ARE YOU NERVOUS ABOUT TODAY?
NERVOUS? NO. EAGER TO DEMONSTRATE MY SKILLS? YES.
I PLAN TO GIVE THE SERGEANT AN EYEFUL. I'LL BE CORPORAL THASSARIAN BEFORE THE DAY IS OUT.
FINALLY SHOWING SOME GUTS, EH? I CAN'T WAIT!

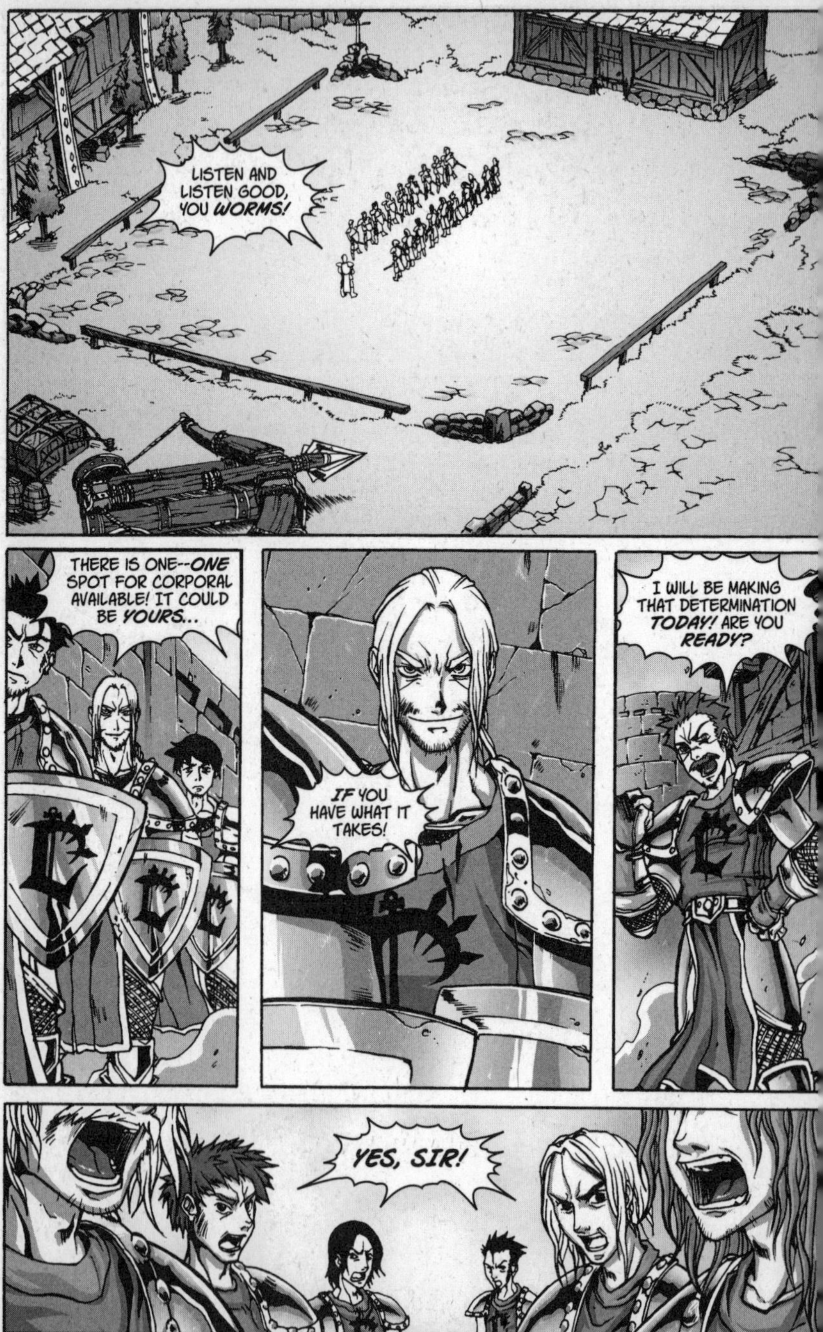
LISTEN AND LISTEN GOOD, YOU WORMS!
THERE IS ONE--ONE SPOT FOR CORPORAL AVAILABLE! IT COULD BE YOURS...
IF YOU HAVE WHAT IT TAKES!
I WILL BE MAKING THAT DETERMINATION TODAY! ARE YOU READY?
YES, SIR!

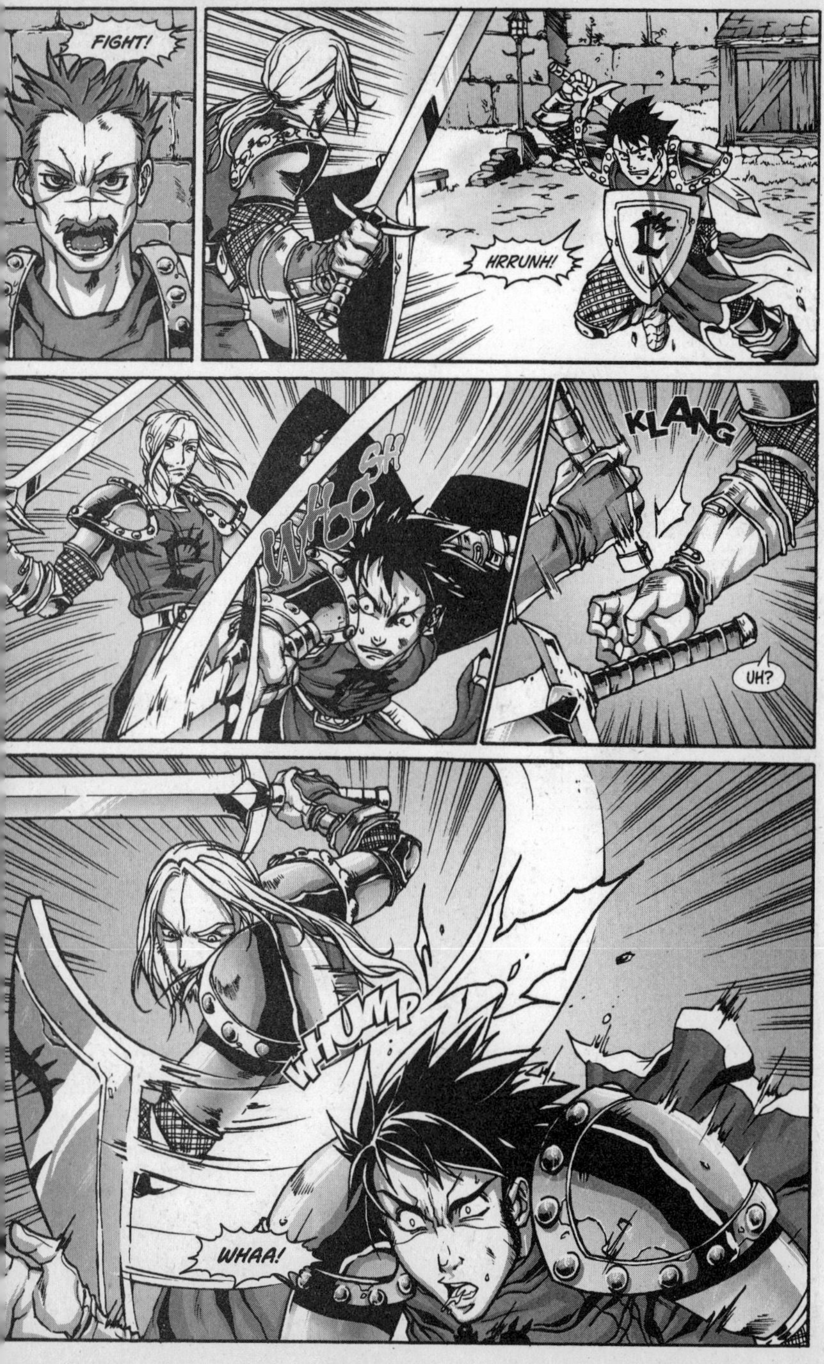
FIGHT!
HRRUNH!
WHOOSH
KLANG
UH?
WHUMP
WHAA!

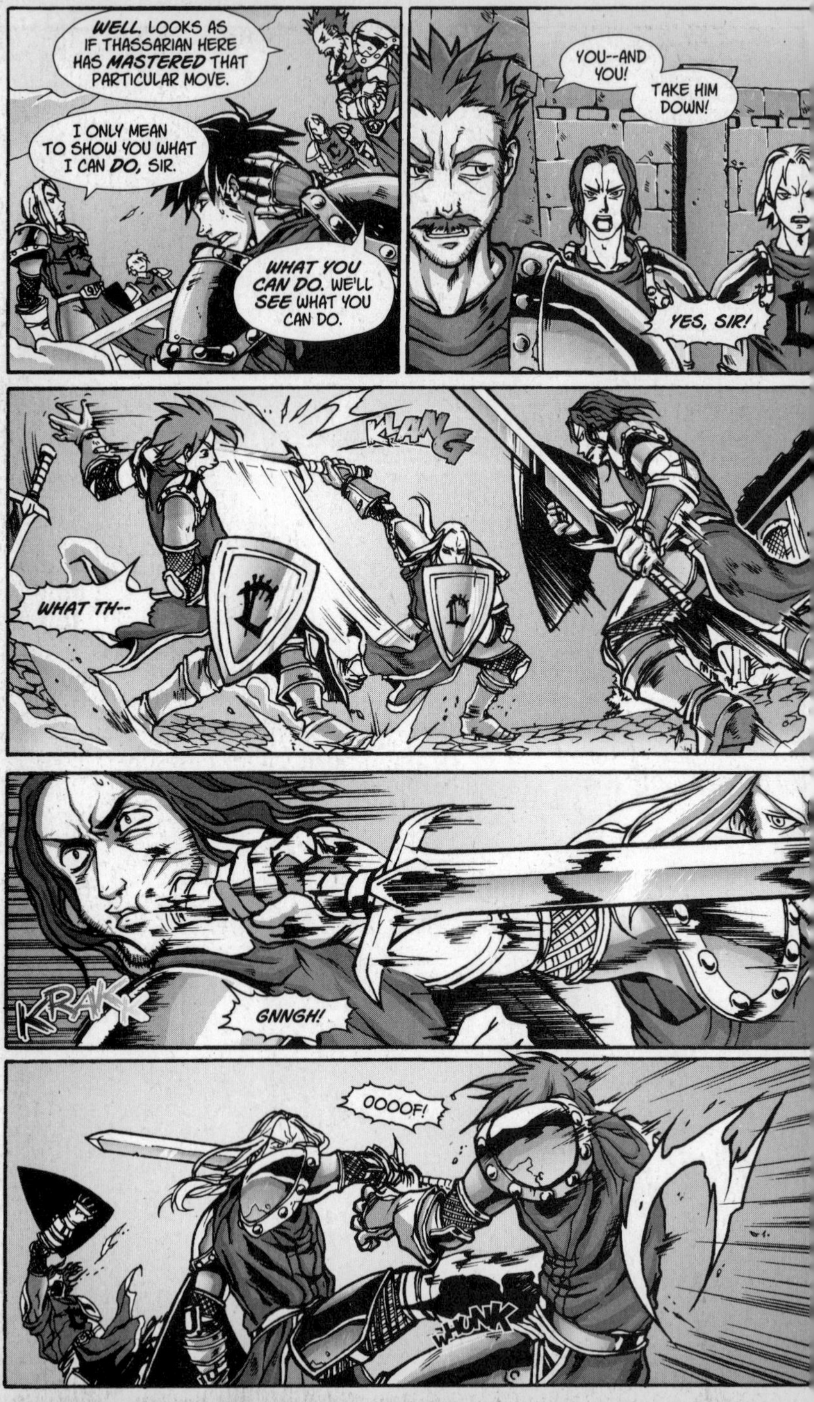
WELL, LOOKS AS IF THASSARIAN HERE HAS MASTERED THAT PARTICULAR MOVE.
I ONLY MEAN TO SHOW YOU WHAT I CAN DO, SIR.
WHAT YOU CAN DO. WE'LL SEE WHAT YOU CAN DO.
YOU--AND YOU!
TAKE HIM DOWN!
YES, SIR!
KLANG
WHAT TH--
KRAKK
GNNGH!
OOOOF!
WHUNK

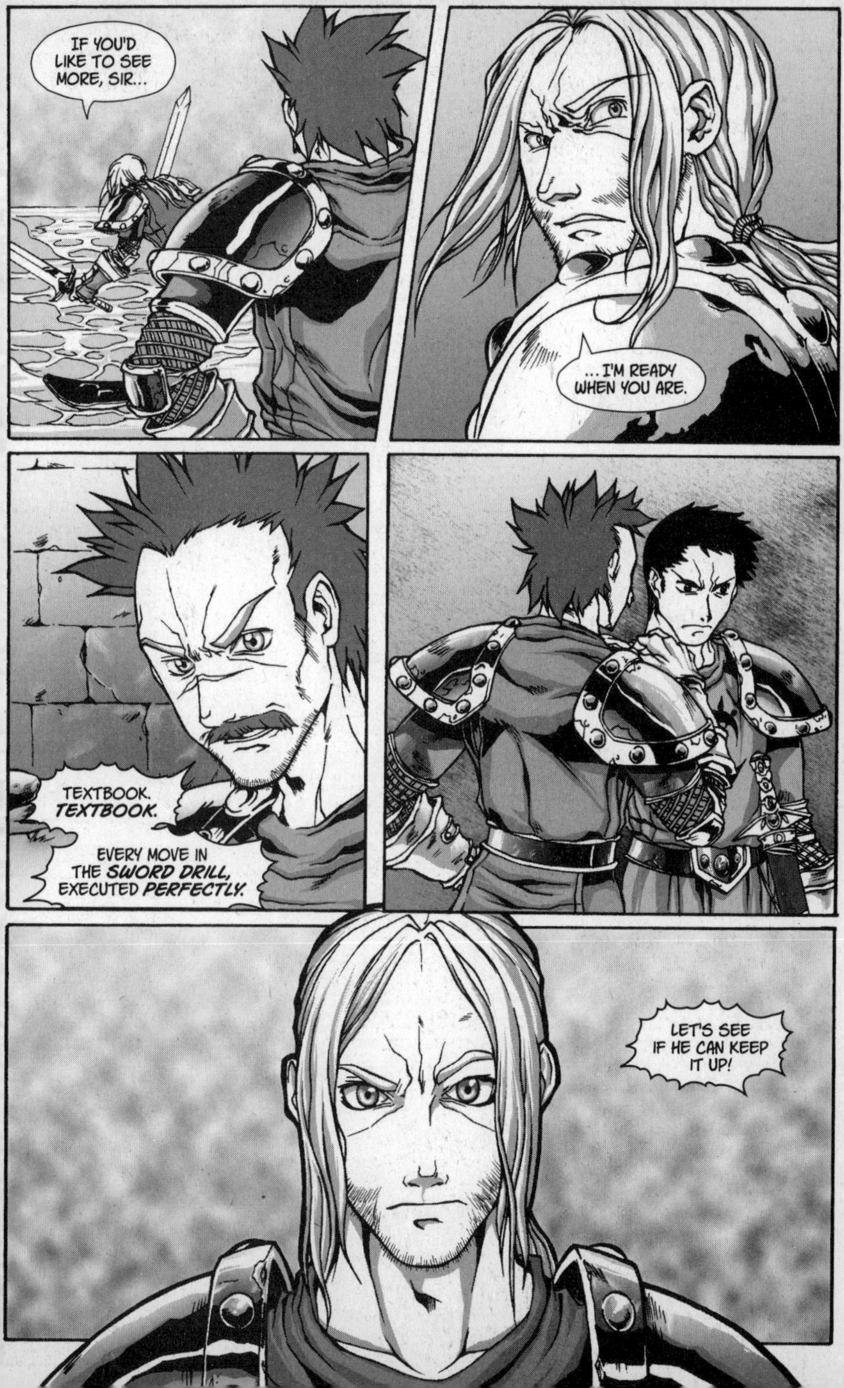
IF YOU'D LIKE TO SEE MORE, SIR...
...I'M READY WHEN YOU ARE.
TEXTBOOK. *TEXTBOOK.*
EVERY MOVE IN THE *SWORD DRILL,* EXECUTED *PERFECTLY.*
LET'S SEE IF HE CAN KEEP IT UP!

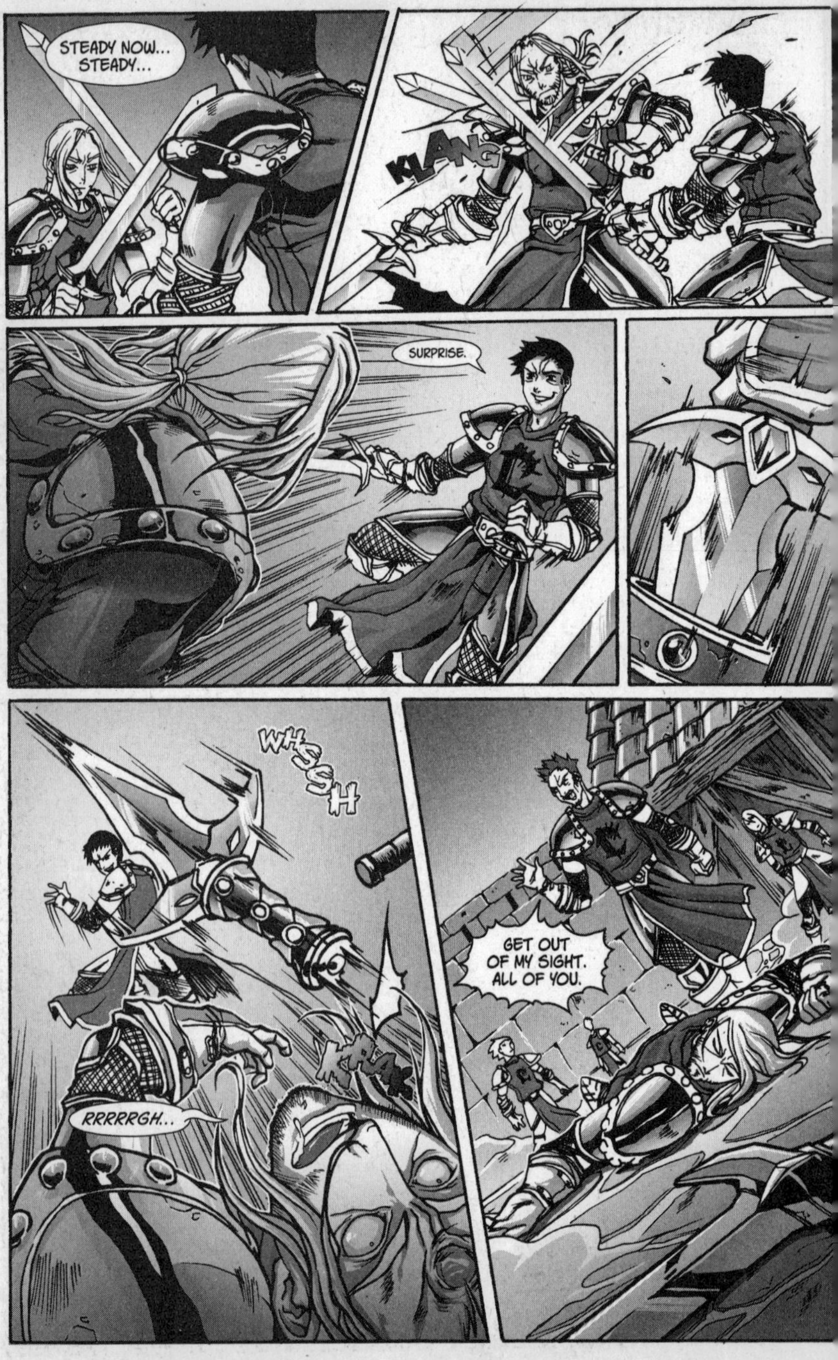
STEADY NOW... STEADY...
KLANG
SURPRISE.
WHSSH
KRAK
RRRRRGH...
GET OUT OF MY SIGHT. ALL OF YOU.

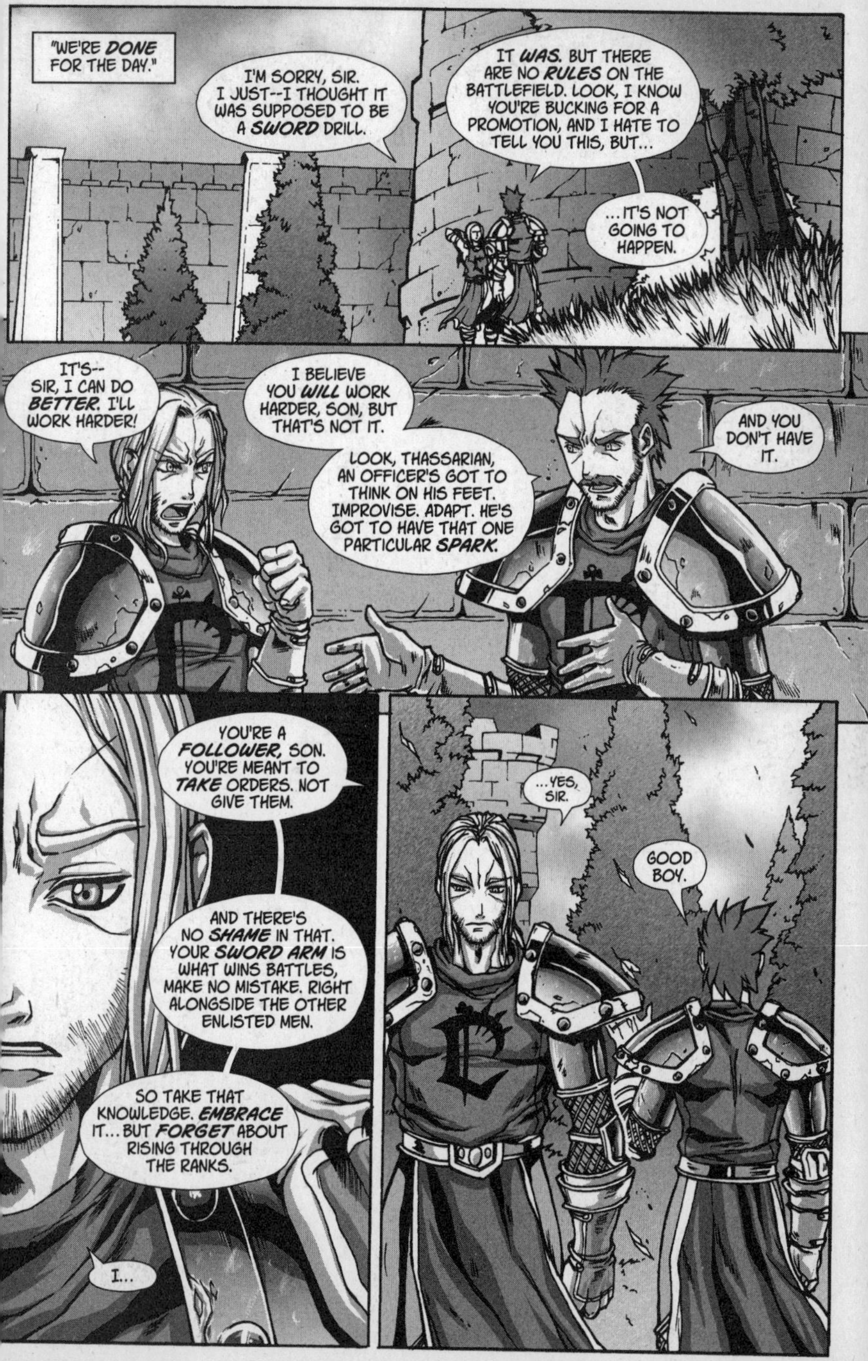
"WE'RE DONE FOR THE DAY."
I'M SORRY, SIR. I JUST--I THOUGHT IT WAS SUPPOSED TO BE A SWORD DRILL.
IT WAS. BUT THERE ARE NO RULES ON THE BATTLEFIELD. LOOK, I KNOW YOU'RE BUCKING FOR A PROMOTION, AND I HATE TO TELL YOU THIS, BUT...
...IT'S NOT GOING TO HAPPEN.
IT'S-- SIR, I CAN DO BETTER. I'LL WORK HARDER!
I BELIEVE YOU WILL WORK HARDER, SON, BUT THAT'S NOT IT.
LOOK, THASSARIAN, AN OFFICER'S GOT TO THINK ON HIS FEET. IMPROVISE. ADAPT. HE'S GOT TO HAVE THAT ONE PARTICULAR SPARK.
AND YOU DON'T HAVE IT.
YOU'RE A FOLLOWER, SON. YOU'RE MEANT TO TAKE ORDERS. NOT GIVE THEM.
AND THERE'S NO SHAME IN THAT. YOUR SWORD ARM IS WHAT WINS BATTLES, MAKE NO MISTAKE. RIGHT ALONGSIDE THE OTHER ENLISTED MEN.
SO TAKE THAT KNOWLEDGE. EMBRACE IT... BUT FORGET ABOUT RISING THROUGH THE RANKS.
I...
...YES, SIR.
GOOD BOY.

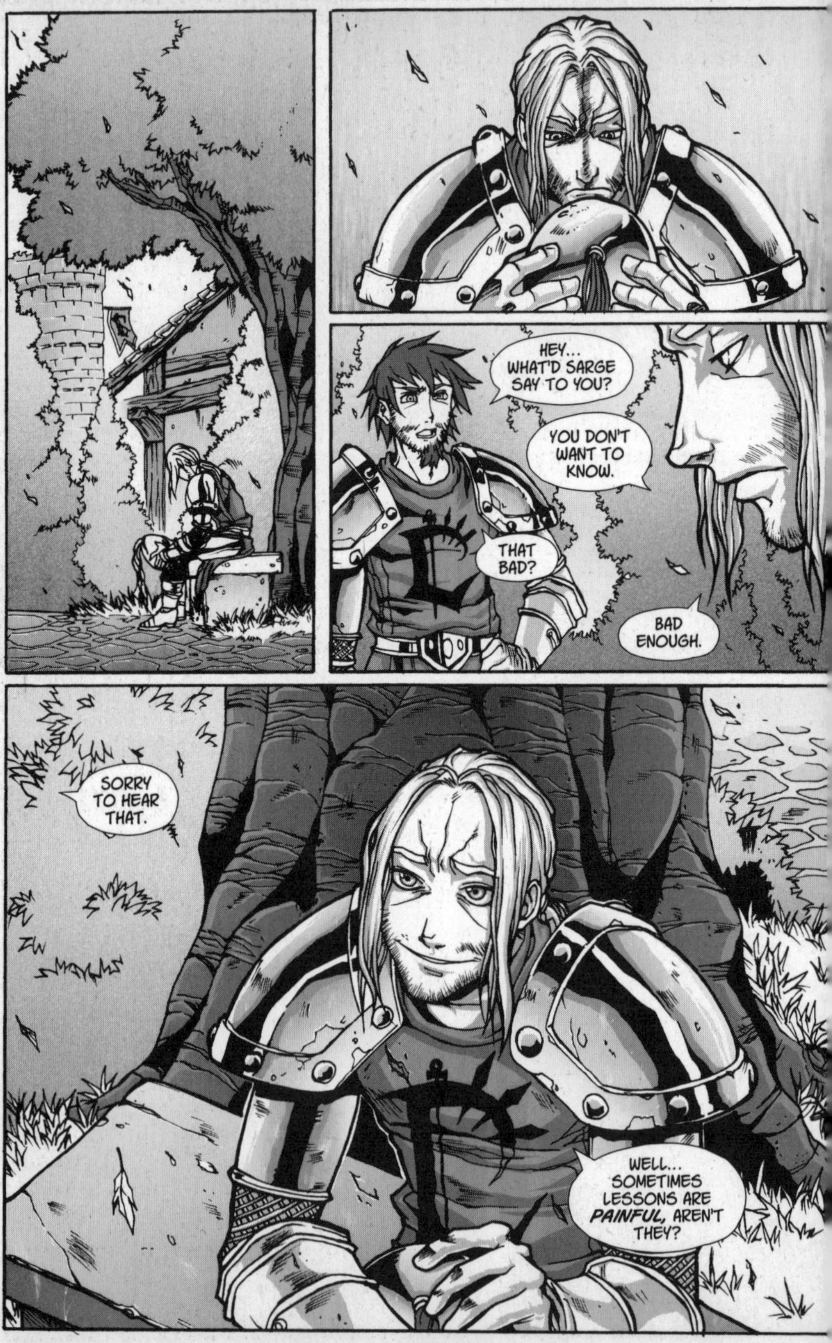
HEY... WHAT'D SARGE SAY TO YOU?
YOU DON'T WANT TO KNOW.
THAT BAD?
BAD ENOUGH.
SORRY TO HEAR THAT.
WELL... SOMETIMES LESSONS ARE *PAINFUL,* AREN'T THEY?

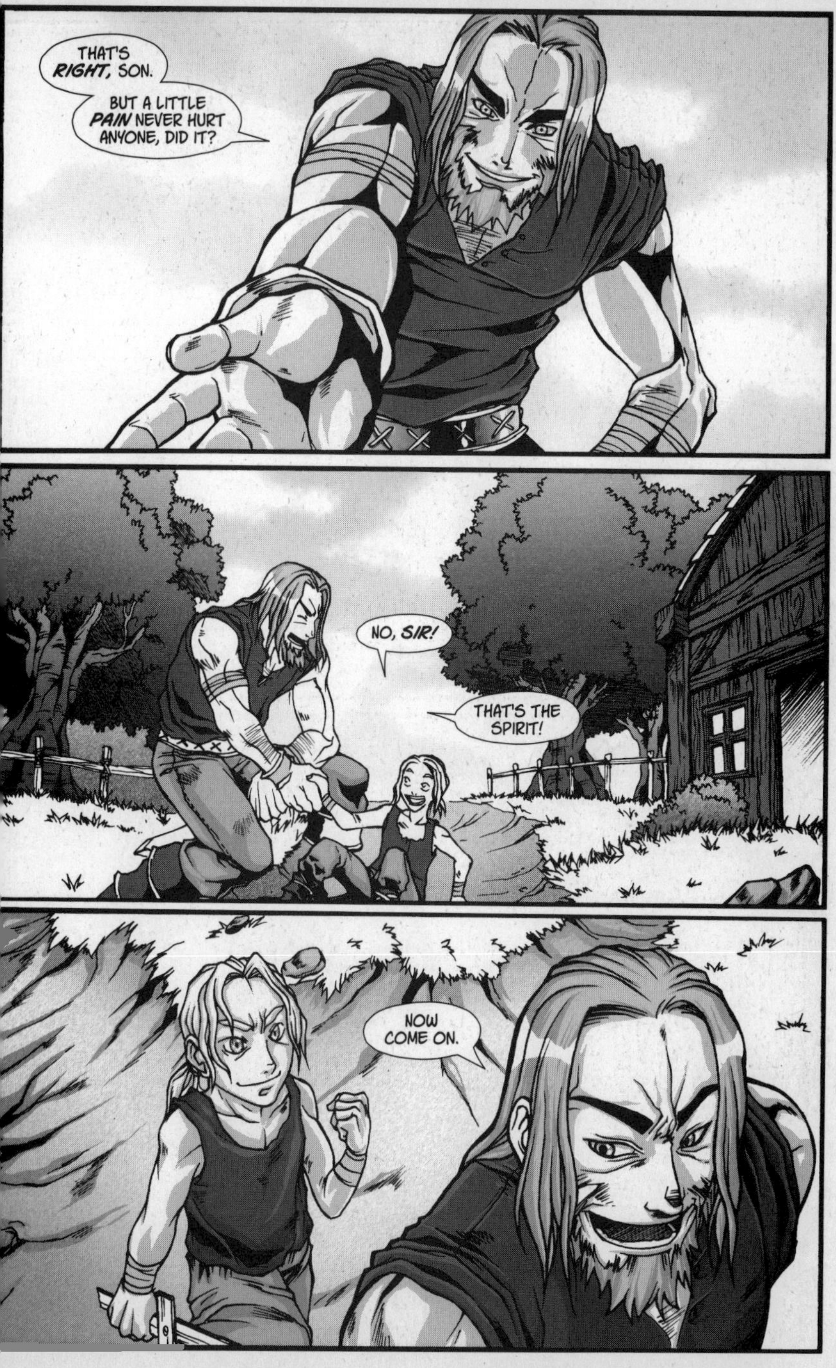
THAT'S *RIGHT,* SON.
BUT A LITTLE *PAIN* NEVER HURT ANYONE, DID IT?
NO, *SIR!*
THAT'S THE SPIRIT!
NOW COME ON.

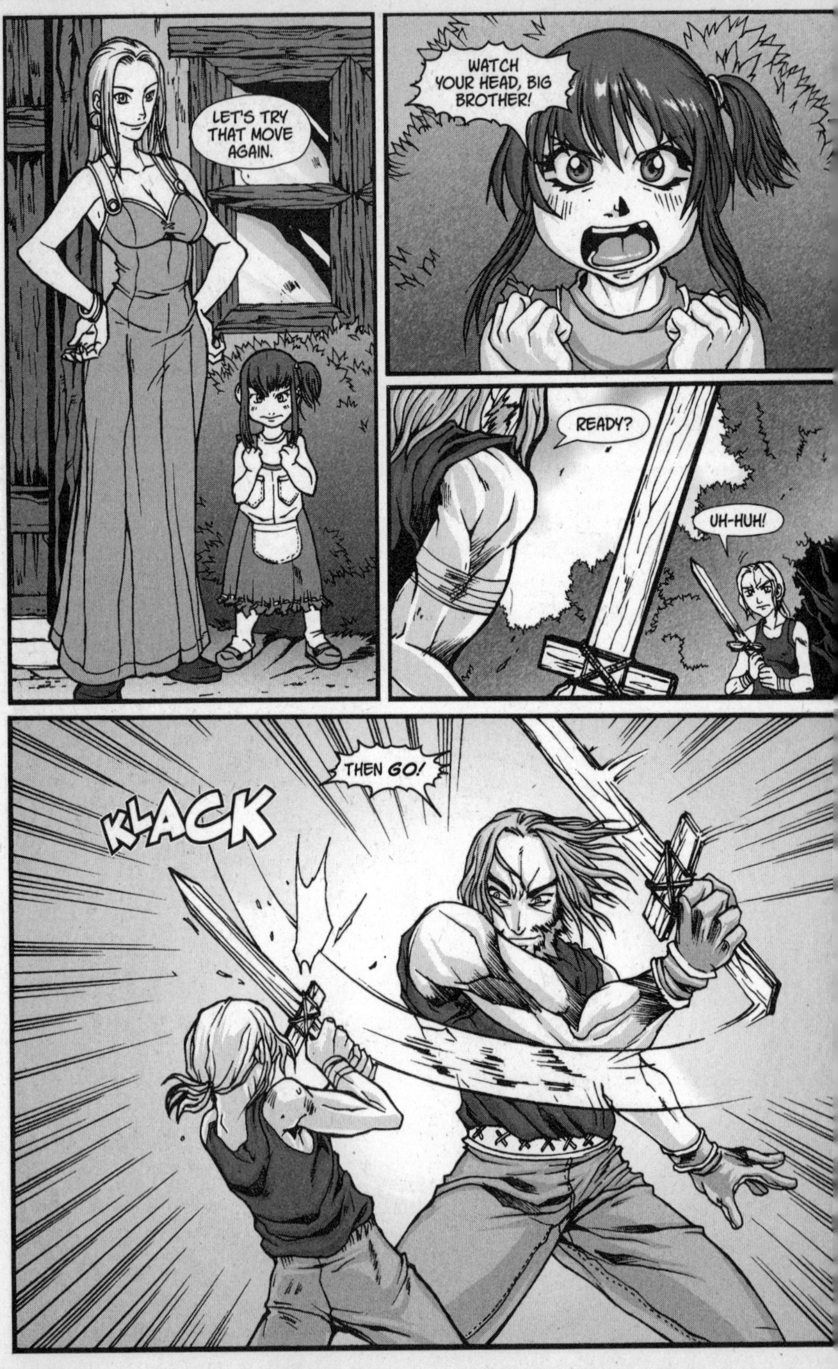
LET'S TRY THAT MOVE AGAIN.
WATCH YOUR HEAD, BIG BROTHER!
READY?
UH-HUH!
THEN GO!
KLACK

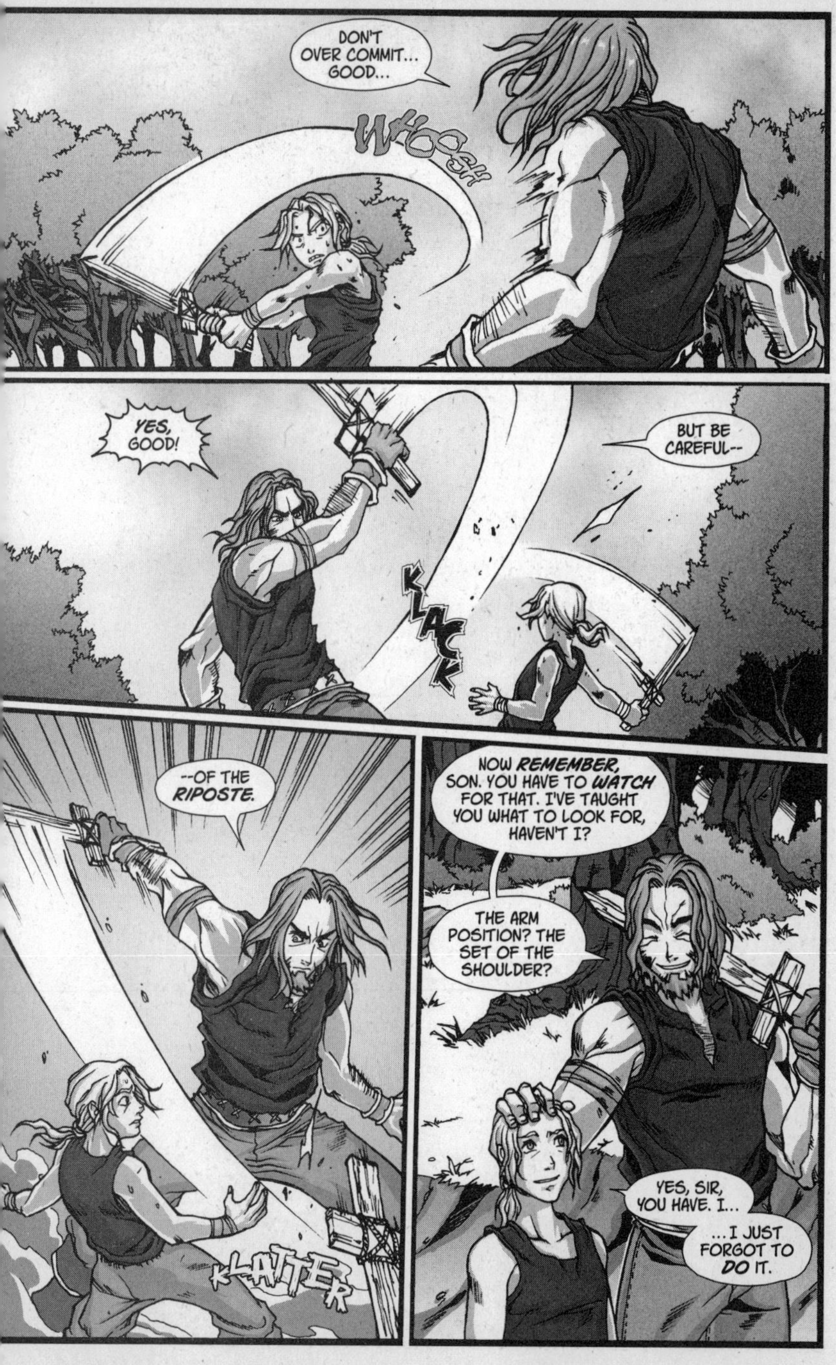
DON'T OVER COMMIT... GOOD...
WHOOSH
YES, GOOD!
BUT BE CAREFUL--
KLACK
--OF THE *RIPOSTE.*
KLATTER
NOW ***REMEMBER,*** SON. YOU HAVE TO ***WATCH*** FOR THAT. I'VE TAUGHT YOU WHAT TO LOOK FOR, HAVEN'T I?
THE ARM POSITION? THE SET OF THE SHOULDER?
YES, SIR, YOU HAVE. I...
...I JUST FORGOT TO ***DO*** IT.

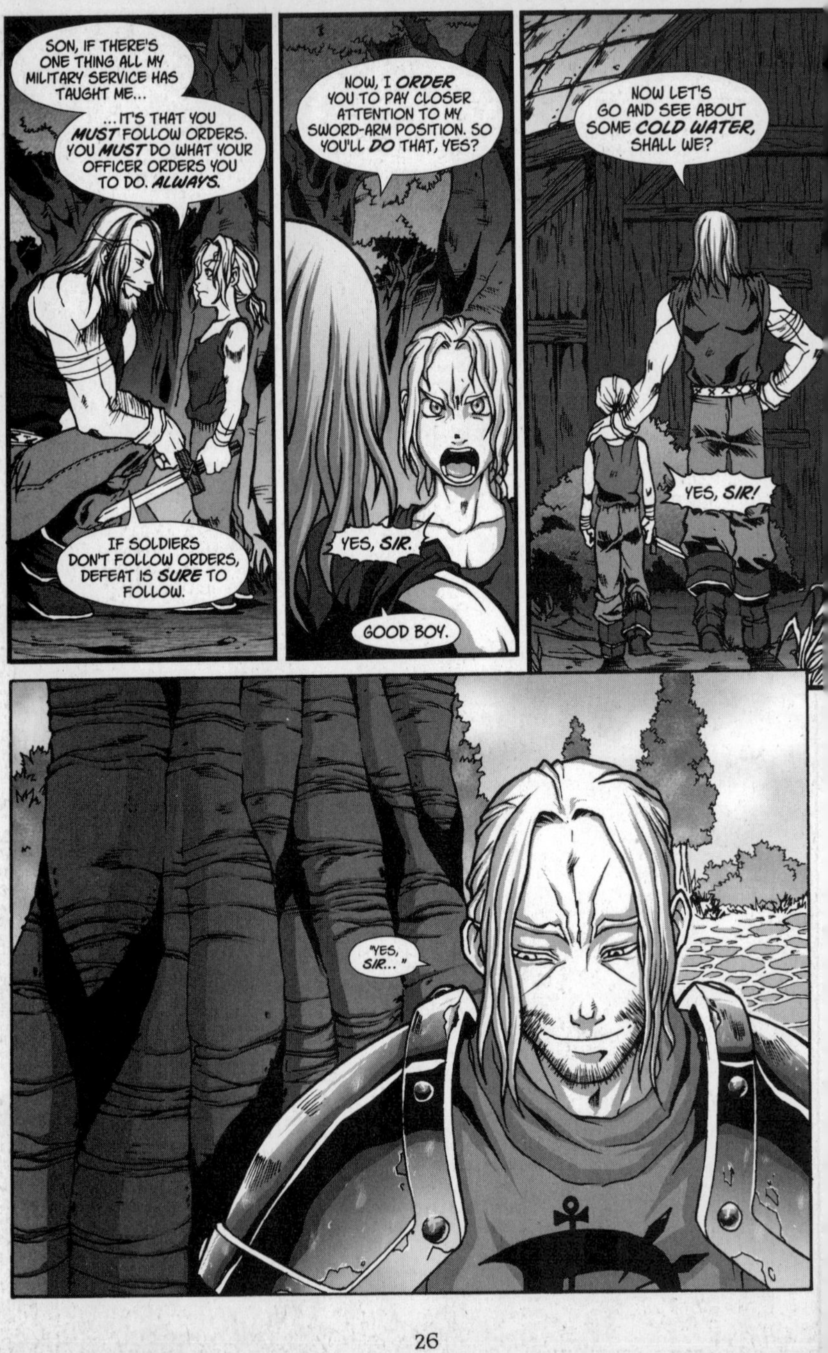
SON, IF THERE'S ONE THING ALL MY MILITARY SERVICE HAS TAUGHT ME...
...IT'S THAT YOU MUST FOLLOW ORDERS. YOU MUST DO WHAT YOUR OFFICER ORDERS YOU TO DO. ALWAYS.
IF SOLDIERS DON'T FOLLOW ORDERS, DEFEAT IS SURE TO FOLLOW.
NOW, I ORDER YOU TO PAY CLOSER ATTENTION TO MY SWORD-ARM POSITION. SO YOU'LL DO THAT, YES?
YES, SIR.
GOOD BOY.
NOW LET'S GO AND SEE ABOUT SOME COLD WATER, SHALL WE?
YES, SIR!
"YES, SIR..."

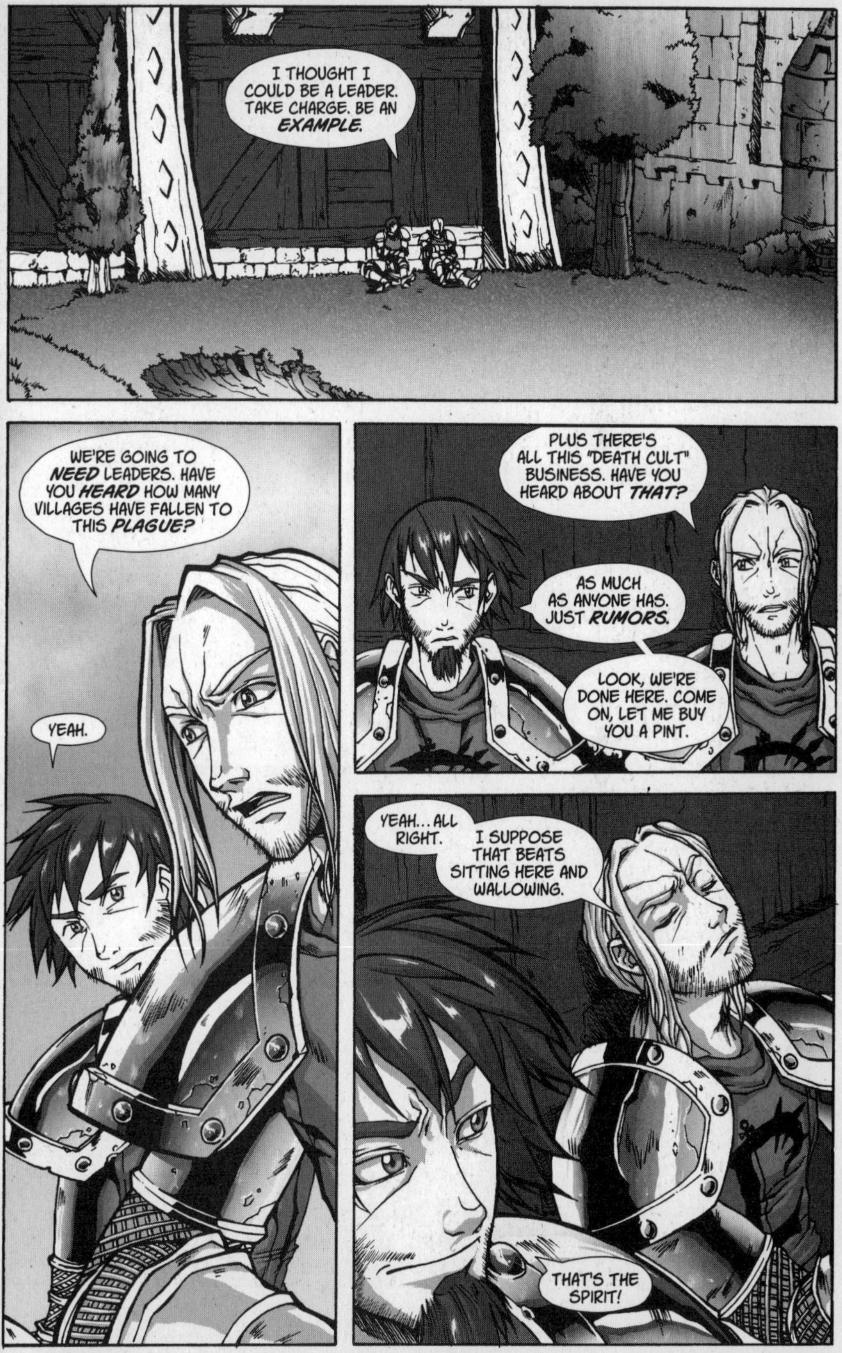
I THOUGHT I COULD BE A LEADER. TAKE CHARGE. BE AN *EXAMPLE.*
WE'RE GOING TO *NEED* LEADERS. HAVE YOU *HEARD* HOW MANY VILLAGES HAVE FALLEN TO THIS *PLAGUE?*
YEAH.
PLUS THERE'S ALL THIS "DEATH CULT" BUSINESS. HAVE YOU HEARD ABOUT *THAT?*
AS MUCH AS ANYONE HAS. JUST *RUMORS.*
LOOK, WE'RE DONE HERE. COME ON, LET ME BUY YOU A PINT.
YEAH... ALL RIGHT.
I SUPPOSE THAT BEATS SITTING HERE AND WALLOWING.
THAT'S THE SPIRIT!

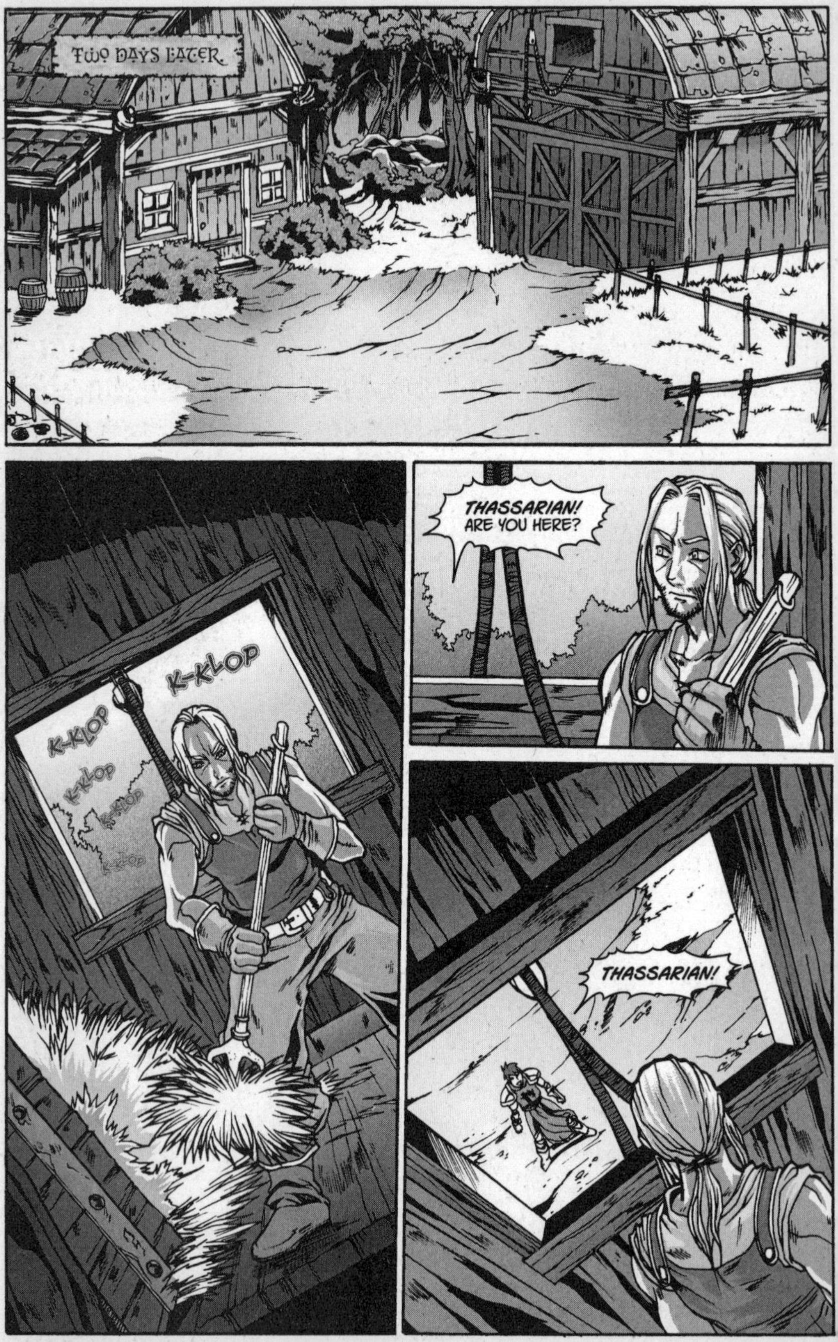
TWO DAYS LATER.
K-KLOP
K-KLOP
K-KLOP
K-KLOP
K-KLOP
THASSARIAN! ARE YOU HERE?
THASSARIAN!

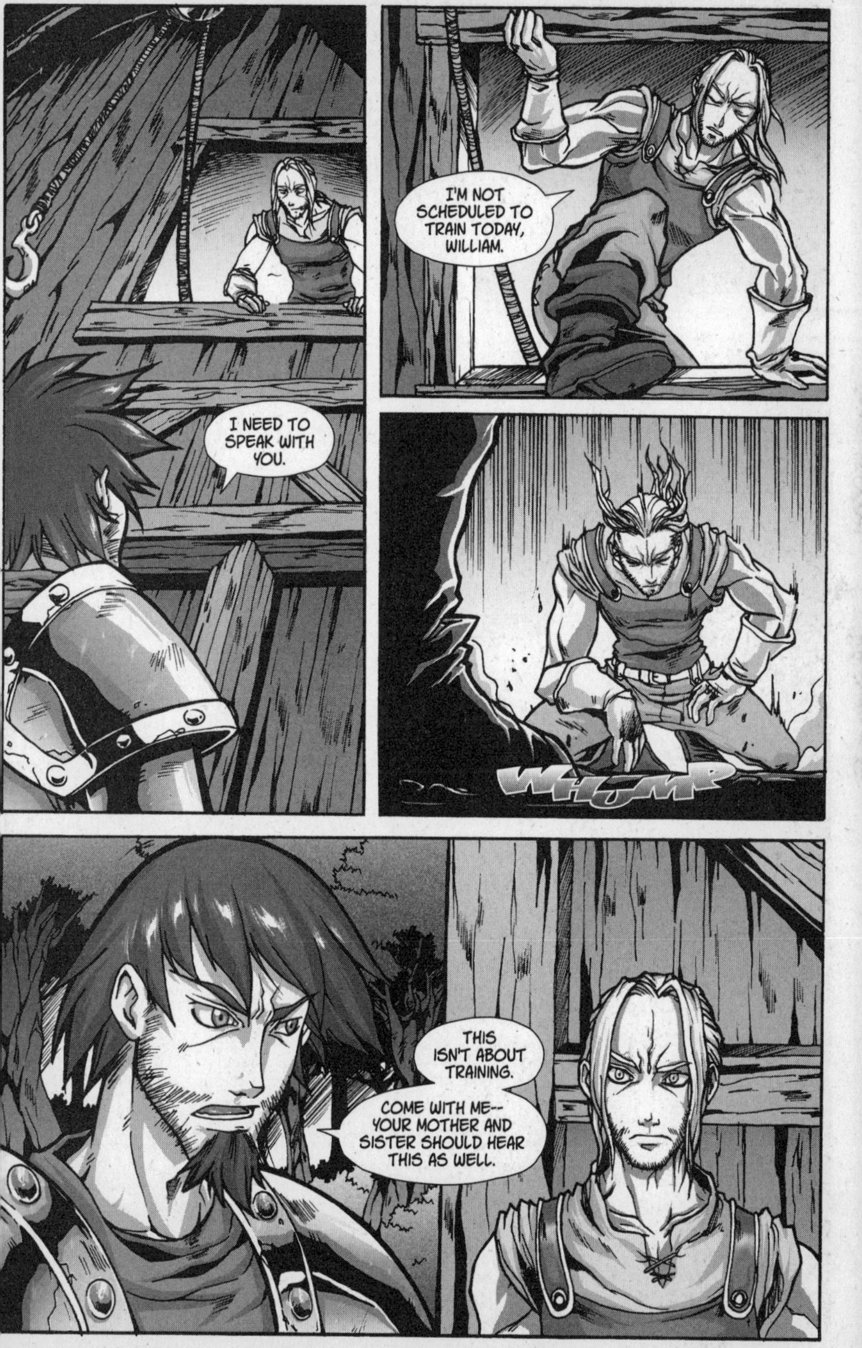
I NEED TO SPEAK WITH YOU.
I'M NOT SCHEDULED TO TRAIN TODAY, WILLIAM.
WHUMP
THIS ISN'T ABOUT TRAINING.
COME WITH ME-- YOUR MOTHER AND SISTER SHOULD HEAR THIS AS WELL.

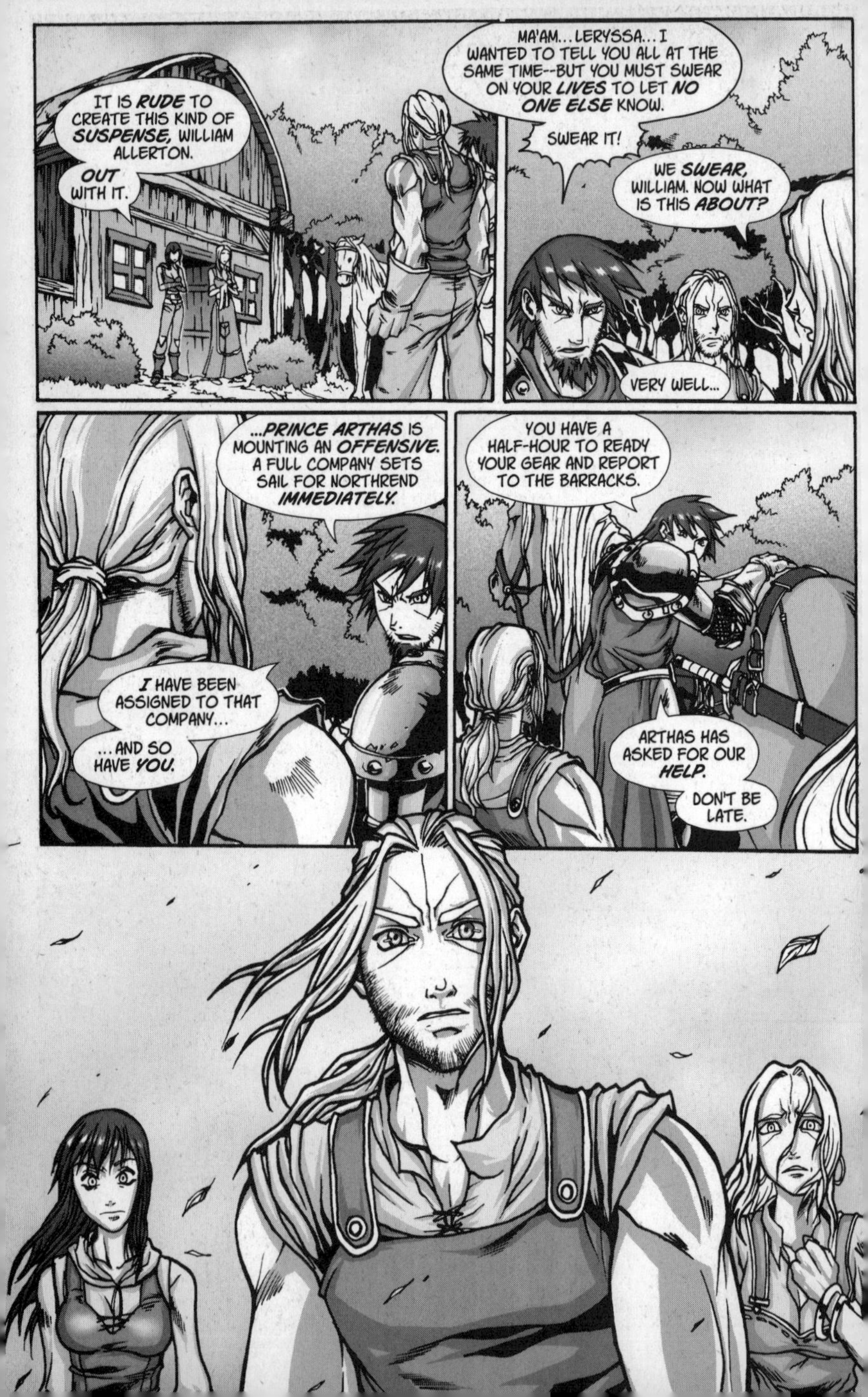
IT IS RUDE TO CREATE THIS KIND OF SUSPENSE, WILLIAM ALLERTON.
OUT WITH IT.
MA'AM... LERYSSA... I WANTED TO TELL YOU ALL AT THE SAME TIME--BUT YOU MUST SWEAR ON YOUR LIVES TO LET NO ONE ELSE KNOW.
SWEAR IT!
WE SWEAR, WILLIAM. NOW WHAT IS THIS ABOUT?
VERY WELL...
...PRINCE ARTHAS IS MOUNTING AN OFFENSIVE. A FULL COMPANY SETS SAIL FOR NORTHREND IMMEDIATELY.
I HAVE BEEN ASSIGNED TO THAT COMPANY...
...AND SO HAVE YOU.
YOU HAVE A HALF-HOUR TO READY YOUR GEAR AND REPORT TO THE BARRACKS.
ARTHAS HAS ASKED FOR OUR HELP.
DON'T BE LATE.

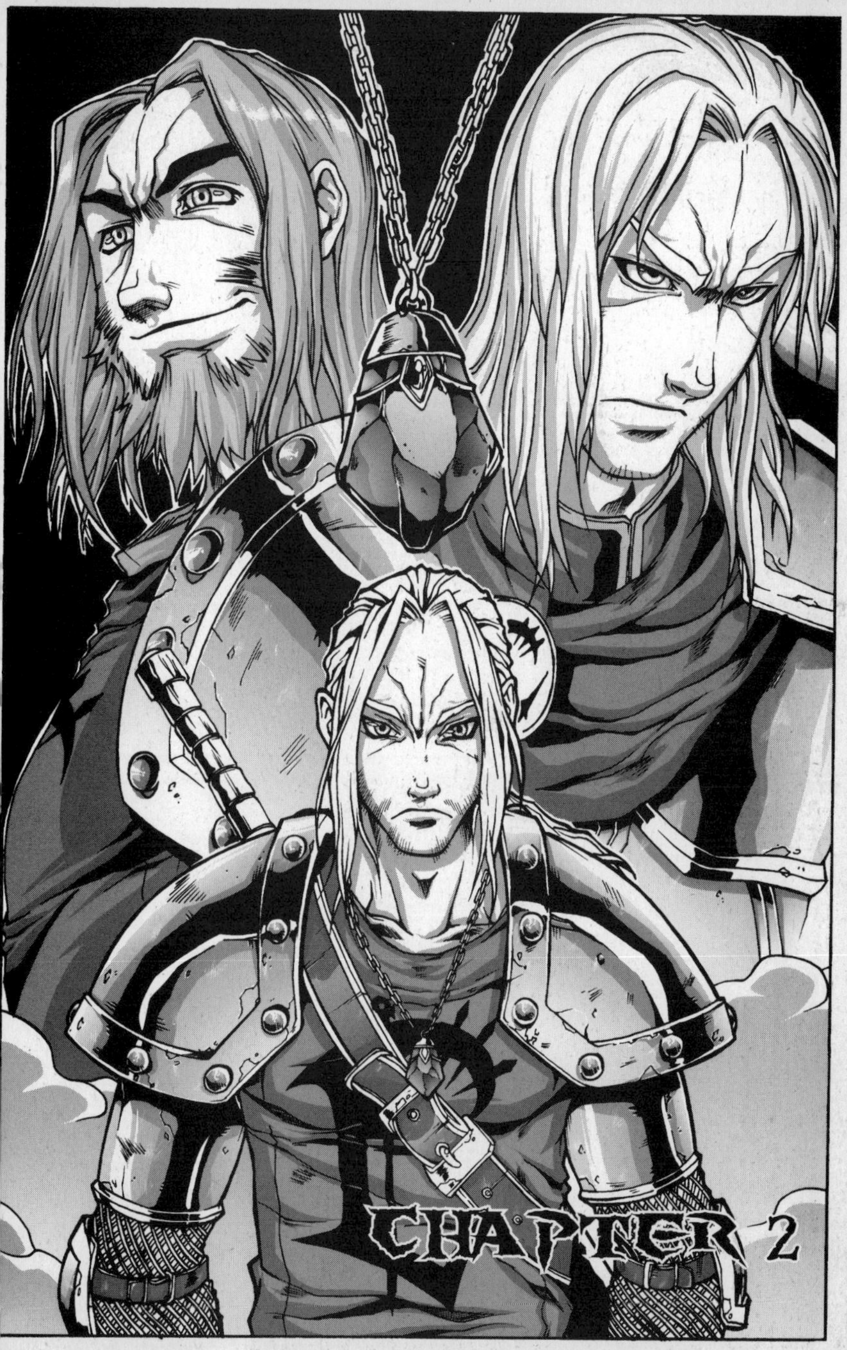
CHAPTER 2

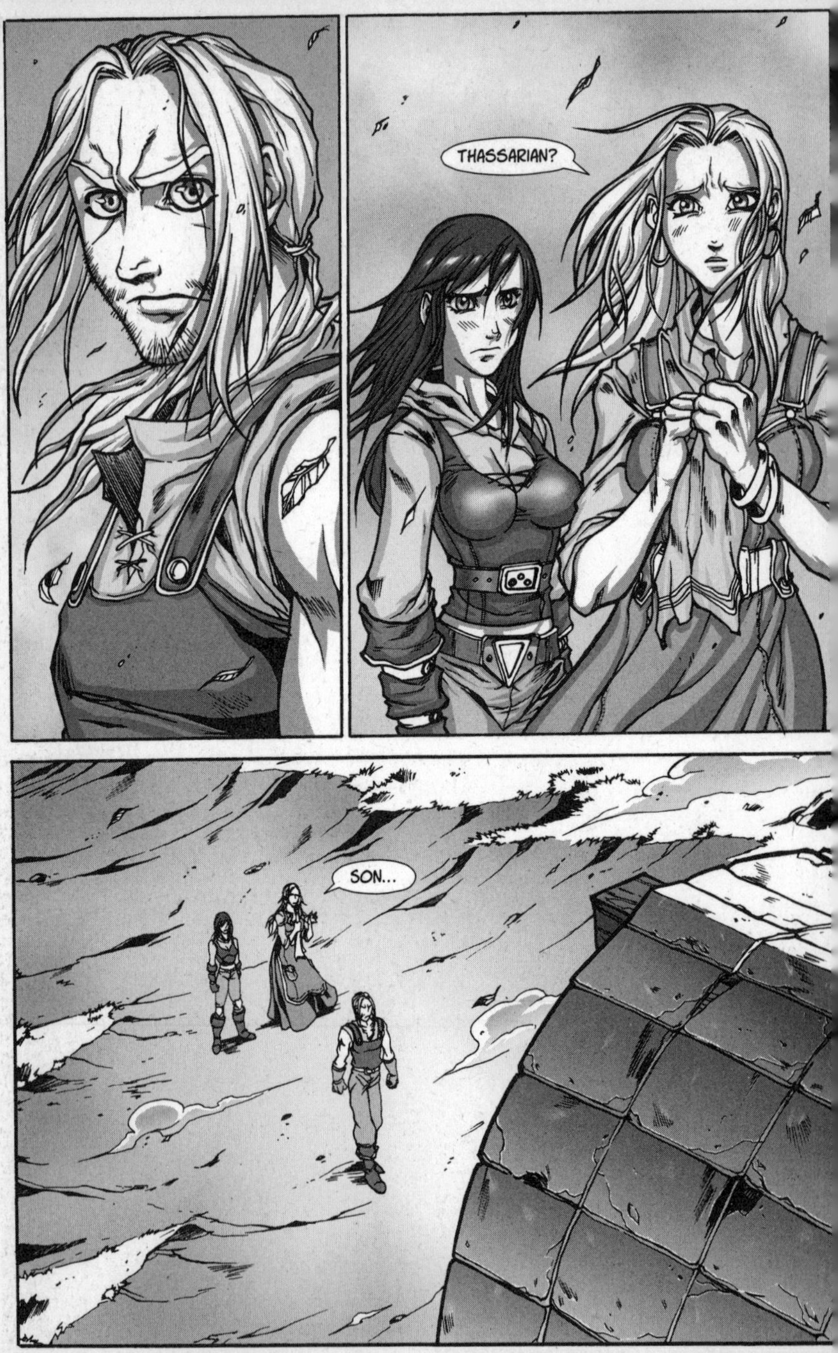
THASSARIAN?
SON...

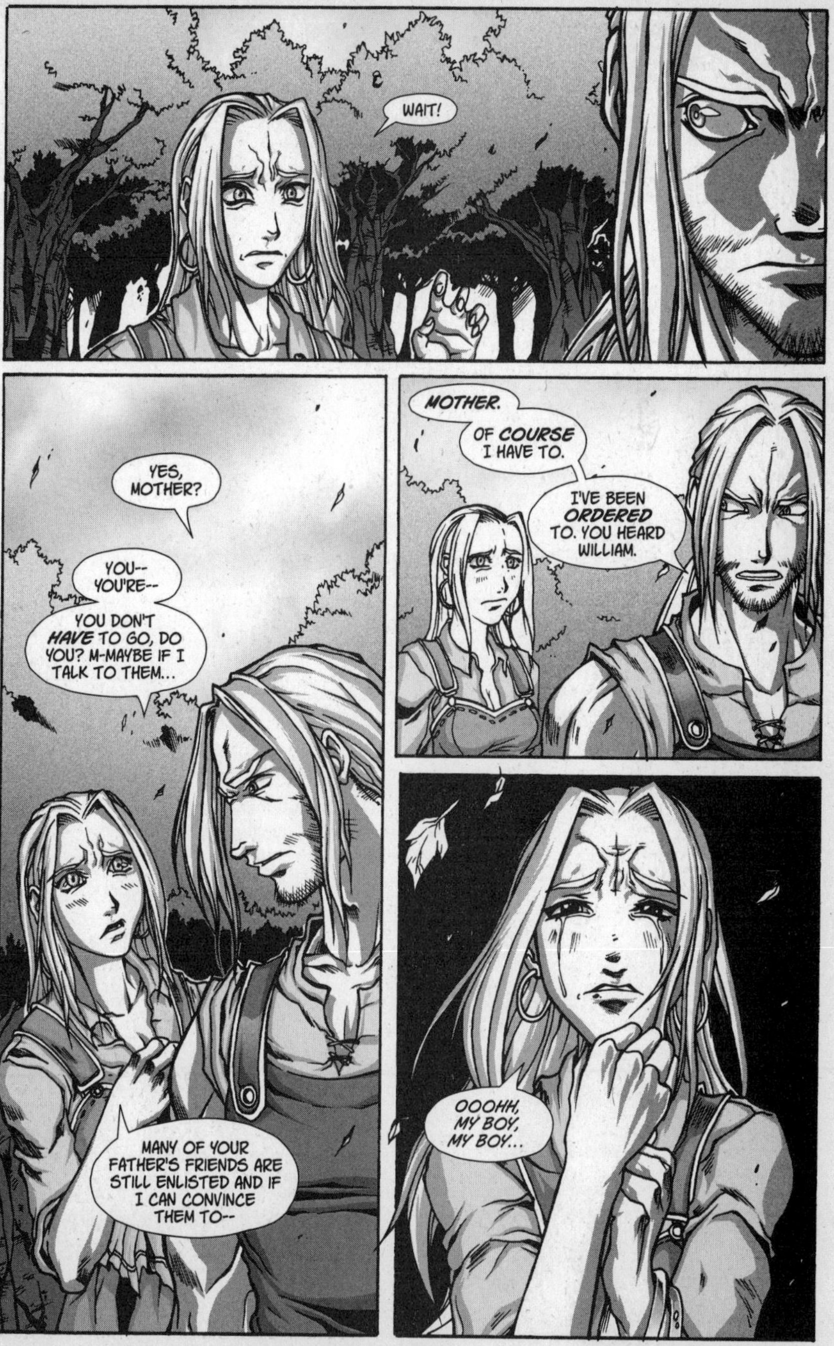
WAIT!
YES, MOTHER?
YOU-- YOU'RE--
YOU DON'T *HAVE* TO GO, DO YOU? M-MAYBE IF I TALK TO THEM...
MANY OF YOUR FATHER'S FRIENDS ARE STILL ENLISTED AND IF I CAN CONVINCE THEM TO--
MOTHER.
OF *COURSE* I HAVE TO.
I'VE BEEN *ORDERED* TO. YOU HEARD WILLIAM.
OOOHH, MY BOY, MY BOY...

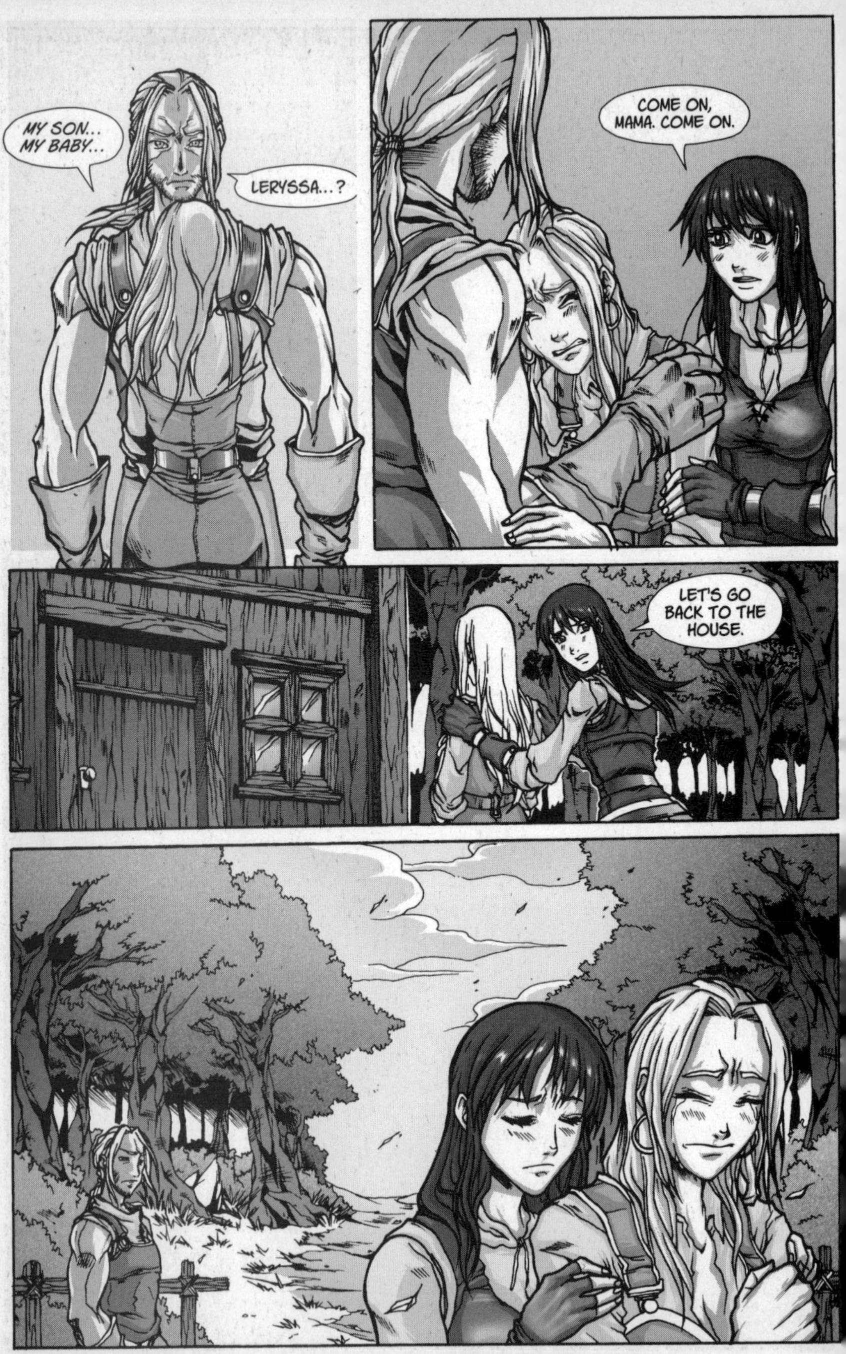
MY SON... MY BABY...
LERYSSA...?
COME ON, MAMA. COME ON.
LET'S GO BACK TO THE HOUSE.

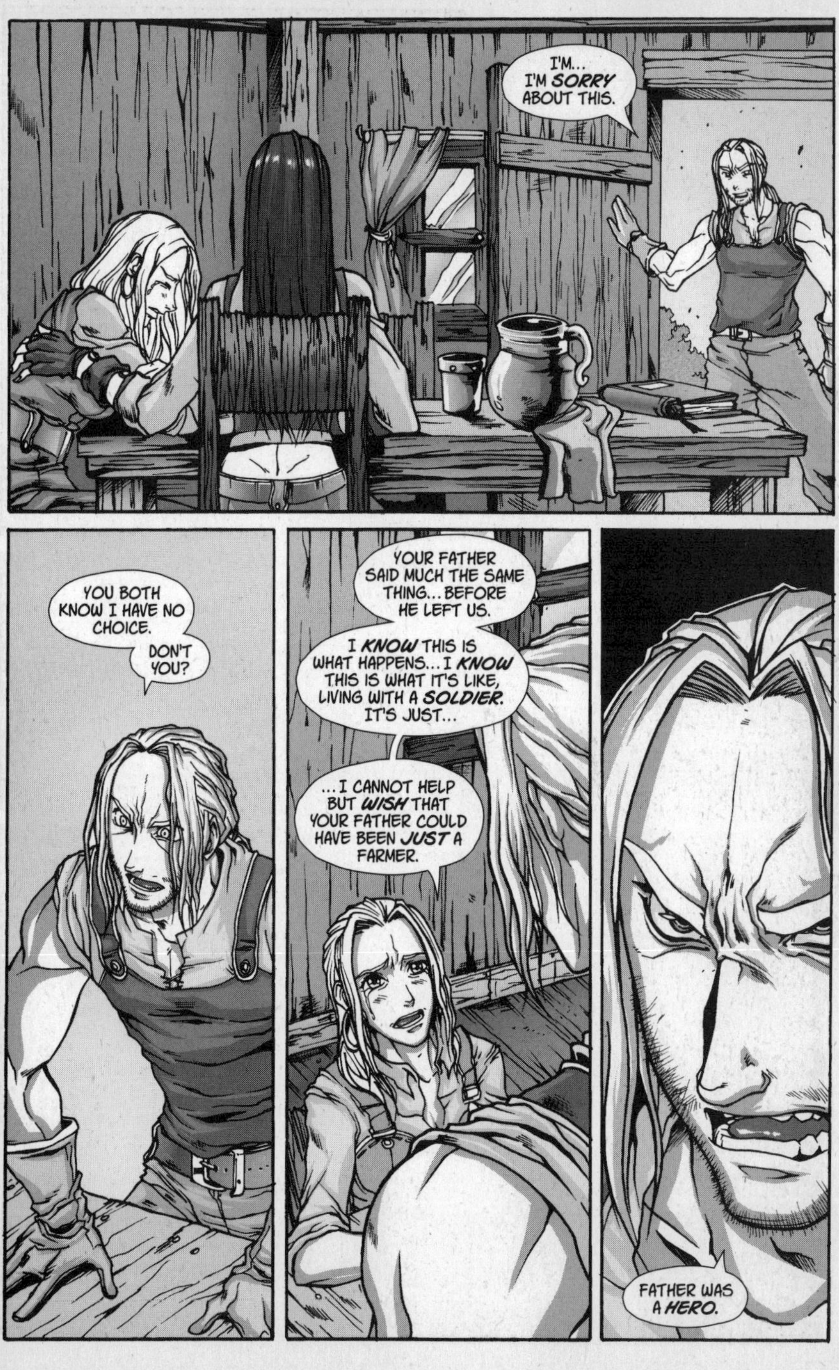
I'M...
I'M SORRY ABOUT THIS.
YOU BOTH KNOW I HAVE NO CHOICE.
DON'T YOU?
YOUR FATHER SAID MUCH THE SAME THING... BEFORE HE LEFT US.
I KNOW THIS IS WHAT HAPPENS... I KNOW THIS IS WHAT IT'S LIKE, LIVING WITH A SOLDIER. IT'S JUST...
...I CANNOT HELP BUT WISH THAT YOUR FATHER COULD HAVE BEEN JUST A FARMER.
FATHER WAS A HERO.

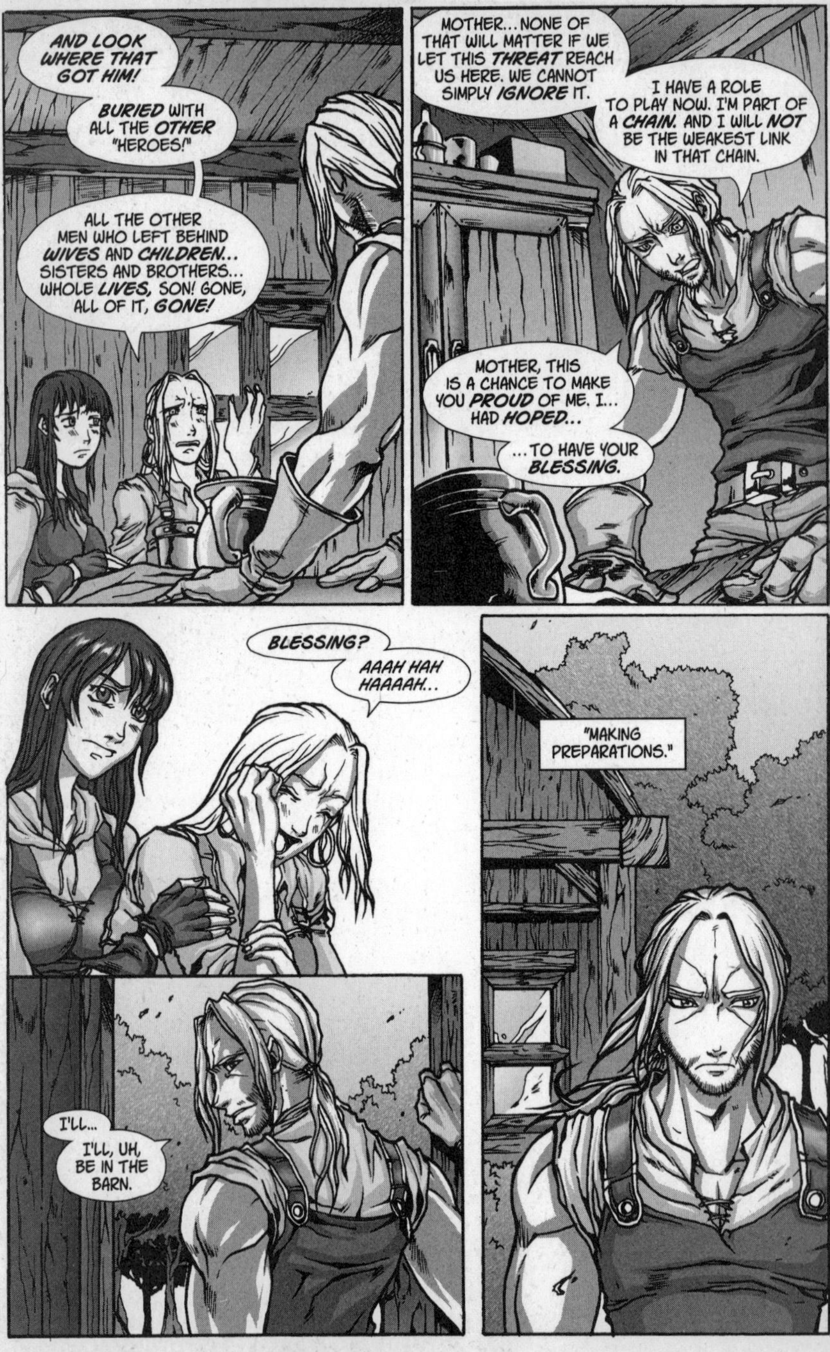
AND LOOK WHERE THAT GOT HIM!
BURIED WITH ALL THE OTHER "HEROES!"
ALL THE OTHER MEN WHO LEFT BEHIND WIVES AND CHILDREN... SISTERS AND BROTHERS... WHOLE LIVES, SON! GONE, ALL OF IT, GONE!
MOTHER... NONE OF THAT WILL MATTER IF WE LET THIS THREAT REACH US HERE. WE CANNOT SIMPLY IGNORE IT.
I HAVE A ROLE TO PLAY NOW. I'M PART OF A CHAIN. AND I WILL NOT BE THE WEAKEST LINK IN THAT CHAIN.
MOTHER, THIS IS A CHANCE TO MAKE YOU PROUD OF ME. I... HAD HOPED...
...TO HAVE YOUR BLESSING.
BLESSING?
AAAH HAH HAAAAH...
I'LL... I'LL, UH, BE IN THE BARN.
"MAKING PREPARATIONS."

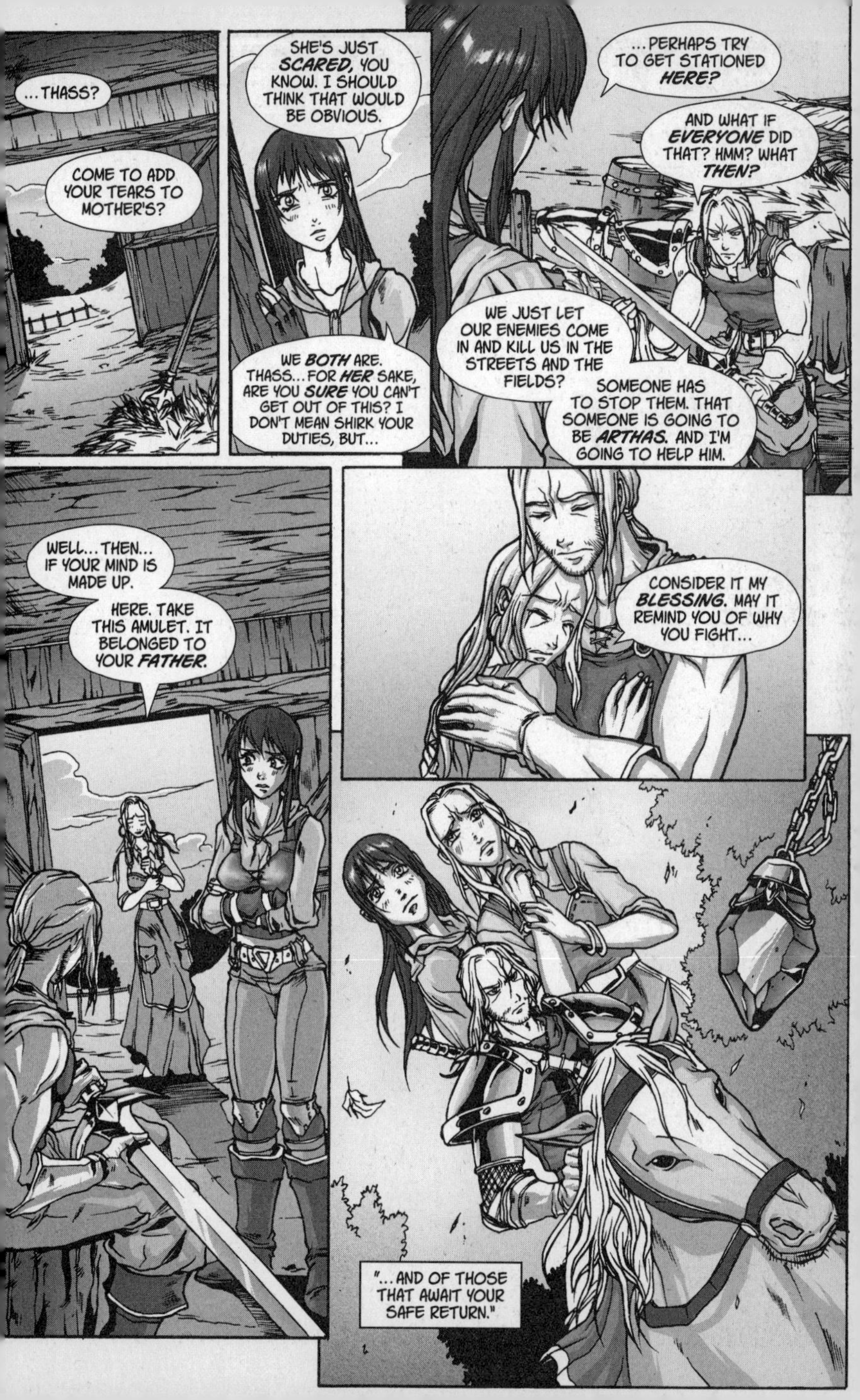
...THASS?
COME TO ADD YOUR TEARS TO MOTHER'S?
SHE'S JUST *SCARED,* YOU KNOW. I SHOULD THINK THAT WOULD BE OBVIOUS.
WE *BOTH* ARE. THASS... FOR *HER* SAKE, ARE YOU *SURE* YOU CAN'T GET OUT OF THIS? I DON'T MEAN SHIRK YOUR DUTIES, BUT...
...PERHAPS TRY TO GET STATIONED *HERE?*
AND WHAT IF *EVERYONE* DID THAT? HMM? WHAT *THEN?*
WE JUST LET OUR ENEMIES COME IN AND KILL US IN THE STREETS AND THE FIELDS?
SOMEONE HAS TO STOP THEM. THAT SOMEONE IS GOING TO BE *ARTHAS.* AND I'M GOING TO HELP HIM.
WELL... THEN... IF YOUR MIND IS MADE UP.
HERE. TAKE THIS AMULET. IT BELONGED TO YOUR *FATHER.*
CONSIDER IT MY *BLESSING.* MAY IT REMIND YOU OF WHY YOU FIGHT...
"...AND OF THOSE THAT AWAIT YOUR SAFE RETURN."

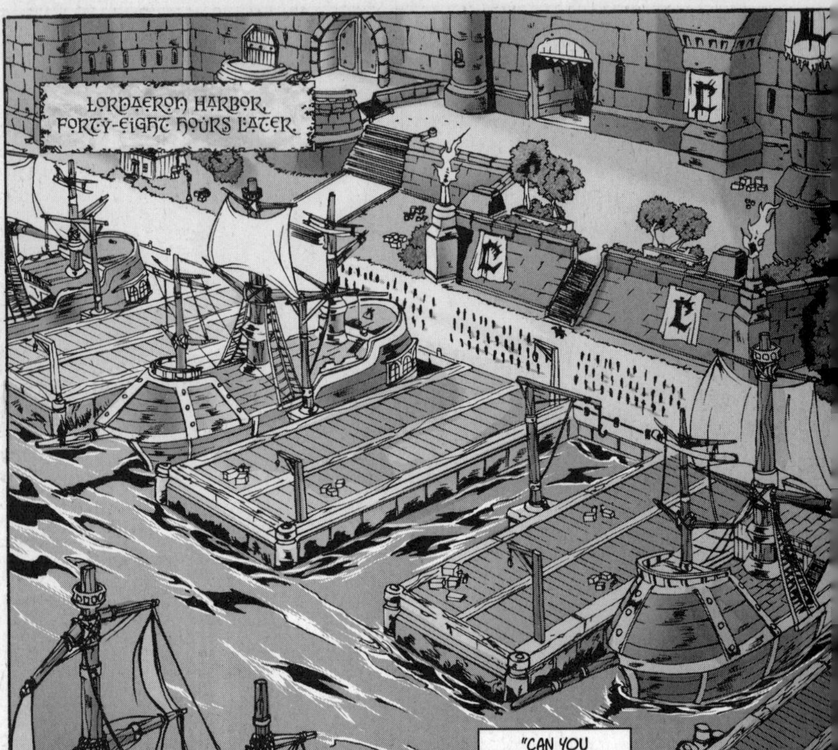
LORDAERON HARBOR, FORTY-EIGHT HOURS LATER.
"CAN YOU BELIEVE THIS?"

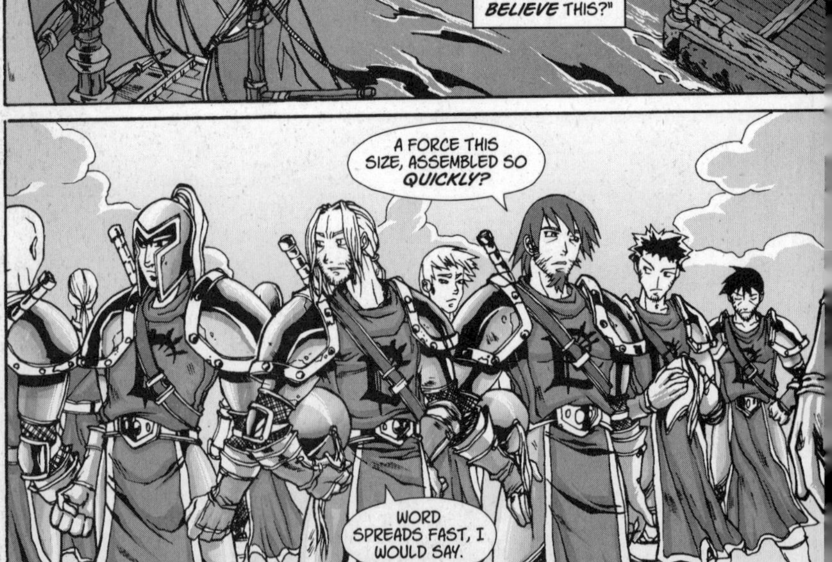
A FORCE THIS SIZE, ASSEMBLED SO QUICKLY?
WORD SPREADS FAST, I WOULD SAY.

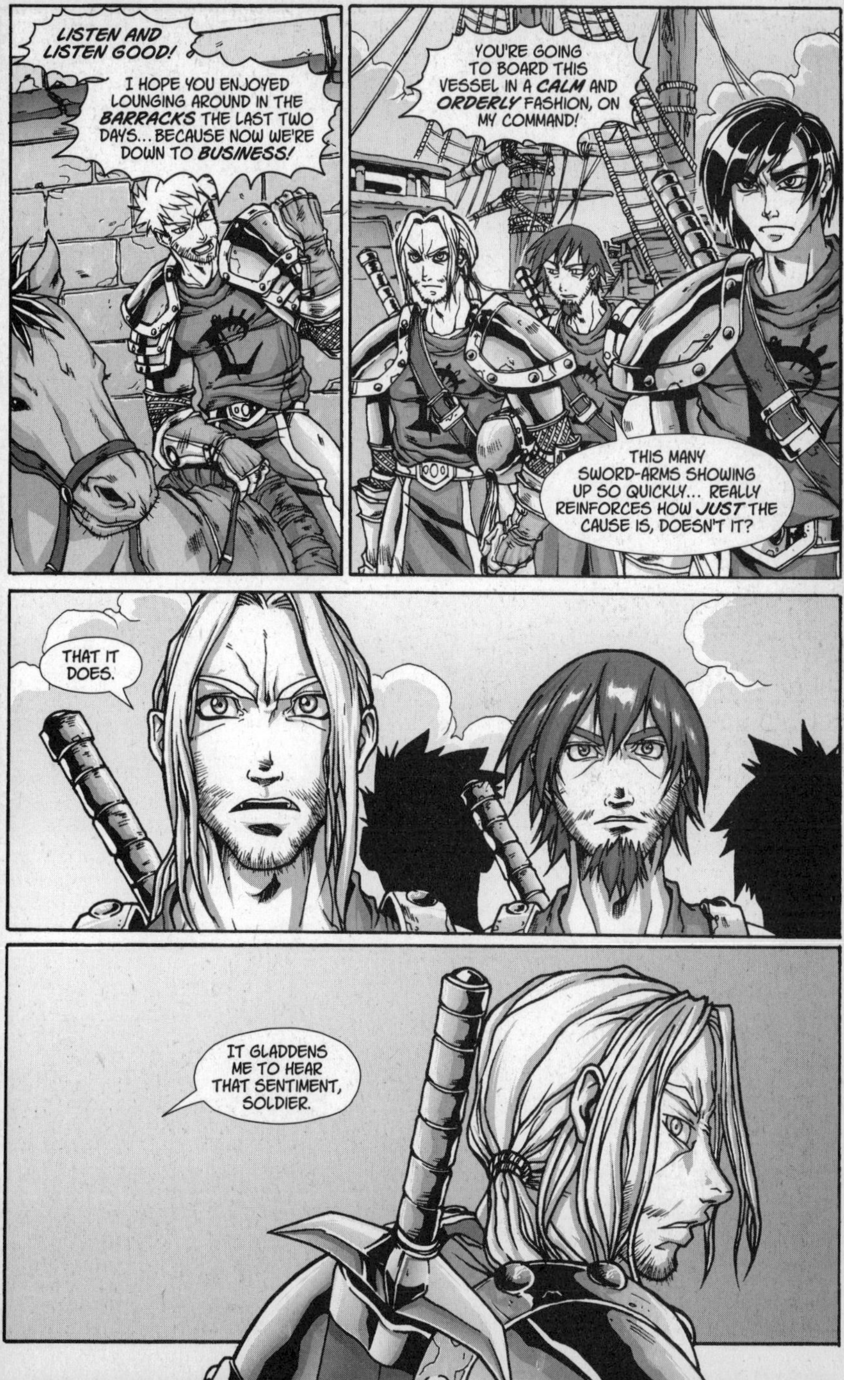
LISTEN AND LISTEN GOOD!
I HOPE YOU ENJOYED LOUNGING AROUND IN THE **BARRACKS** THE LAST TWO DAYS... BECAUSE NOW WE'RE DOWN TO **BUSINESS!**
YOU'RE GOING TO BOARD THIS VESSEL IN A **CALM** AND **ORDERLY** FASHION, ON MY COMMAND!
THIS MANY SWORD-ARMS SHOWING UP SO QUICKLY... REALLY REINFORCES HOW **JUST** THE CAUSE IS, DOESN'T IT?
THAT IT DOES.
IT GLADDENS ME TO HEAR THAT SENTIMENT, SOLDIER.

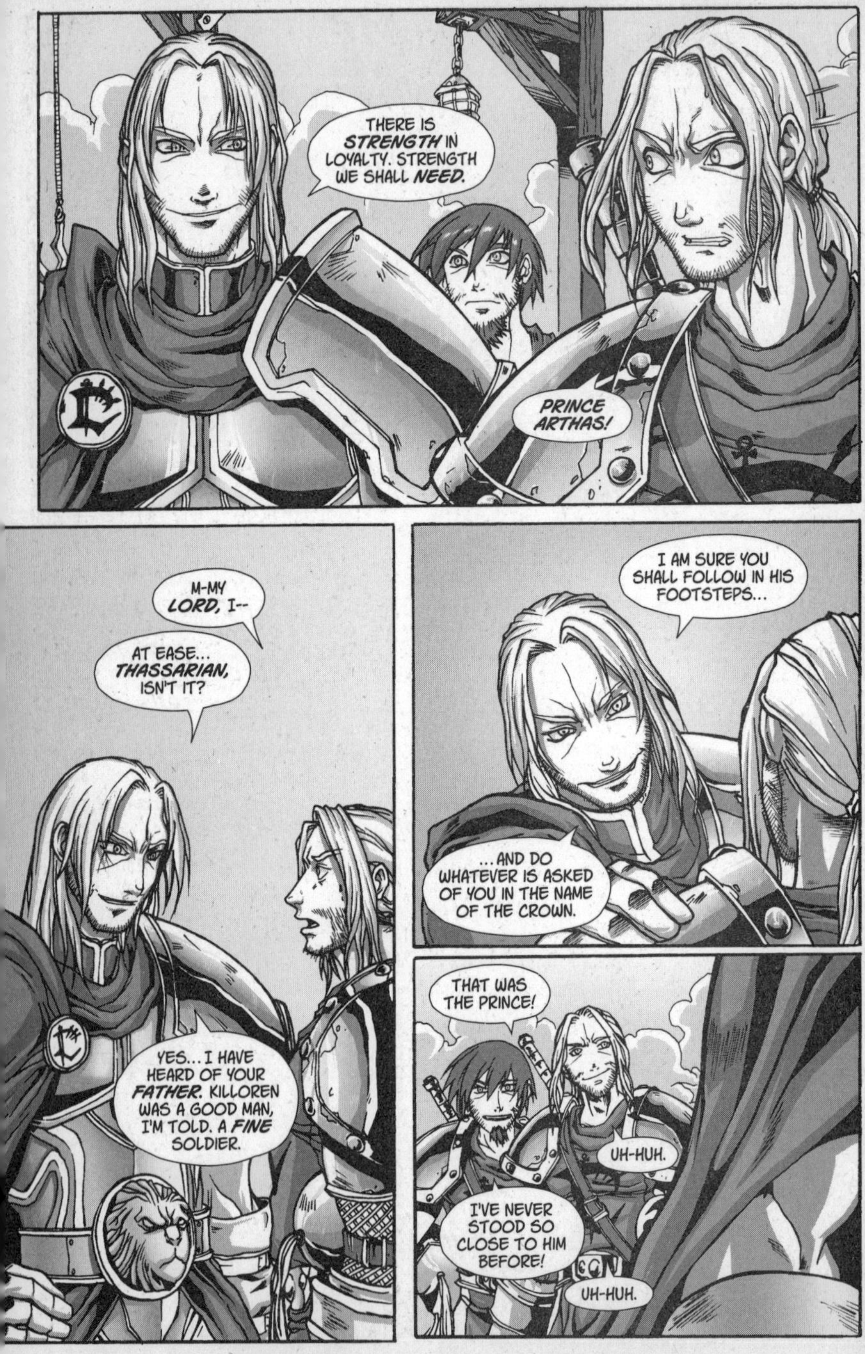
THERE IS STRENGTH IN LOYALTY. STRENGTH WE SHALL NEED.
PRINCE ARTHAS!
M-MY LORD, I--
AT EASE... THASSARIAN, ISN'T IT?
YES... I HAVE HEARD OF YOUR FATHER. KILLOREN WAS A GOOD MAN, I'M TOLD. A FINE SOLDIER.
I AM SURE YOU SHALL FOLLOW IN HIS FOOTSTEPS...
...AND DO WHATEVER IS ASKED OF YOU IN THE NAME OF THE CROWN.
THAT WAS THE PRINCE!
UH-HUH.
I'VE NEVER STOOD SO CLOSE TO HIM BEFORE!
UH-HUH.

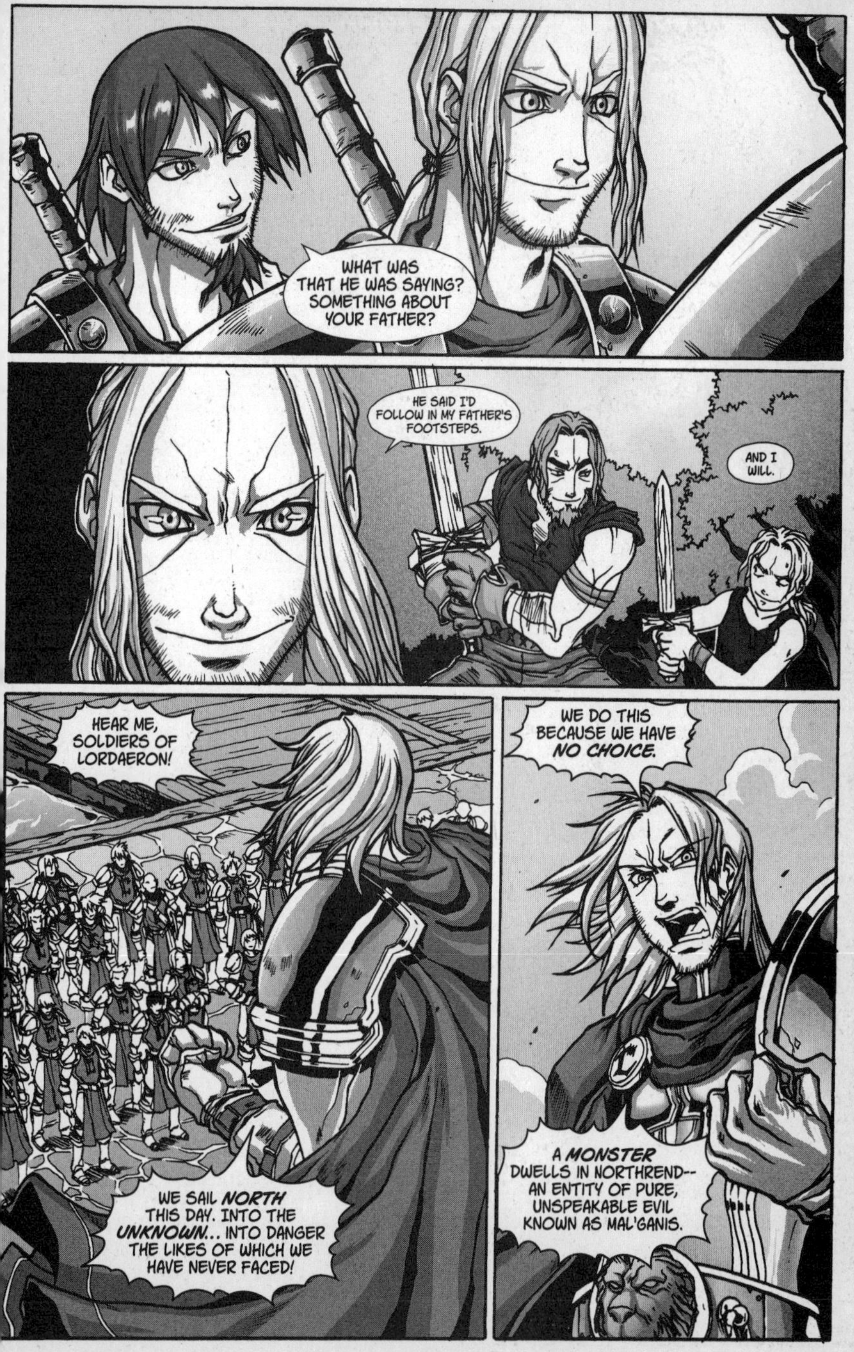
WHAT WAS THAT HE WAS SAYING? SOMETHING ABOUT YOUR FATHER?
HE SAID I'D FOLLOW IN MY FATHER'S FOOTSTEPS.
AND I WILL.
HEAR ME, SOLDIERS OF LORDAERON!
WE SAIL **NORTH** THIS DAY. INTO THE **UNKNOWN**... INTO DANGER THE LIKES OF WHICH WE HAVE NEVER FACED!
WE DO THIS BECAUSE WE HAVE **NO CHOICE**.
A **MONSTER** DWELLS IN NORTHREND-- AN ENTITY OF PURE, UNSPEAKABLE EVIL KNOWN AS MAL'GANIS.

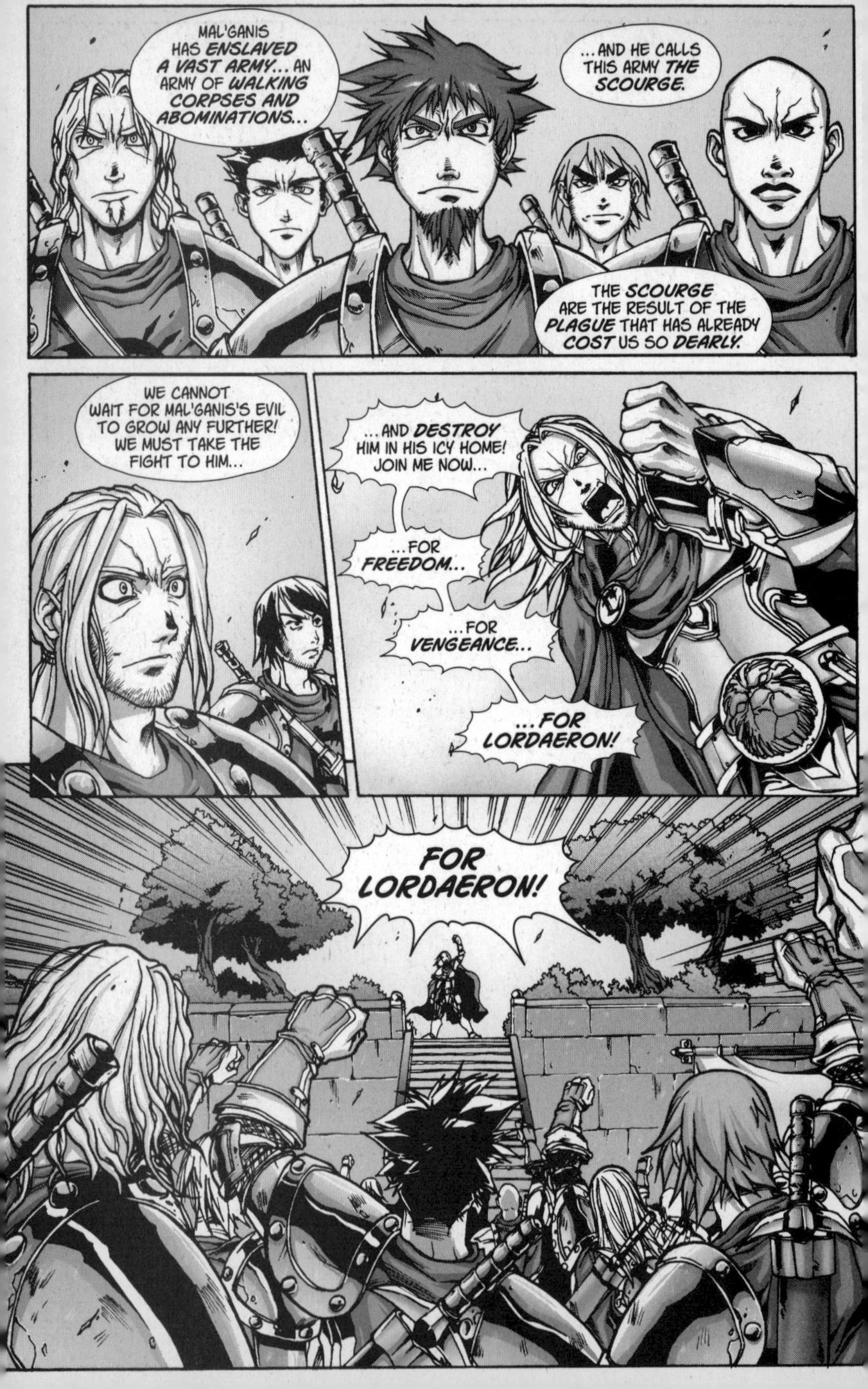
MAL'GANIS HAS ENSLAVED A VAST ARMY... AN ARMY OF WALKING CORPSES AND ABOMINATIONS...
...AND HE CALLS THIS ARMY THE SCOURGE.
THE SCOURGE ARE THE RESULT OF THE PLAGUE THAT HAS ALREADY COST US SO DEARLY.
WE CANNOT WAIT FOR MAL'GANIS'S EVIL TO GROW ANY FURTHER! WE MUST TAKE THE FIGHT TO HIM...
...AND DESTROY HIM IN HIS ICY HOME! JOIN ME NOW...
...FOR FREEDOM...
...FOR VENGEANCE...
...FOR LORDAERON!
FOR LORDAERON!

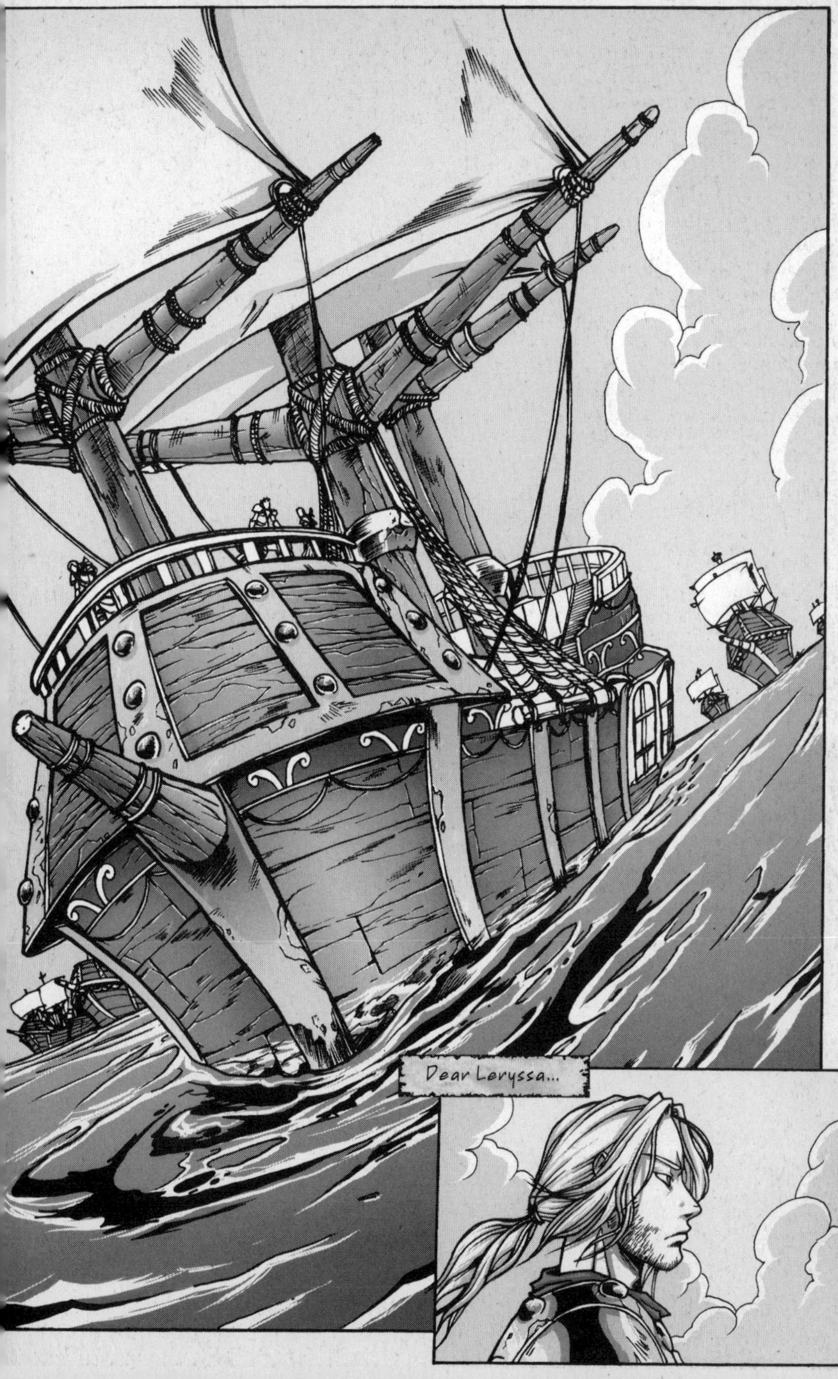
Dear Leryssa...

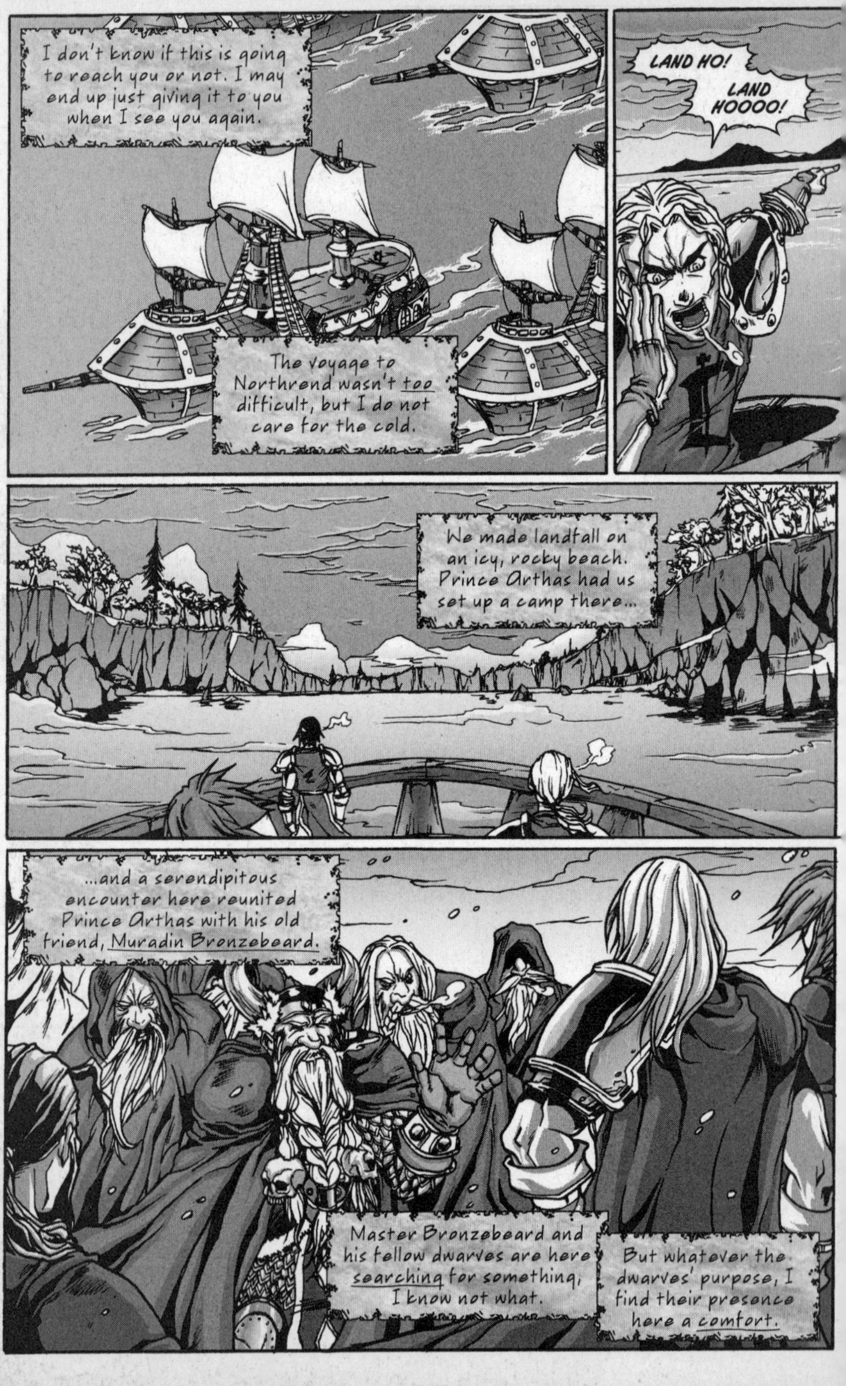
I don't know if this is going to reach you or not. I may end up just giving it to you when I see you again.
The voyage to Northrend wasn't too difficult, but I do not care for the cold.
LAND HO!
LAND HOOOO!
We made landfall on an icy, rocky beach. Prince Arthas had us set up a camp there...
...and a serendipitous encounter here reunited Prince Arthas with his old friend, Muradin Bronzebeard.
Master Bronzebeard and his fellow dwarves are here searching for something, I know not what.
But whatever the dwarves' purpose, I find their presence here a comfort.

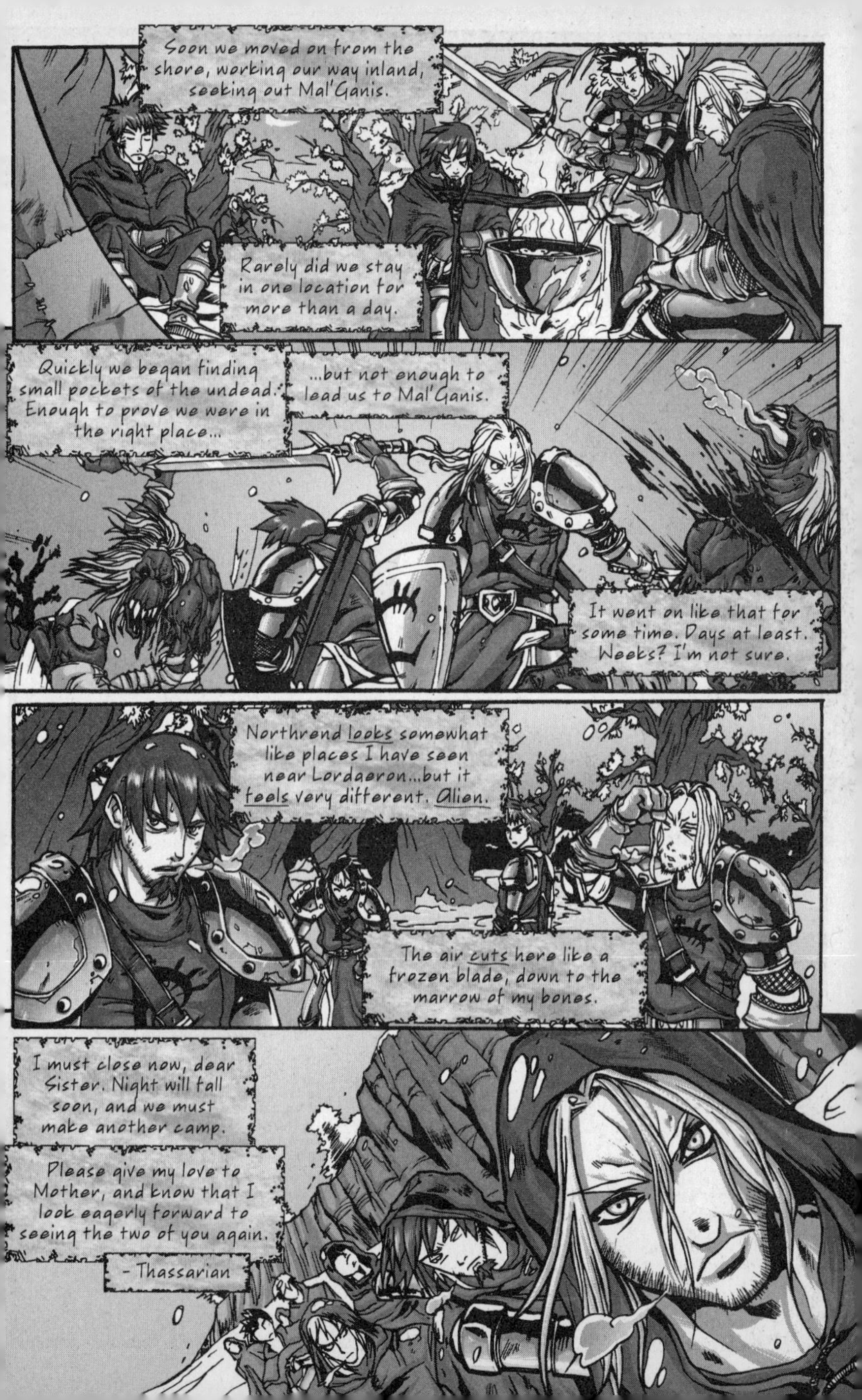
Soon we moved on from the shore, working our way inland, seeking out Mal'Ganis.
Rarely did we stay in one location for more than a day.
Quickly we began finding small pockets of the undead. Enough to prove we were in the right place...
...but not enough to lead us to Mal'Ganis.
It went on like that for some time. Days at least. Weeks? I'm not sure.
Northrend looks somewhat like places I have seen near Lordaeron...but it feels very different. Alien.
The air cuts here like a frozen blade, down to the marrow of my bones.
I must close now, dear Sister. Night will fall soon, and we must make another camp.
Please give my love to Mother, and know that I look eagerly forward to seeing the two of you again.
- Thassarian

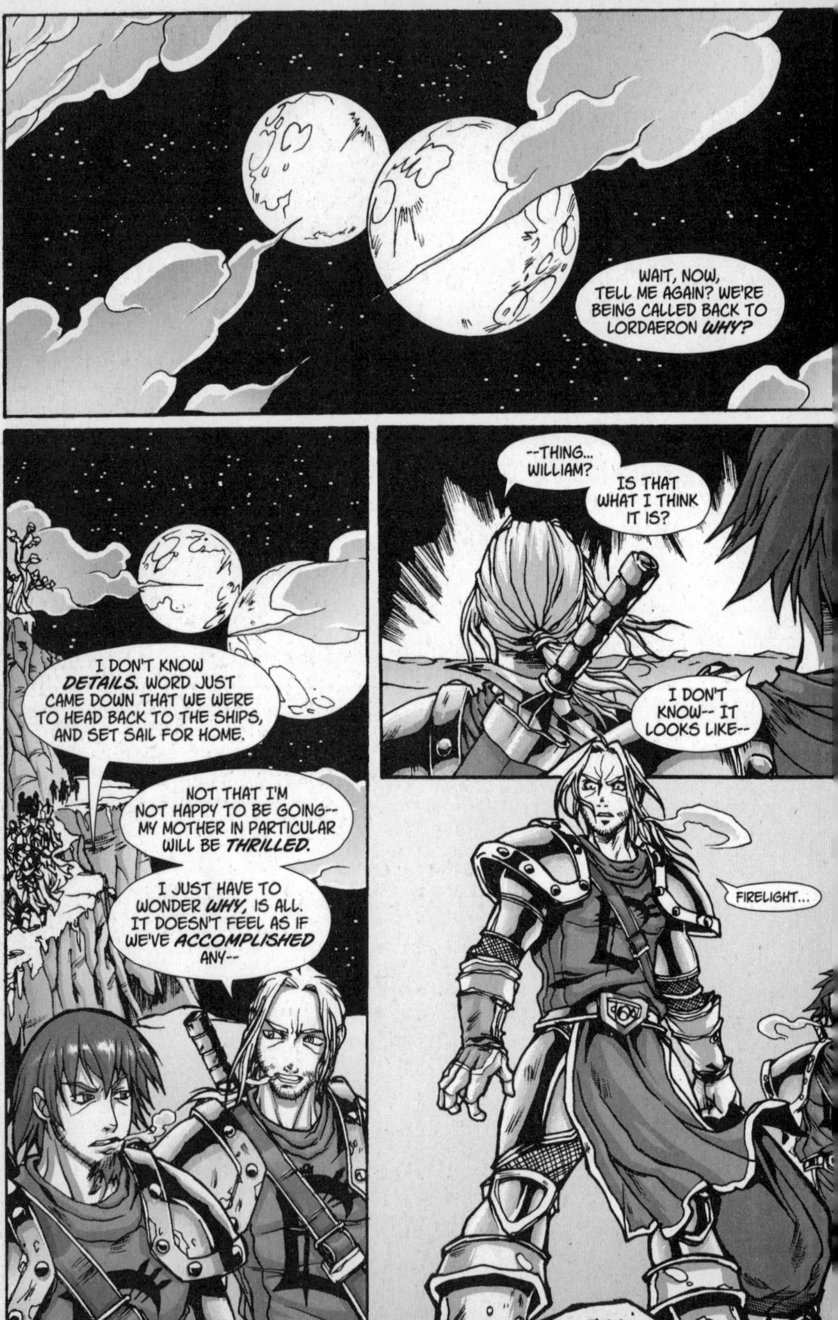
WAIT, NOW, TELL ME AGAIN? WE'RE BEING CALLED BACK TO LORDAERON *WHY?*
I DON'T KNOW *DETAILS.* WORD JUST CAME DOWN THAT WE WERE TO HEAD BACK TO THE SHIPS, AND SET SAIL FOR HOME.
NOT THAT I'M NOT HAPPY TO BE GOING-- MY MOTHER IN PARTICULAR WILL BE *THRILLED.*
I JUST HAVE TO WONDER *WHY,* IS ALL. IT DOESN'T FEEL AS IF WE'VE *ACCOMPLISHED* ANY--
--THING... WILLIAM?
IS THAT WHAT I THINK IT IS?
I DON'T KNOW-- IT LOOKS LIKE--
FIRELIGHT...

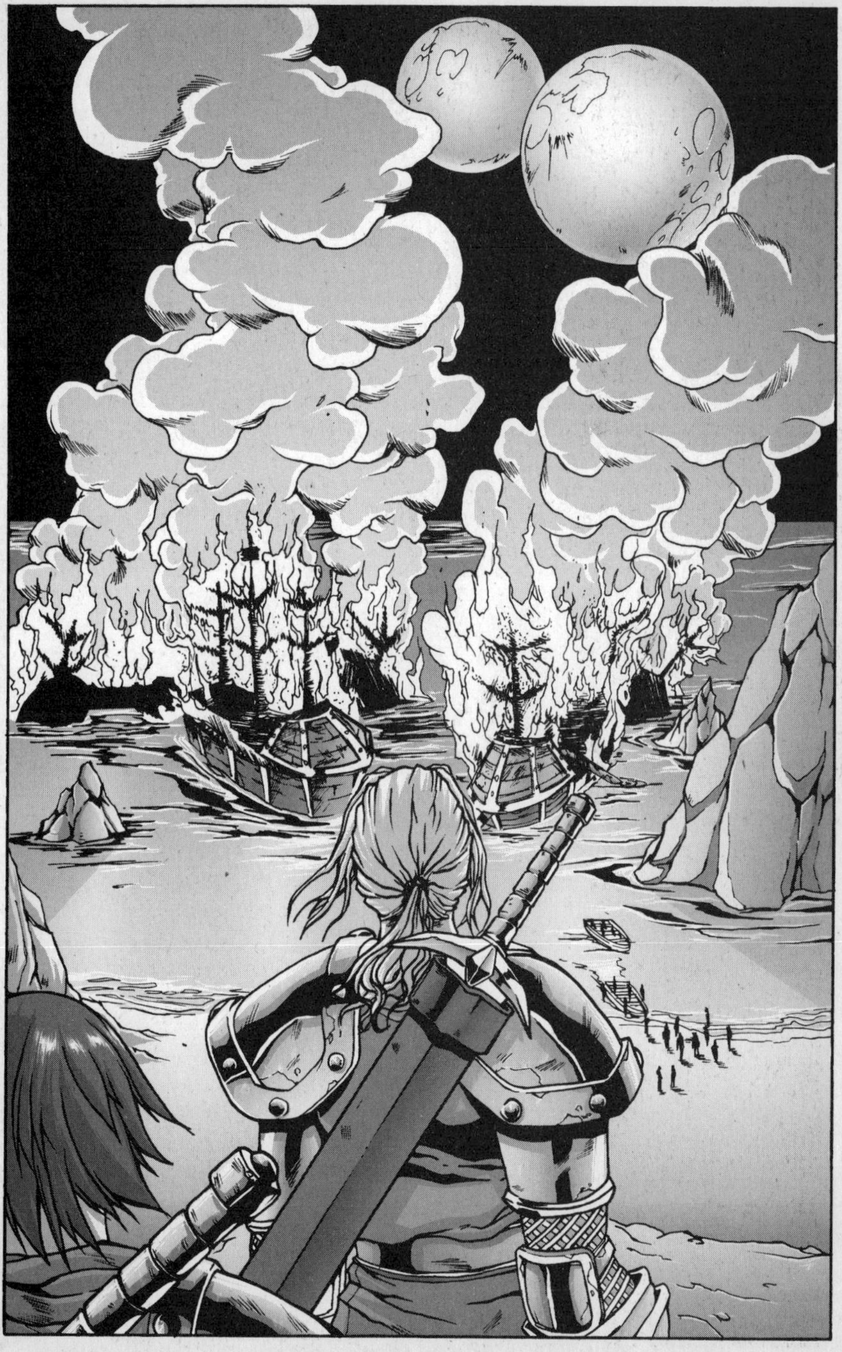

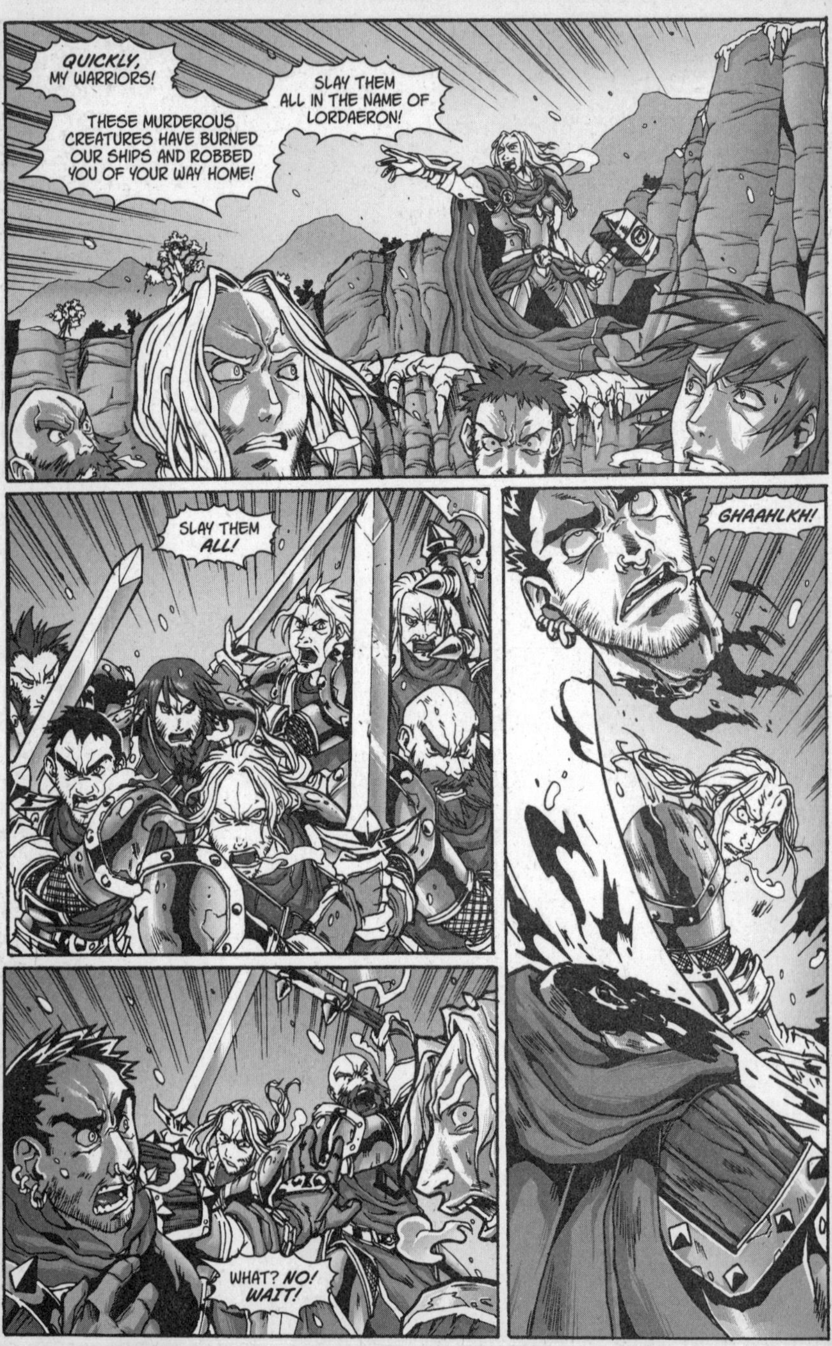
QUICKLY, MY WARRIORS!
THESE MURDEROUS CREATURES HAVE BURNED OUR SHIPS AND ROBBED YOU OF YOUR WAY HOME!
SLAY THEM ALL IN THE NAME OF LORDAERON!
SLAY THEM ALL!
WHAT? NO! WAIT!
GHAAHLKH!

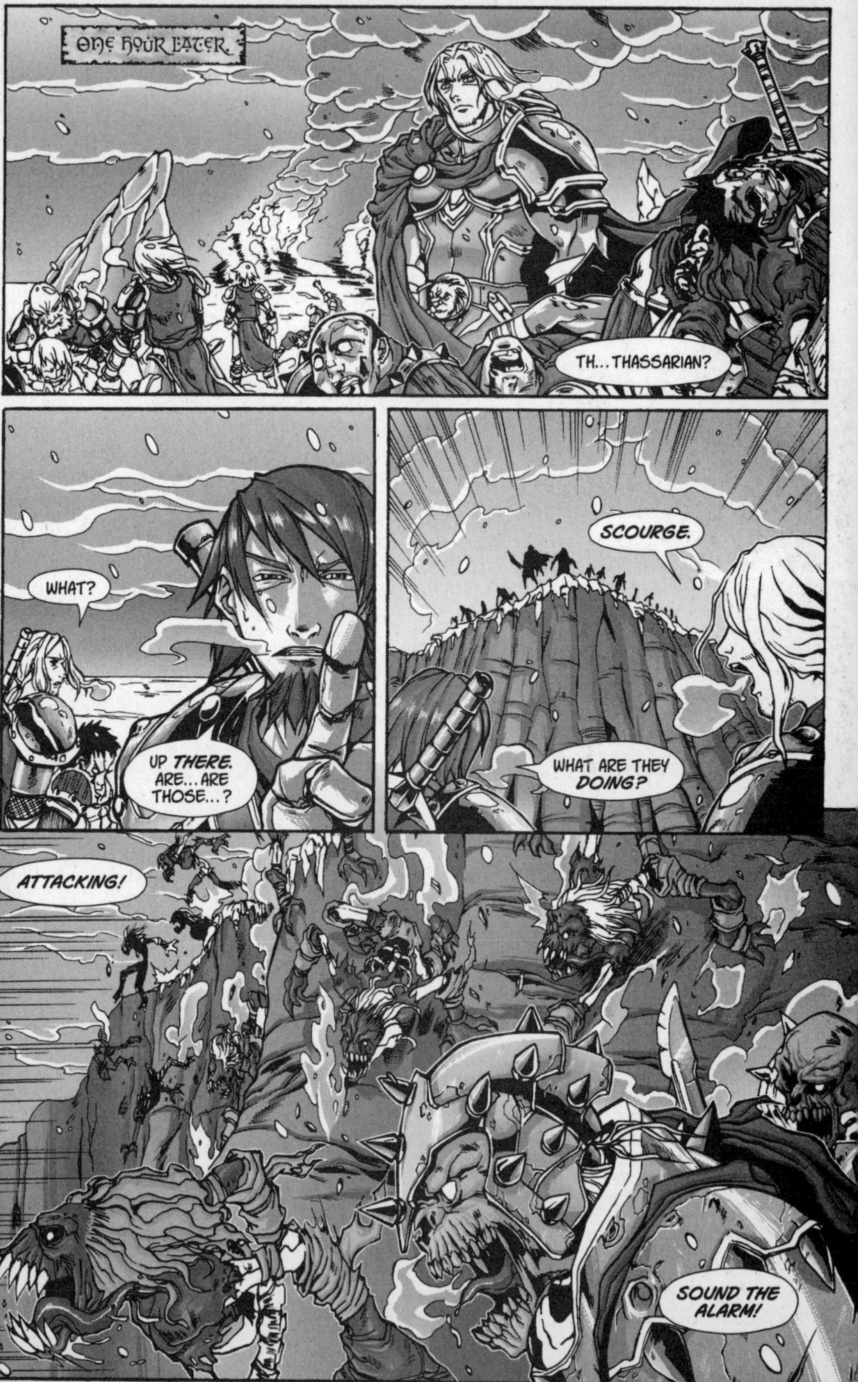
ONE HOUR LATER.
TH...THASSARIAN?
WHAT?
UP THERE. ARE...ARE THOSE...?
SCOURGE.
WHAT ARE THEY DOING?
ATTACKING!
SOUND THE ALARM!

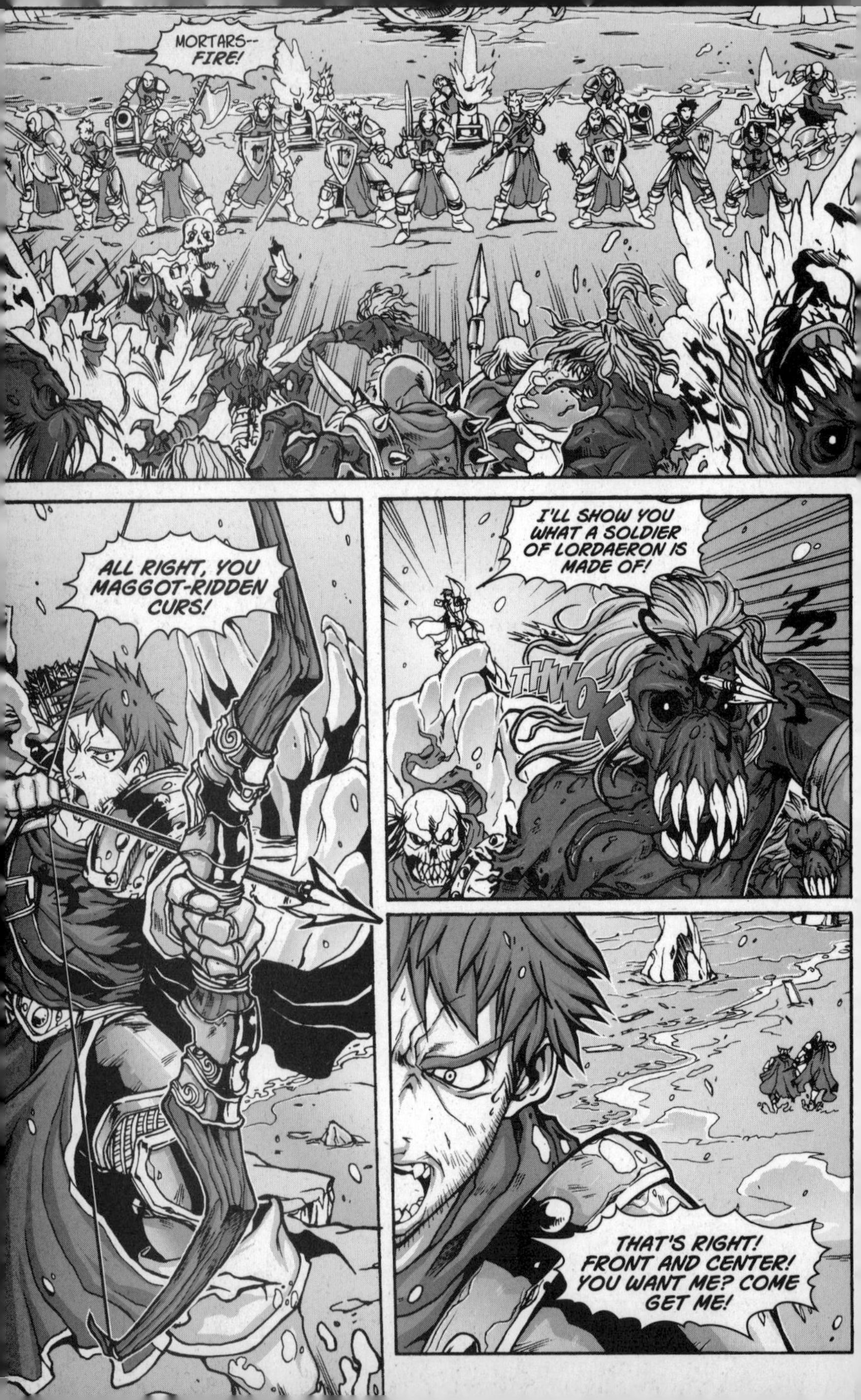
MORTARS--
FIRE!
ALL RIGHT, YOU MAGGOT-RIDDEN CURS!
I'LL SHOW YOU WHAT A SOLDIER OF LORDAERON IS MADE OF!
THWOK
THAT'S RIGHT! FRONT AND CENTER! YOU WANT ME? COME GET ME!

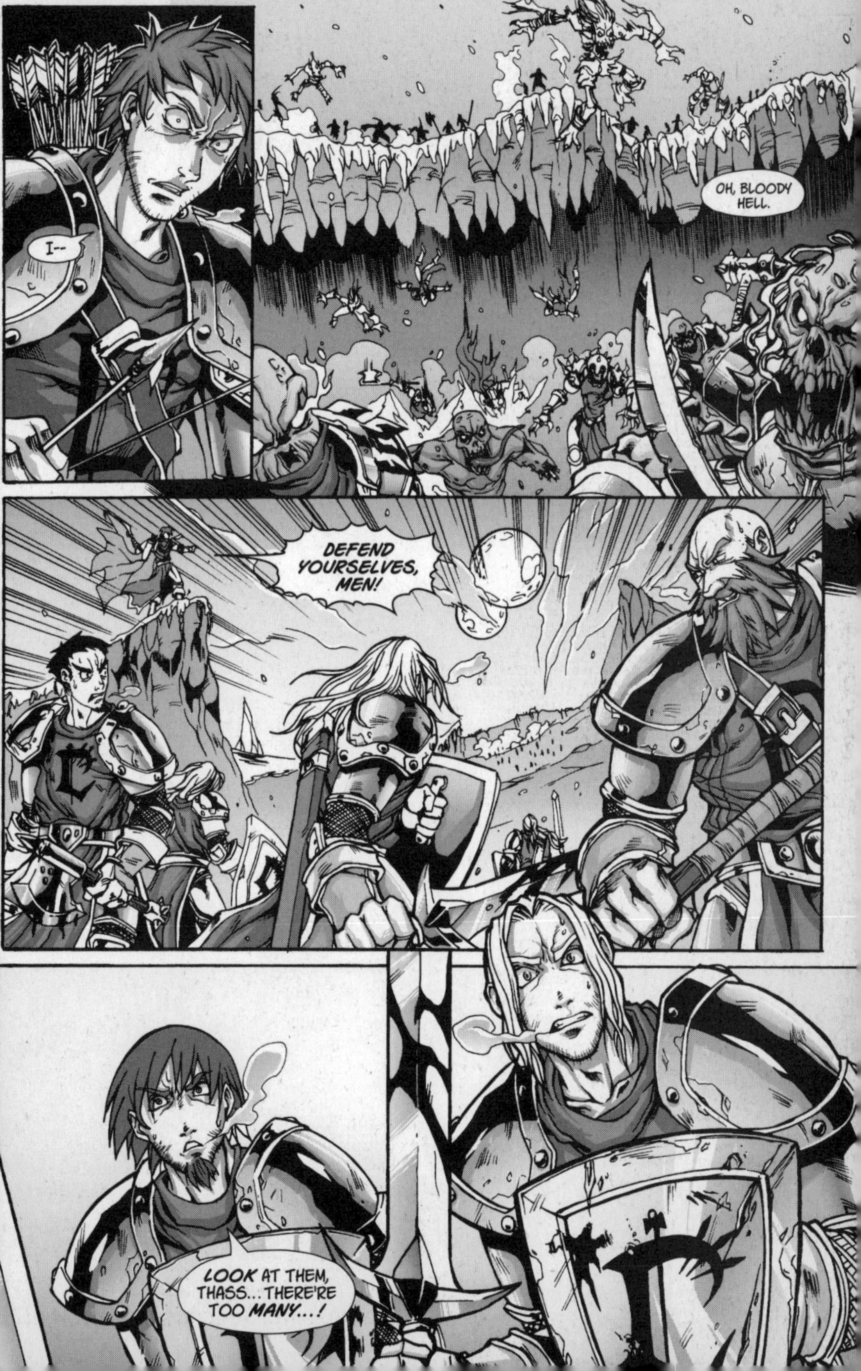
I--
OH, BLOODY HELL.
DEFEND YOURSELVES, MEN!
LOOK AT THEM, THASS... THERE'RE TOO MANY...!

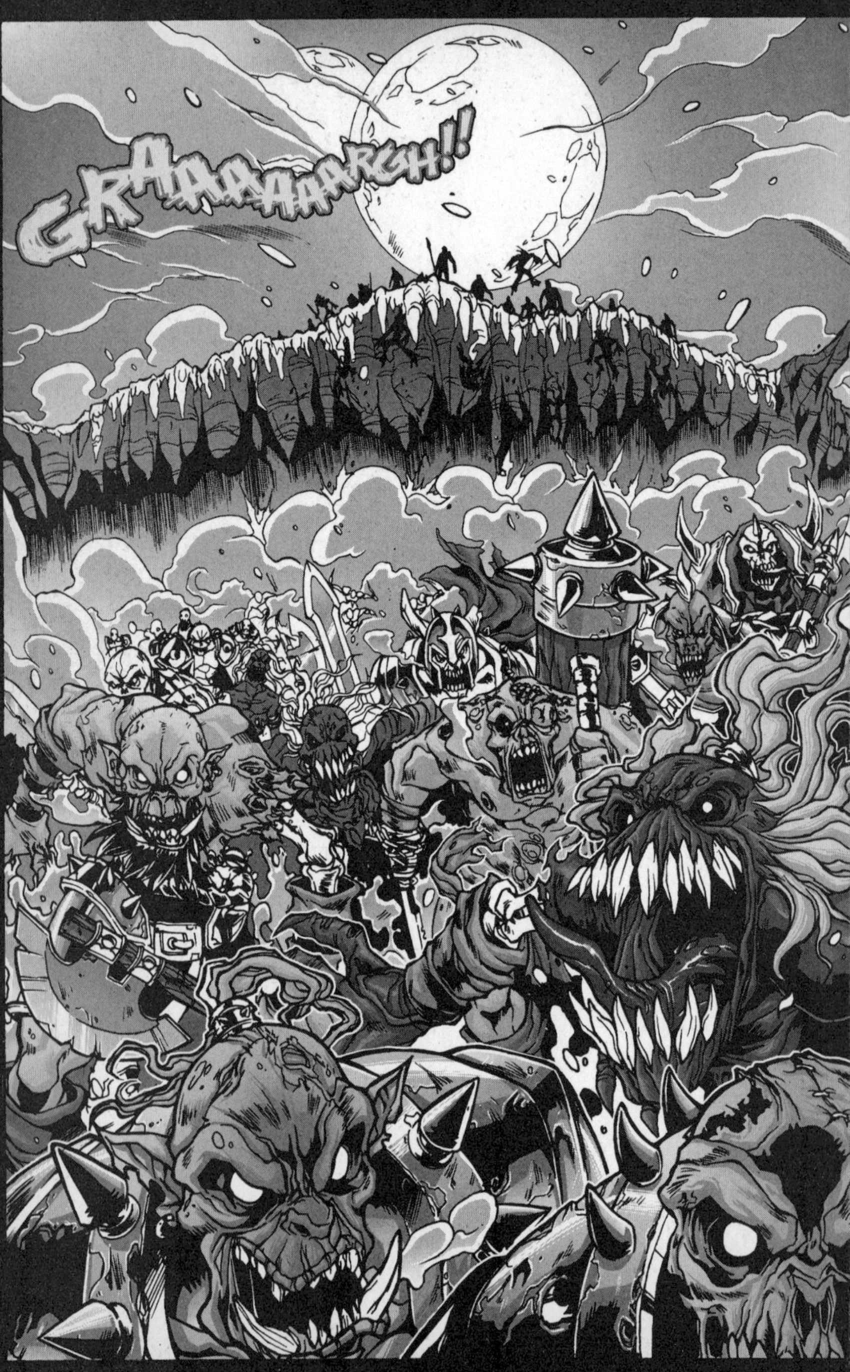
GRAAAAAARGH!!

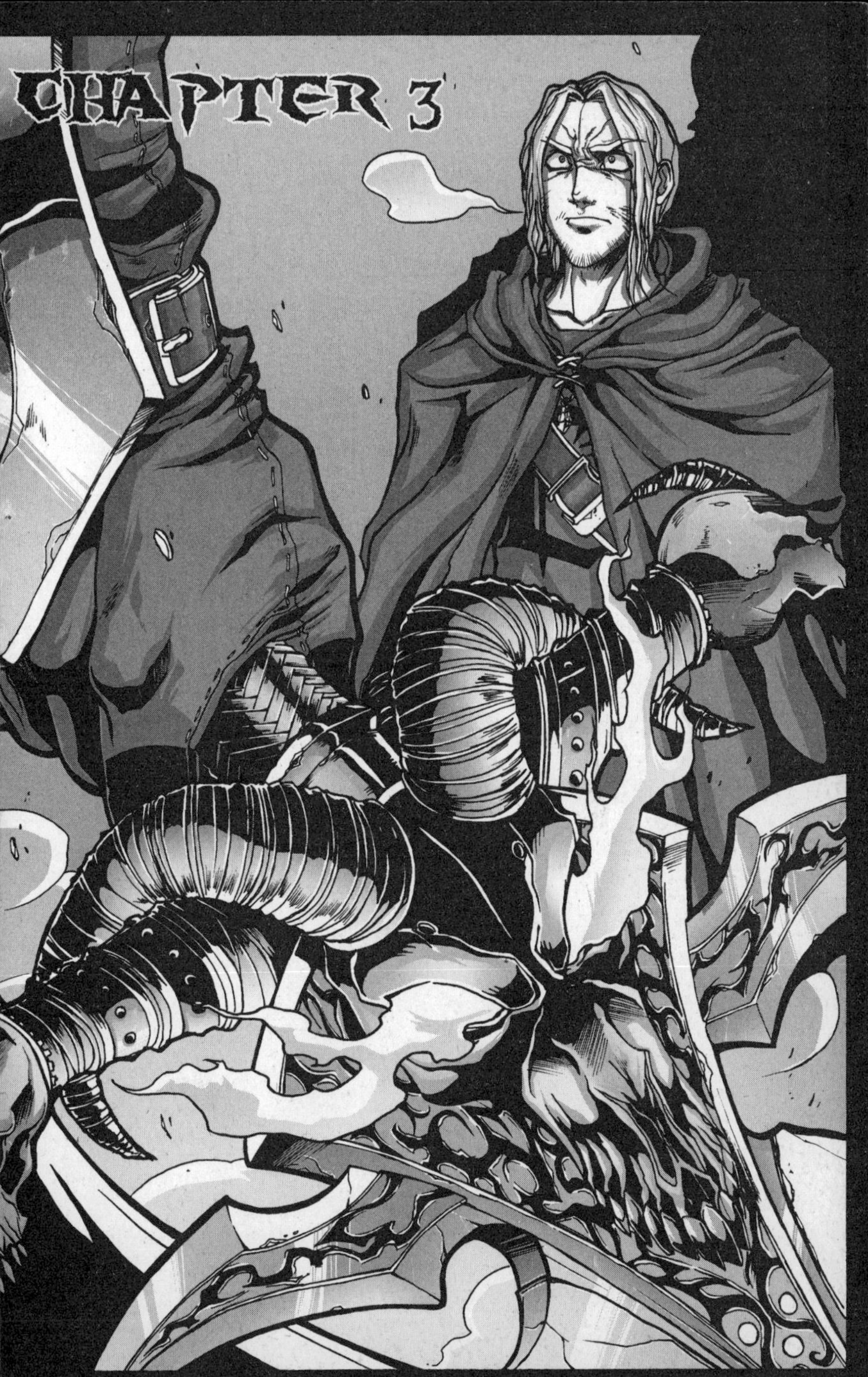
CHAPTER 3

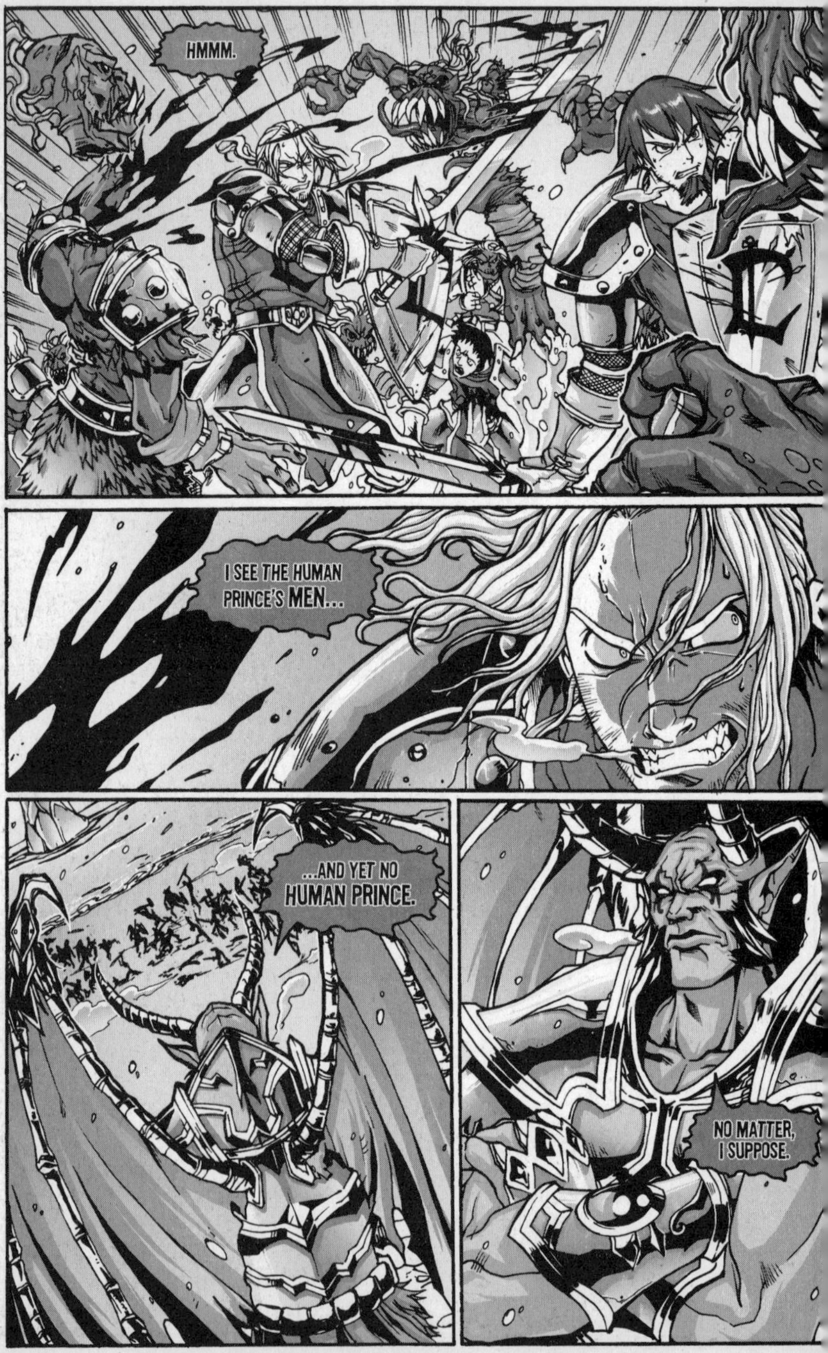
HMMM.
I SEE THE HUMAN PRINCE'S MEN...
...AND YET NO HUMAN PRINCE.
NO MATTER, I SUPPOSE.

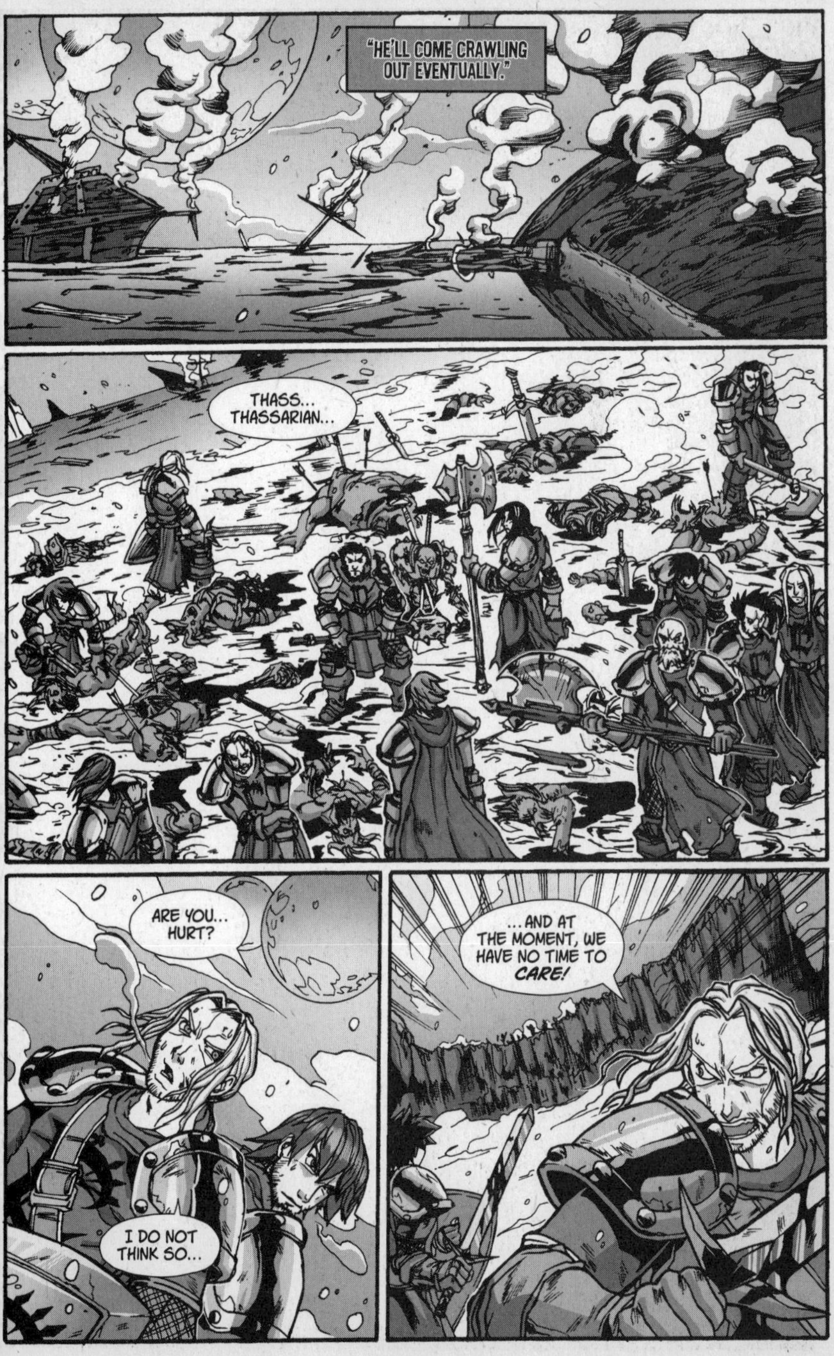
"HE'LL COME CRAWLING OUT EVENTUALLY."
THASS... THASSARIAN...
ARE YOU... HURT?
I DO NOT THINK SO...
...AND AT THE MOMENT, WE HAVE NO TIME TO CARE!

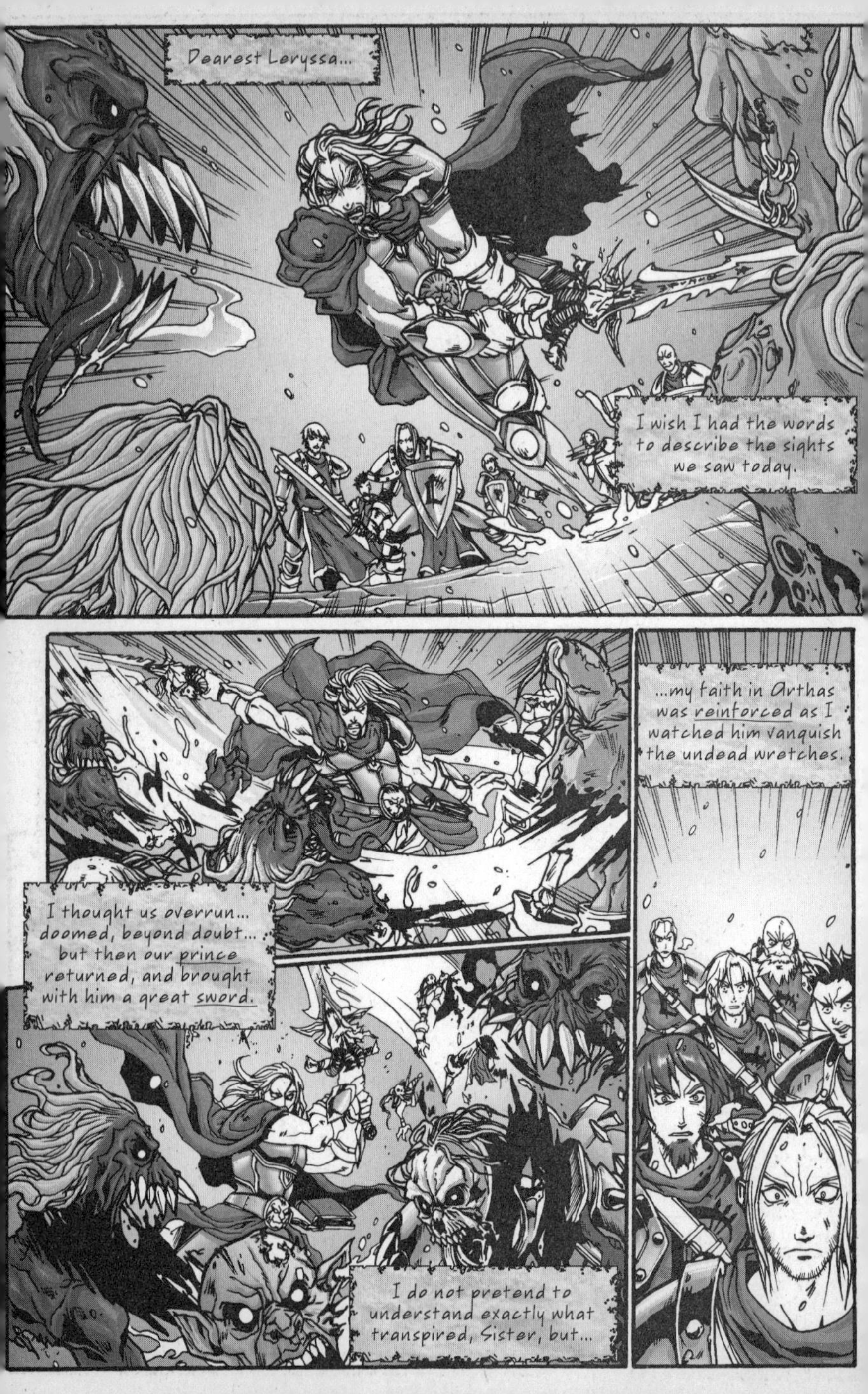
Dearest Leryssa...
I wish I had the words to describe the sights we saw today.
I thought us overrun... doomed, beyond doubt... but then our prince returned, and brought with him a great sword.
I do not pretend to understand exactly what transpired, Sister, but...
...my faith in Arthas was reinforced as I watched him vanquish the undead wretches.

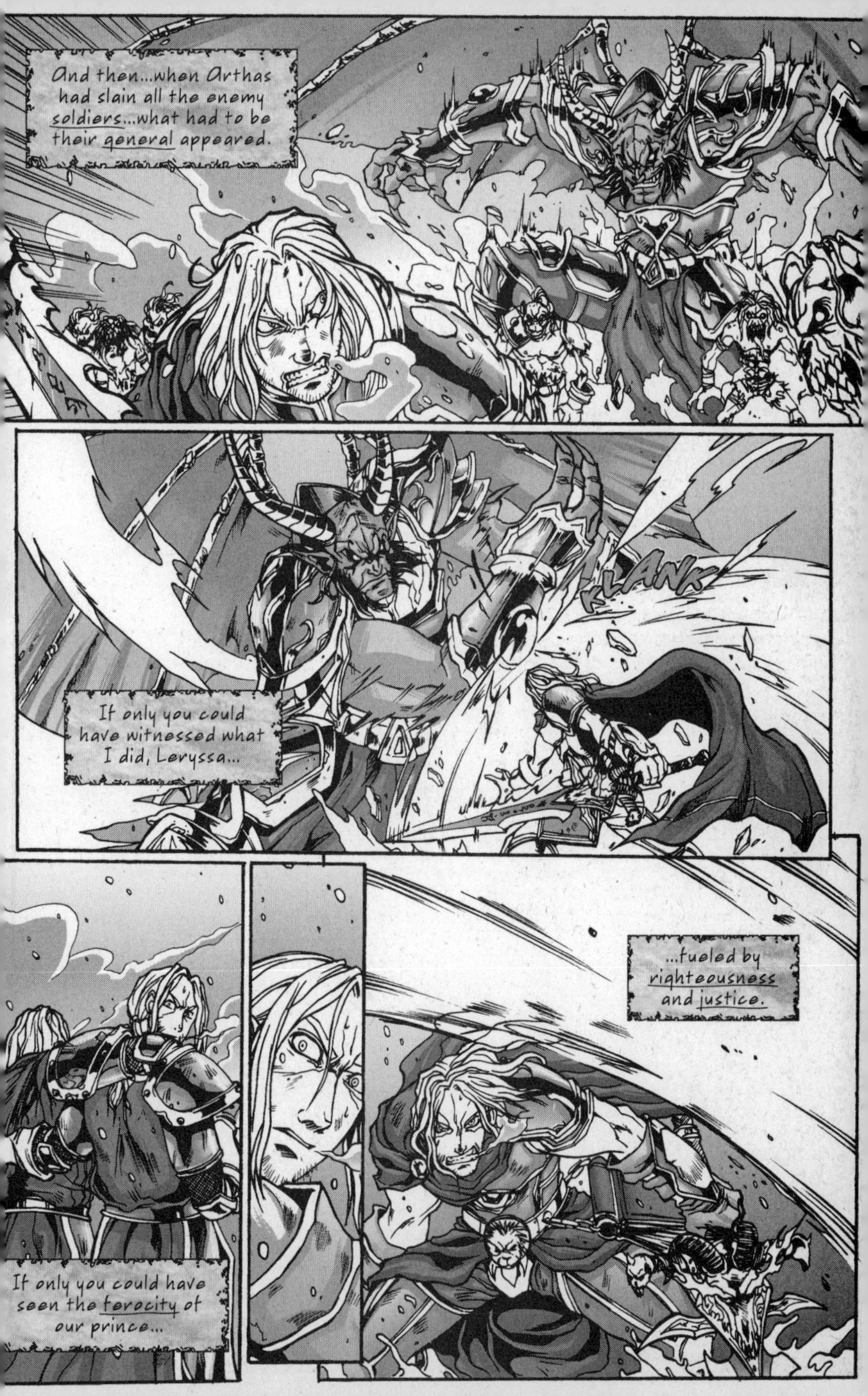
And then...when Arthas had slain all the enemy soldiers...what had to be their general appeared.
KLANK
If only you could have witnessed what I did, Leryssa...
If only you could have seen the ferocity of our prince...
...fueled by righteousness and justice.

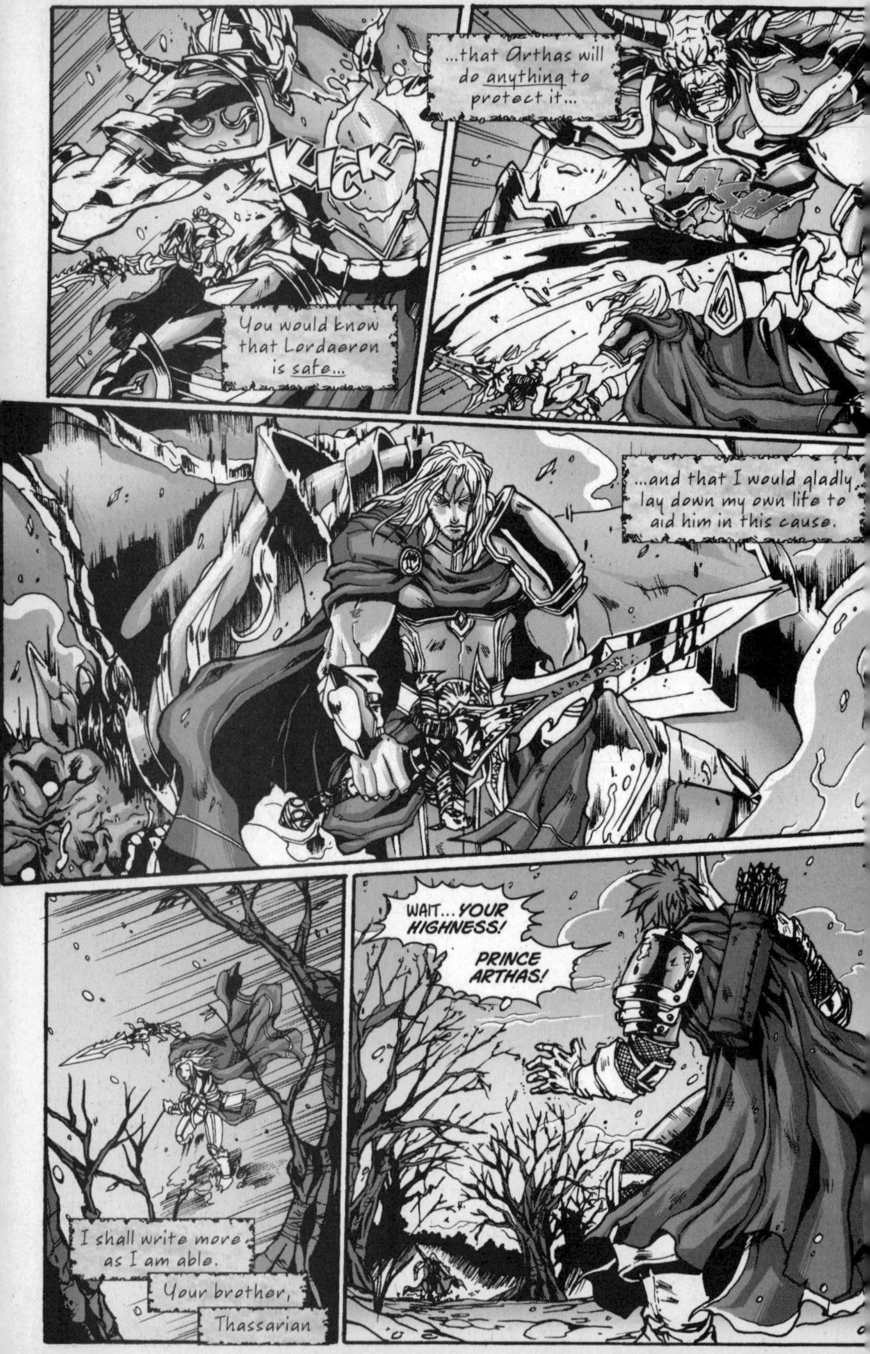
KICK!
You would know that Lordaeron is safe...
...that Arthas will do anything to protect it...
SLASH
...and that I would gladly lay down my own life to aid him in this cause.
I shall write more as I am able.
Your brother,
Thassarian
WAIT... YOUR HIGHNESS!
PRINCE ARTHAS!

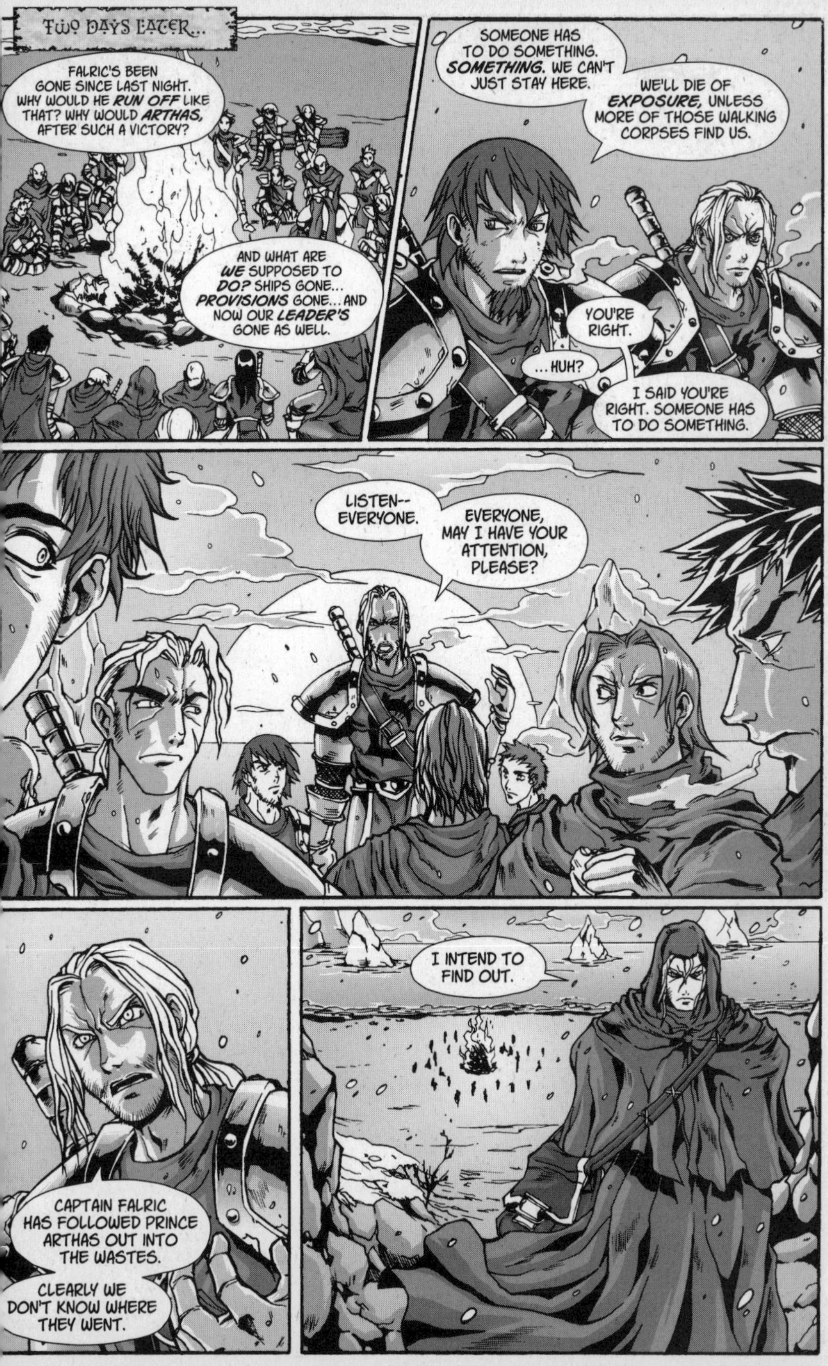
TWO DAYS LATER...
FALRIC'S BEEN GONE SINCE LAST NIGHT. WHY WOULD HE RUN OFF LIKE THAT? WHY WOULD ARTHAS, AFTER SUCH A VICTORY?
AND WHAT ARE WE SUPPOSED TO DO? SHIPS GONE... PROVISIONS GONE... AND NOW OUR LEADER'S GONE AS WELL.
SOMEONE HAS TO DO SOMETHING. SOMETHING. WE CAN'T JUST STAY HERE.
WE'LL DIE OF EXPOSURE, UNLESS MORE OF THOSE WALKING CORPSES FIND US.
YOU'RE RIGHT.
...HUH?
I SAID YOU'RE RIGHT. SOMEONE HAS TO DO SOMETHING.
LISTEN-- EVERYONE.
EVERYONE, MAY I HAVE YOUR ATTENTION, PLEASE?
CAPTAIN FALRIC HAS FOLLOWED PRINCE ARTHAS OUT INTO THE WASTES.
CLEARLY WE DON'T KNOW WHERE THEY WENT.
I INTEND TO FIND OUT.

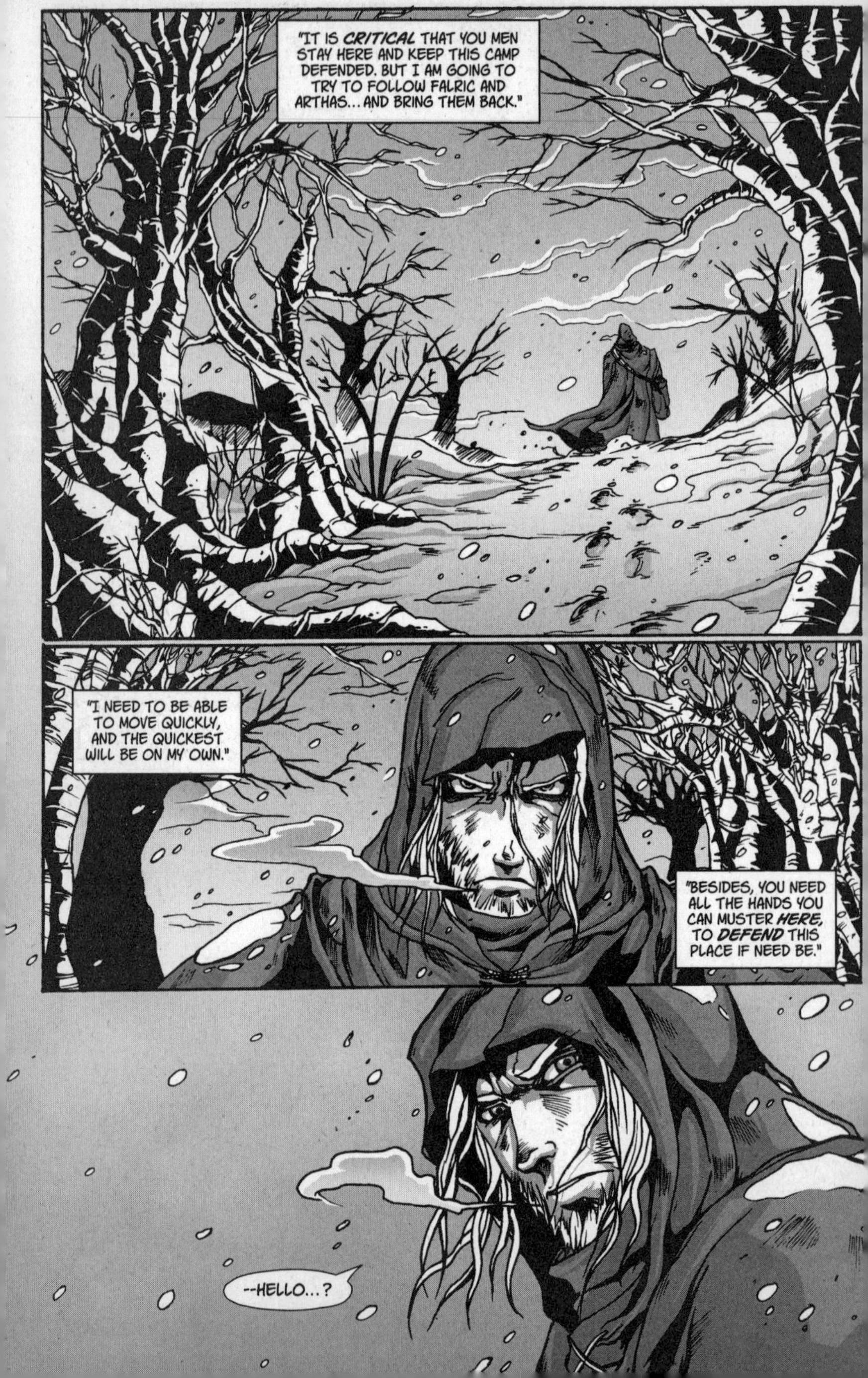
"IT IS *CRITICAL* THAT YOU MEN STAY HERE AND KEEP THIS CAMP DEFENDED. BUT I AM GOING TO TRY TO FOLLOW FALRIC AND ARTHAS... AND BRING THEM BACK."
"I NEED TO BE ABLE TO MOVE QUICKLY, AND THE QUICKEST WILL BE ON MY OWN."
"BESIDES, YOU NEED ALL THE HANDS YOU CAN MUSTER *HERE*, TO *DEFEND* THIS PLACE IF NEED BE."
--HELLO...?

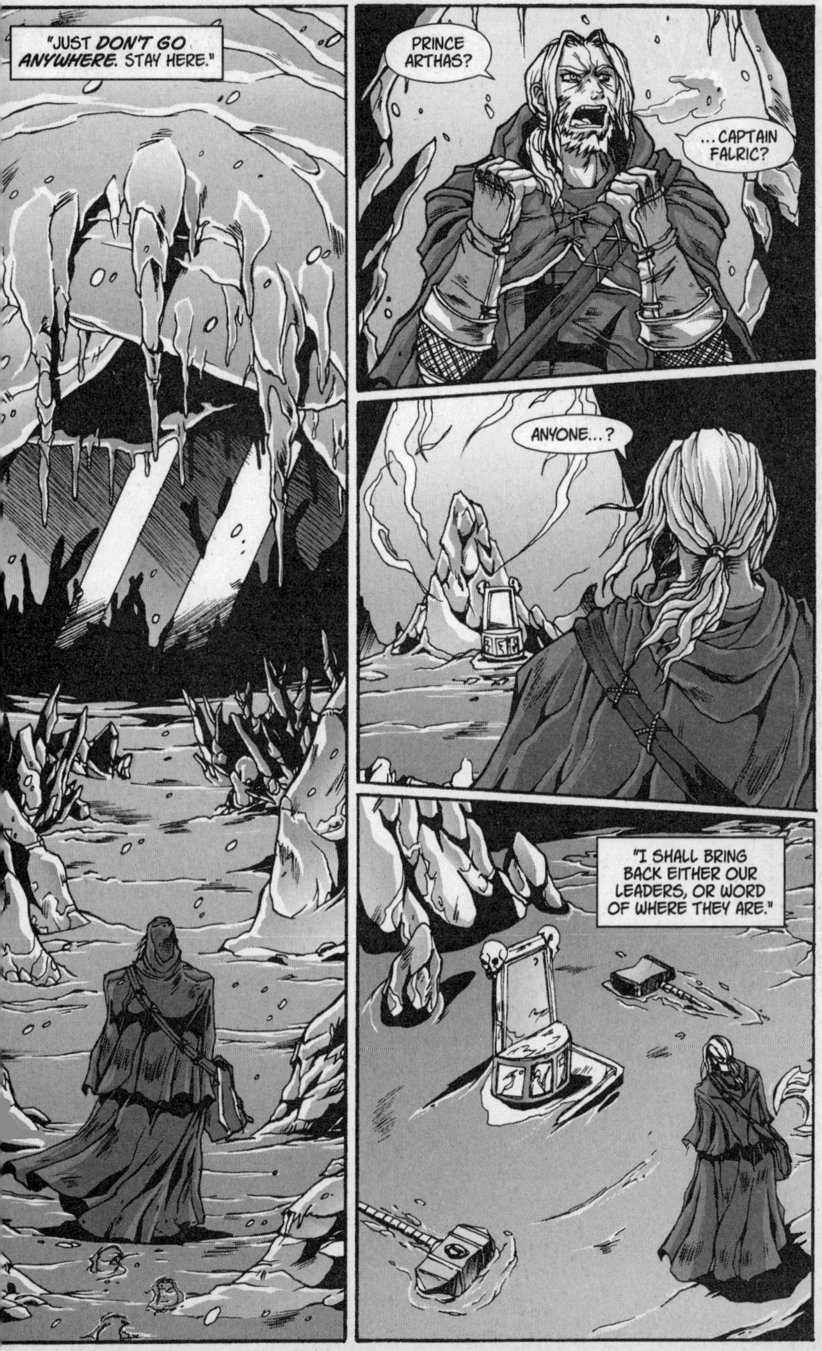
"JUST DON'T GO ANYWHERE. STAY HERE."
PRINCE ARTHAS?
...CAPTAIN FALRIC?
ANYONE...?
"I SHALL BRING BACK EITHER OUR LEADERS, OR WORD OF WHERE THEY ARE."

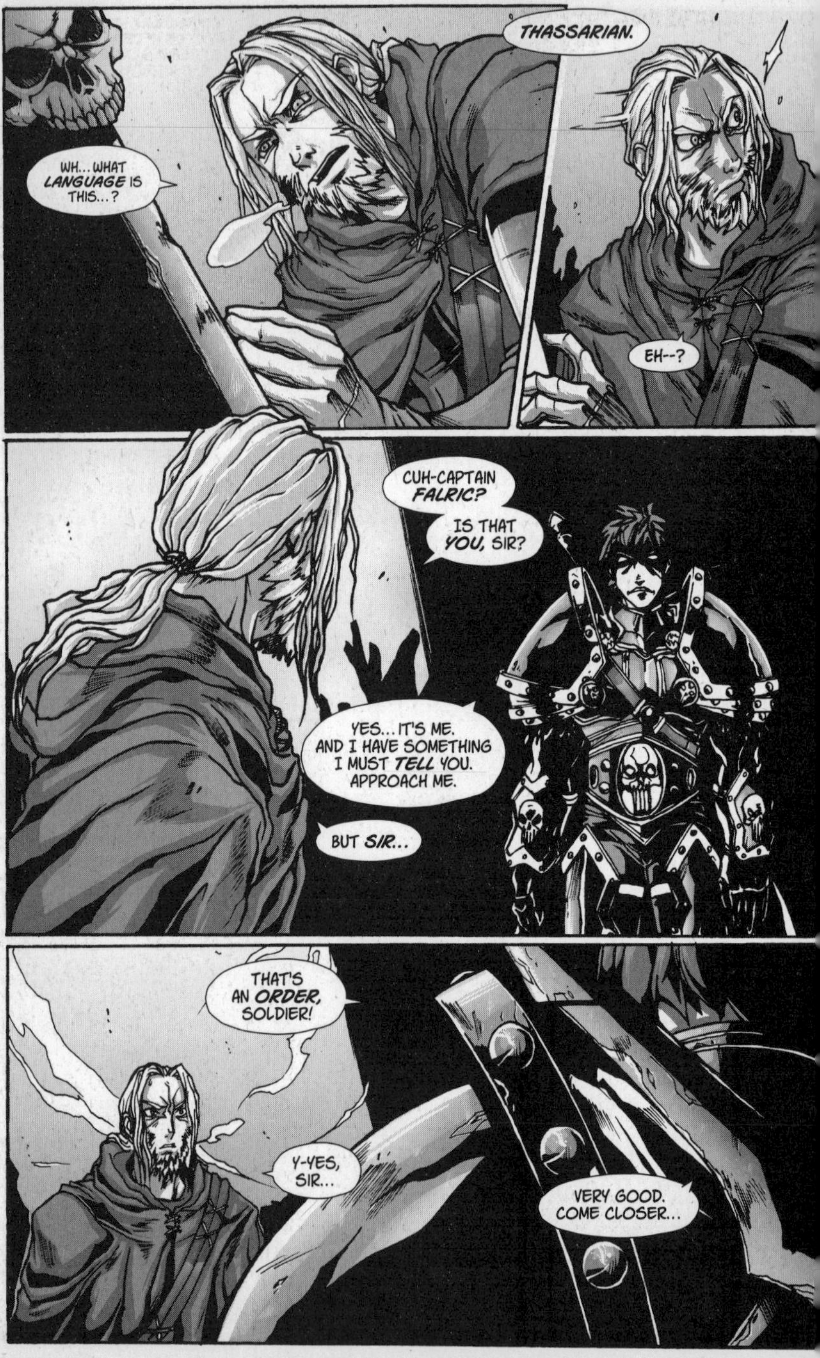
WH... WHAT LANGUAGE IS THIS...?
THASSARIAN.
EH--?
CUH-CAPTAIN FALRIC?
IS THAT YOU, SIR?
YES... IT'S ME. AND I HAVE SOMETHING I MUST TELL YOU. APPROACH ME.
BUT SIR...
THAT'S AN ORDER, SOLDIER!
Y-YES, SIR...
VERY GOOD. COME CLOSER...

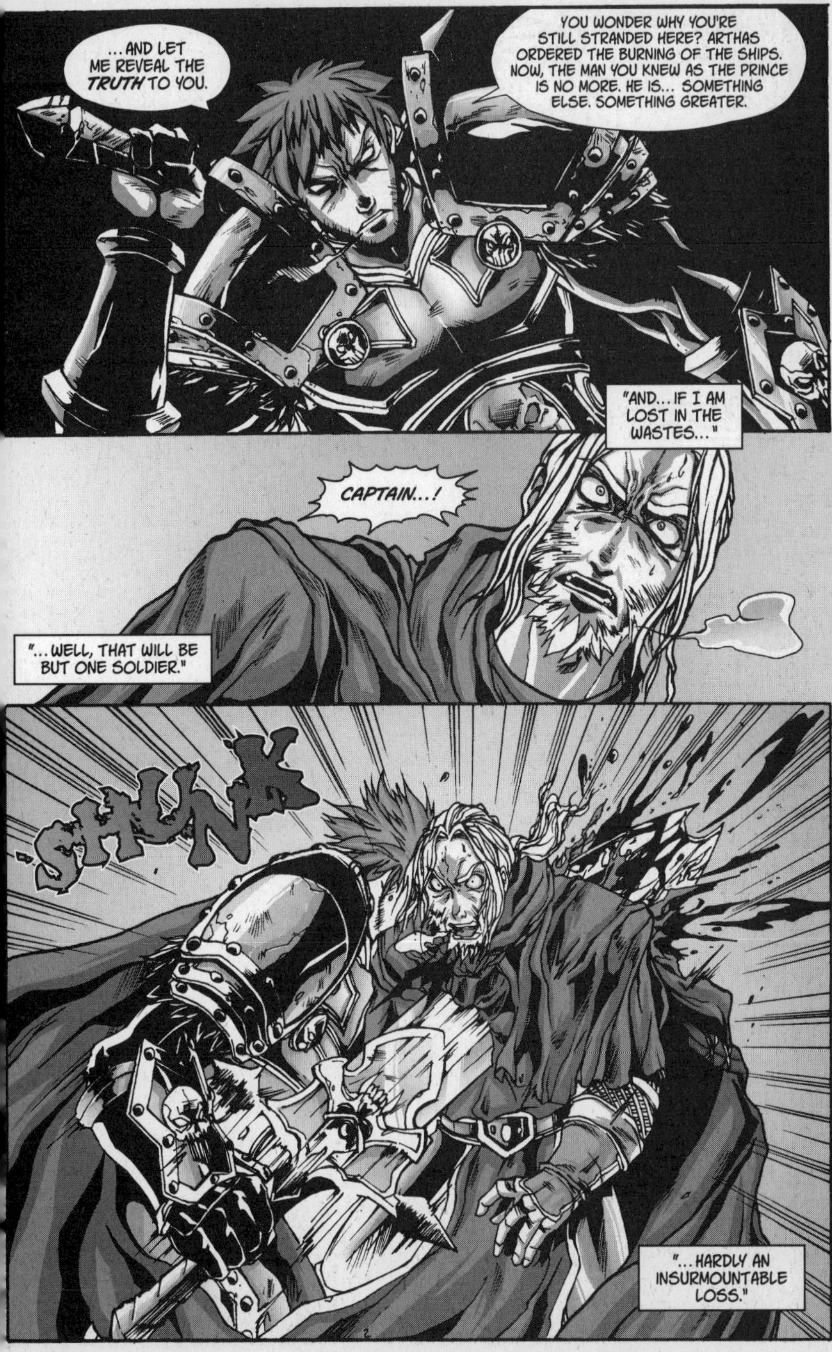
...AND LET ME REVEAL THE *TRUTH* TO YOU.
YOU WONDER WHY YOU'RE STILL STRANDED HERE? ARTHAS ORDERED THE BURNING OF THE SHIPS. NOW, THE MAN YOU KNEW AS THE PRINCE IS NO MORE. HE IS... SOMETHING ELSE. SOMETHING GREATER.
"AND... IF I AM LOST IN THE WASTES..."
CAPTAIN...!
"...WELL, THAT WILL BE BUT ONE SOLDIER."
SHUNK
"...HARDLY AN INSURMOUNTABLE LOSS."

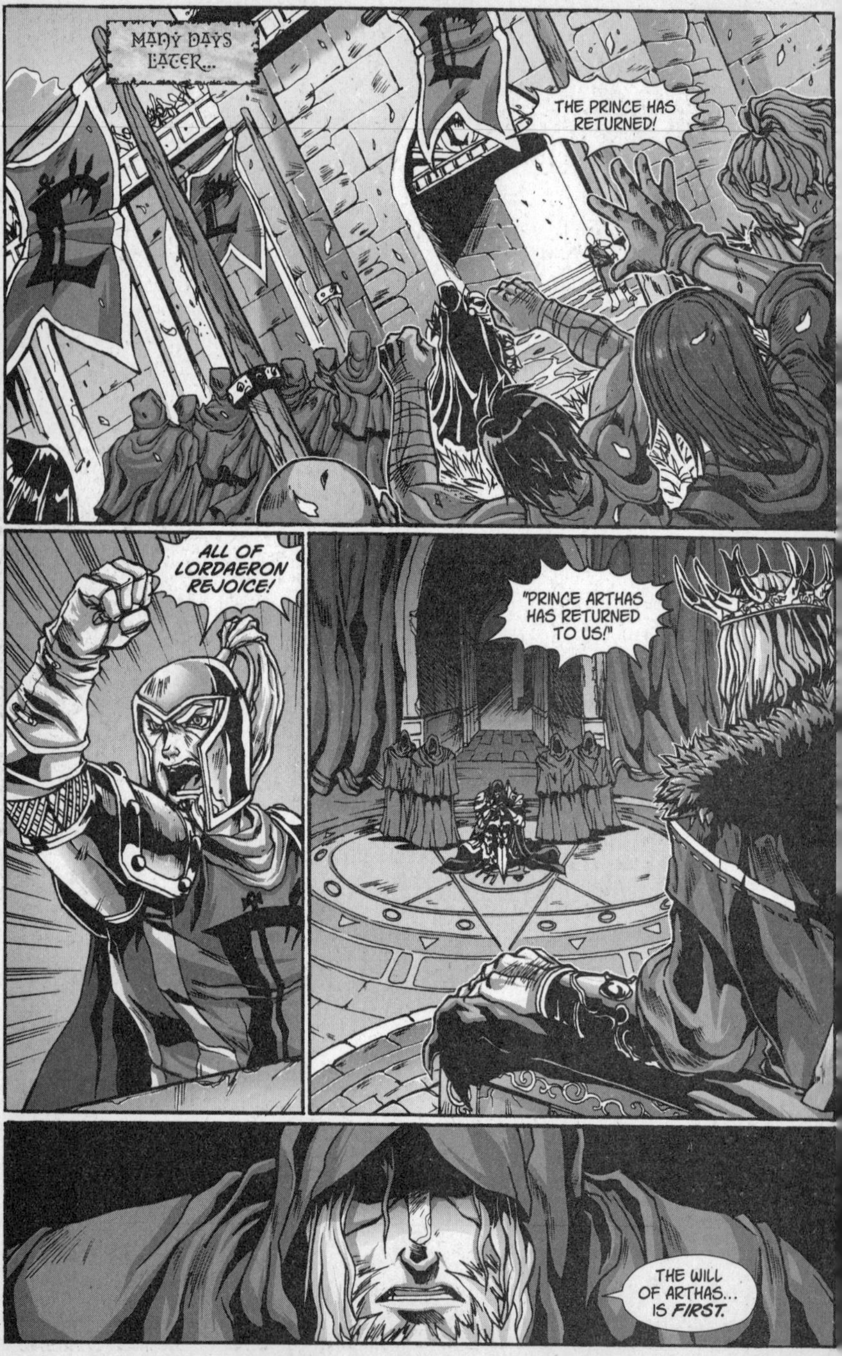

MANY DAYS LATER...
THE PRINCE HAS RETURNED!
ALL OF LORDAERON REJOICE!
"PRINCE ARTHAS HAS RETURNED TO US!"
THE WILL OF ARTHAS... IS *FIRST.*

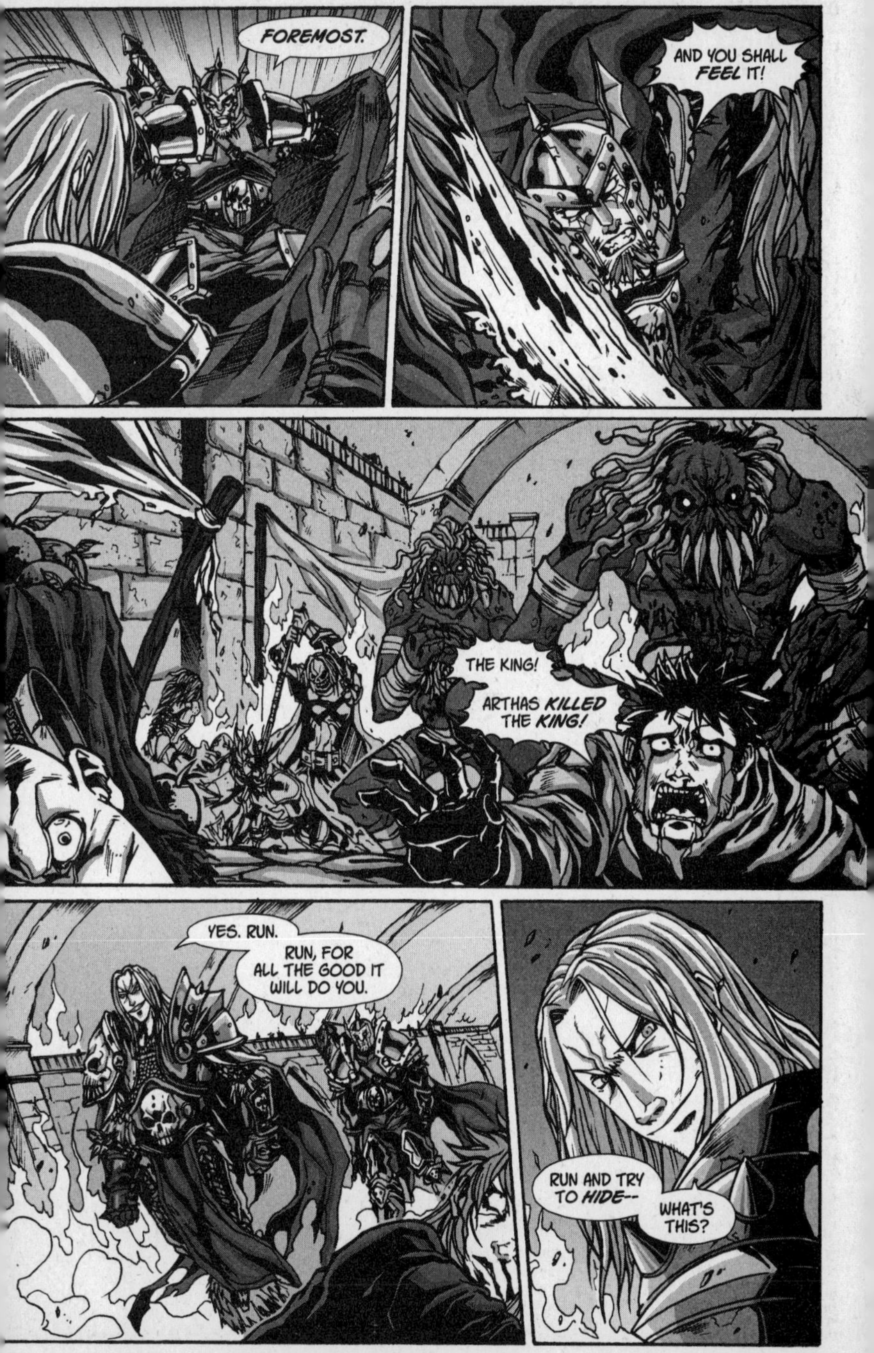
FOREMOST.
AND YOU SHALL *FEEL* IT!
THE KING!
ARTHAS *KILLED* THE *KING*!
YES. RUN.
RUN, FOR ALL THE GOOD IT WILL DO YOU.
RUN AND TRY TO *HIDE*--
WHAT'S THIS?

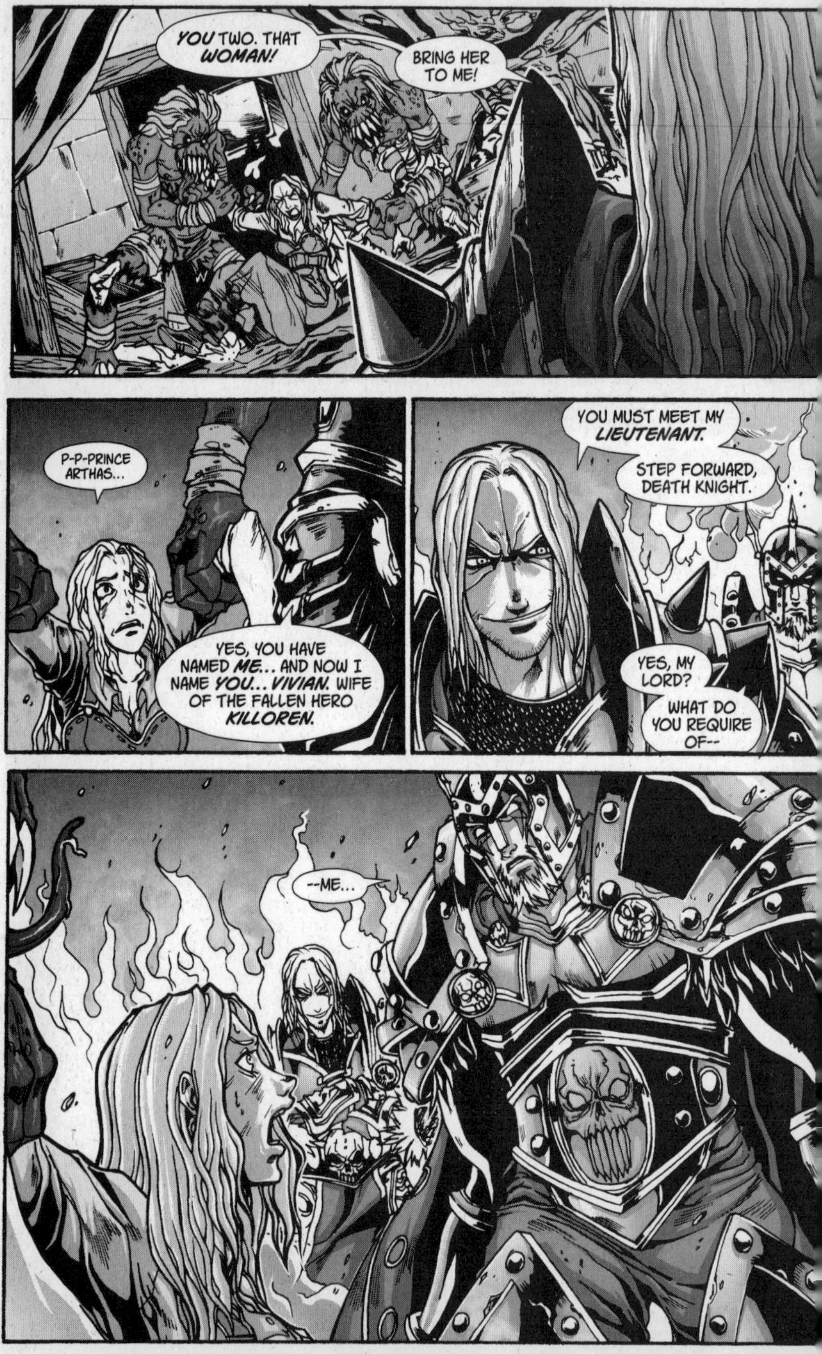
YOU TWO. THAT WOMAN!
BRING HER TO ME!
P-P-PRINCE ARTHAS...
YES, YOU HAVE NAMED ME... AND NOW I NAME YOU... VIVIAN. WIFE OF THE FALLEN HERO KILLOREN.
YOU MUST MEET MY LIEUTENANT.
STEP FORWARD, DEATH KNIGHT.
YES, MY LORD?
WHAT DO YOU REQUIRE OF--
--ME...

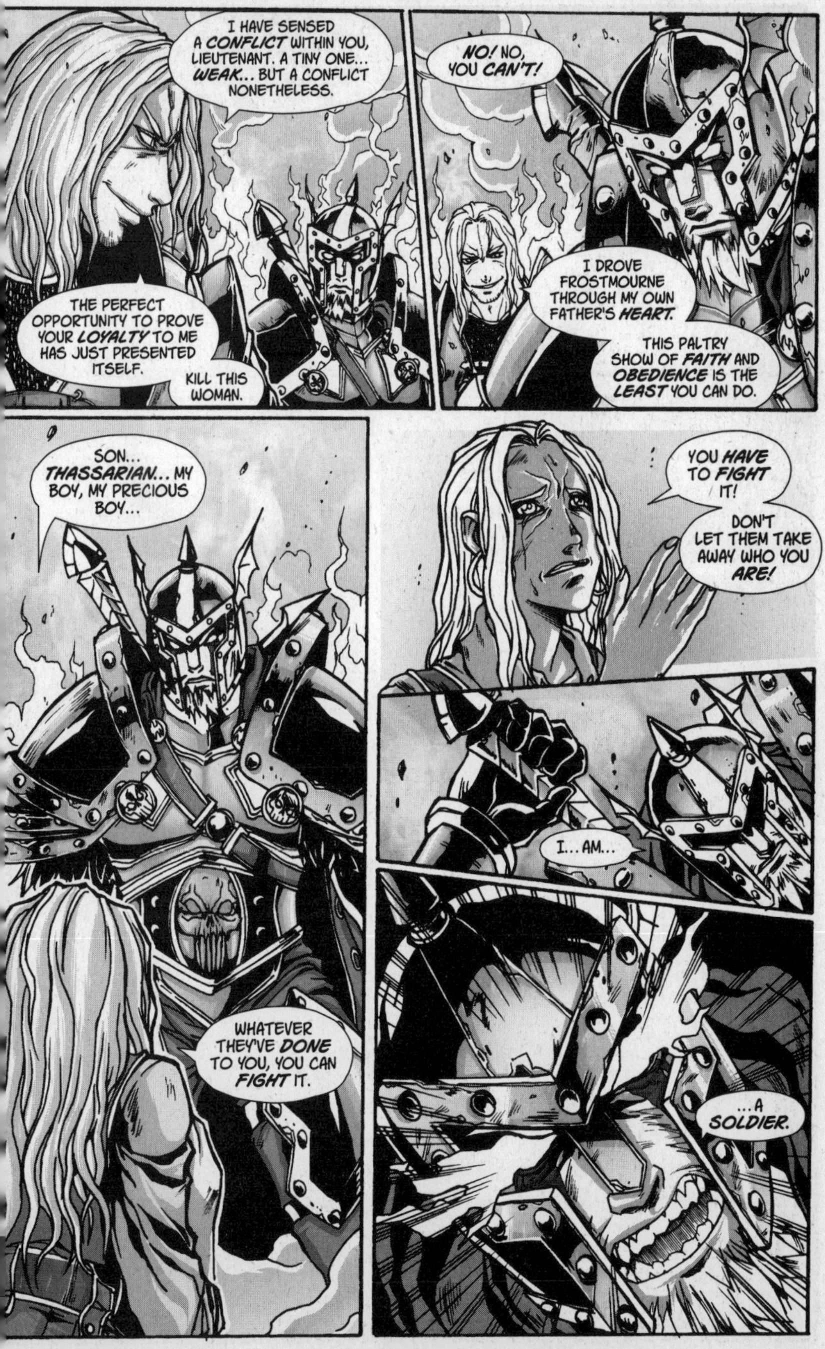
I HAVE SENSED A CONFLICT WITHIN YOU, LIEUTENANT. A TINY ONE... WEAK... BUT A CONFLICT NONETHELESS.
THE PERFECT OPPORTUNITY TO PROVE YOUR LOYALTY TO ME HAS JUST PRESENTED ITSELF.
KILL THIS WOMAN.
NO! NO, YOU CAN'T!
I DROVE FROSTMOURNE THROUGH MY OWN FATHER'S HEART.
THIS PALTRY SHOW OF FAITH AND OBEDIENCE IS THE LEAST YOU CAN DO.
SON... THASSARIAN... MY BOY, MY PRECIOUS BOY...
WHATEVER THEY'VE DONE TO YOU, YOU CAN FIGHT IT.
YOU HAVE TO FIGHT IT!
DON'T LET THEM TAKE AWAY WHO YOU ARE!
I... AM...
...A SOLDIER.

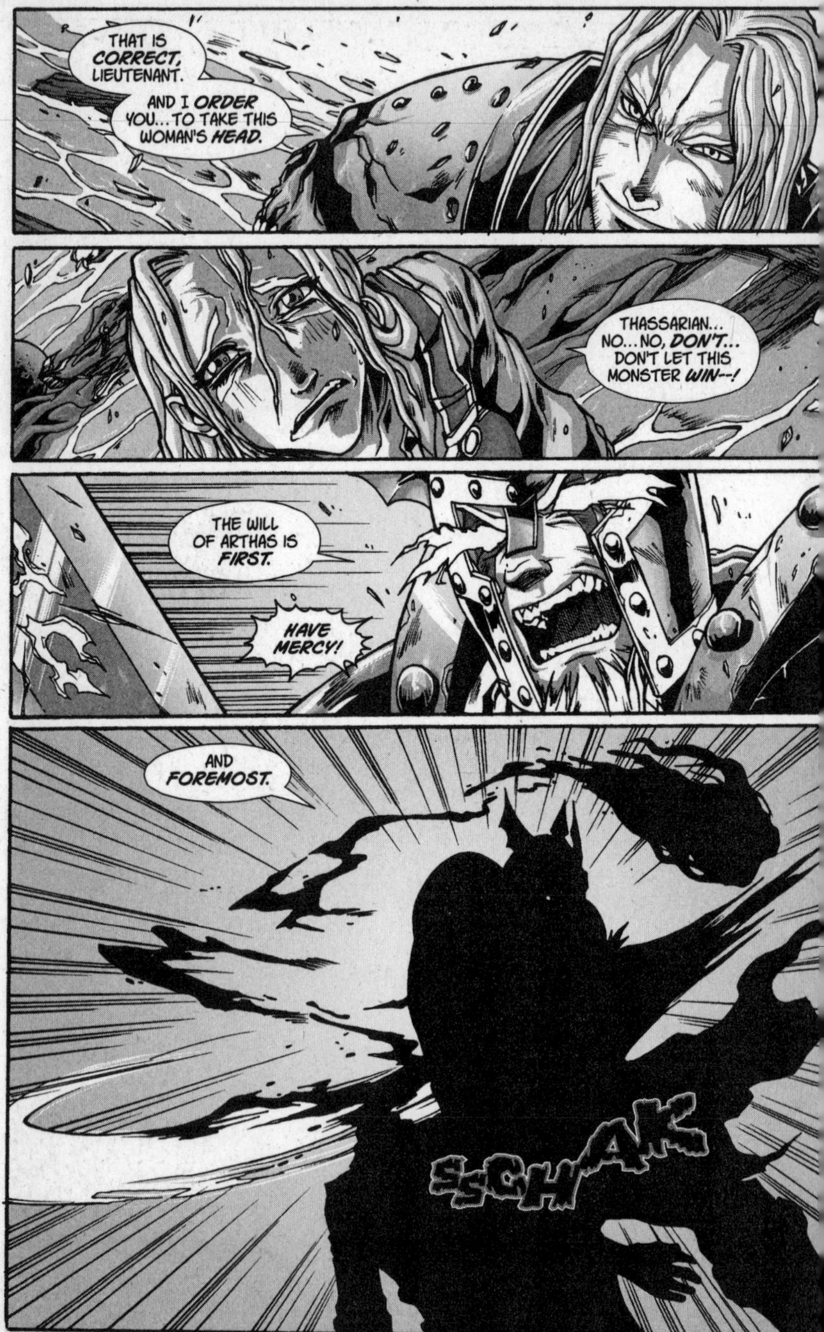
THAT IS CORRECT, LIEUTENANT.
AND I ORDER YOU... TO TAKE THIS WOMAN'S HEAD.
THASSARIAN... NO...NO, DON'T... DON'T LET THIS MONSTER WIN--!
THE WILL OF ARTHAS IS FIRST.
HAVE MERCY!
AND FOREMOST.
SSCHAK

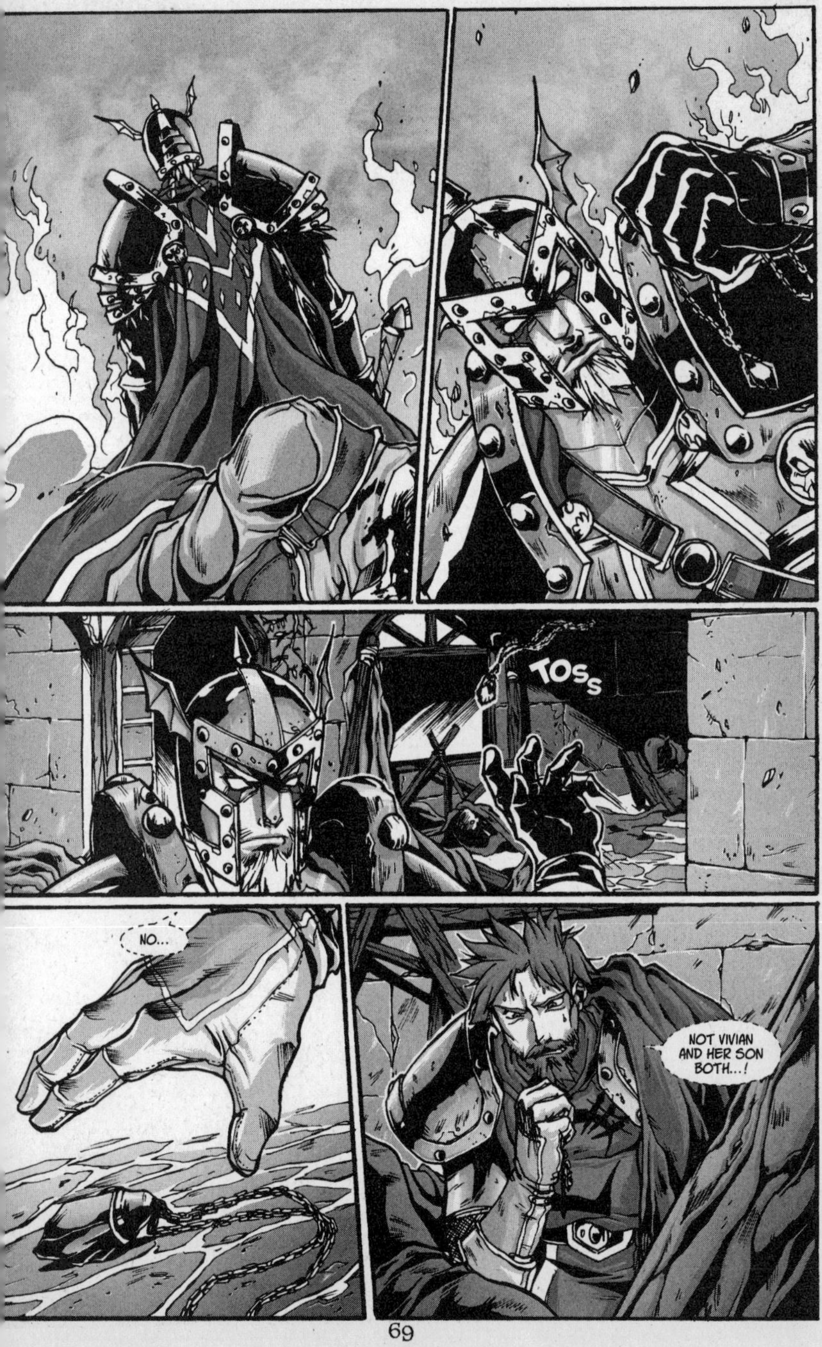
TOSS
NO...
NOT VIVIAN AND HER SON BOTH...!

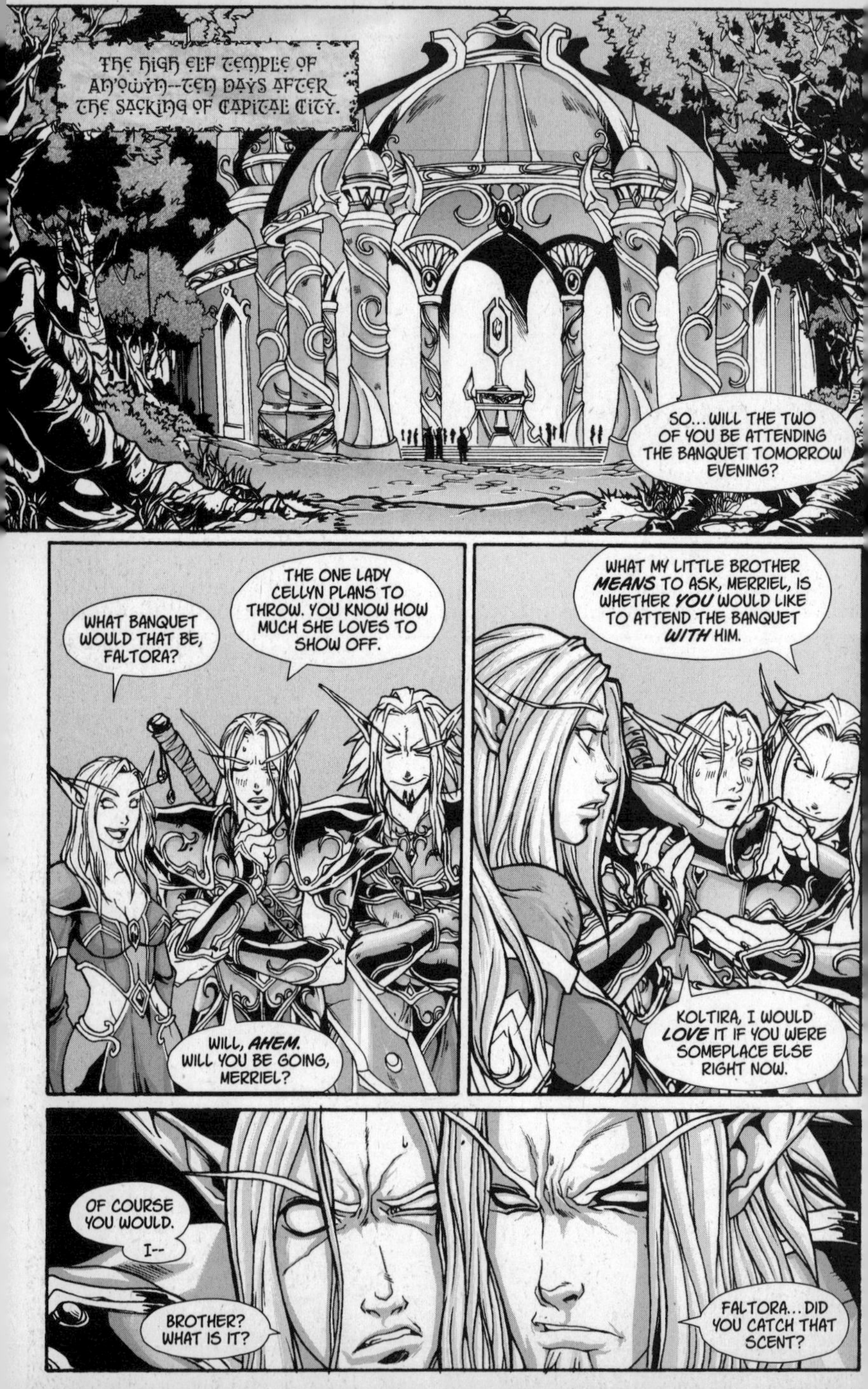
THE HIGH ELF TEMPLE OF AN'OWYN--TEN DAYS AFTER THE SACKING OF CAPITAL CITY.
SO... WILL THE TWO OF YOU BE ATTENDING THE BANQUET TOMORROW EVENING?
WHAT BANQUET WOULD THAT BE, FALTORA?
THE ONE LADY CELLYN PLANS TO THROW. YOU KNOW HOW MUCH SHE LOVES TO SHOW OFF.
WILL, *AHEM.* WILL YOU BE GOING, MERRIEL?
WHAT MY LITTLE BROTHER *MEANS* TO ASK, MERRIEL, IS WHETHER *YOU* WOULD LIKE TO ATTEND THE BANQUET *WITH* HIM.
KOLTIRA, I WOULD *LOVE* IT IF YOU WERE SOMEPLACE ELSE RIGHT NOW.
OF COURSE YOU WOULD.
I--
BROTHER? WHAT IS IT?
FALTORA... DID YOU CATCH THAT SCENT?

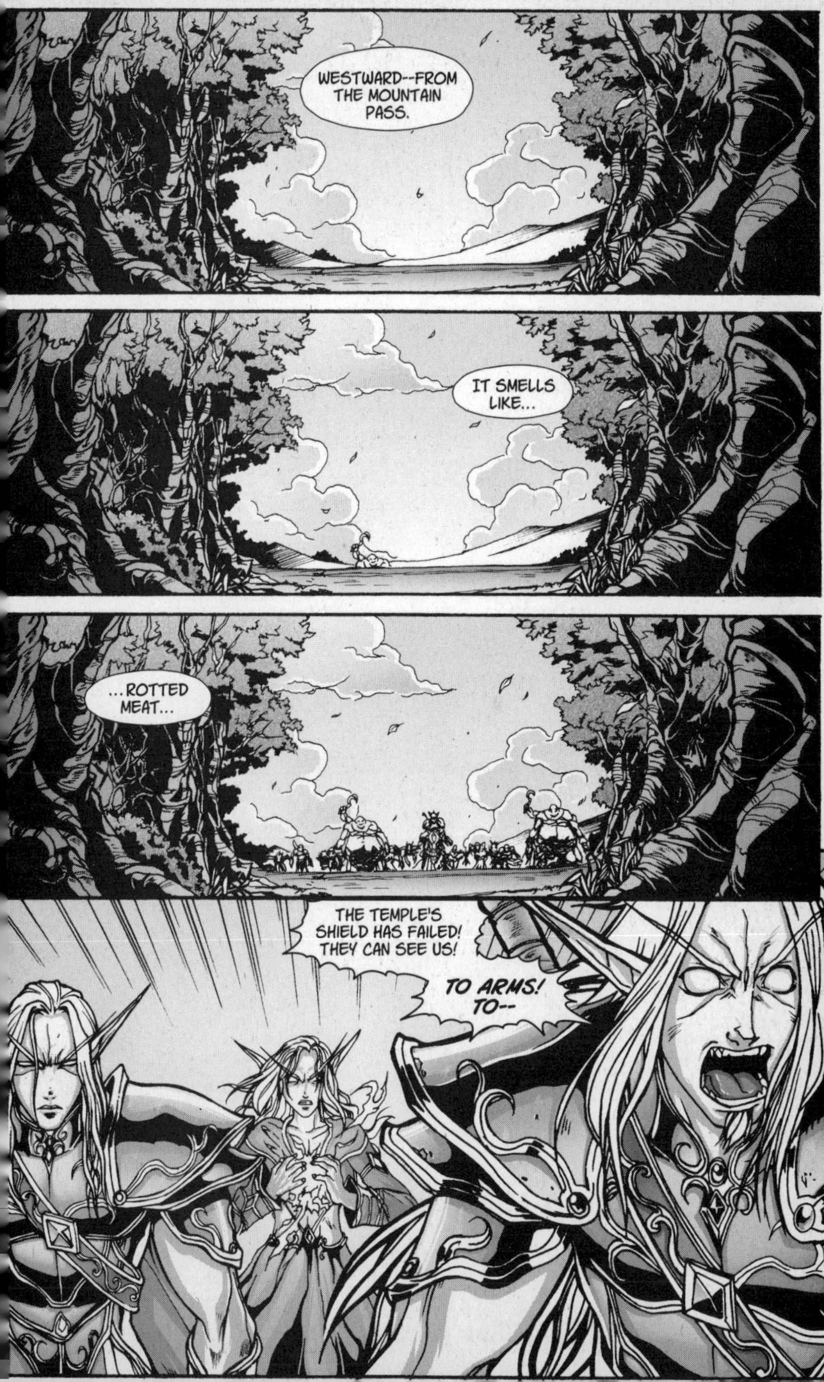
WESTWARD--FROM THE MOUNTAIN PASS.
IT SMELLS LIKE...
...ROTTED MEAT...
THE TEMPLE'S SHIELD HAS FAILED! THEY CAN SEE US!
TO ARMS! TO--

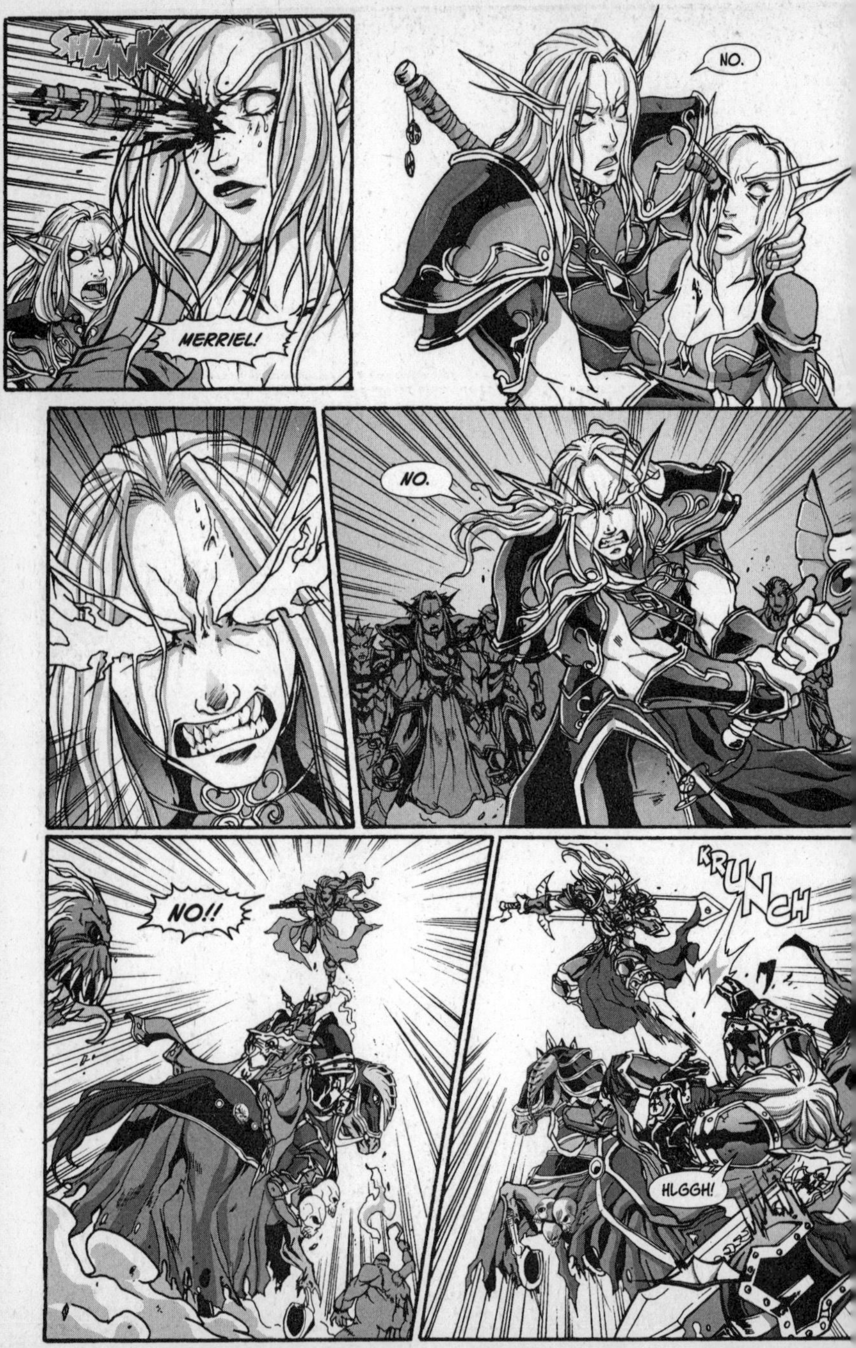
SHUNK
MERRIEL!
NO.
NO.
NO!!
KRUNCH
HLGGH!

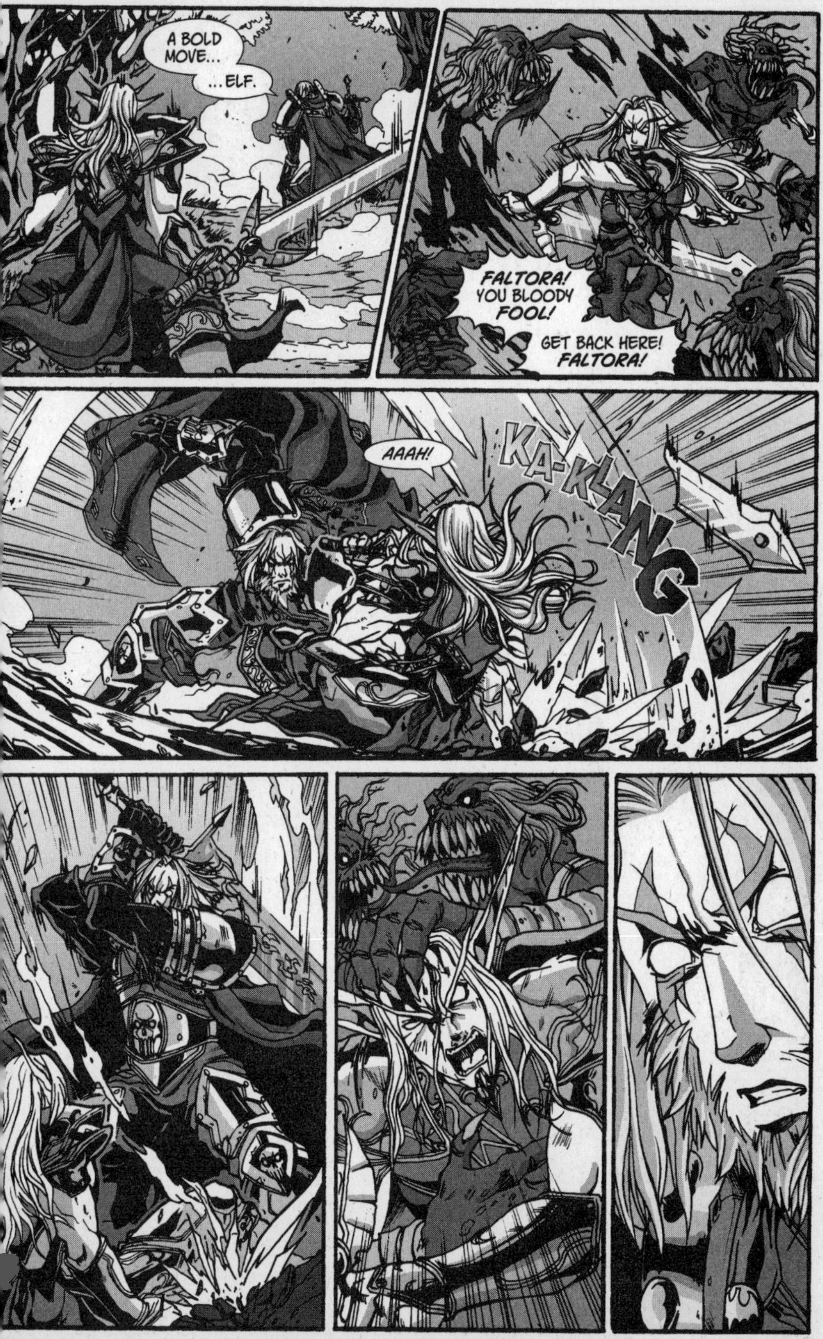
A BOLD MOVE...
...ELF.
FALTORA! YOU BLOODY FOOL!
GET BACK HERE! FALTORA!
AAAH!
KA-KLANG

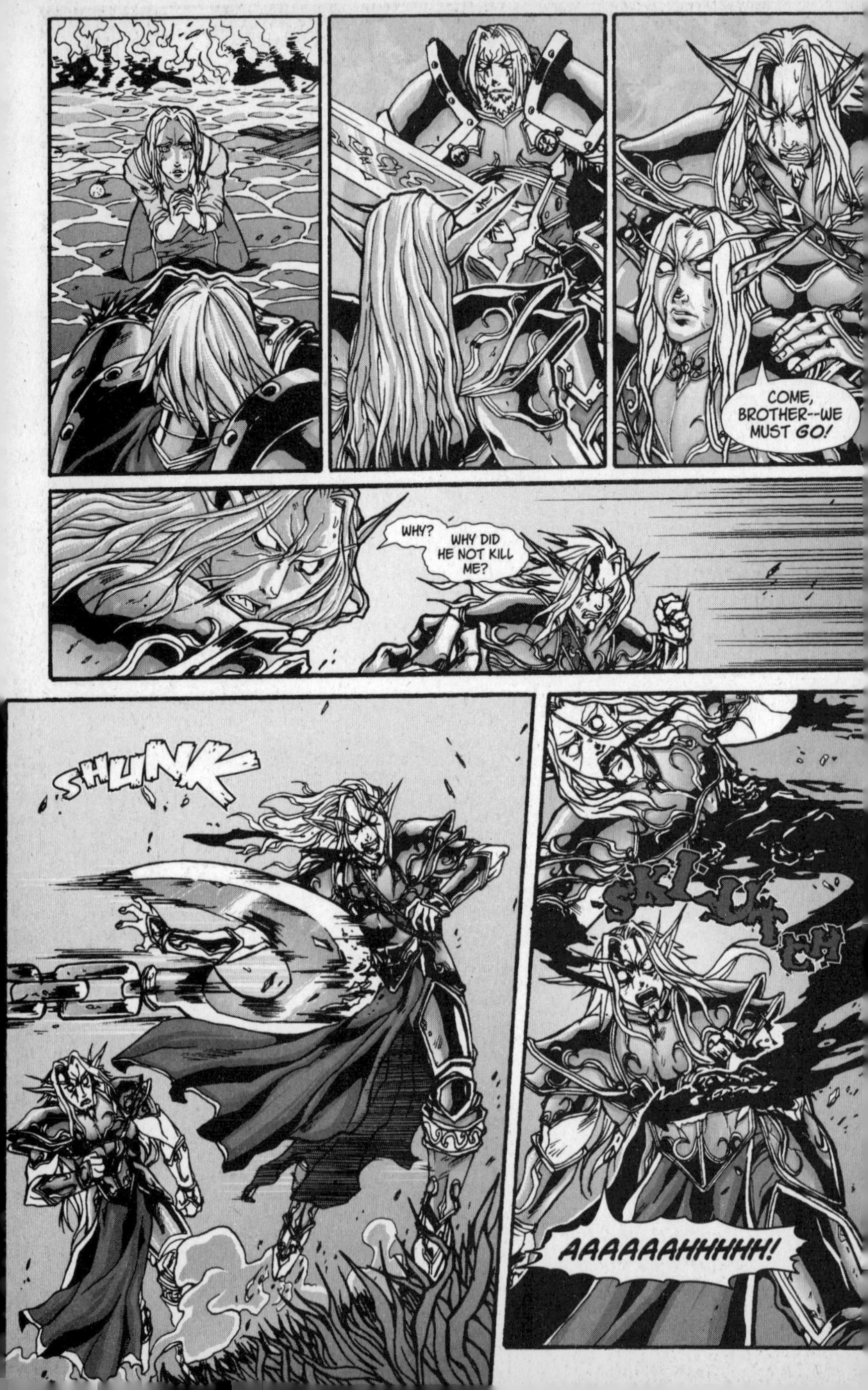
COME, BROTHER--WE MUST GO!
WHY?
WHY DID HE NOT KILL ME?
SHUNK
SKLUTCH
AAAAAAHHHHH!

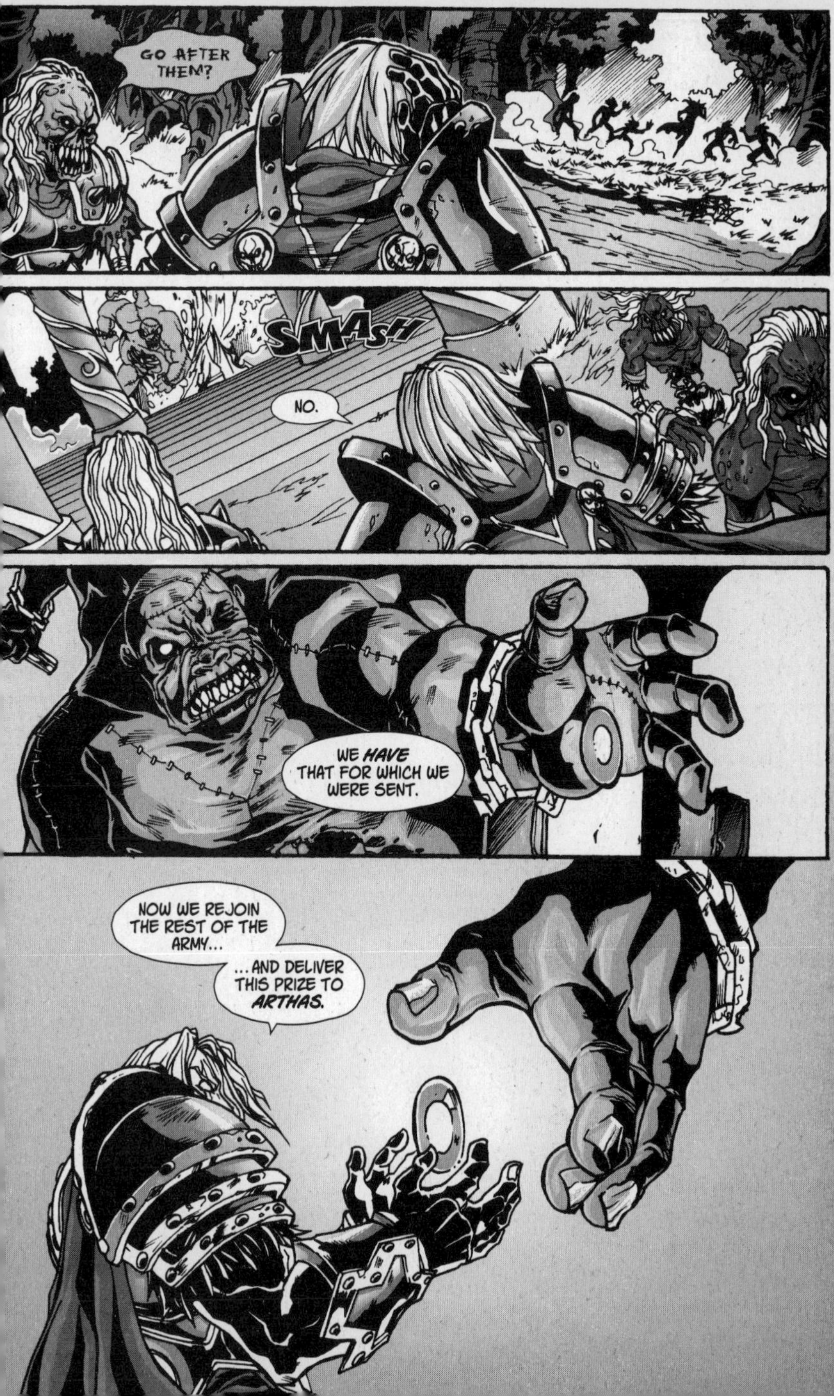
GO AFTER THEM?
SMASH
NO.
WE HAVE THAT FOR WHICH WE WERE SENT.
NOW WE REJOIN THE REST OF THE ARMY...
...AND DELIVER THIS PRIZE TO ARTHAS.

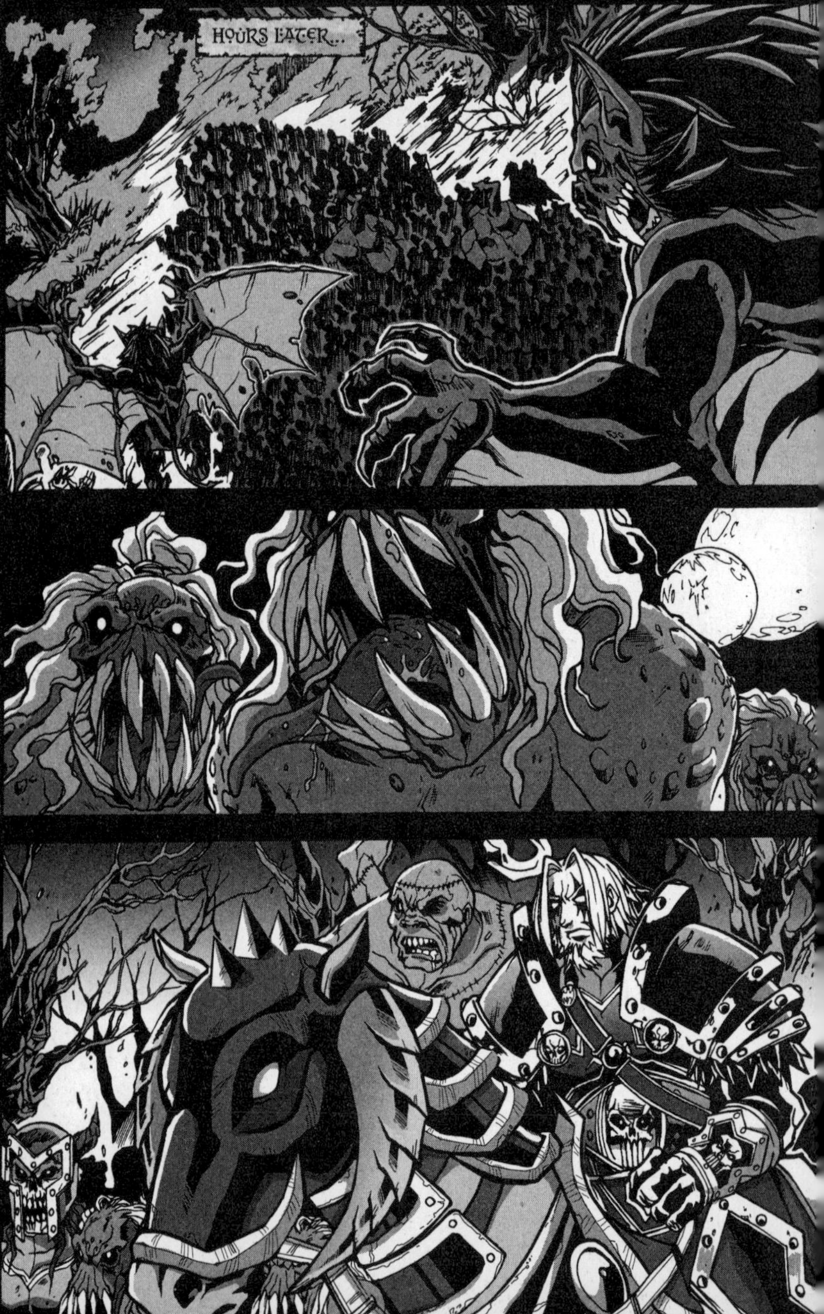
HOURS LATER...

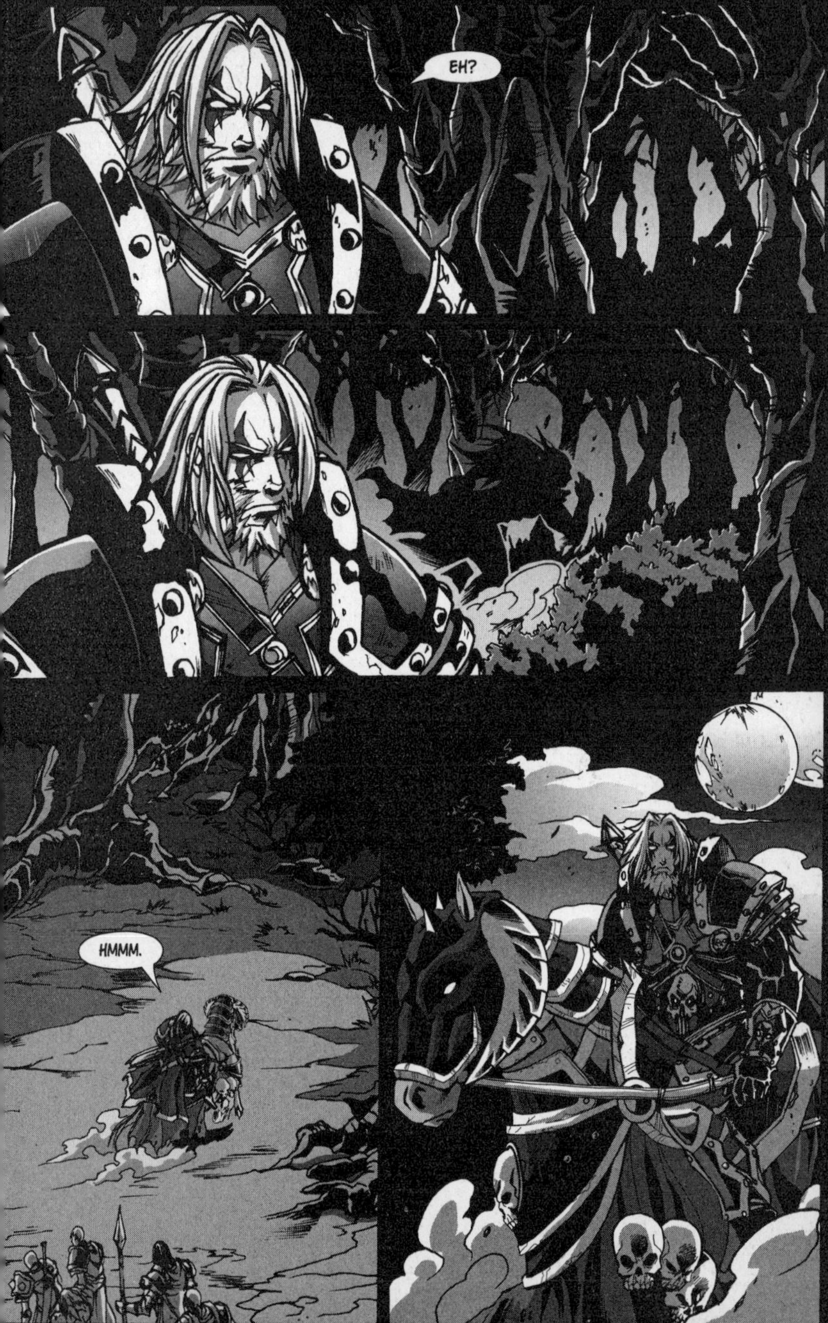
EH?
HMMM.

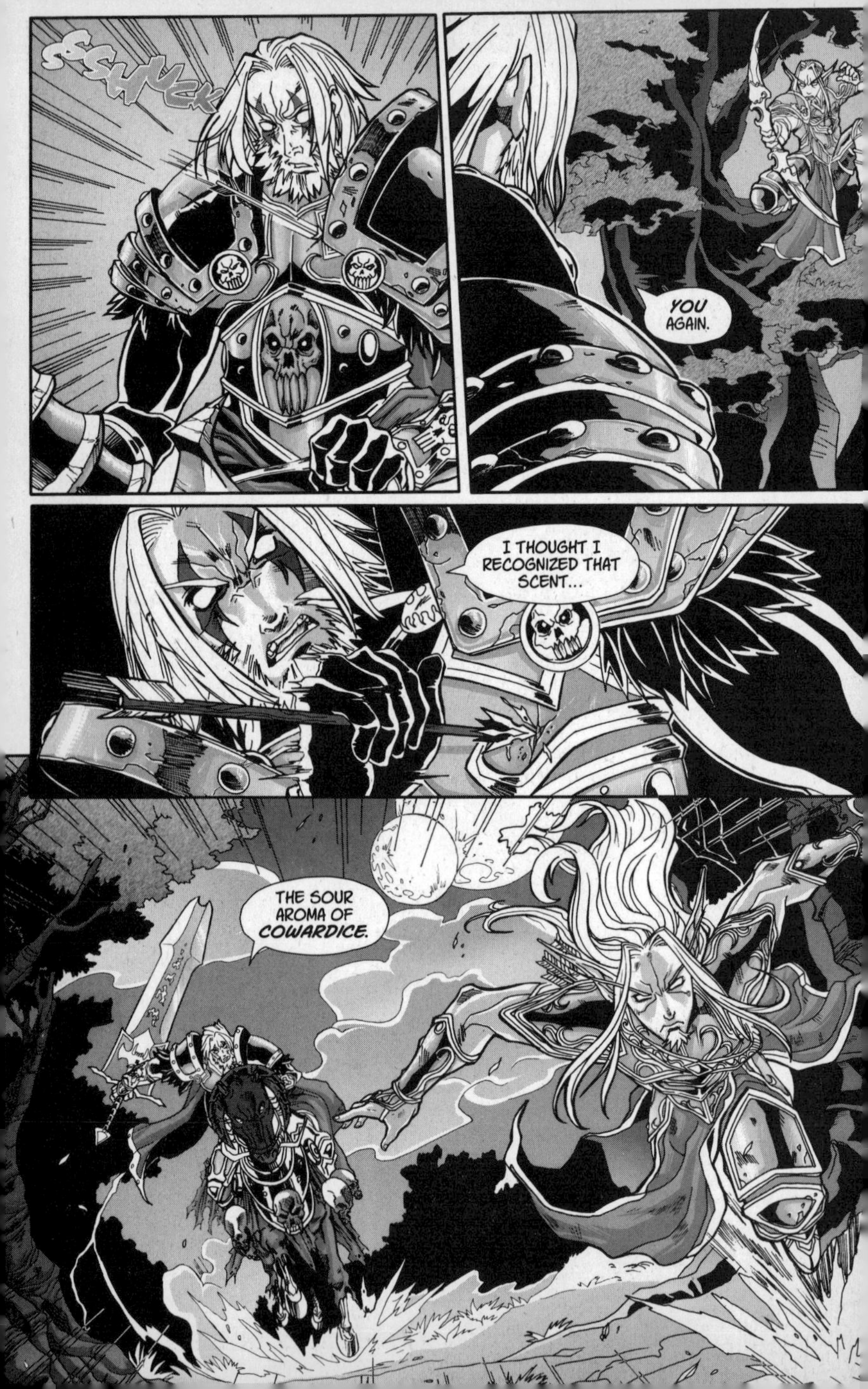
SSSHUCK
YOU AGAIN.
I THOUGHT I RECOGNIZED THAT SCENT...
THE SOUR AROMA OF COWARDICE.

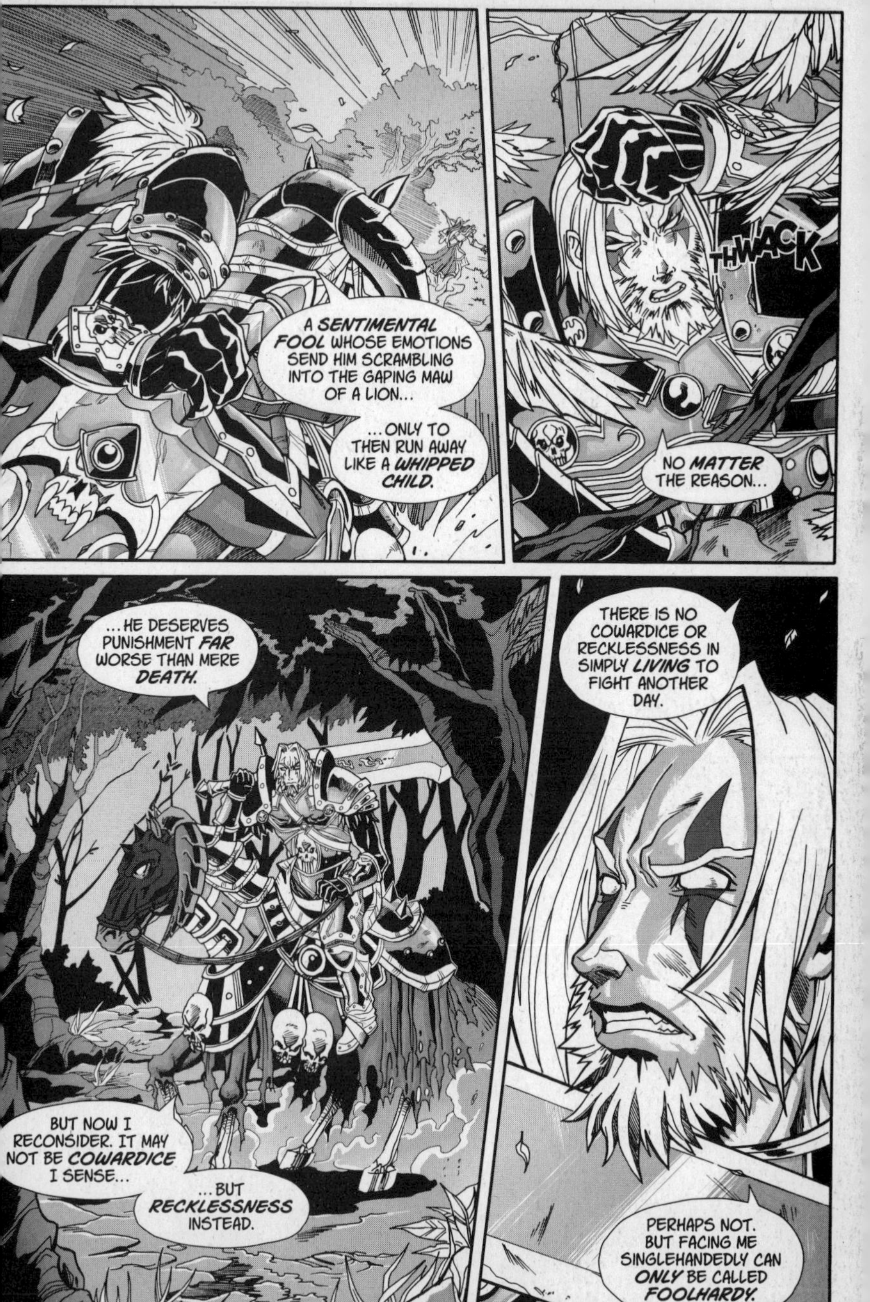
A SENTIMENTAL FOOL WHOSE EMOTIONS SEND HIM SCRAMBLING INTO THE GAPING MAW OF A LION...
...ONLY TO THEN RUN AWAY LIKE A WHIPPED CHILD.
THWACK
NO MATTER THE REASON...
...HE DESERVES PUNISHMENT FAR WORSE THAN MERE DEATH.
BUT NOW I RECONSIDER. IT MAY NOT BE COWARDICE I SENSE...
...BUT RECKLESSNESS INSTEAD.
THERE IS NO COWARDICE OR RECKLESSNESS IN SIMPLY LIVING TO FIGHT ANOTHER DAY.
PERHAPS NOT. BUT FACING ME SINGLEHANDEDLY CAN ONLY BE CALLED FOOLHARDY.

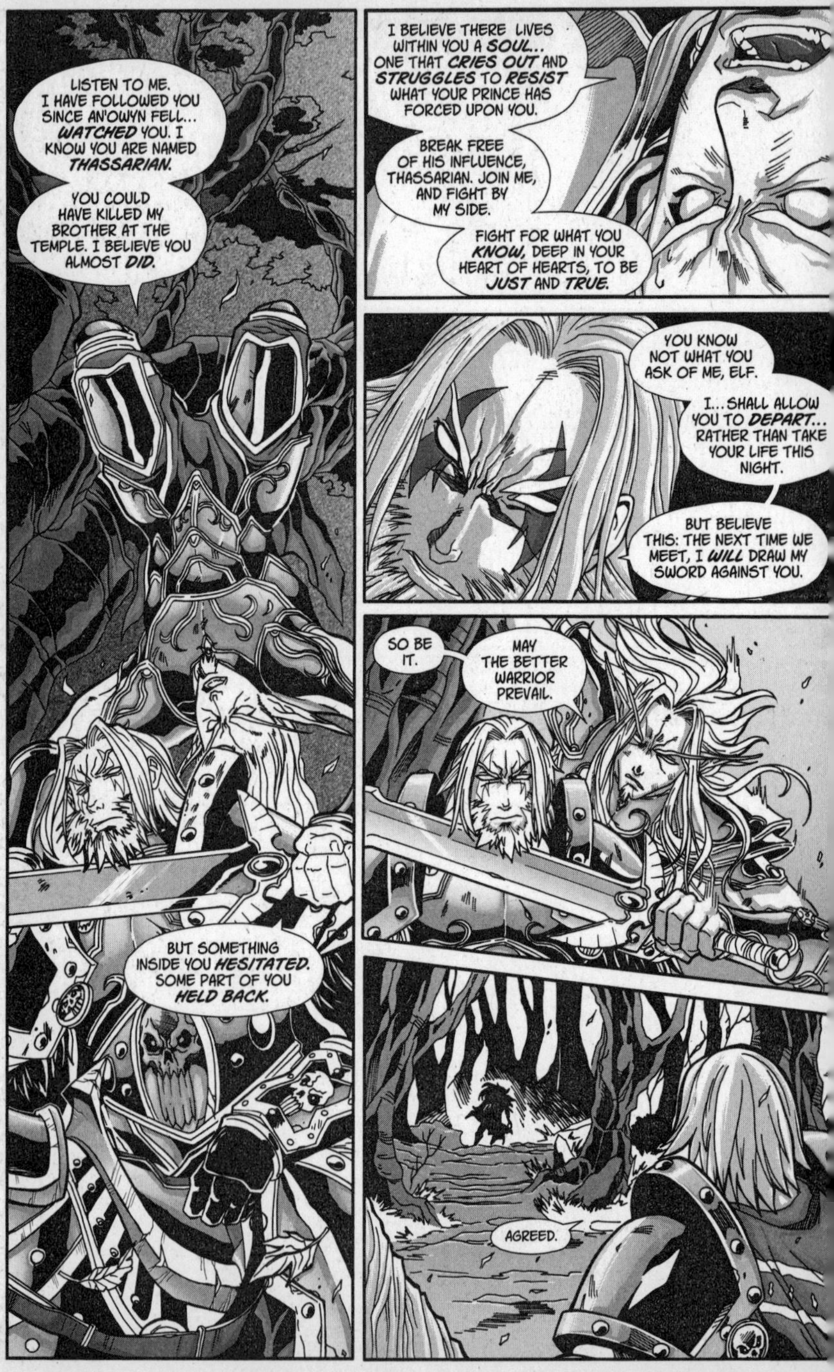
LISTEN TO ME. I HAVE FOLLOWED YOU SINCE AN'OWYN FELL... WATCHED YOU. I KNOW YOU ARE NAMED THASSARIAN.
YOU COULD HAVE KILLED MY BROTHER AT THE TEMPLE. I BELIEVE YOU ALMOST DID.
BUT SOMETHING INSIDE YOU HESITATED. SOME PART OF YOU HELD BACK.
I BELIEVE THERE LIVES WITHIN YOU A SOUL... ONE THAT CRIES OUT AND STRUGGLES TO RESIST WHAT YOUR PRINCE HAS FORCED UPON YOU.
BREAK FREE OF HIS INFLUENCE, THASSARIAN. JOIN ME, AND FIGHT BY MY SIDE.
FIGHT FOR WHAT YOU KNOW, DEEP IN YOUR HEART OF HEARTS, TO BE JUST AND TRUE.
YOU KNOW NOT WHAT YOU ASK OF ME, ELF.
I... SHALL ALLOW YOU TO DEPART... RATHER THAN TAKE YOUR LIFE THIS NIGHT.
BUT BELIEVE THIS: THE NEXT TIME WE MEET, I WILL DRAW MY SWORD AGAINST YOU.
SO BE IT.
MAY THE BETTER WARRIOR PREVAIL.
AGREED.

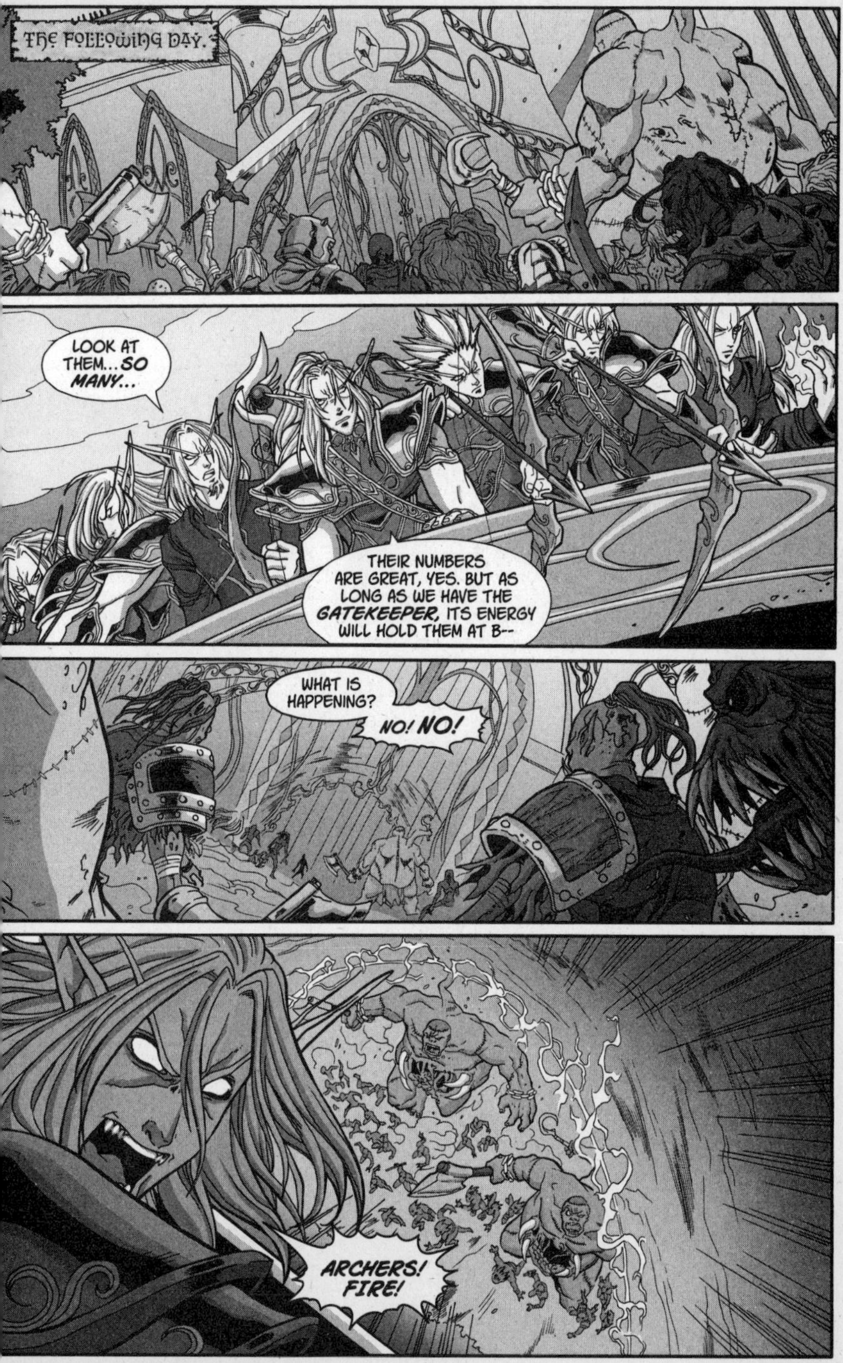

THE FOLLOWING DAY.
LOOK AT THEM...SO MANY...
THEIR NUMBERS ARE GREAT, YES. BUT AS LONG AS WE HAVE THE GATEKEEPER, ITS ENERGY WILL HOLD THEM AT B--
WHAT IS HAPPENING?
NO! NO!
ARCHERS! FIRE!

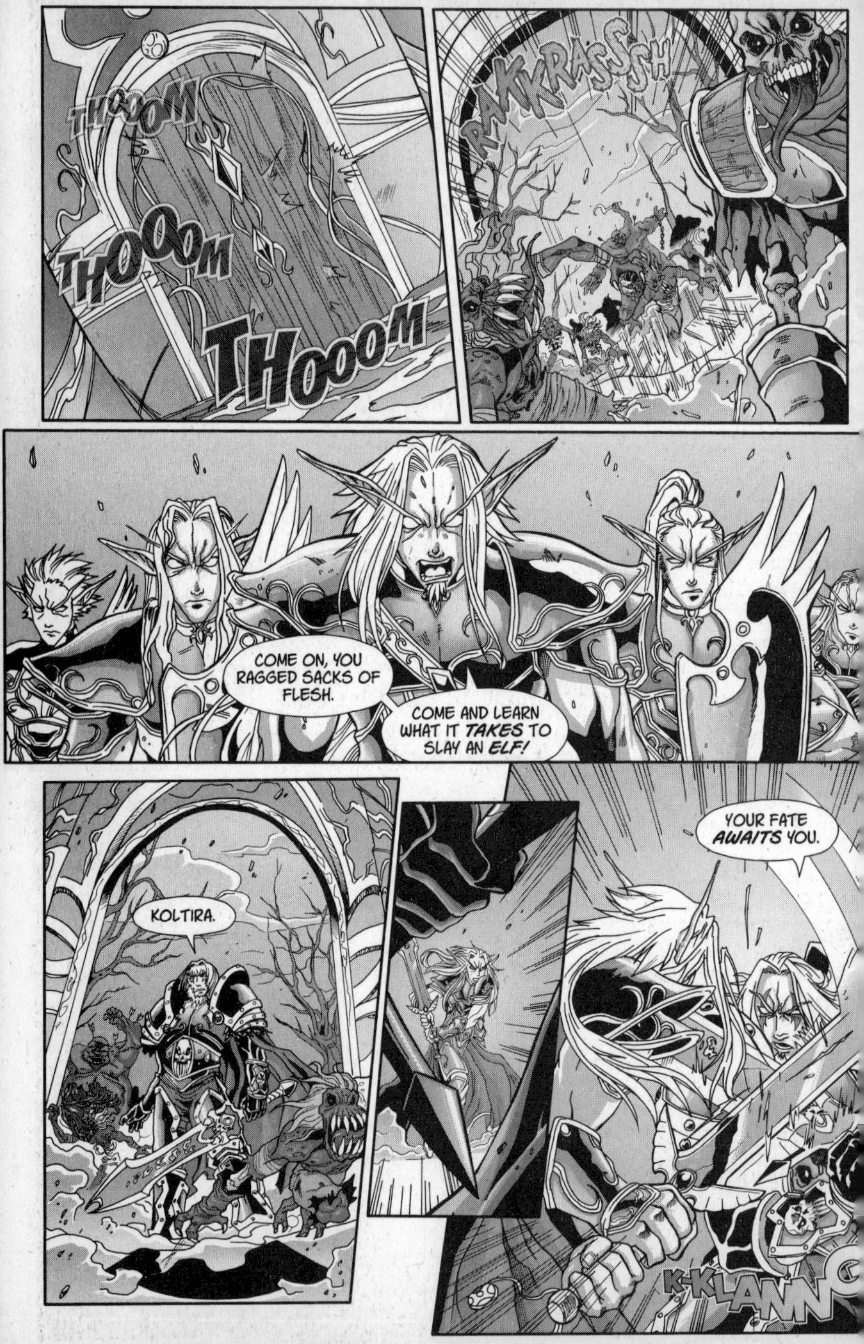
THOOOM
THOOOM
THOOOM
RAKKRASSSH
COME ON, YOU RAGGED SACKS OF FLESH.
COME AND LEARN WHAT IT *TAKES* TO SLAY AN *ELF!*
KOLTIRA.
YOUR FATE *AWAITS* YOU.
K-KLANN

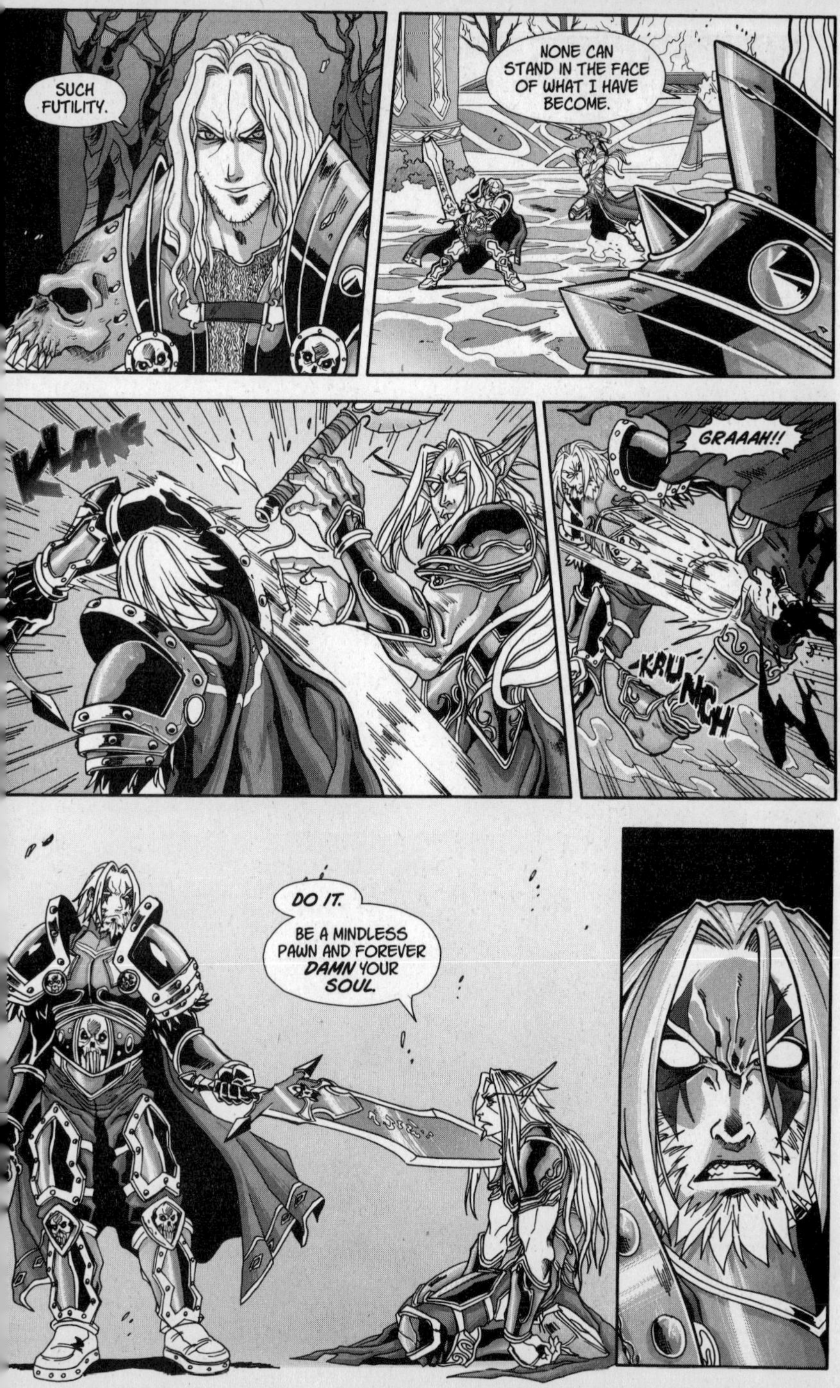
SUCH FUTILITY.
NONE CAN STAND IN THE FACE OF WHAT I HAVE BECOME.
KLANG
GRAAAH!!
KRUNCH
DO IT.
BE A MINDLESS PAWN AND FOREVER DAMN YOUR SOUL.

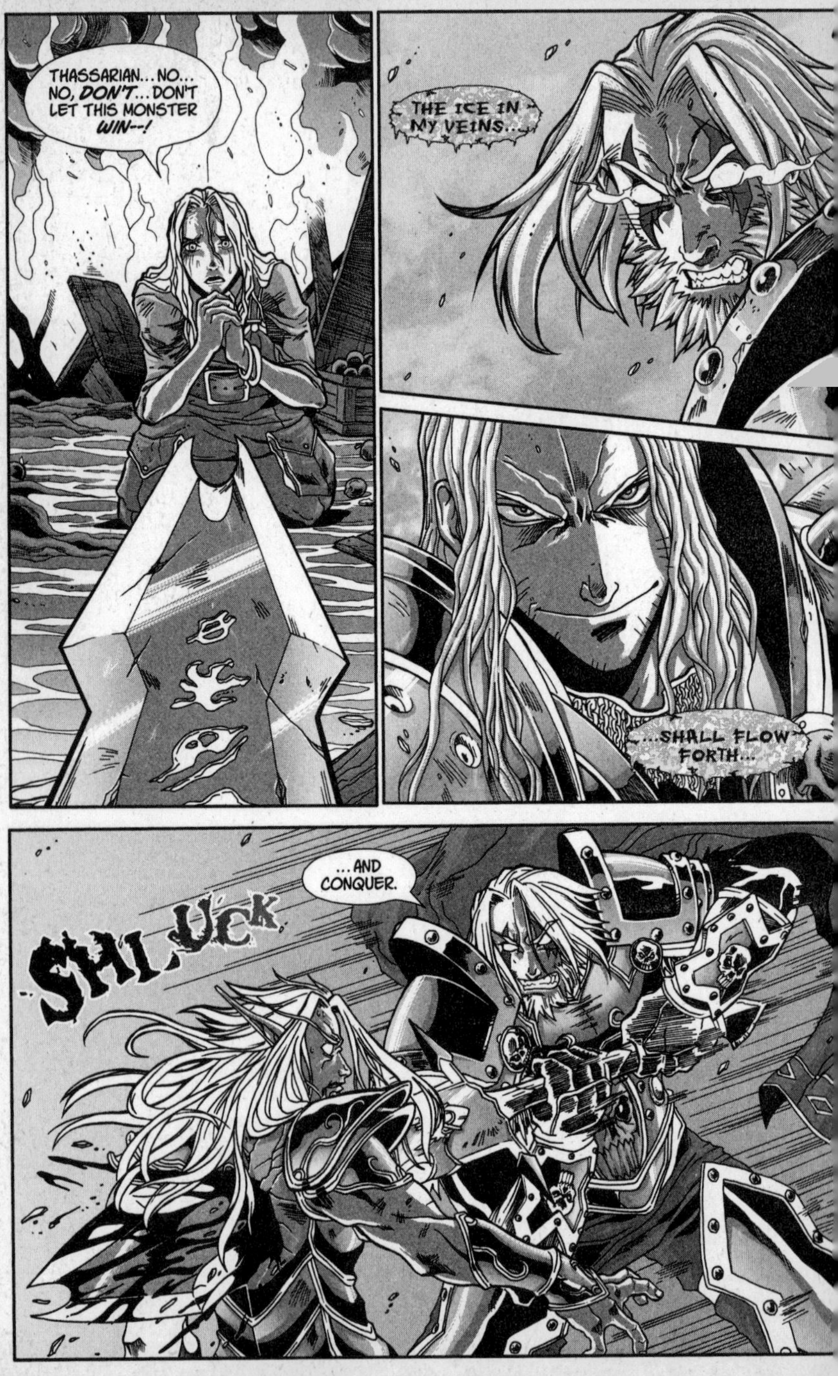
THASSARIAN... NO... NO, DON'T... DON'T LET THIS MONSTER WIN--!
THE ICE IN MY VEINS...
...SHALL FLOW FORTH...
...AND CONQUER.
SHLUCK

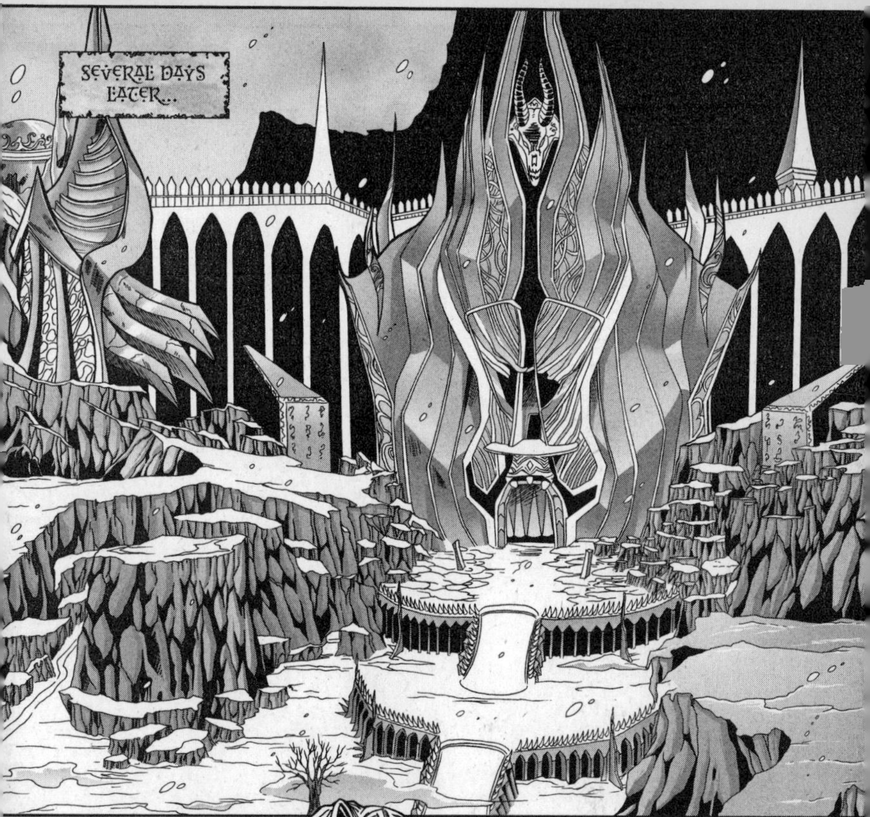
SEVERAL DAYS LATER...

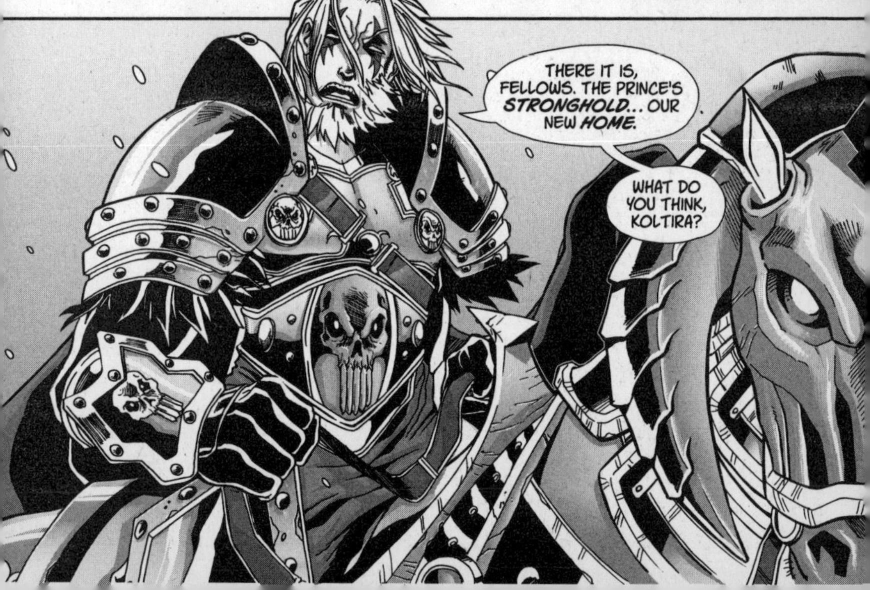
THERE IT IS, FELLOWS. THE PRINCE'S **STRONGHOLD**... OUR NEW **HOME**.
WHAT DO YOU THINK, KOLTIRA?

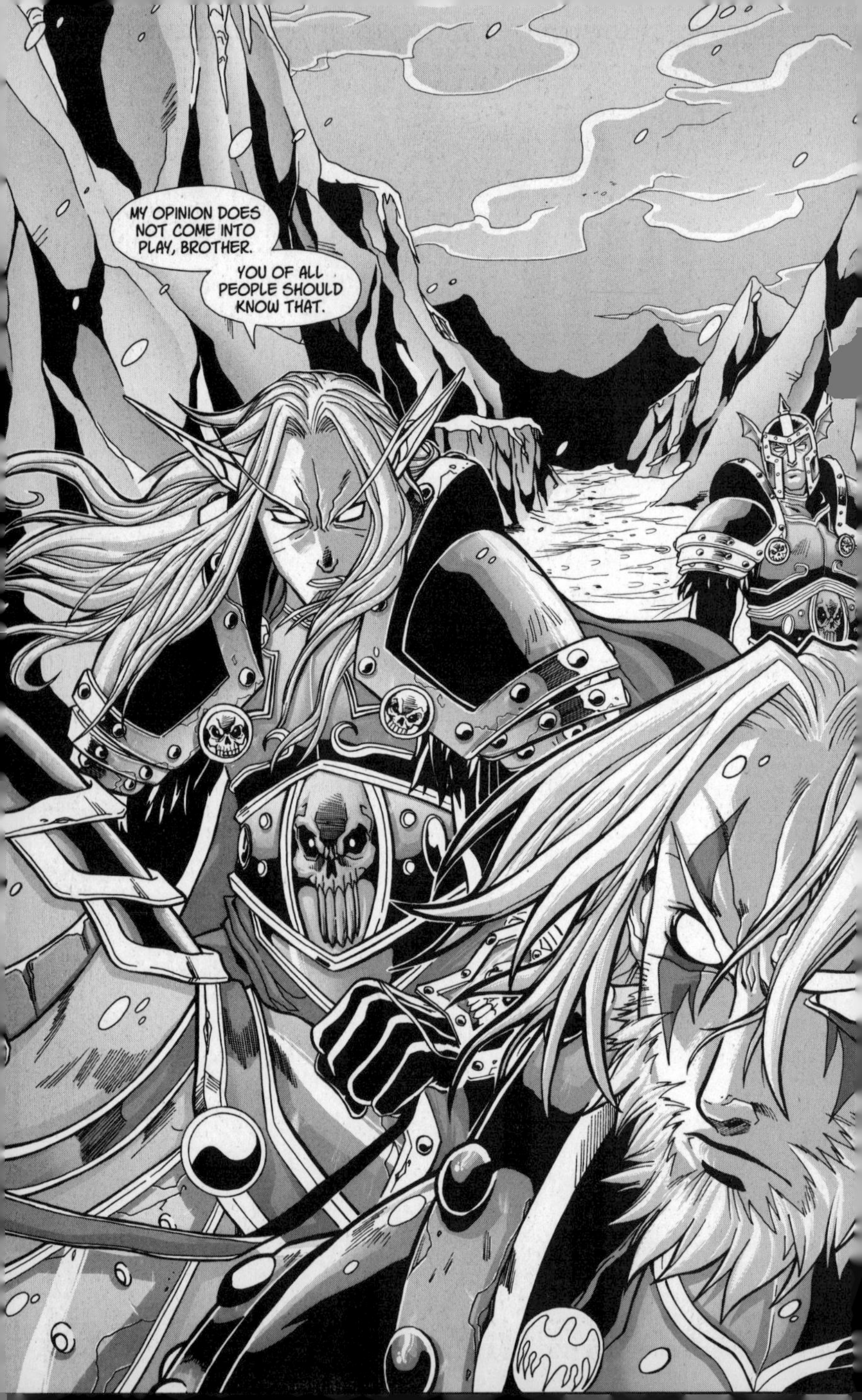
MY OPINION DOES NOT COME INTO PLAY, BROTHER.
YOU OF ALL PEOPLE SHOULD KNOW THAT.

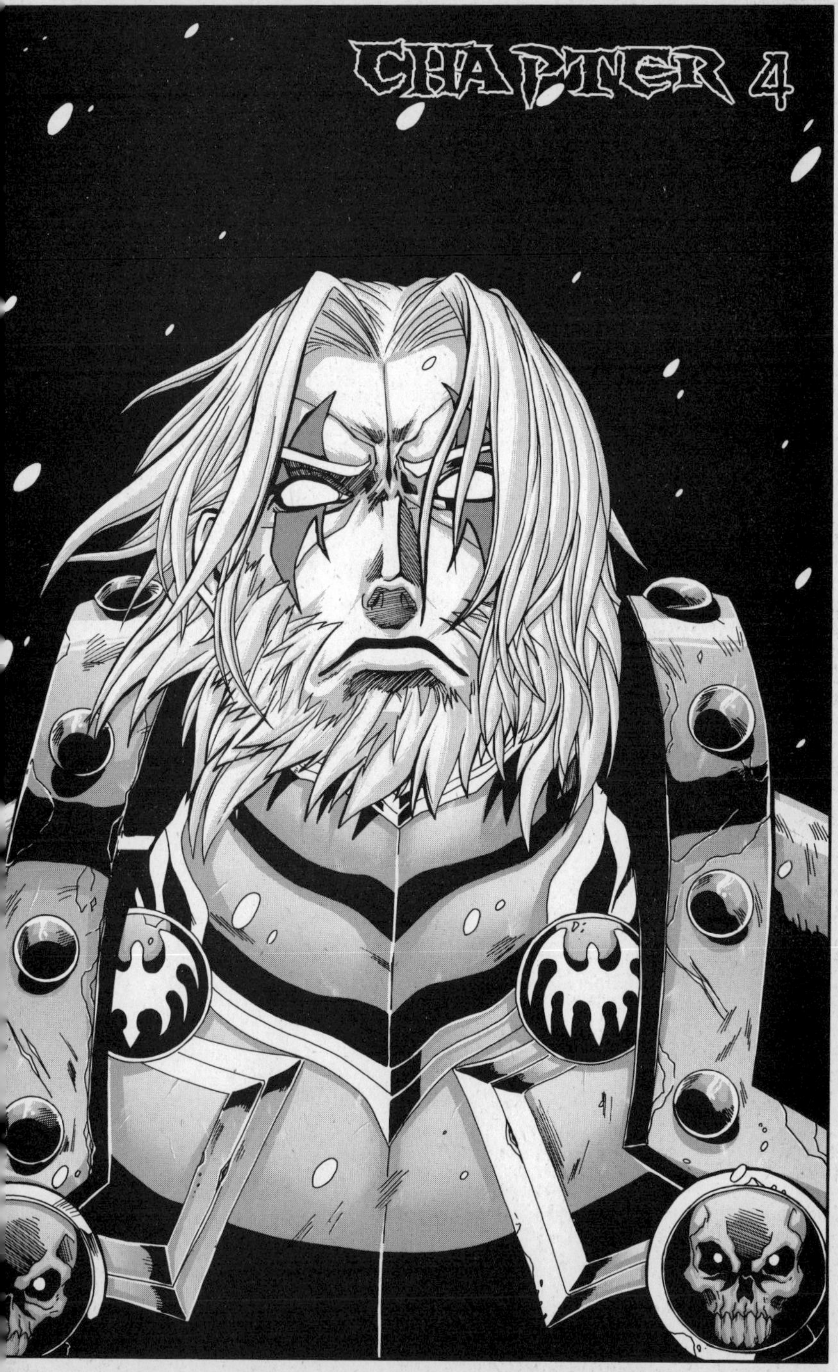
CHAPTER 4

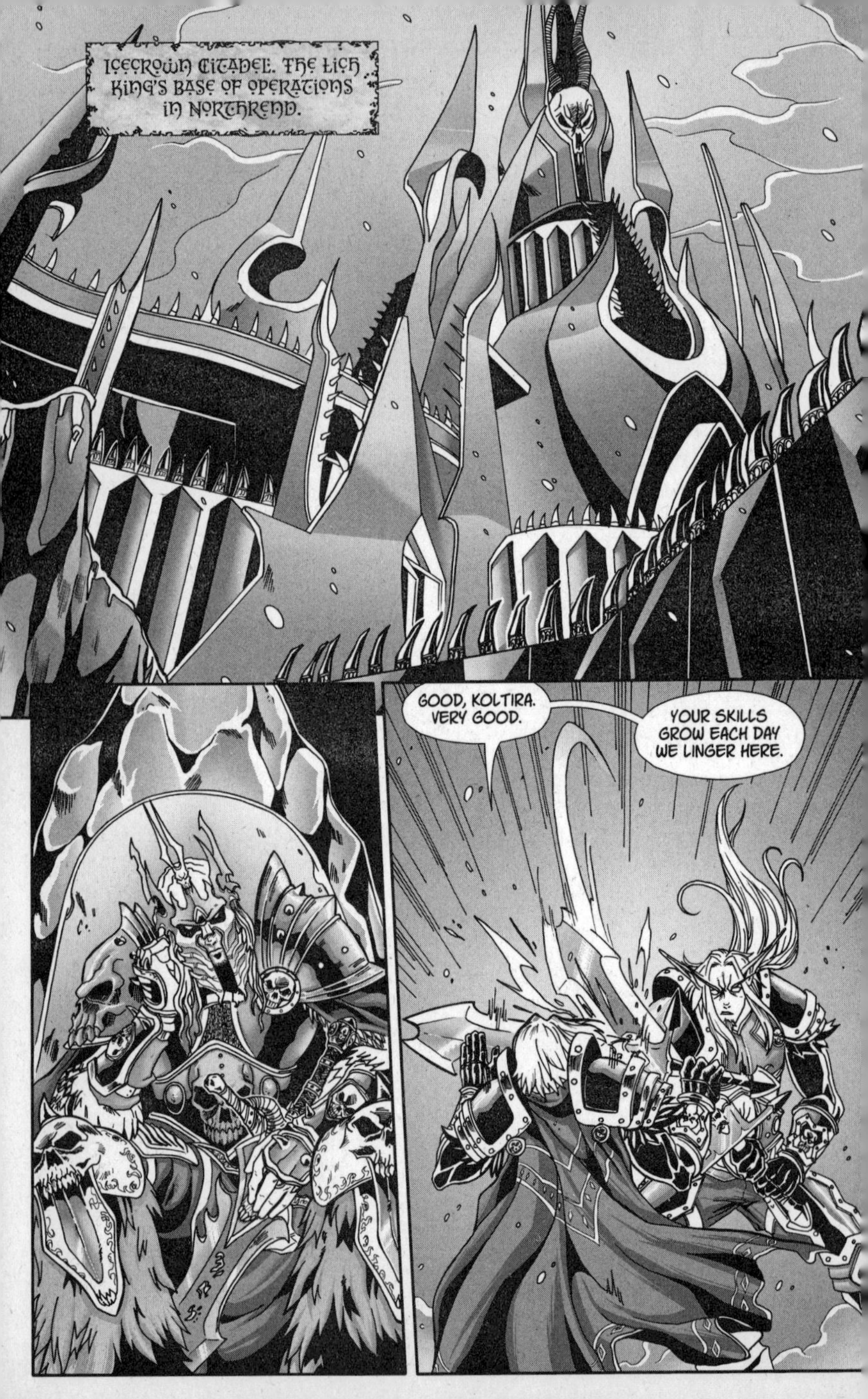
ICECROWN CITADEL. THE LICH KING'S BASE OF OPERATIONS IN NORTHREND.
GOOD, KOLTIRA. VERY GOOD.
YOUR SKILLS GROW EACH DAY WE LINGER HERE.

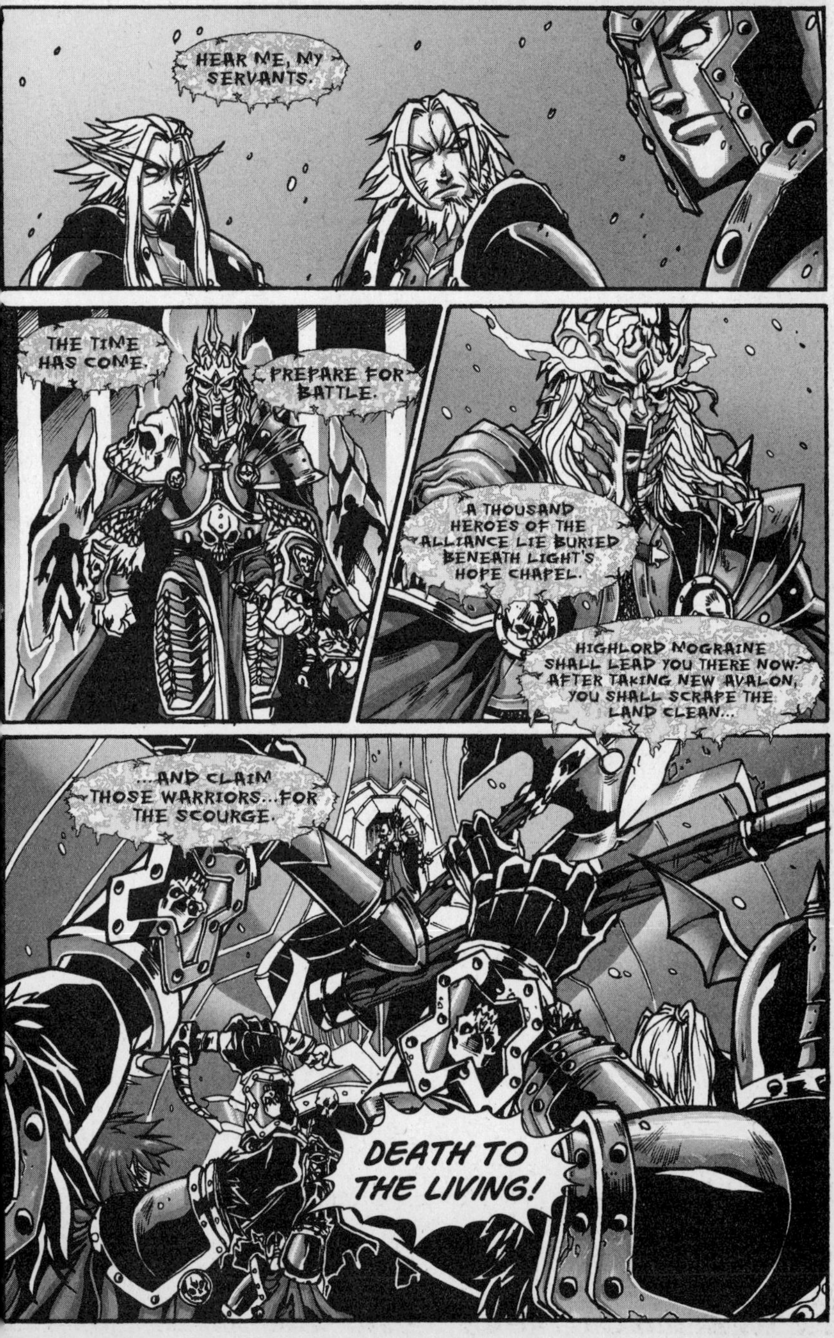
HEAR ME, MY SERVANTS.
THE TIME HAS COME.
PREPARE FOR BATTLE.
A THOUSAND HEROES OF THE ALLIANCE LIE BURIED BENEATH LIGHT'S HOPE CHAPEL.
HIGHLORD MOGRAINE SHALL LEAD YOU THERE NOW. AFTER TAKING NEW AVALON, YOU SHALL SCRAPE THE LAND CLEAN...
...AND CLAIM THOSE WARRIORS...FOR THE SCOURGE.
DEATH TO THE LIVING!

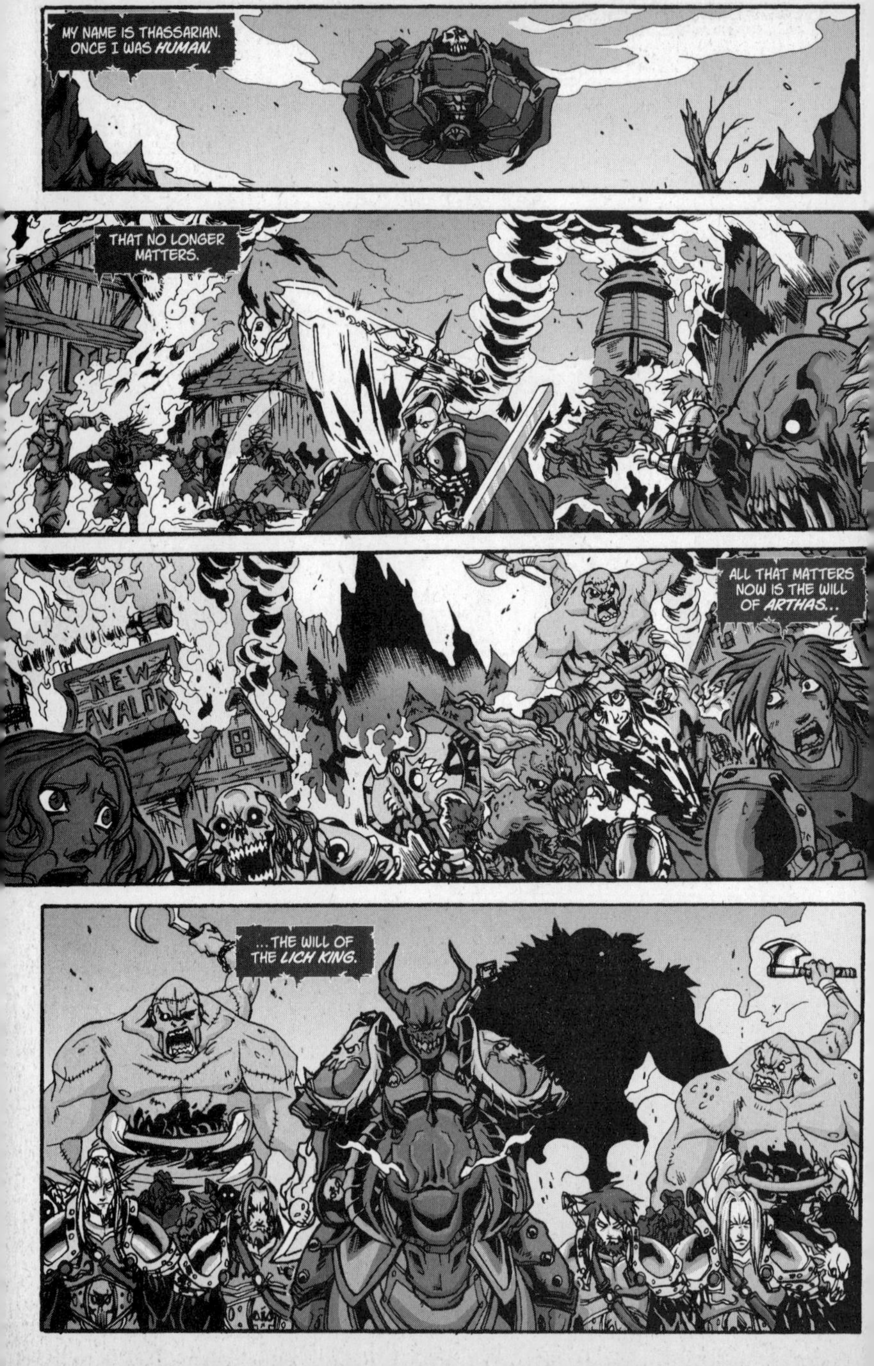

MY NAME IS THASSARIAN. ONCE I WAS *HUMAN.*
THAT NO LONGER MATTERS.
NEW AVALON
ALL THAT MATTERS NOW IS THE WILL OF *ARTHAS*...
...THE WILL OF THE *LICH KING.*

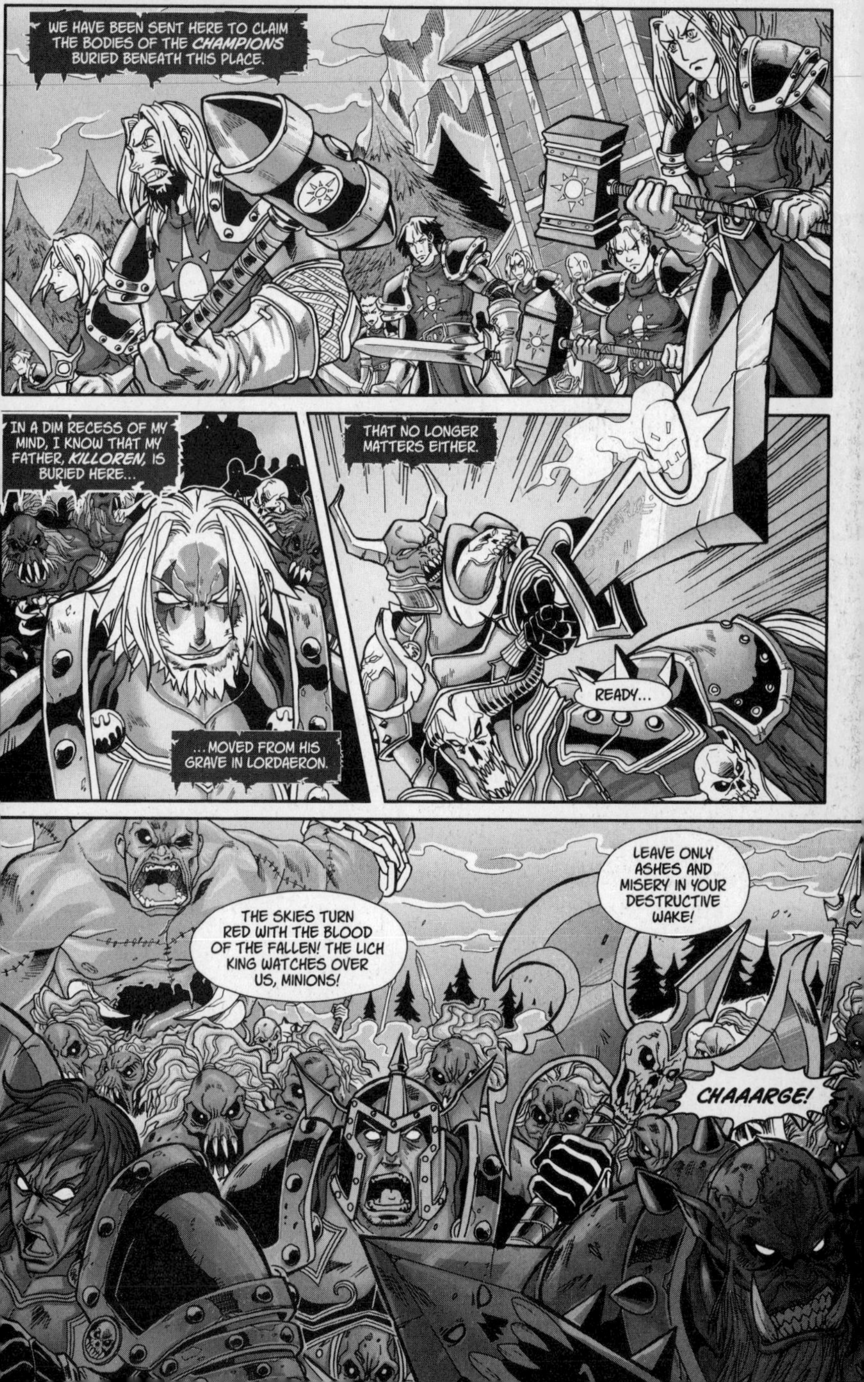
WE HAVE BEEN SENT HERE TO CLAIM THE BODIES OF THE CHAMPIONS BURIED BENEATH THIS PLACE.
IN A DIM RECESS OF MY MIND, I KNOW THAT MY FATHER, KILLOREN, IS BURIED HERE...
...MOVED FROM HIS GRAVE IN LORDAERON.
THAT NO LONGER MATTERS EITHER.
READY...
THE SKIES TURN RED WITH THE BLOOD OF THE FALLEN! THE LICH KING WATCHES OVER US, MINIONS!
LEAVE ONLY ASHES AND MISERY IN YOUR DESTRUCTIVE WAKE!
CHAAARGE!

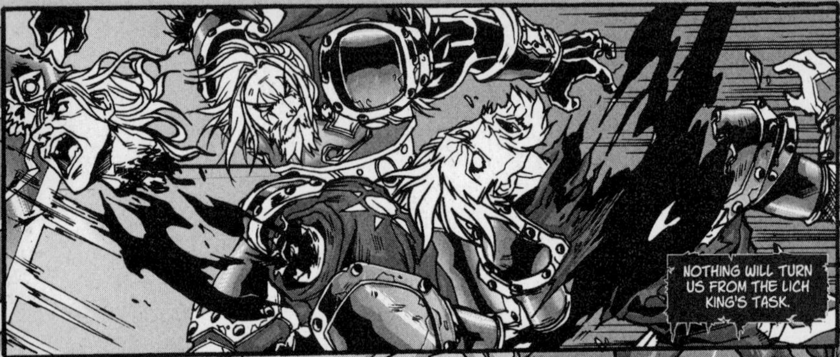
NOTHING WILL TURN US FROM THE LICH KING'S TASK.

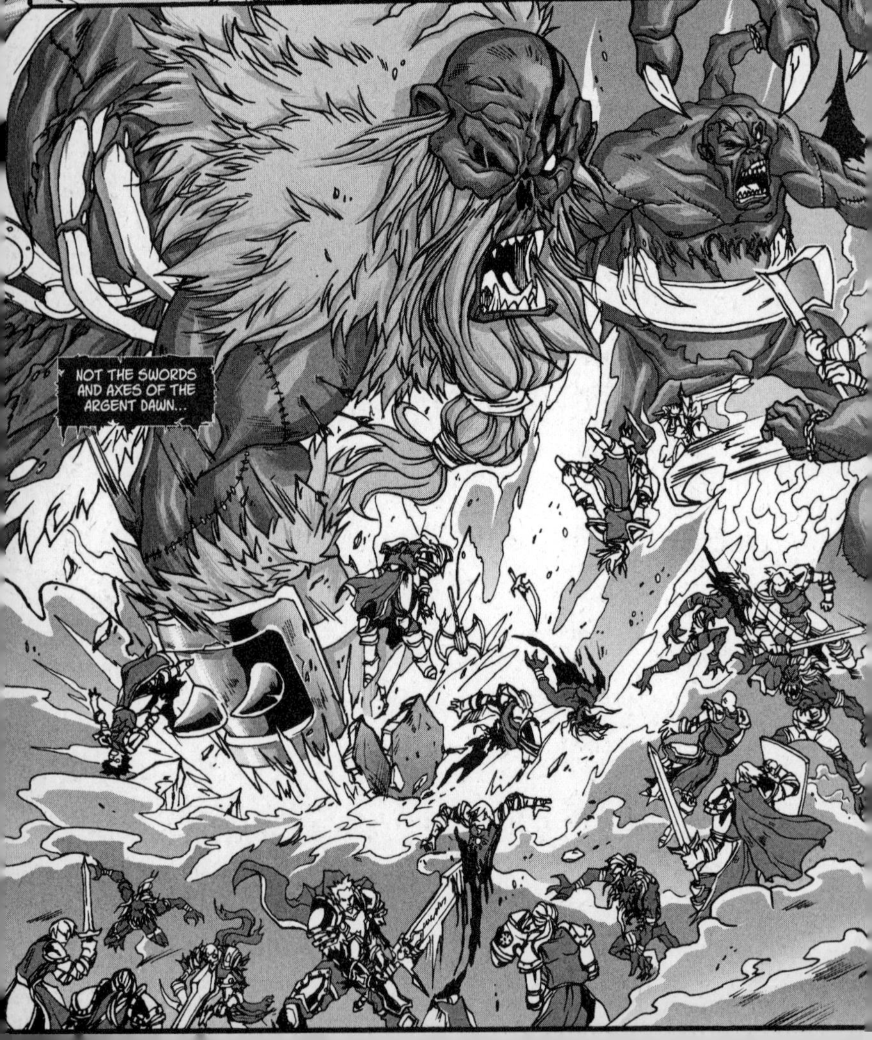
NOT THE SWORDS AND AXES OF THE ARGENT DAWN...

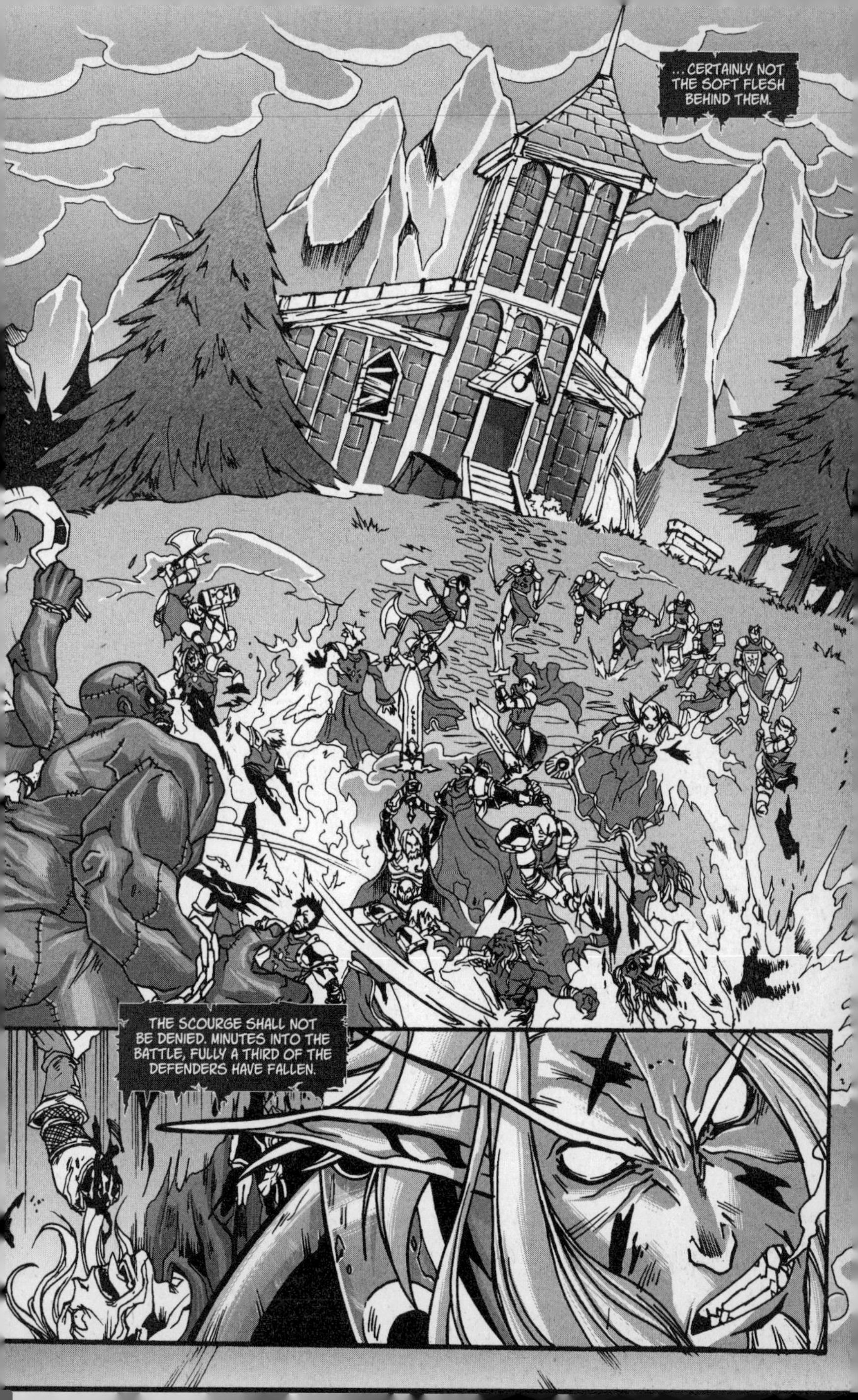
...CERTAINLY NOT THE SOFT FLESH BEHIND THEM.
THE SCOURGE SHALL NOT BE DENIED. MINUTES INTO THE BATTLE, FULLY A THIRD OF THE DEFENDERS HAVE FALLEN.

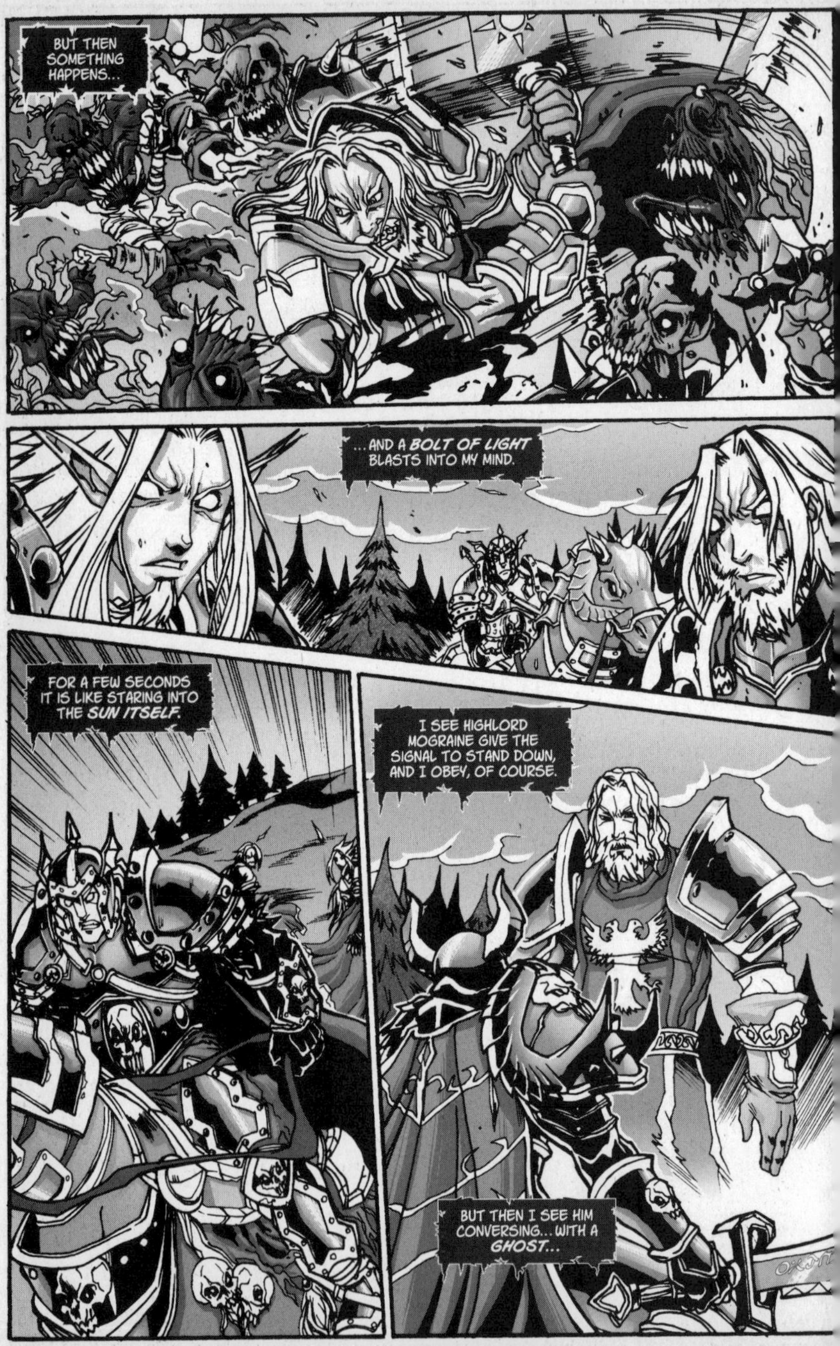
BUT THEN SOMETHING HAPPENS...
...AND A *BOLT OF LIGHT* BLASTS INTO MY MIND.
FOR A FEW SECONDS IT IS LIKE STARING INTO THE *SUN ITSELF*.
I SEE HIGHLORD MOGRAINE GIVE THE SIGNAL TO STAND DOWN, AND I OBEY, OF COURSE.
BUT THEN I SEE HIM CONVERSING... WITH A *GHOST*...

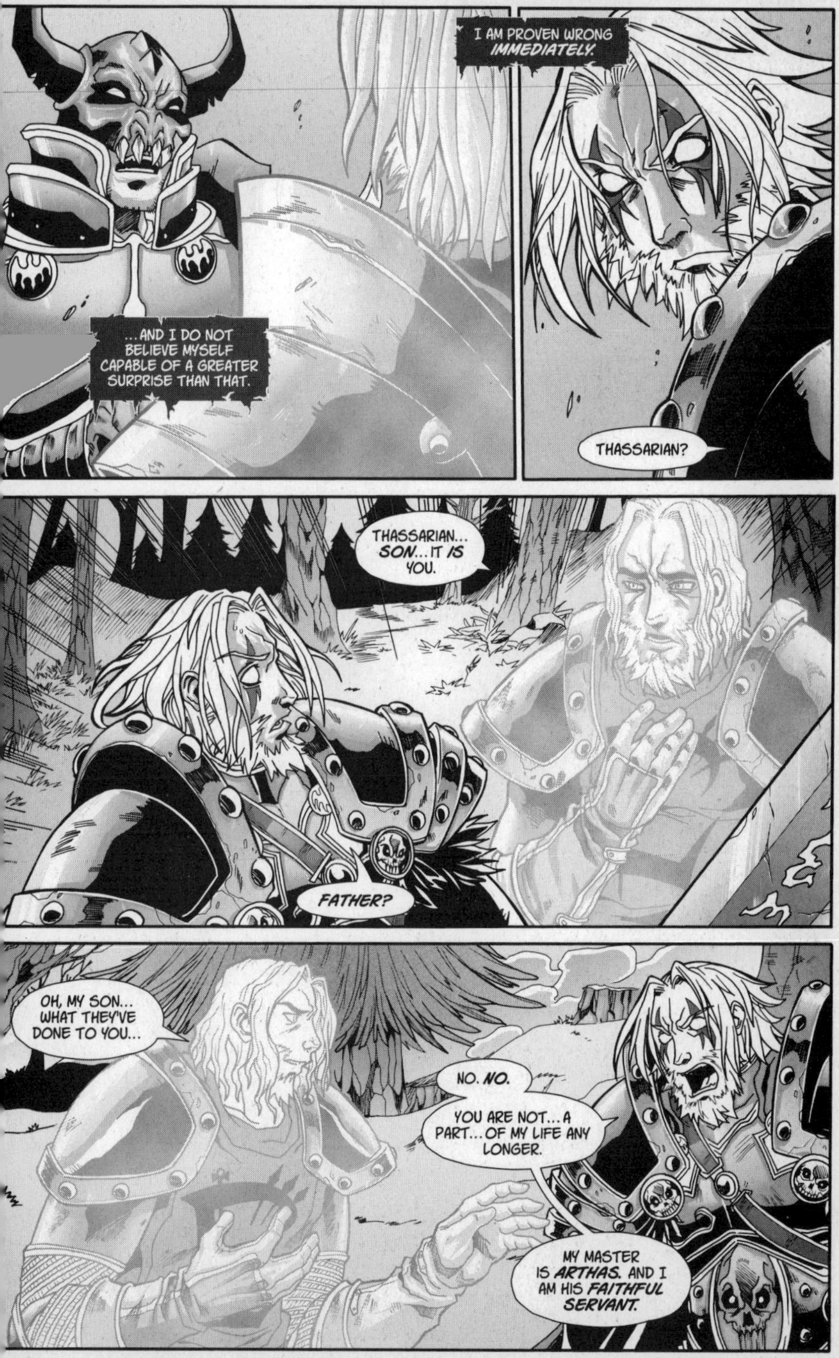
...AND I DO NOT BELIEVE MYSELF CAPABLE OF A GREATER SURPRISE THAN THAT.
I AM PROVEN WRONG IMMEDIATELY.
THASSARIAN?
THASSARIAN... SON... IT IS YOU.
FATHER?
OH, MY SON... WHAT THEY'VE DONE TO YOU...
NO. NO.
YOU ARE NOT... A PART... OF MY LIFE ANY LONGER.
MY MASTER IS ARTHAS. AND I AM HIS FAITHFUL SERVANT.

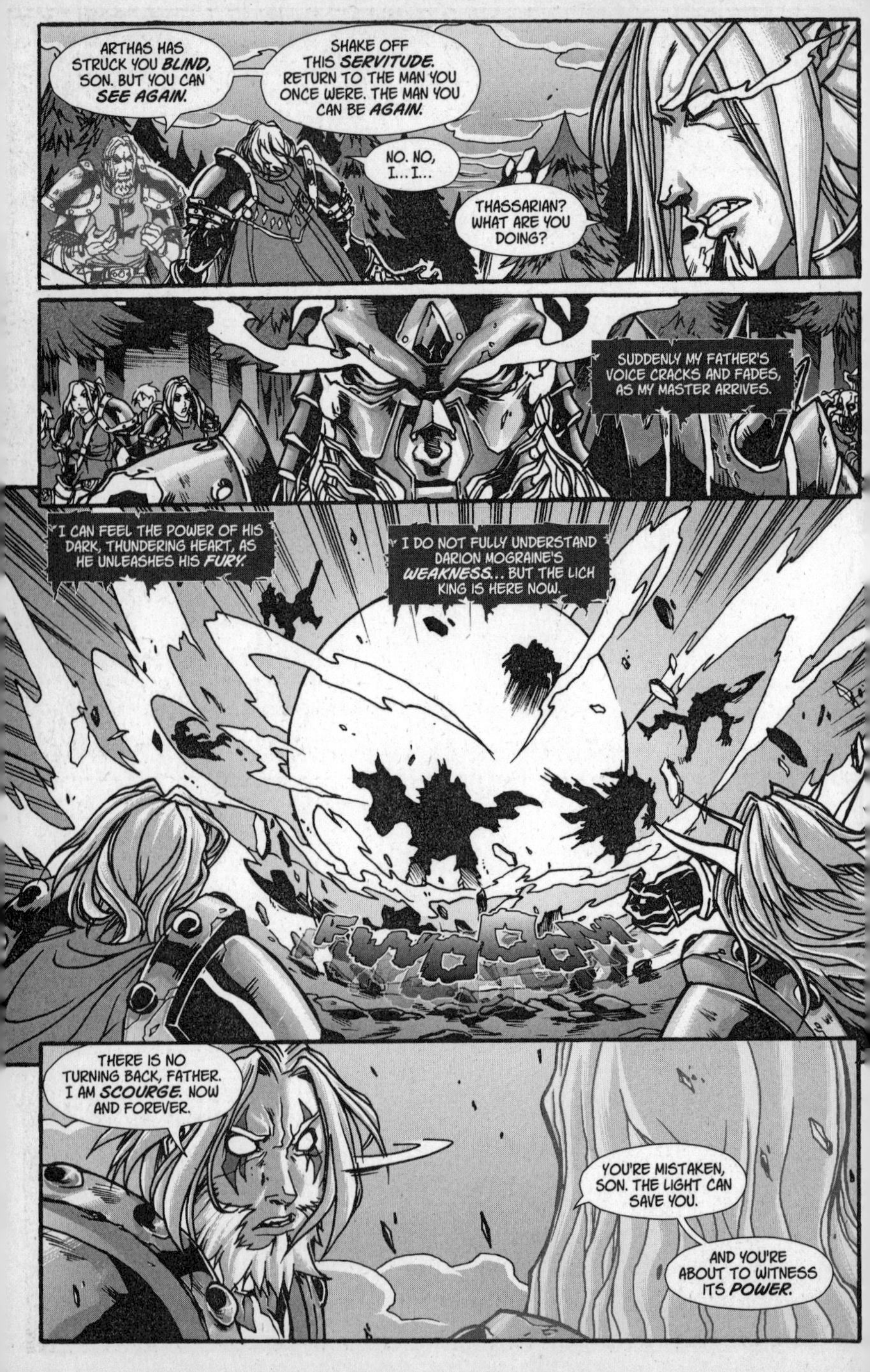
ARTHAS HAS STRUCK YOU *BLIND*, SON. BUT YOU CAN *SEE AGAIN.*
SHAKE OFF THIS *SERVITUDE.* RETURN TO THE MAN YOU ONCE WERE. THE MAN YOU CAN BE *AGAIN.*
NO. NO, I... I...
THASSARIAN? WHAT ARE YOU DOING?
SUDDENLY MY FATHER'S VOICE CRACKS AND FADES, AS MY MASTER ARRIVES.
I CAN FEEL THE POWER OF HIS DARK, THUNDERING HEART, AS HE UNLEASHES HIS *FURY.*
I DO NOT FULLY UNDERSTAND DARION MOGRAINE'S *WEAKNESS*... BUT THE LICH KING IS HERE NOW.
FWOOM
THERE IS NO TURNING BACK, FATHER. I AM *SCOURGE.* NOW AND FOREVER.
YOU'RE MISTAKEN, SON. THE LIGHT CAN SAVE YOU.
AND YOU'RE ABOUT TO WITNESS ITS *POWER.*

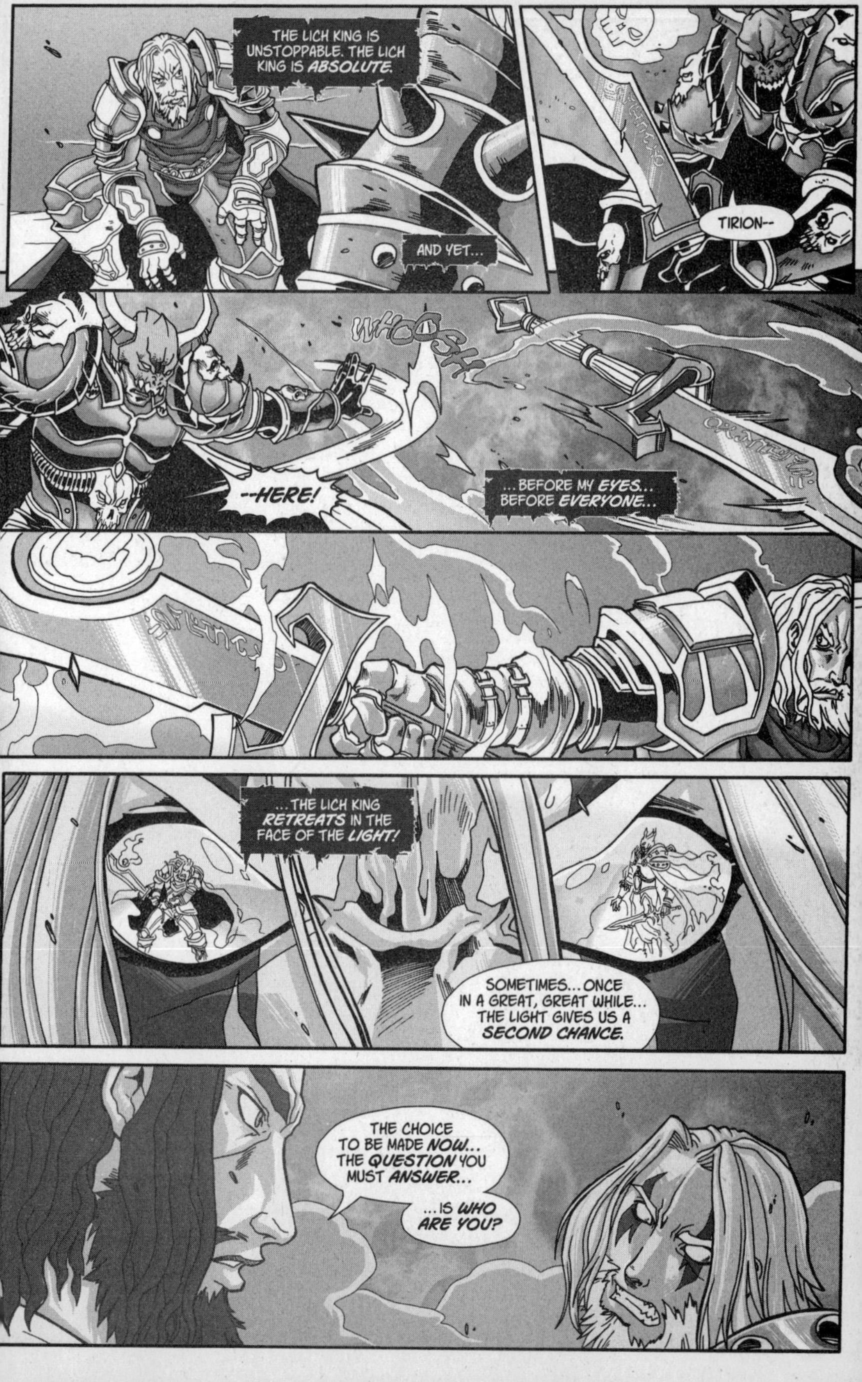
THE LICH KING IS UNSTOPPABLE. THE LICH KING IS *ABSOLUTE.*
AND YET...
TIRION--
WHOOSH
--HERE!
...BEFORE MY *EYES*... BEFORE *EVERYONE*...
...THE LICH KING *RETREATS* IN THE FACE OF THE *LIGHT!*
SOMETIMES... ONCE IN A GREAT, GREAT WHILE... THE LIGHT GIVES US A *SECOND CHANCE.*
THE CHOICE TO BE MADE *NOW*... THE *QUESTION* YOU MUST *ANSWER*...
...IS *WHO ARE YOU?*

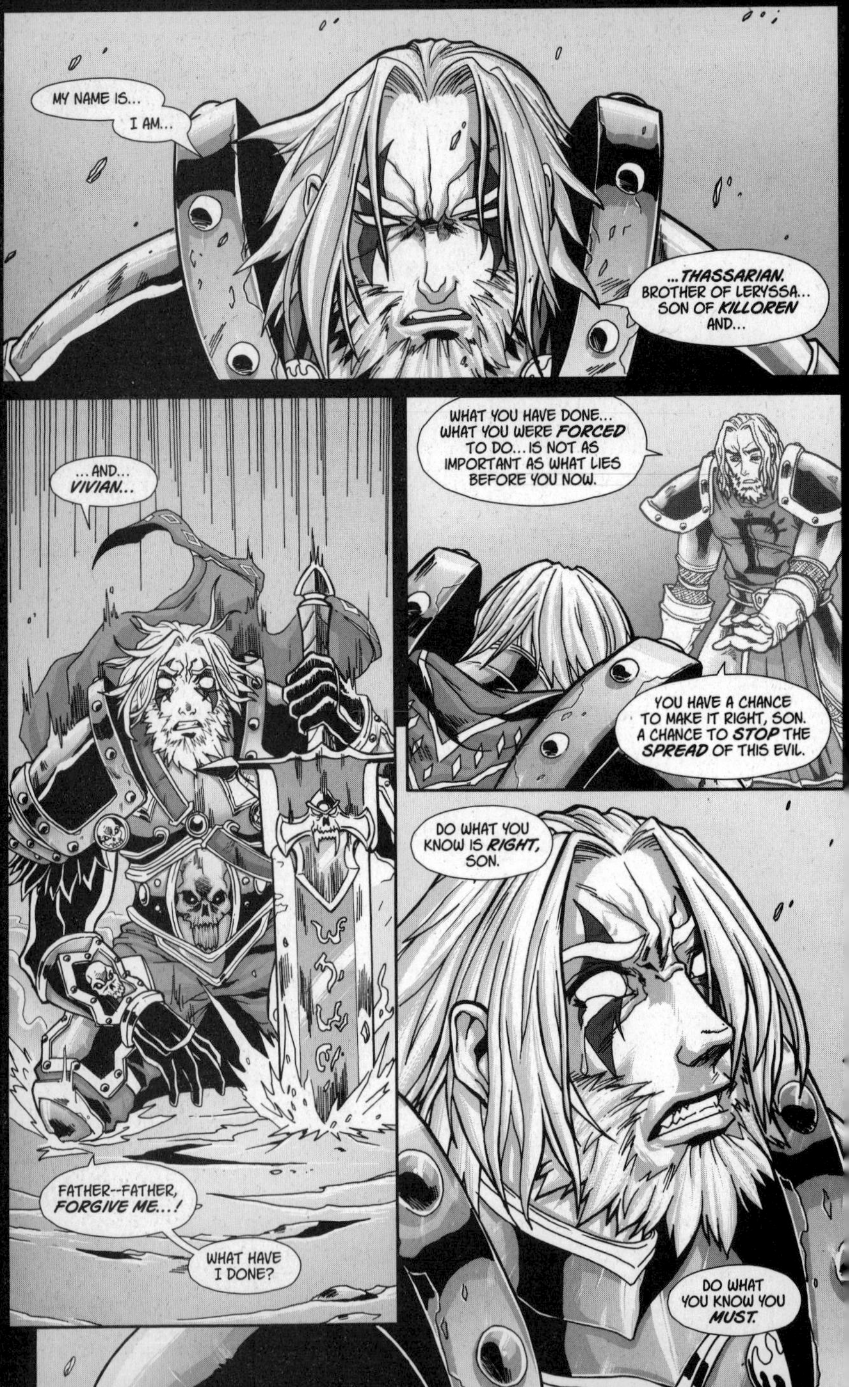
MY NAME IS...
I AM...
...THASSARIAN. BROTHER OF LERYSSA... SON OF KILLOREN AND...
...AND... VIVIAN...
FATHER--FATHER, FORGIVE ME...!
WHAT HAVE I DONE?
WHAT YOU HAVE DONE... WHAT YOU WERE FORCED TO DO... IS NOT AS IMPORTANT AS WHAT LIES BEFORE YOU NOW.
YOU HAVE A CHANCE TO MAKE IT RIGHT, SON. A CHANCE TO STOP THE SPREAD OF THIS EVIL.
DO WHAT YOU KNOW IS RIGHT, SON.
DO WHAT YOU KNOW YOU MUST.

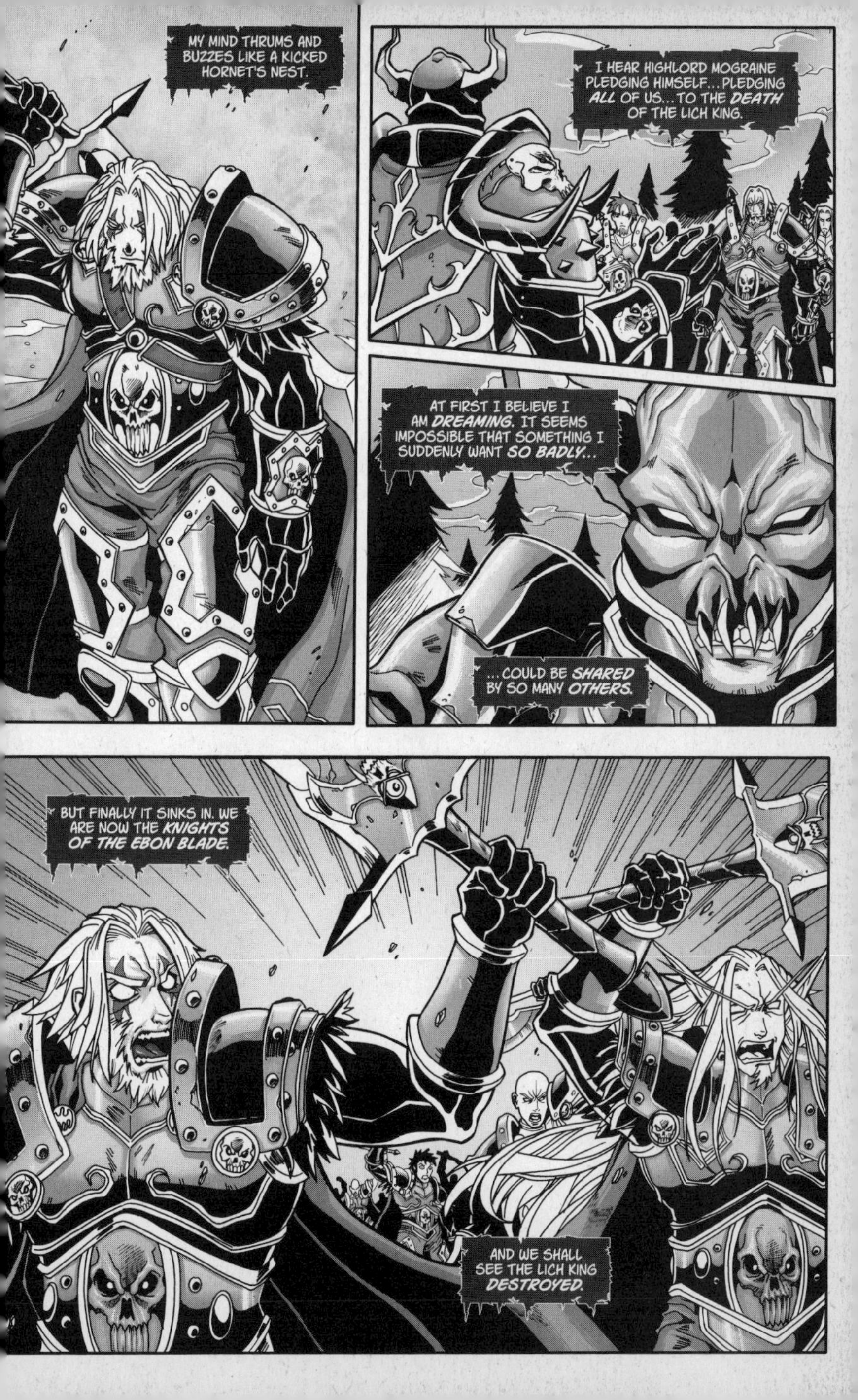
MY MIND THRUMS AND BUZZES LIKE A KICKED HORNET'S NEST.
I HEAR HIGHLORD MOGRAINE PLEDGING HIMSELF...PLEDGING ALL OF US...TO THE DEATH OF THE LICH KING.
AT FIRST I BELIEVE I AM DREAMING. IT SEEMS IMPOSSIBLE THAT SOMETHING I SUDDENLY WANT SO BADLY...
...COULD BE SHARED BY SO MANY OTHERS.
BUT FINALLY IT SINKS IN. WE ARE NOW THE KNIGHTS OF THE EBON BLADE.
AND WE SHALL SEE THE LICH KING DESTROYED.

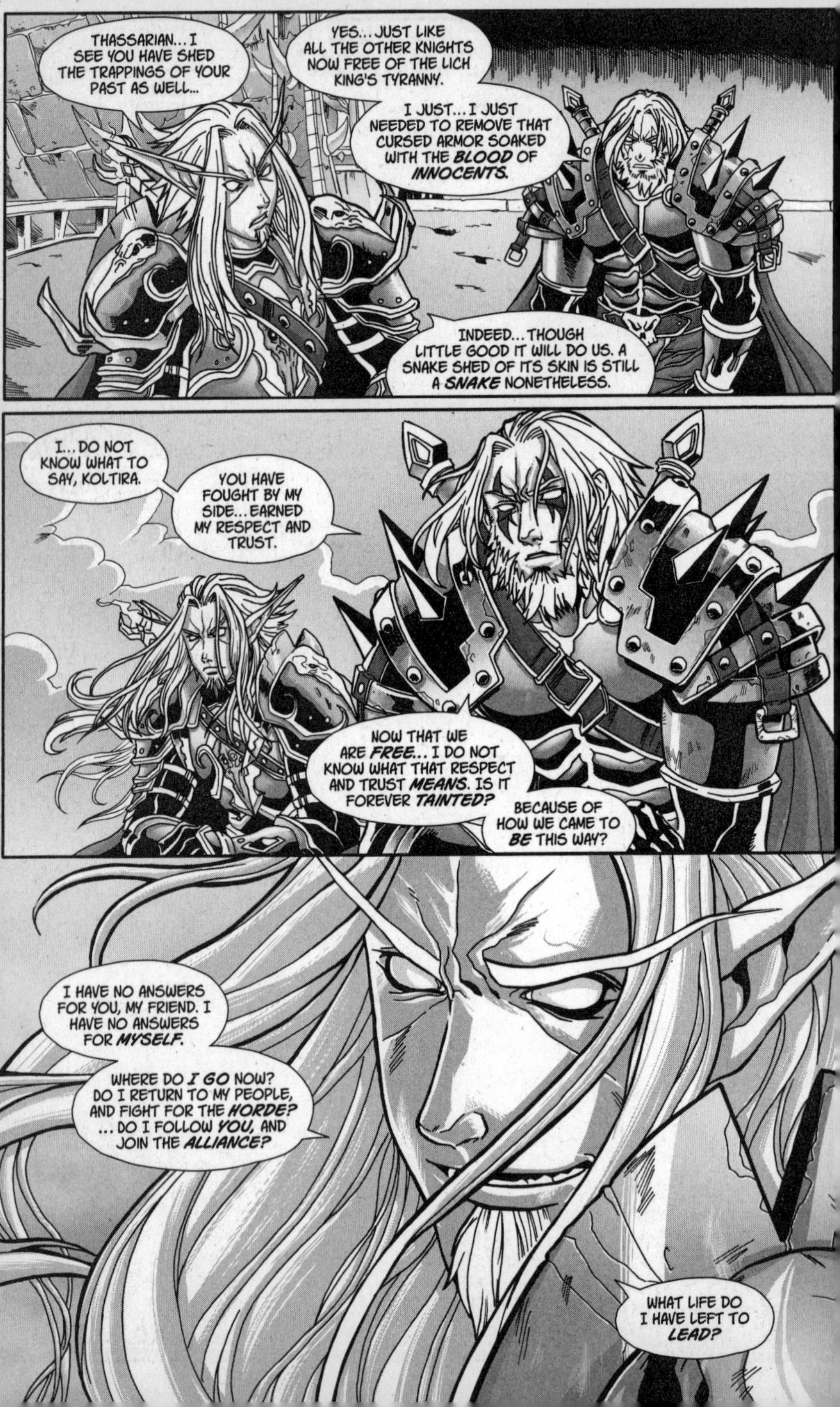
THASSARIAN... I SEE YOU HAVE SHED THE TRAPPINGS OF YOUR PAST AS WELL...
YES... JUST LIKE ALL THE OTHER KNIGHTS NOW FREE OF THE LICH KING'S TYRANNY.
I JUST... I JUST NEEDED TO REMOVE THAT CURSED ARMOR SOAKED WITH THE BLOOD OF INNOCENTS.
INDEED... THOUGH LITTLE GOOD IT WILL DO US. A SNAKE SHED OF ITS SKIN IS STILL A SNAKE NONETHELESS.
I... DO NOT KNOW WHAT TO SAY, KOLTIRA.
YOU HAVE FOUGHT BY MY SIDE... EARNED MY RESPECT AND TRUST.
NOW THAT WE ARE FREE... I DO NOT KNOW WHAT THAT RESPECT AND TRUST MEANS. IS IT FOREVER TAINTED?
BECAUSE OF HOW WE CAME TO BE THIS WAY?
I HAVE NO ANSWERS FOR YOU, MY FRIEND. I HAVE NO ANSWERS FOR MYSELF.
WHERE DO I GO NOW? DO I RETURN TO MY PEOPLE, AND FIGHT FOR THE HORDE? ...DO I FOLLOW YOU, AND JOIN THE ALLIANCE?
WHAT LIFE DO I HAVE LEFT TO LEAD?

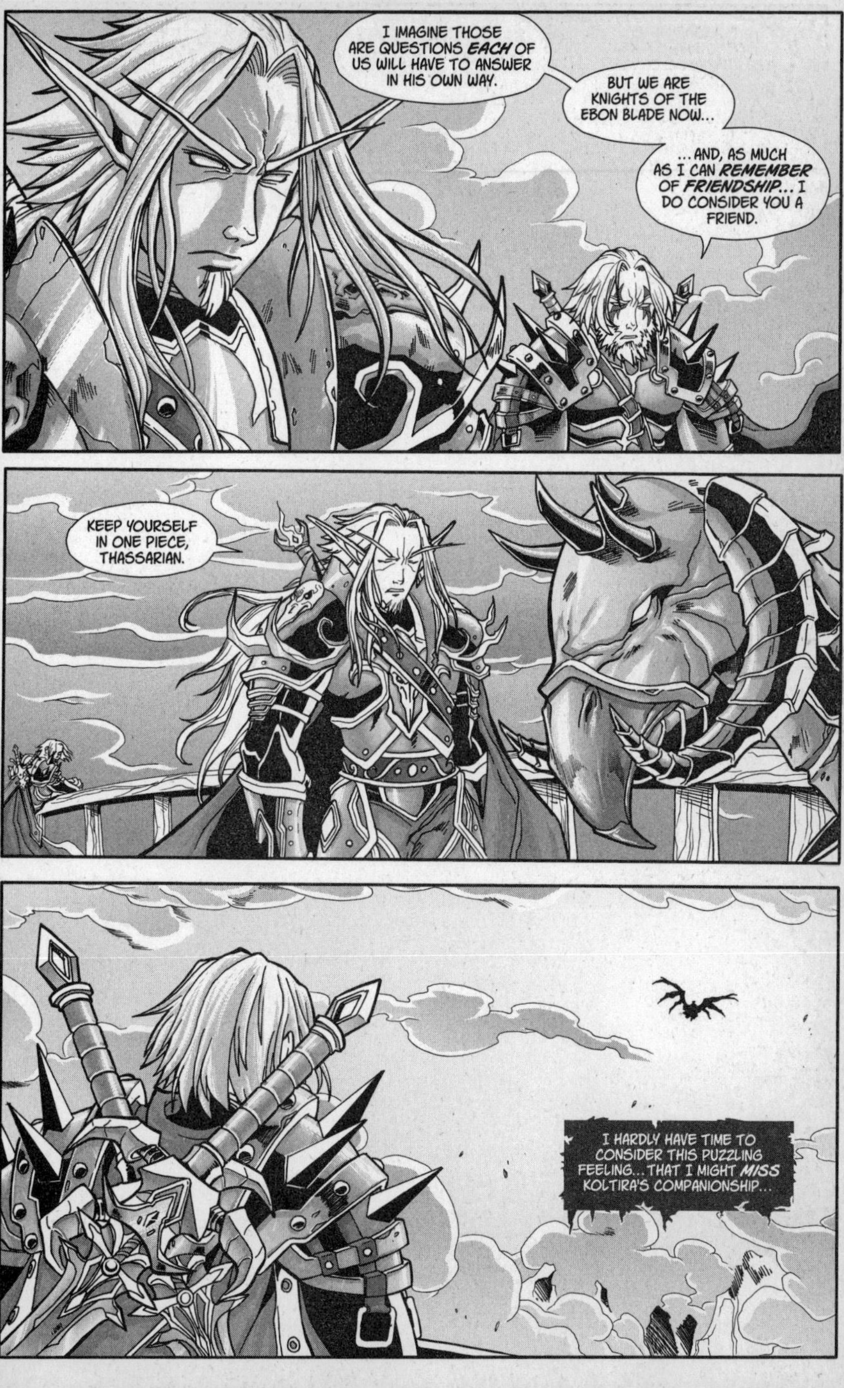
I IMAGINE THOSE ARE QUESTIONS *EACH* OF US WILL HAVE TO ANSWER IN HIS OWN WAY.
BUT WE ARE KNIGHTS OF THE EBON BLADE NOW...
...AND, AS MUCH AS I CAN *REMEMBER* OF *FRIENDSHIP*... I DO CONSIDER YOU A FRIEND.
KEEP YOURSELF IN ONE PIECE, THASSARIAN.
I HARDLY HAVE TIME TO CONSIDER THIS PUZZLING FEELING...THAT I MIGHT *MISS* KOLTIRA'S COMPANIONSHIP...

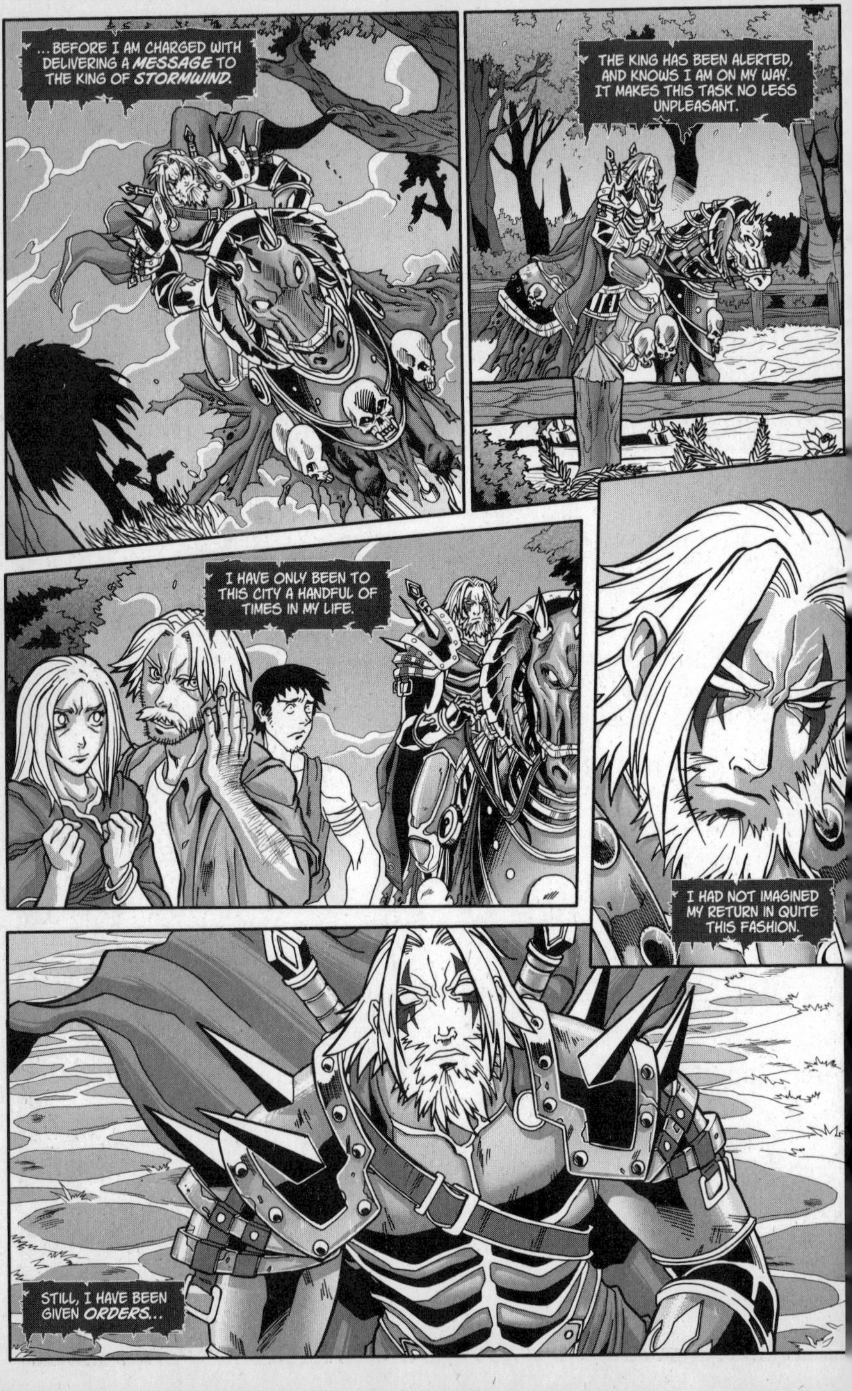
...BEFORE I AM CHARGED WITH DELIVERING A MESSAGE TO THE KING OF STORMWIND.
THE KING HAS BEEN ALERTED, AND KNOWS I AM ON MY WAY. IT MAKES THIS TASK NO LESS UNPLEASANT.
I HAVE ONLY BEEN TO THIS CITY A HANDFUL OF TIMES IN MY LIFE.
I HAD NOT IMAGINED MY RETURN IN QUITE THIS FASHION.
STILL, I HAVE BEEN GIVEN ORDERS...

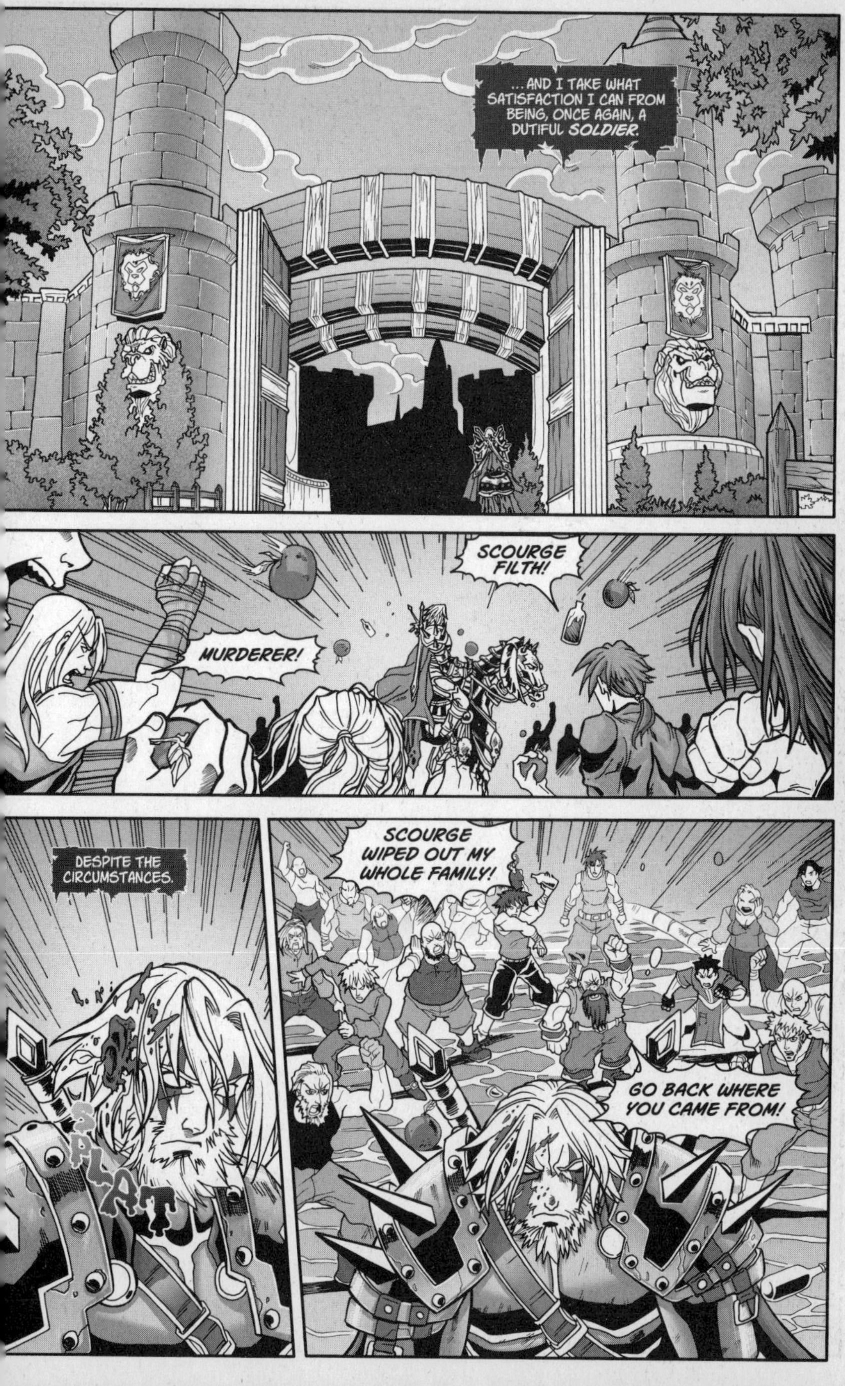
...AND I TAKE WHAT SATISFACTION I CAN FROM BEING, ONCE AGAIN, A DUTIFUL SOLDIER.
MURDERER!
SCOURGE FILTH!
DESPITE THE CIRCUMSTANCES.
SPLAT
SCOURGE WIPED OUT MY WHOLE FAMILY!
GO BACK WHERE YOU CAME FROM!

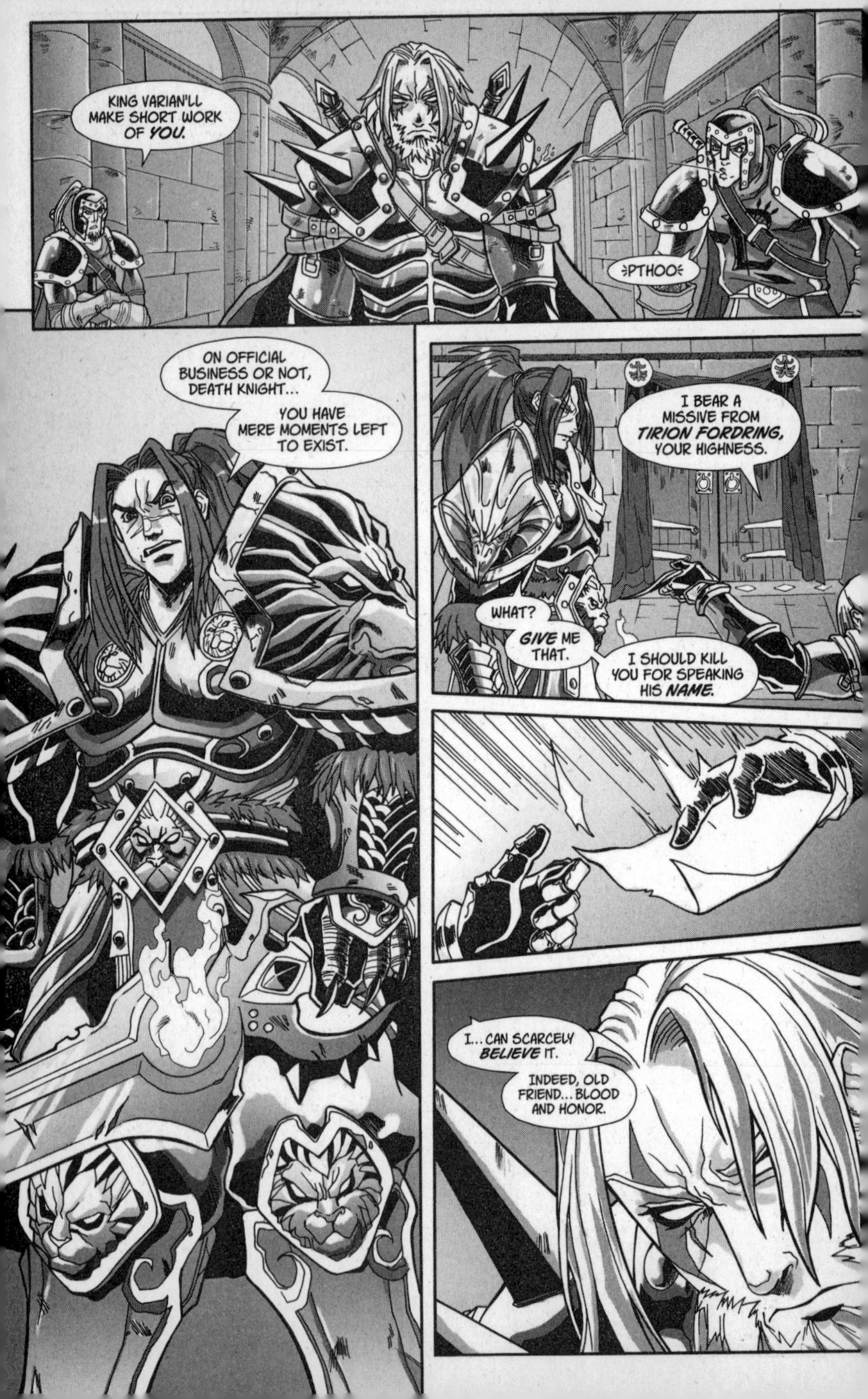
KING VARIAN'LL MAKE SHORT WORK OF YOU.
PTHOO
ON OFFICIAL BUSINESS OR NOT, DEATH KNIGHT...
YOU HAVE MERE MOMENTS LEFT TO EXIST.
I BEAR A MISSIVE FROM TIRION FORDRING, YOUR HIGHNESS.
WHAT?
GIVE ME THAT.
I SHOULD KILL YOU FOR SPEAKING HIS NAME.
I...CAN SCARCELY BELIEVE IT.
INDEED, OLD FRIEND...BLOOD AND HONOR.

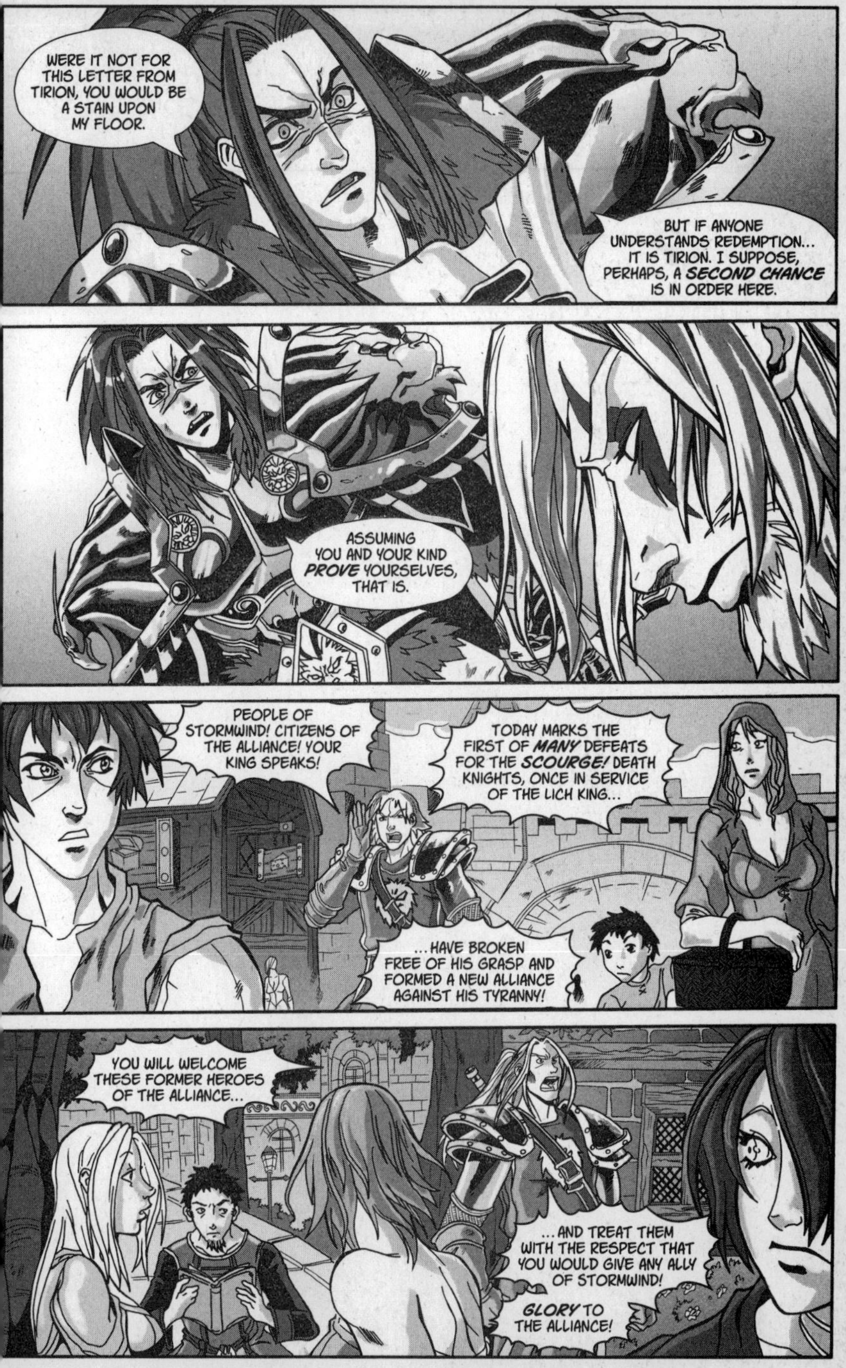

WERE IT NOT FOR THIS LETTER FROM TIRION, YOU WOULD BE A STAIN UPON MY FLOOR.
BUT IF ANYONE UNDERSTANDS REDEMPTION... IT IS TIRION. I SUPPOSE, PERHAPS, A **SECOND CHANCE** IS IN ORDER HERE.
ASSUMING YOU AND YOUR KIND **PROVE** YOURSELVES, THAT IS.
PEOPLE OF STORMWIND! CITIZENS OF THE ALLIANCE! YOUR KING SPEAKS!
TODAY MARKS THE FIRST OF **MANY** DEFEATS FOR THE **SCOURGE!** DEATH KNIGHTS, ONCE IN SERVICE OF THE LICH KING...
...HAVE BROKEN FREE OF HIS GRASP AND FORMED A NEW ALLIANCE AGAINST HIS TYRANNY!
YOU WILL WELCOME THESE FORMER HEROES OF THE ALLIANCE...
...AND TREAT THEM WITH THE RESPECT THAT YOU WOULD GIVE ANY ALLY OF STORMWIND!
GLORY TO THE ALLIANCE!

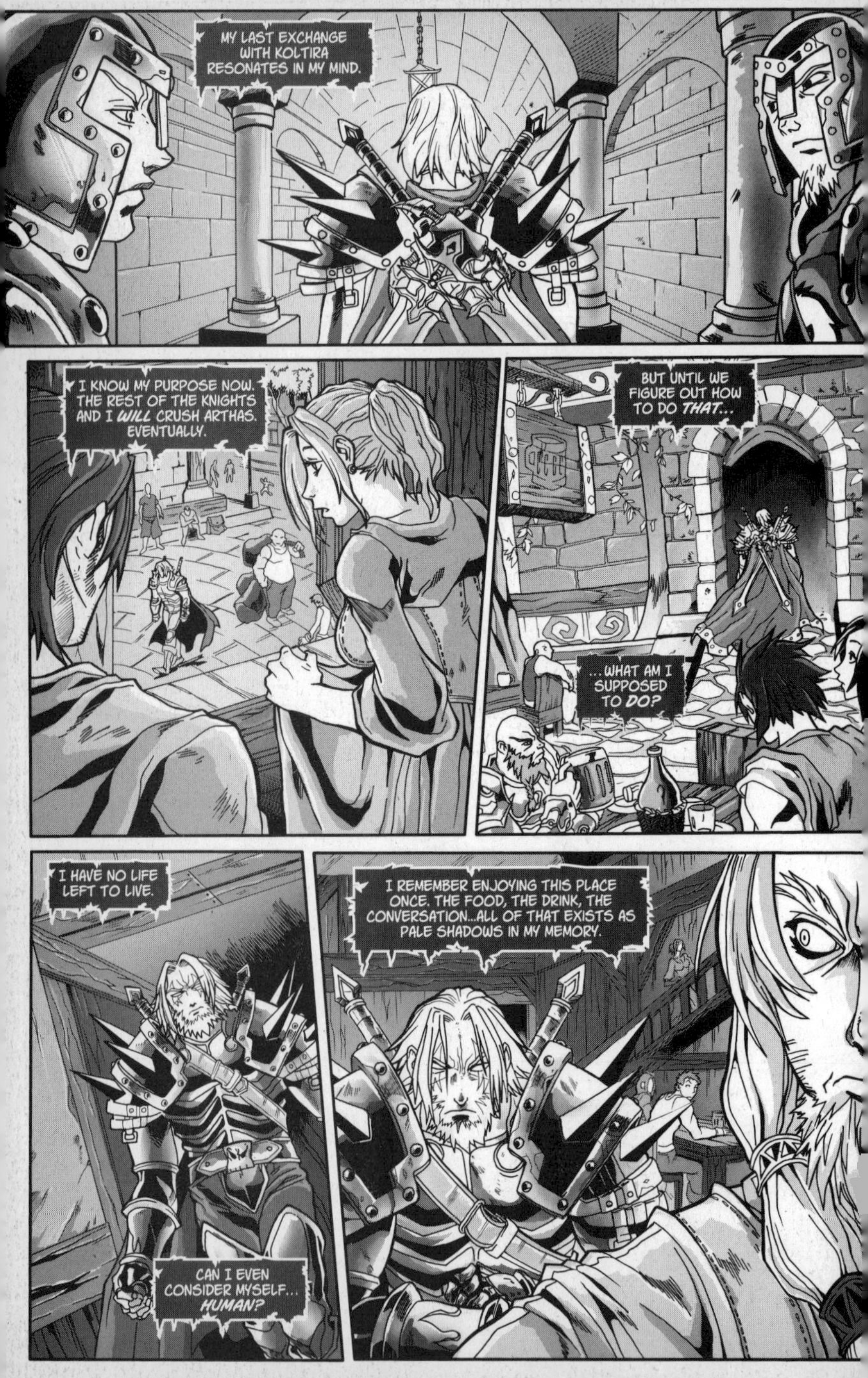
MY LAST EXCHANGE WITH KOLTIRA RESONATES IN MY MIND.
I KNOW MY PURPOSE NOW. THE REST OF THE KNIGHTS AND I *WILL* CRUSH ARTHAS. EVENTUALLY.
BUT UNTIL WE FIGURE OUT HOW TO DO *THAT*...
...WHAT AM I SUPPOSED TO *DO*?
I HAVE NO LIFE LEFT TO LIVE.
CAN I EVEN CONSIDER MYSELF... *HUMAN*?
I REMEMBER ENJOYING THIS PLACE ONCE. THE FOOD, THE DRINK, THE CONVERSATION...ALL OF THAT EXISTS AS PALE SHADOWS IN MY MEMORY.

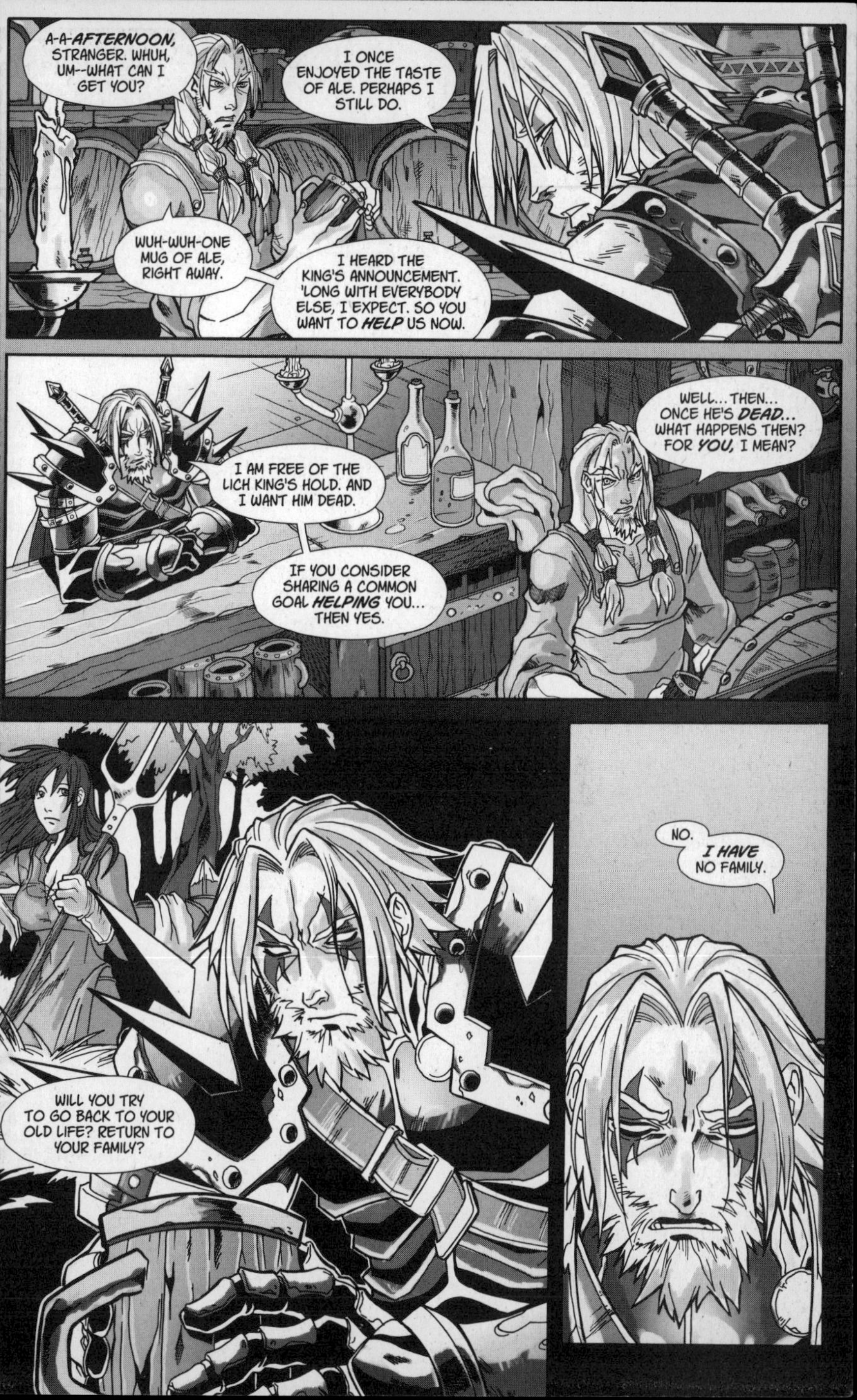
A-A-*AFTERNOON,* STRANGER. WHUH, UM--WHAT CAN I GET YOU?
I ONCE ENJOYED THE TASTE OF ALE. PERHAPS I STILL DO.
WUH-WUH-ONE MUG OF ALE, RIGHT AWAY.
I HEARD THE KING'S ANNOUNCEMENT. 'LONG WITH EVERYBODY ELSE, I EXPECT. SO YOU WANT TO *HELP* US NOW.
I AM FREE OF THE LICH KING'S HOLD. AND I WANT HIM DEAD.
IF YOU CONSIDER SHARING A COMMON GOAL *HELPING* YOU... THEN YES.
WELL... THEN... ONCE HE'S *DEAD...* WHAT HAPPENS THEN? FOR *YOU,* I MEAN?
WILL YOU TRY TO GO BACK TO YOUR OLD LIFE? RETURN TO YOUR FAMILY?
NO. *I HAVE* NO FAMILY.

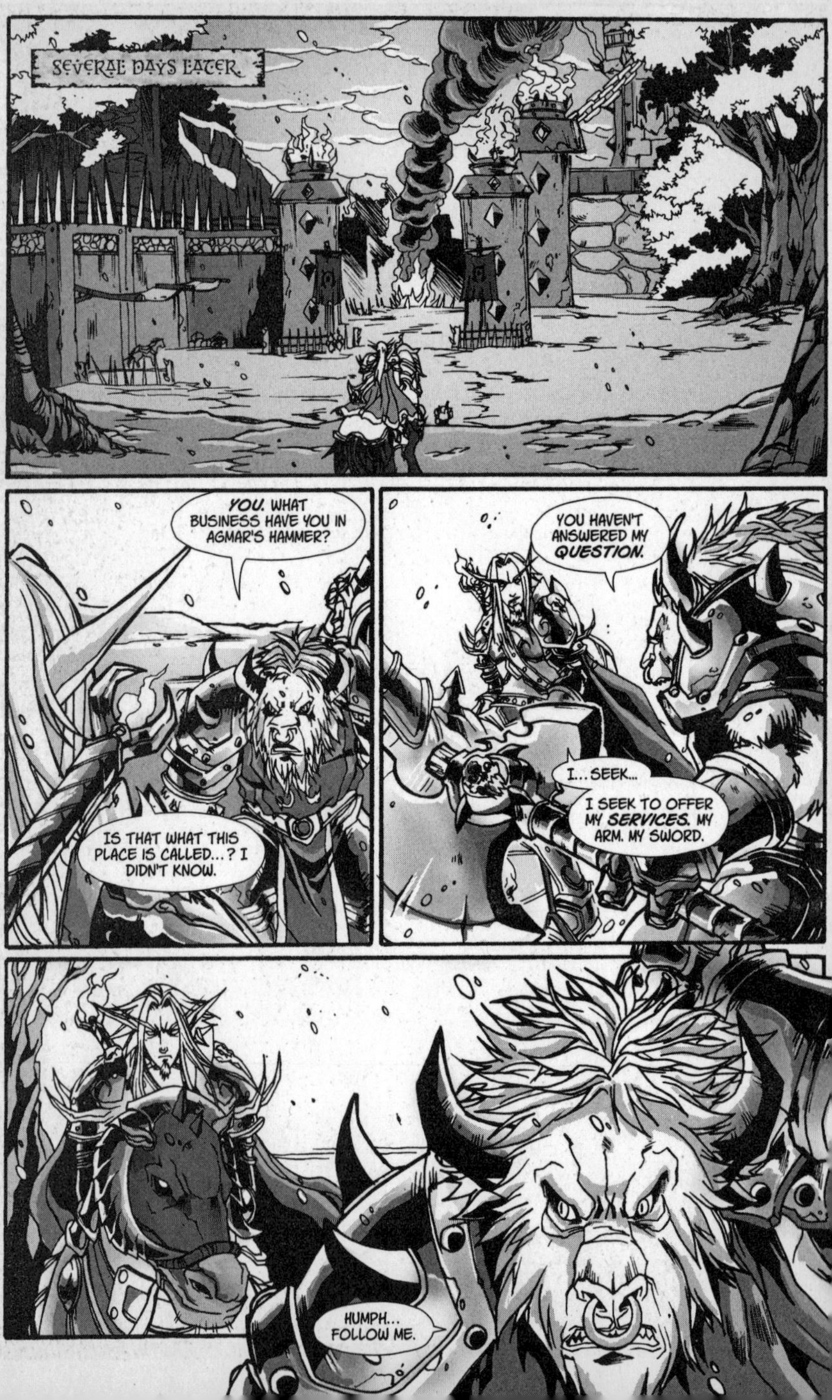
SEVERAL DAYS LATER.
YOU. WHAT BUSINESS HAVE YOU IN AGMAR'S HAMMER?
IS THAT WHAT THIS PLACE IS CALLED...? I DIDN'T KNOW.
YOU HAVEN'T ANSWERED MY QUESTION.
I... SEEK...
I SEEK TO OFFER MY SERVICES. MY ARM. MY SWORD.
HUMPH... FOLLOW ME.

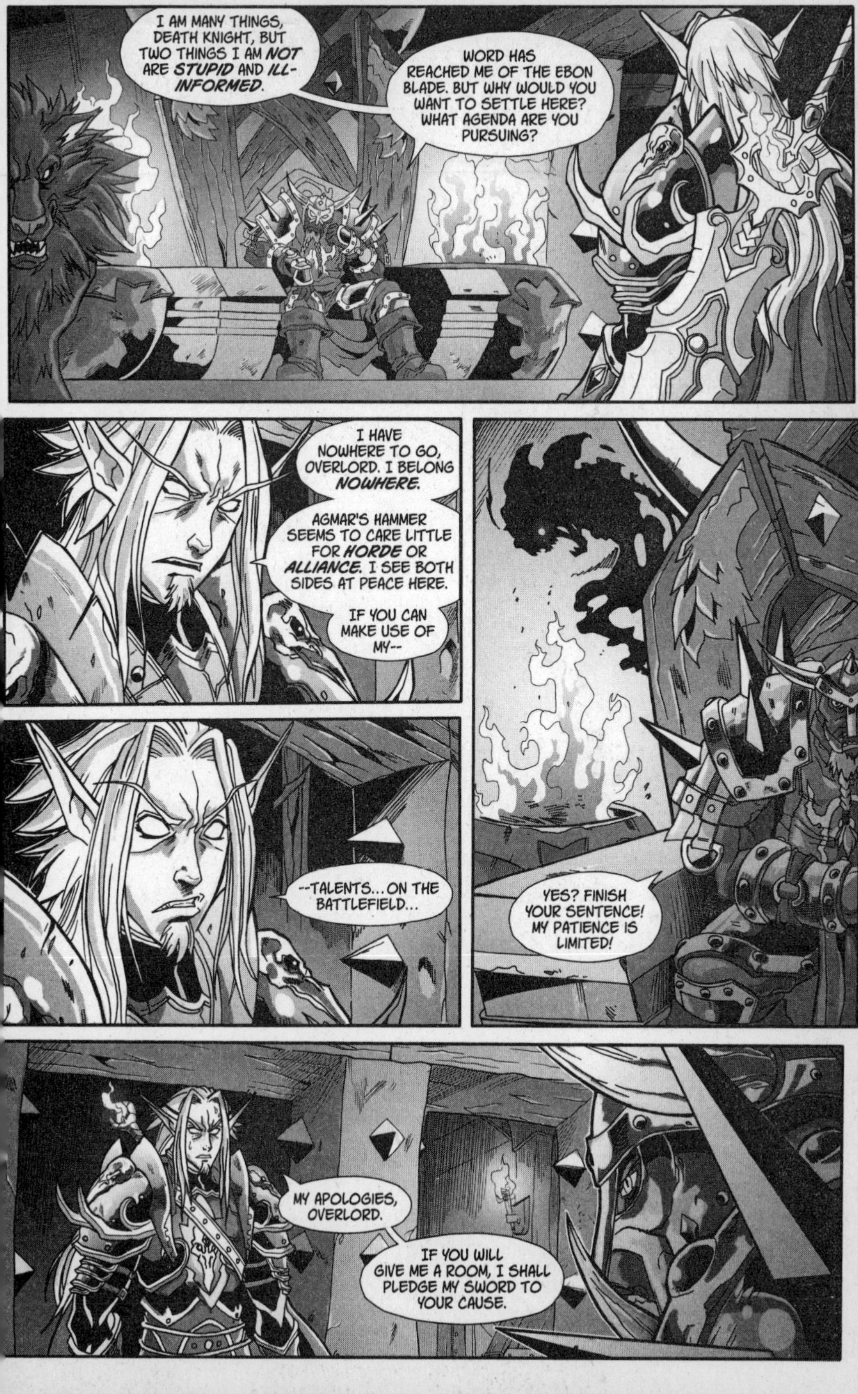
I AM MANY THINGS, DEATH KNIGHT, BUT TWO THINGS I AM *NOT* ARE *STUPID* AND *ILL-INFORMED*.
WORD HAS REACHED ME OF THE EBON BLADE. BUT WHY WOULD YOU WANT TO SETTLE HERE? WHAT AGENDA ARE YOU PURSUING?
I HAVE NOWHERE TO GO, OVERLORD. I BELONG *NOWHERE*.
AGMAR'S HAMMER SEEMS TO CARE LITTLE FOR *HORDE* OR *ALLIANCE*. I SEE BOTH SIDES AT PEACE HERE.
IF YOU CAN MAKE USE OF MY--
--TALENTS...ON THE BATTLEFIELD...
YES? FINISH YOUR SENTENCE! MY PATIENCE IS LIMITED!
MY APOLOGIES, OVERLORD.
IF YOU WILL GIVE ME A ROOM, I SHALL PLEDGE MY SWORD TO YOUR CAUSE.

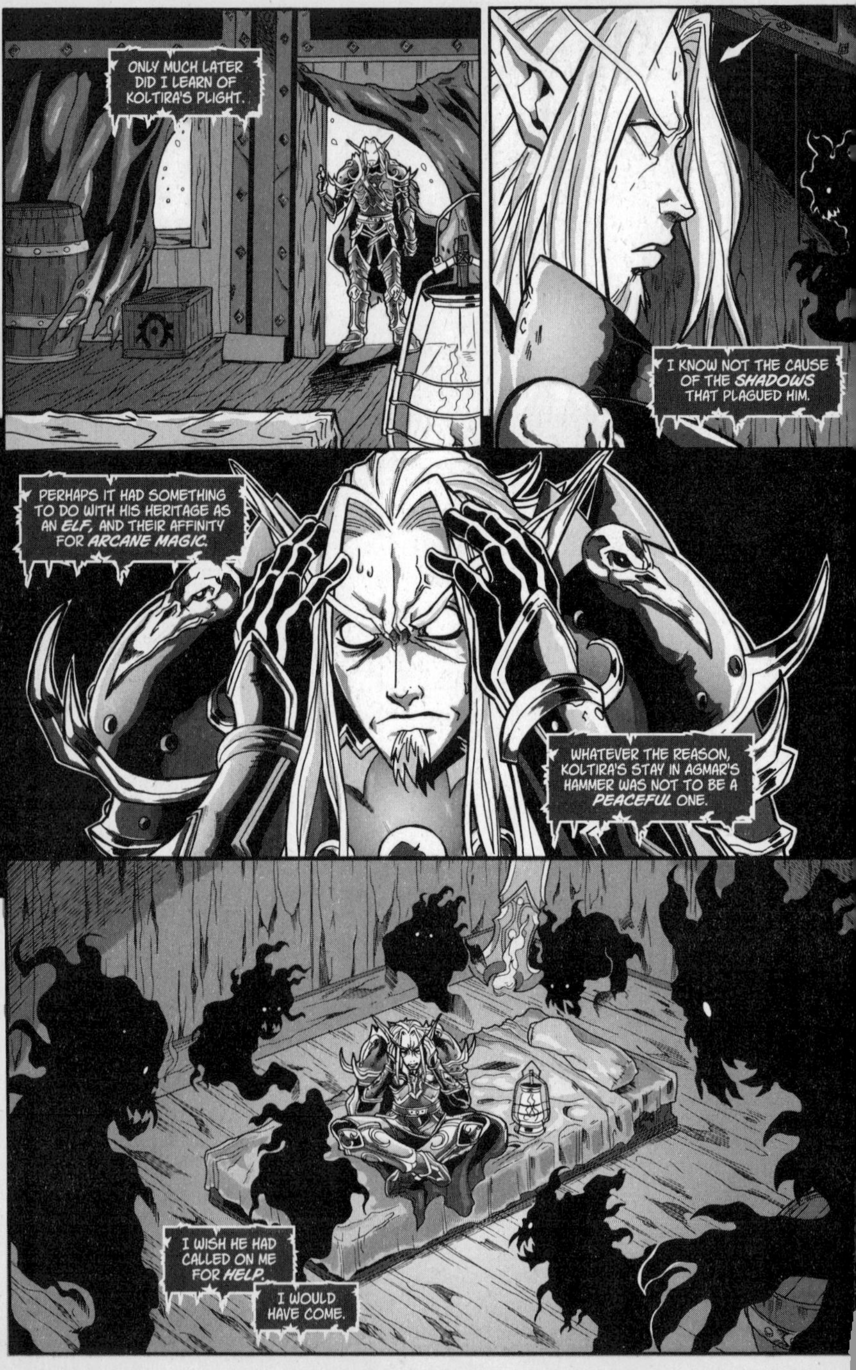
ONLY MUCH LATER DID I LEARN OF KOLTIRA'S PLIGHT.
I KNOW NOT THE CAUSE OF THE SHADOWS THAT PLAGUED HIM.
PERHAPS IT HAD SOMETHING TO DO WITH HIS HERITAGE AS AN ELF, AND THEIR AFFINITY FOR ARCANE MAGIC.
WHATEVER THE REASON, KOLTIRA'S STAY IN AGMAR'S HAMMER WAS NOT TO BE A PEACEFUL ONE.
I WISH HE HAD CALLED ON ME FOR HELP.
I WOULD HAVE COME.

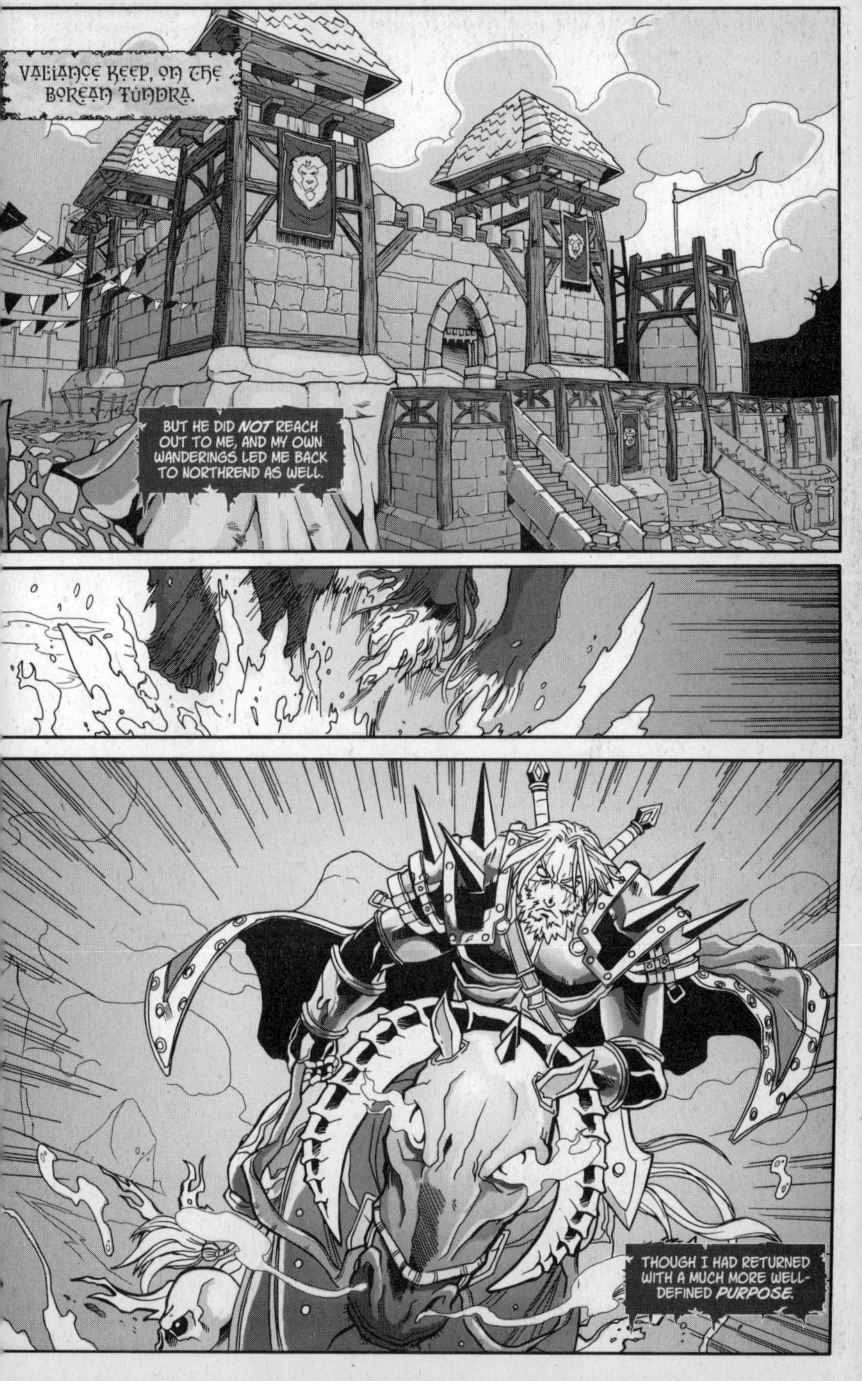
VALIANCE KEEP, ON THE BOREAN TUNDRA.
BUT HE DID *NOT* REACH OUT TO ME, AND MY OWN WANDERINGS LED ME BACK TO NORTHREND AS WELL.
THOUGH I HAD RETURNED WITH A MUCH MORE WELL-DEFINED *PURPOSE*.

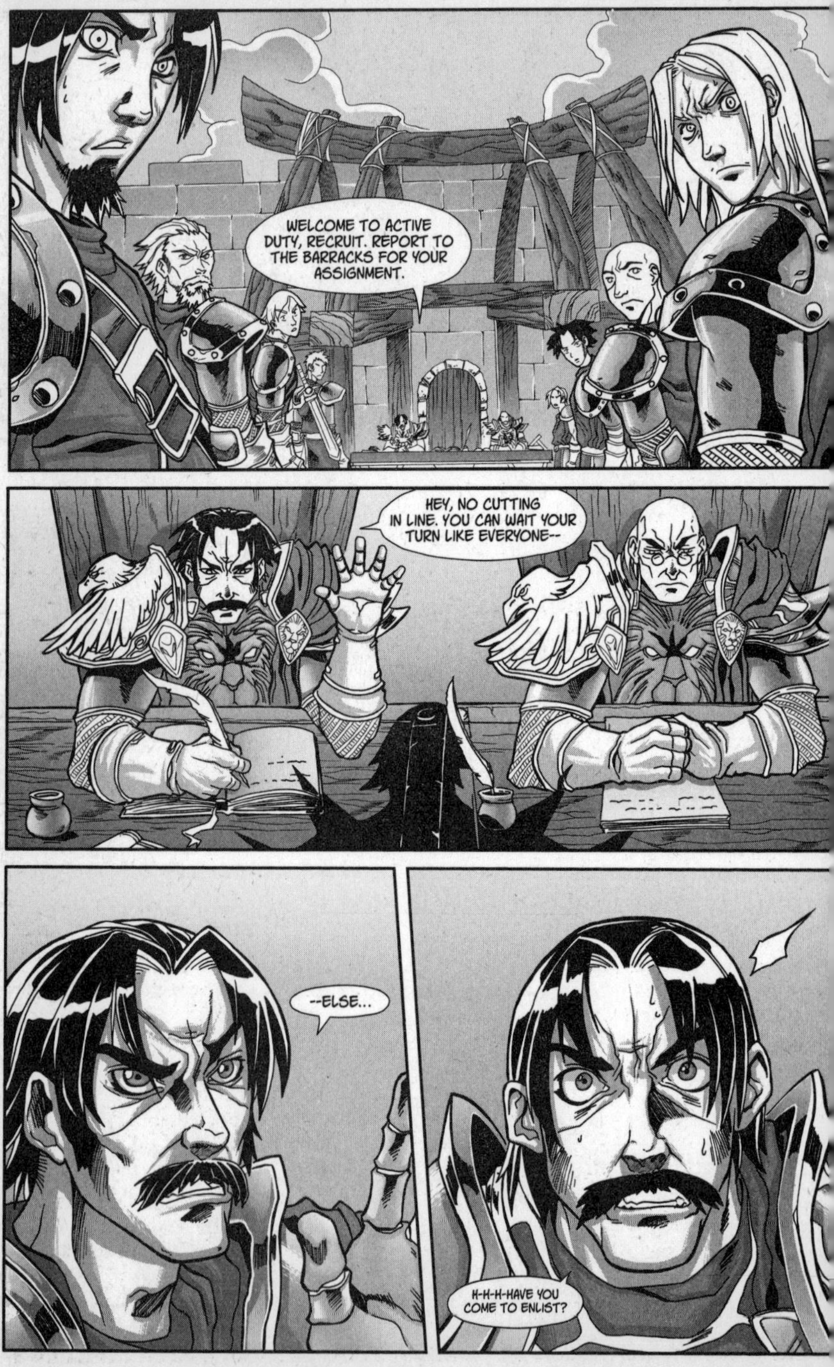
WELCOME TO ACTIVE DUTY, RECRUIT. REPORT TO THE BARRACKS FOR YOUR ASSIGNMENT.
HEY, NO CUTTING IN LINE. YOU CAN WAIT YOUR TURN LIKE EVERYONE--
--ELSE...
H-H-H-HAVE YOU COME TO ENLIST?

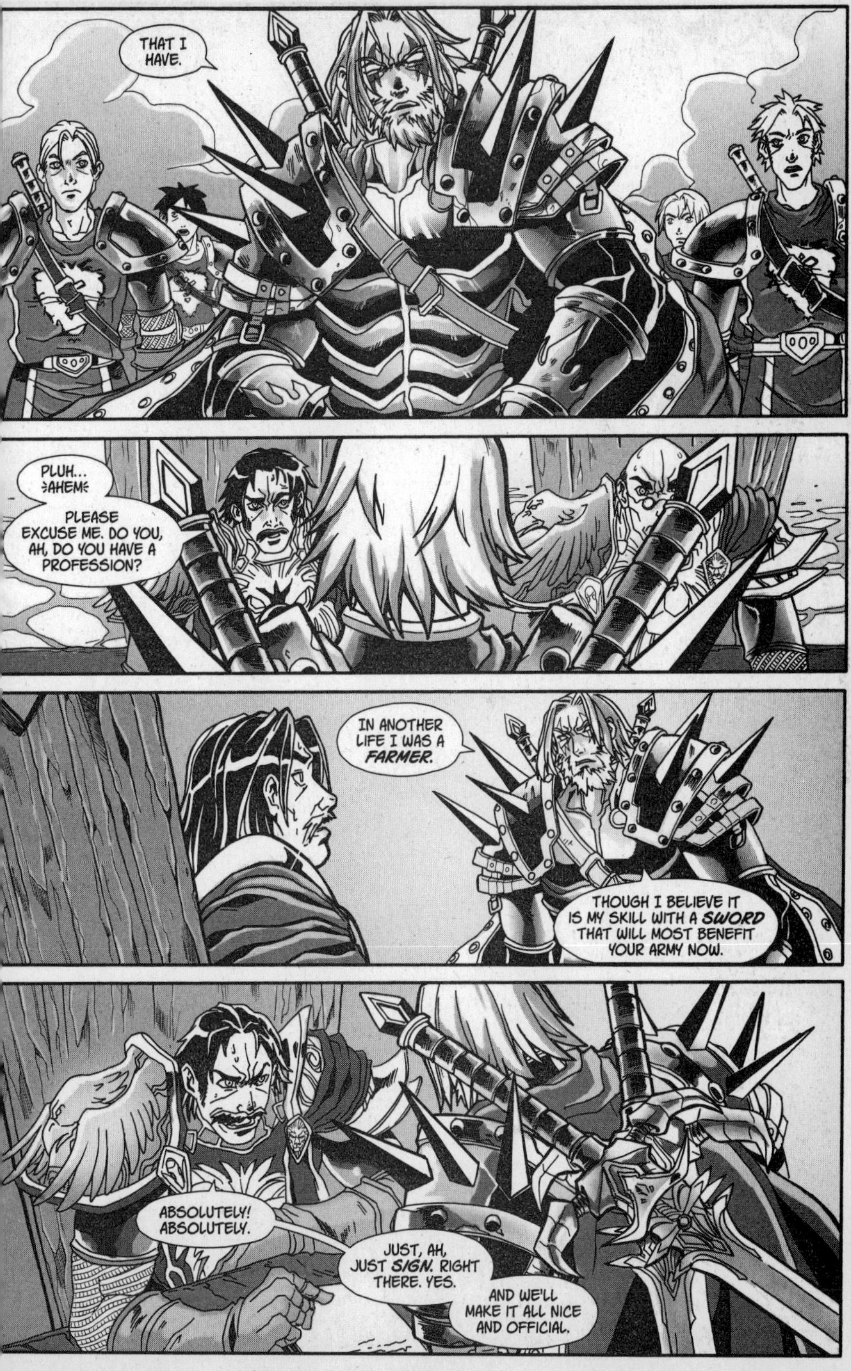
THAT I HAVE.
PLUH... AHEM
PLEASE EXCUSE ME. DO YOU, AH, DO YOU HAVE A PROFESSION?
IN ANOTHER LIFE I WAS A FARMER.
THOUGH I BELIEVE IT IS MY SKILL WITH A SWORD THAT WILL MOST BENEFIT YOUR ARMY NOW.
ABSOLUTELY! ABSOLUTELY.
JUST, AH, JUST SIGN. RIGHT THERE. YES.
AND WE'LL MAKE IT ALL NICE AND OFFICIAL.

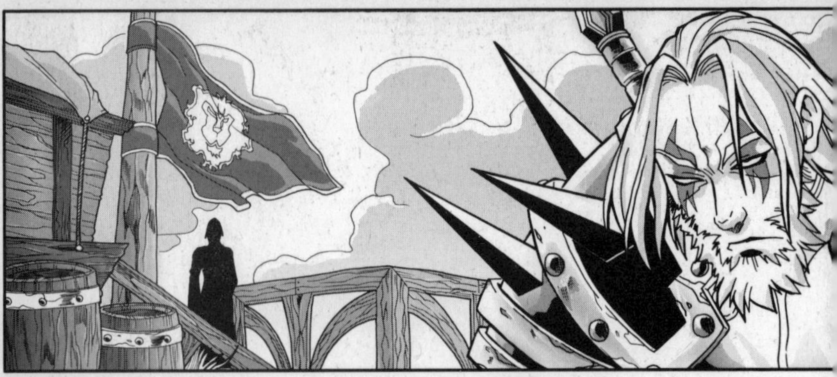
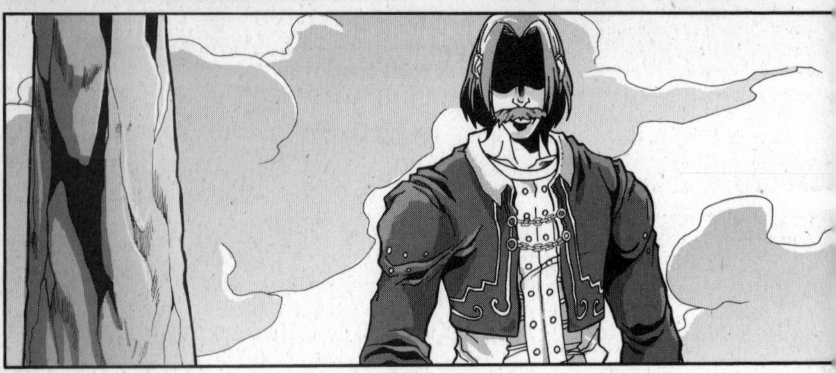
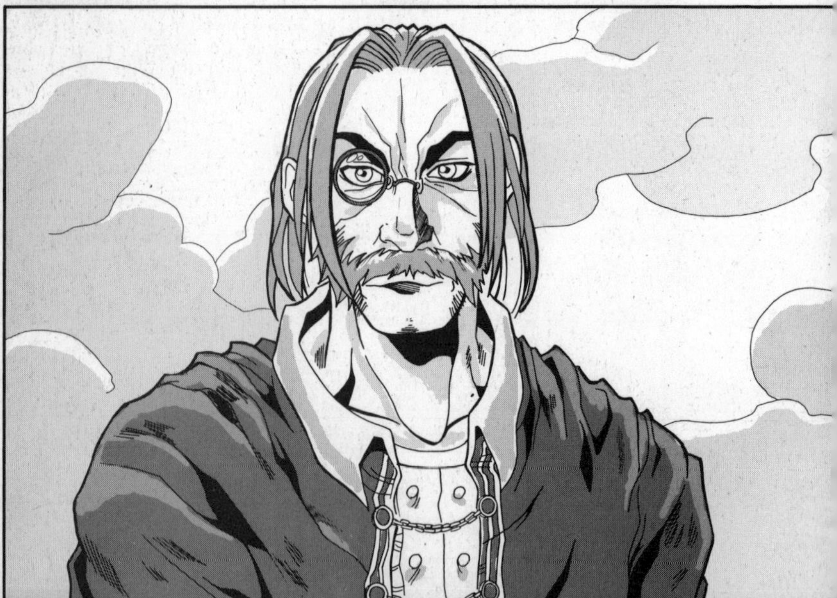

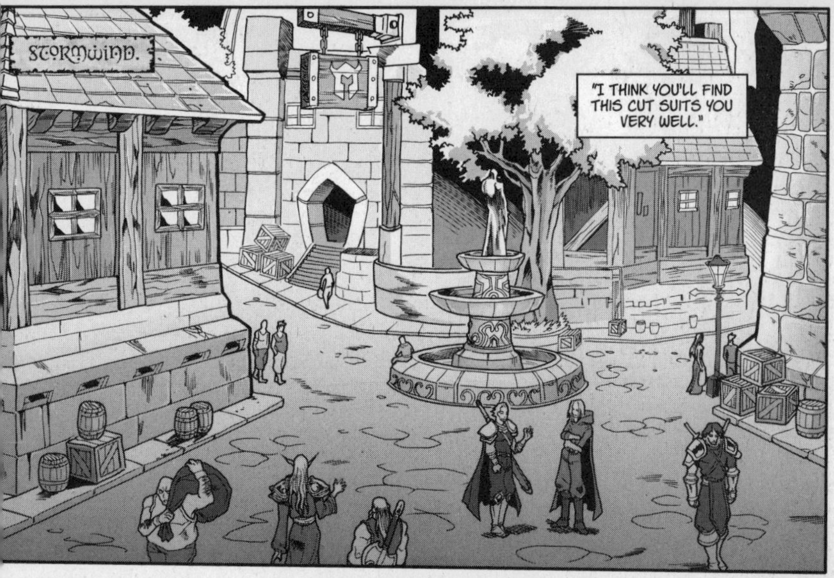
STORMWIND.
"I THINK YOU'LL FIND THIS CUT SUITS YOU VERY WELL."

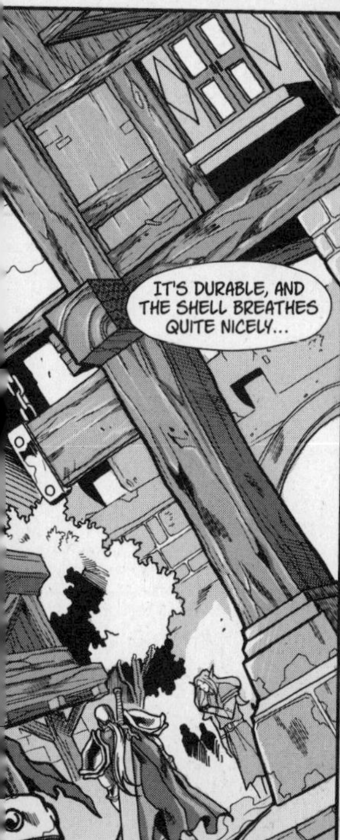
IT'S DURABLE, AND THE SHELL BREATHES QUITE NICELY...

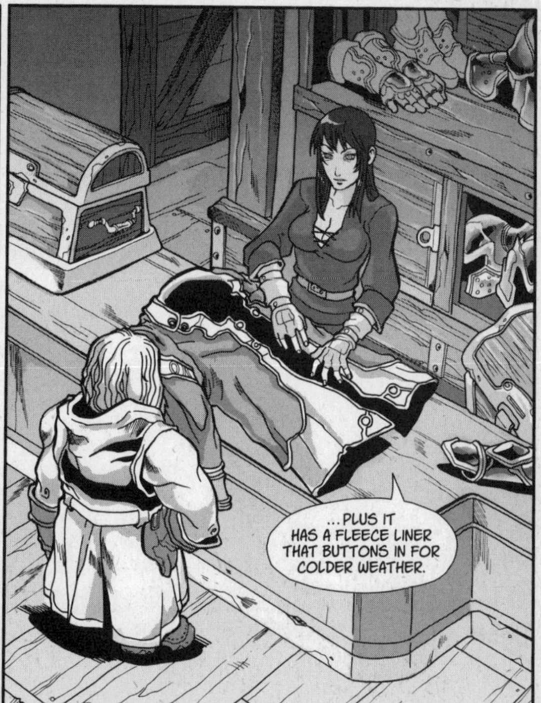
...PLUS IT HAS A FLEECE LINER THAT BUTTONS IN FOR COLDER WEATHER.

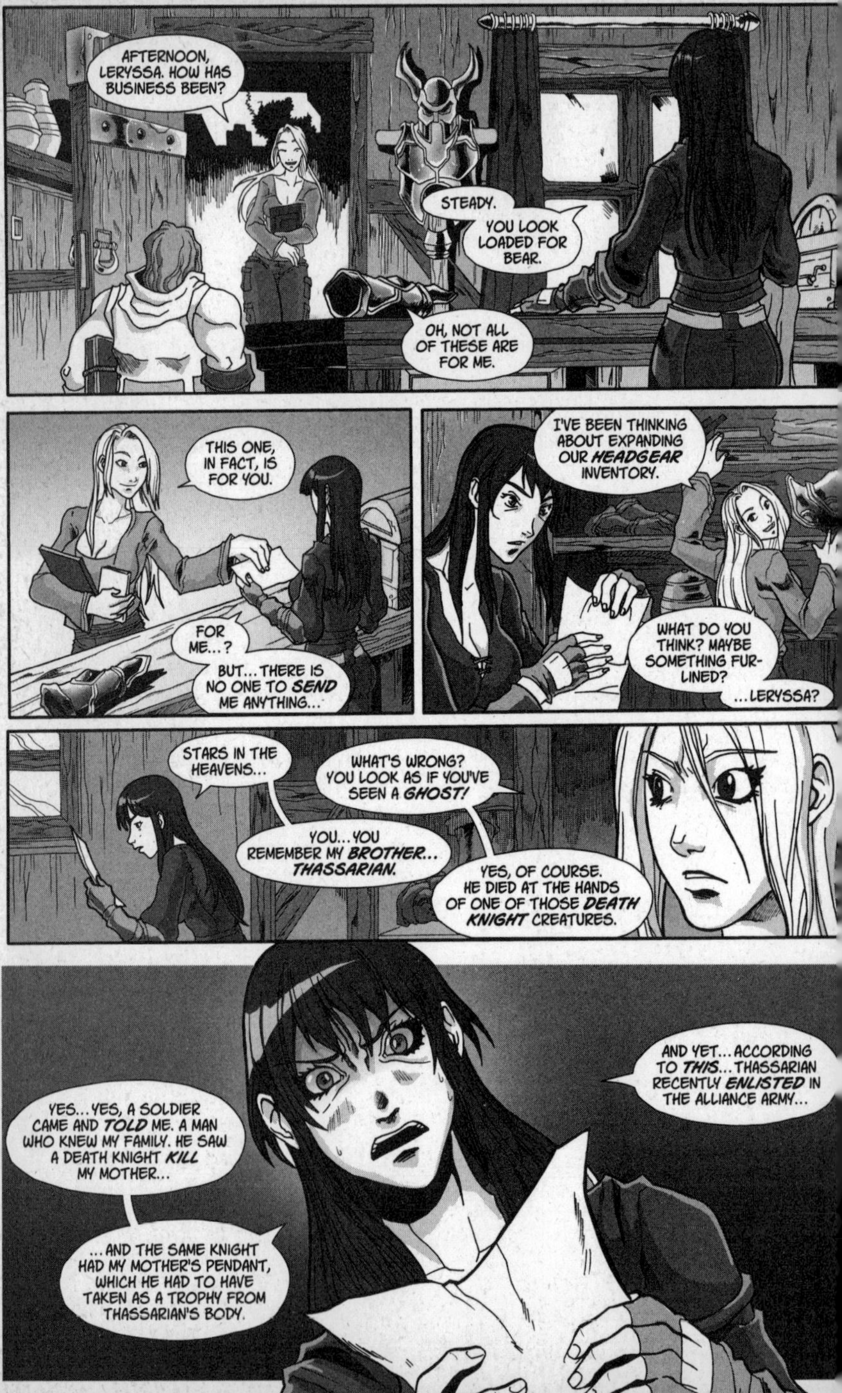
AFTERNOON, LERYSSA. HOW HAS BUSINESS BEEN?
STEADY.
YOU LOOK LOADED FOR BEAR.
OH, NOT ALL OF THESE ARE FOR ME.
THIS ONE, IN FACT, IS FOR YOU.
FOR ME...?
BUT... THERE IS NO ONE TO SEND ME ANYTHING...
I'VE BEEN THINKING ABOUT EXPANDING OUR HEADGEAR INVENTORY.
WHAT DO YOU THINK? MAYBE SOMETHING FUR-LINED?
...LERYSSA?
STARS IN THE HEAVENS...
WHAT'S WRONG? YOU LOOK AS IF YOU'VE SEEN A GHOST!
YOU... YOU REMEMBER MY BROTHER... THASSARIAN.
YES, OF COURSE. HE DIED AT THE HANDS OF ONE OF THOSE DEATH KNIGHT CREATURES.
AND YET... ACCORDING TO THIS... THASSARIAN RECENTLY ENLISTED IN THE ALLIANCE ARMY...
YES... YES, A SOLDIER CAME AND TOLD ME. A MAN WHO KNEW MY FAMILY. HE SAW A DEATH KNIGHT KILL MY MOTHER...
...AND THE SAME KNIGHT HAD MY MOTHER'S PENDANT, WHICH HE HAD TO HAVE TAKEN AS A TROPHY FROM THASSARIAN'S BODY.

CHAPTER 5

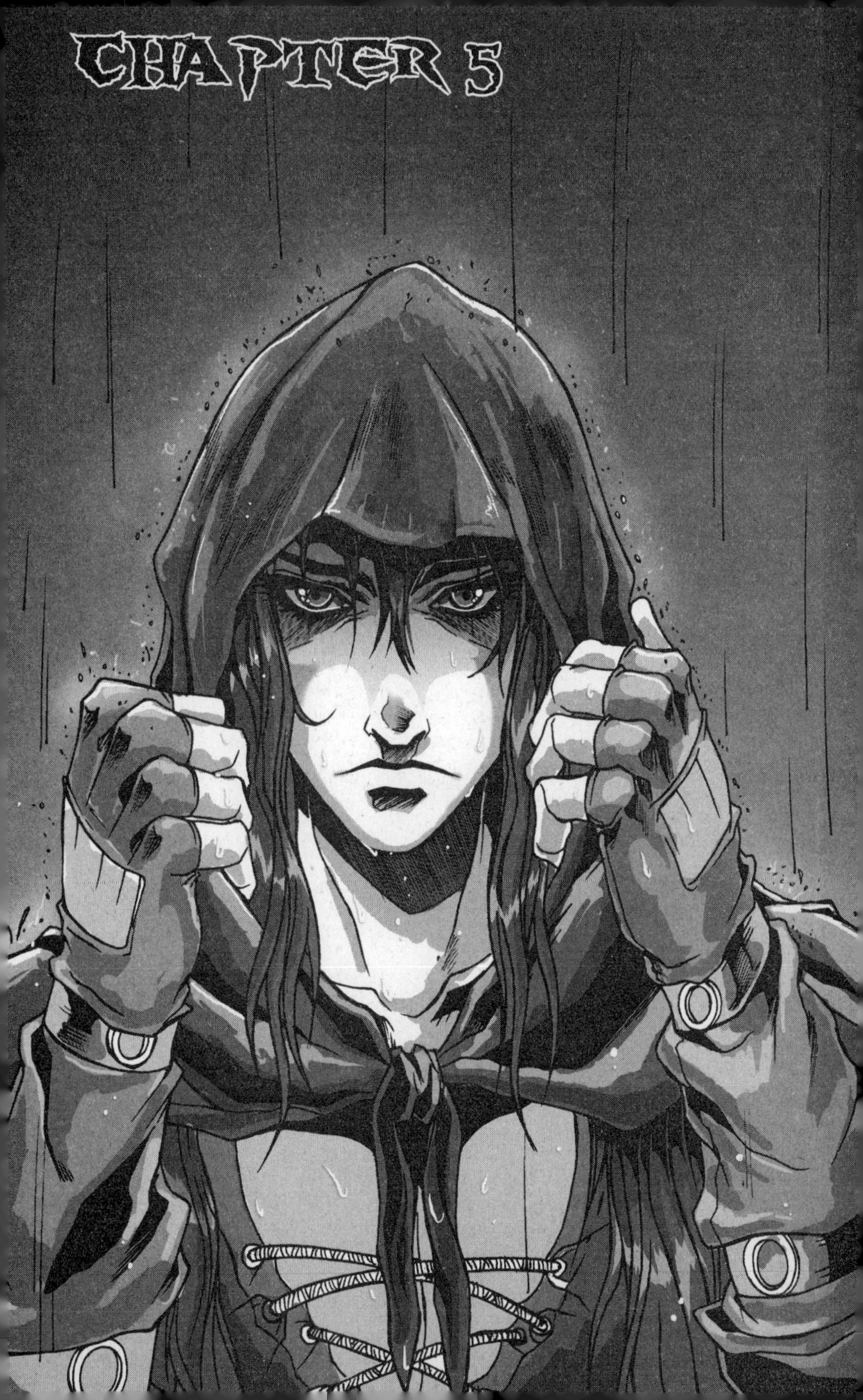

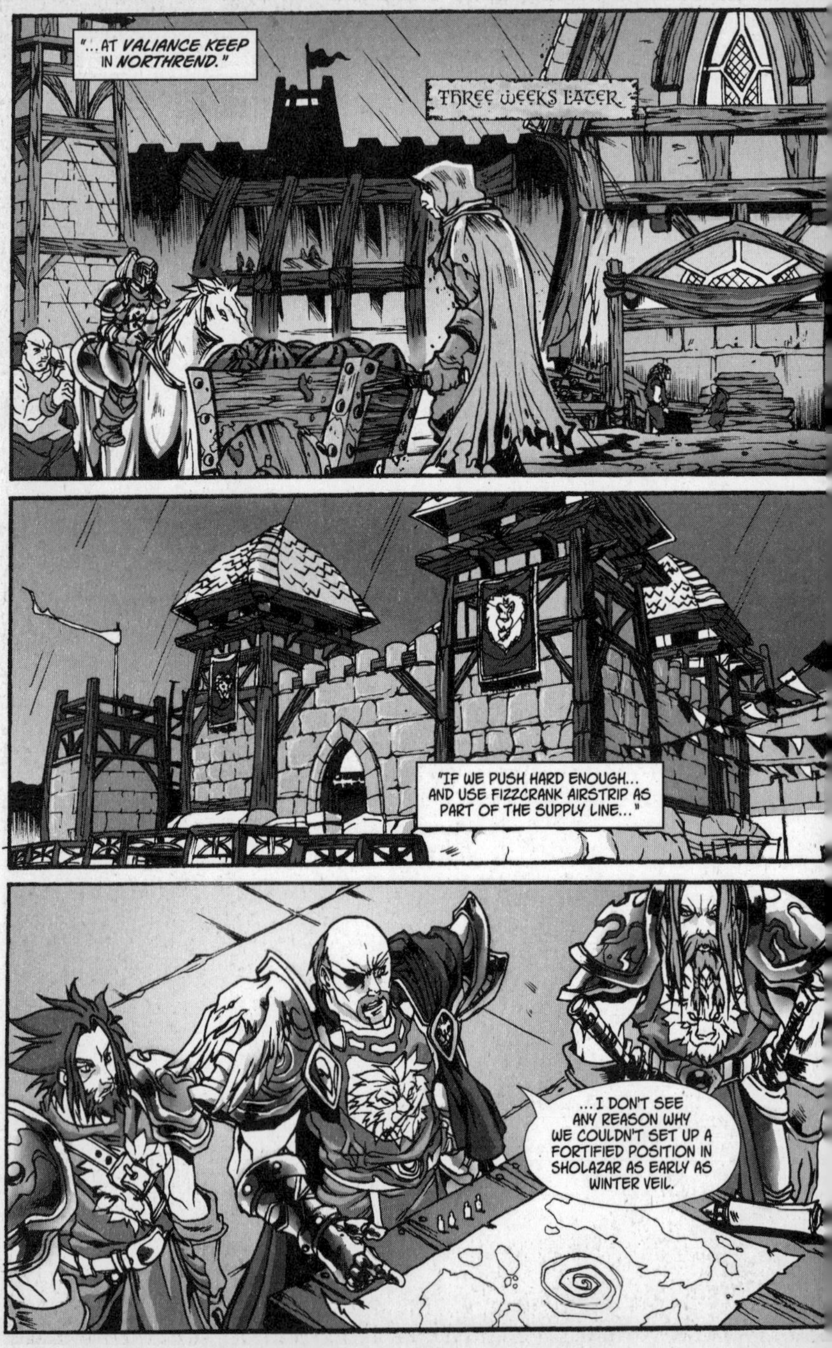
"...AT VALIANCE KEEP IN NORTHREND."
THREE WEEKS LATER.
"IF WE PUSH HARD ENOUGH... AND USE FIZZCRANK AIRSTRIP AS PART OF THE SUPPLY LINE..."
...I DON'T SEE ANY REASON WHY WE COULDN'T SET UP A FORTIFIED POSITION IN SHOLAZAR AS EARLY AS WINTER VEIL.

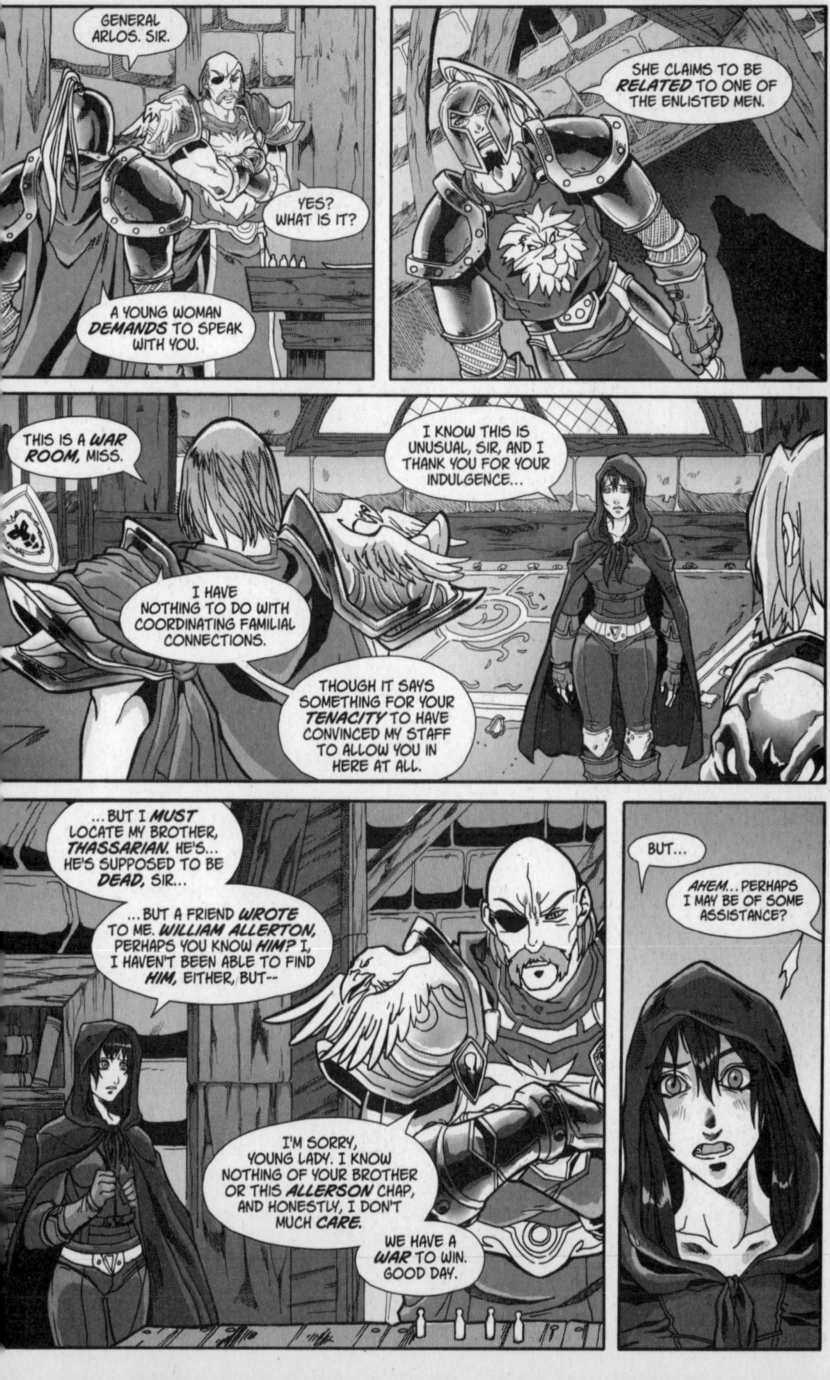
GENERAL ARLOS. SIR.
YES? WHAT IS IT?
A YOUNG WOMAN DEMANDS TO SPEAK WITH YOU.
SHE CLAIMS TO BE RELATED TO ONE OF THE ENLISTED MEN.
THIS IS A WAR ROOM, MISS.
I KNOW THIS IS UNUSUAL, SIR, AND I THANK YOU FOR YOUR INDULGENCE...
I HAVE NOTHING TO DO WITH COORDINATING FAMILIAL CONNECTIONS.
THOUGH IT SAYS SOMETHING FOR YOUR TENACITY TO HAVE CONVINCED MY STAFF TO ALLOW YOU IN HERE AT ALL.
...BUT I MUST LOCATE MY BROTHER, THASSARIAN. HE'S... HE'S SUPPOSED TO BE DEAD, SIR...
...BUT A FRIEND WROTE TO ME. WILLIAM ALLERTON, PERHAPS YOU KNOW HIM? I, I HAVEN'T BEEN ABLE TO FIND HIM, EITHER, BUT--
I'M SORRY, YOUNG LADY. I KNOW NOTHING OF YOUR BROTHER OR THIS ALLERSON CHAP, AND HONESTLY, I DON'T MUCH CARE.
WE HAVE A WAR TO WIN. GOOD DAY.
BUT...
AHEM... PERHAPS I MAY BE OF SOME ASSISTANCE?

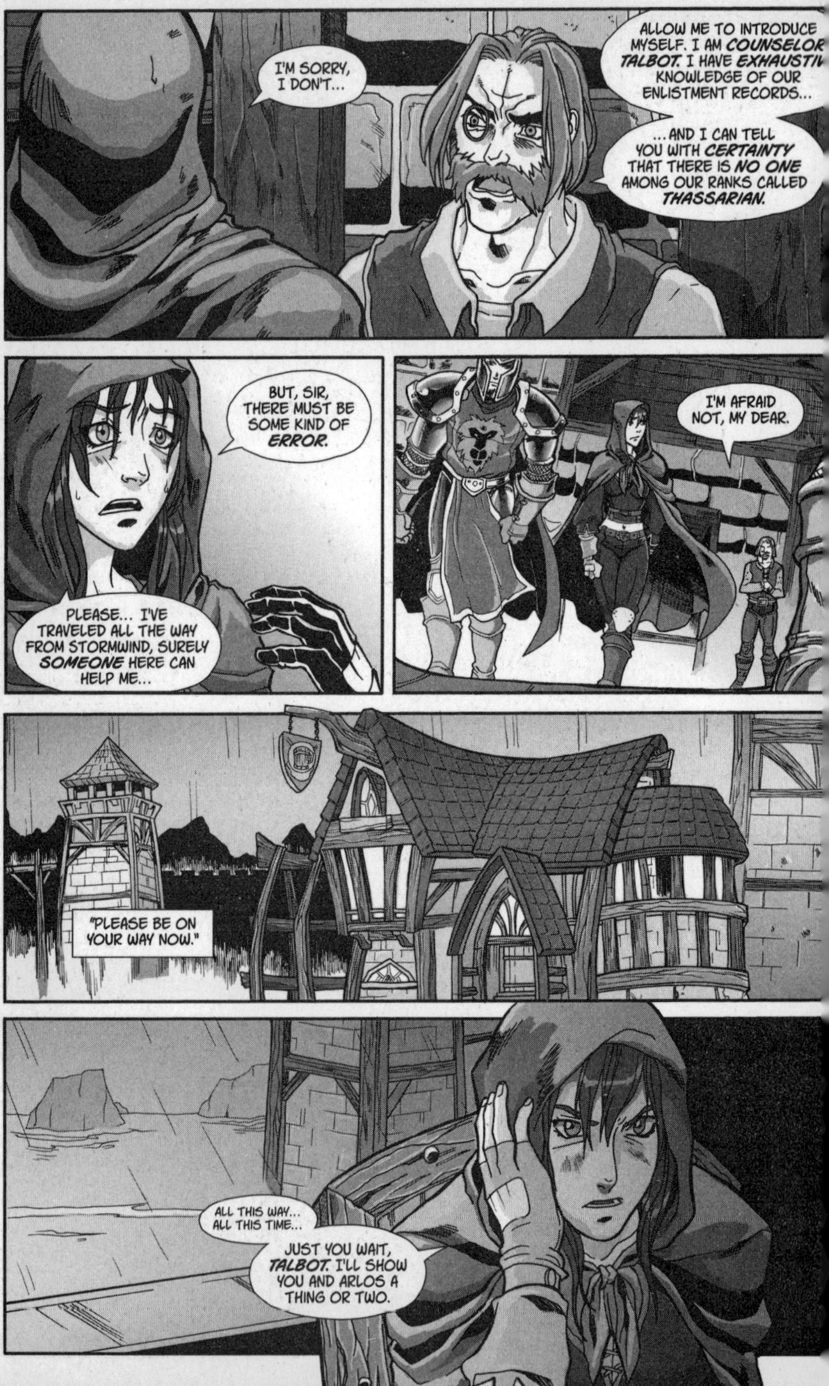
I'M SORRY, I DON'T...
ALLOW ME TO INTRODUCE MYSELF. I AM COUNSELOR TALBOT. I HAVE EXHAUSTIVE KNOWLEDGE OF OUR ENLISTMENT RECORDS...
...AND I CAN TELL YOU WITH CERTAINTY THAT THERE IS NO ONE AMONG OUR RANKS CALLED THASSARIAN.
BUT, SIR, THERE MUST BE SOME KIND OF ERROR.
PLEASE... I'VE TRAVELED ALL THE WAY FROM STORMWIND, SURELY SOMEONE HERE CAN HELP ME...
I'M AFRAID NOT, MY DEAR.
"PLEASE BE ON YOUR WAY NOW."
ALL THIS WAY... ALL THIS TIME...
JUST YOU WAIT, TALBOT. I'LL SHOW YOU AND ARLOS A THING OR TWO.

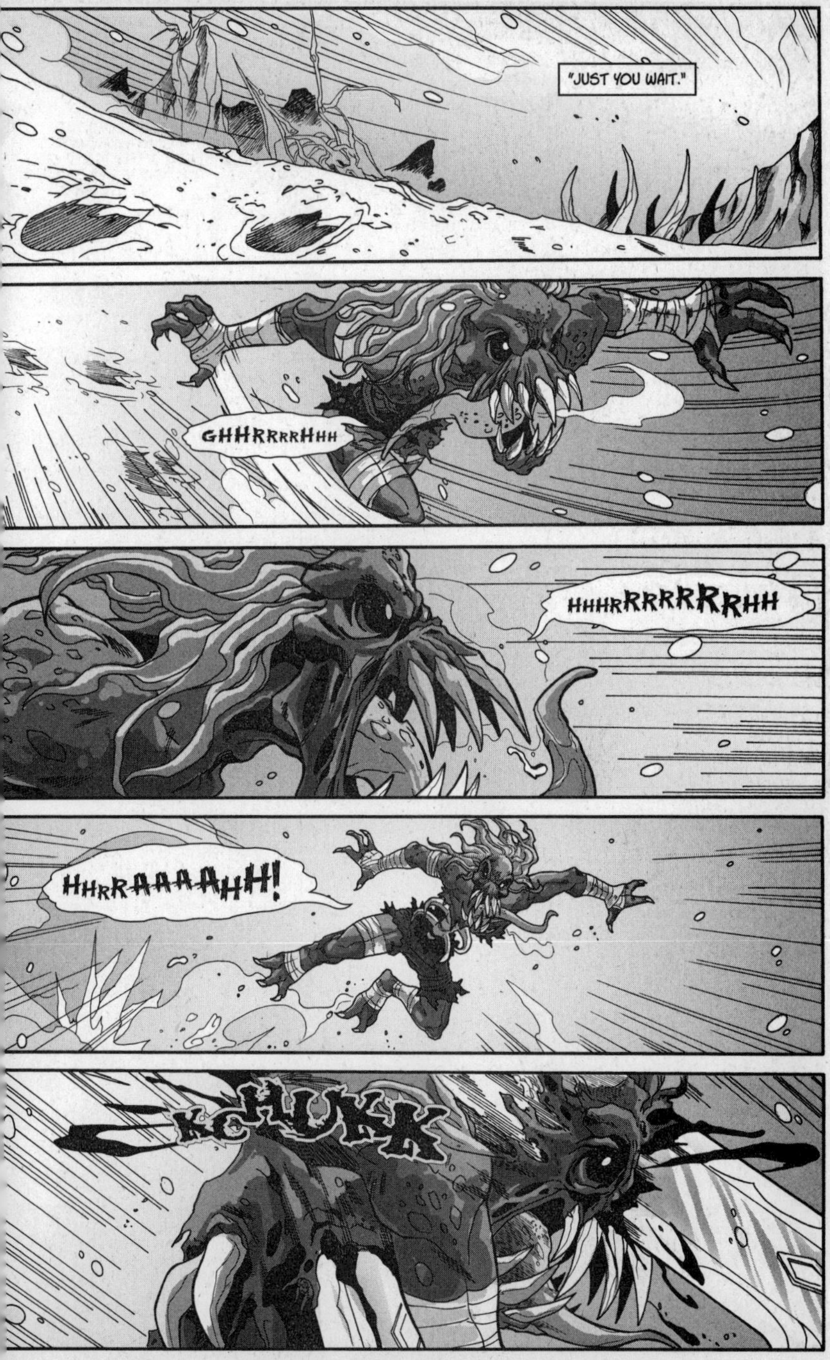
"JUST YOU WAIT."
GHHRRRRHHH
HHHRRRRRRRHH
HHRRAAAAAHH!
KCHUKK

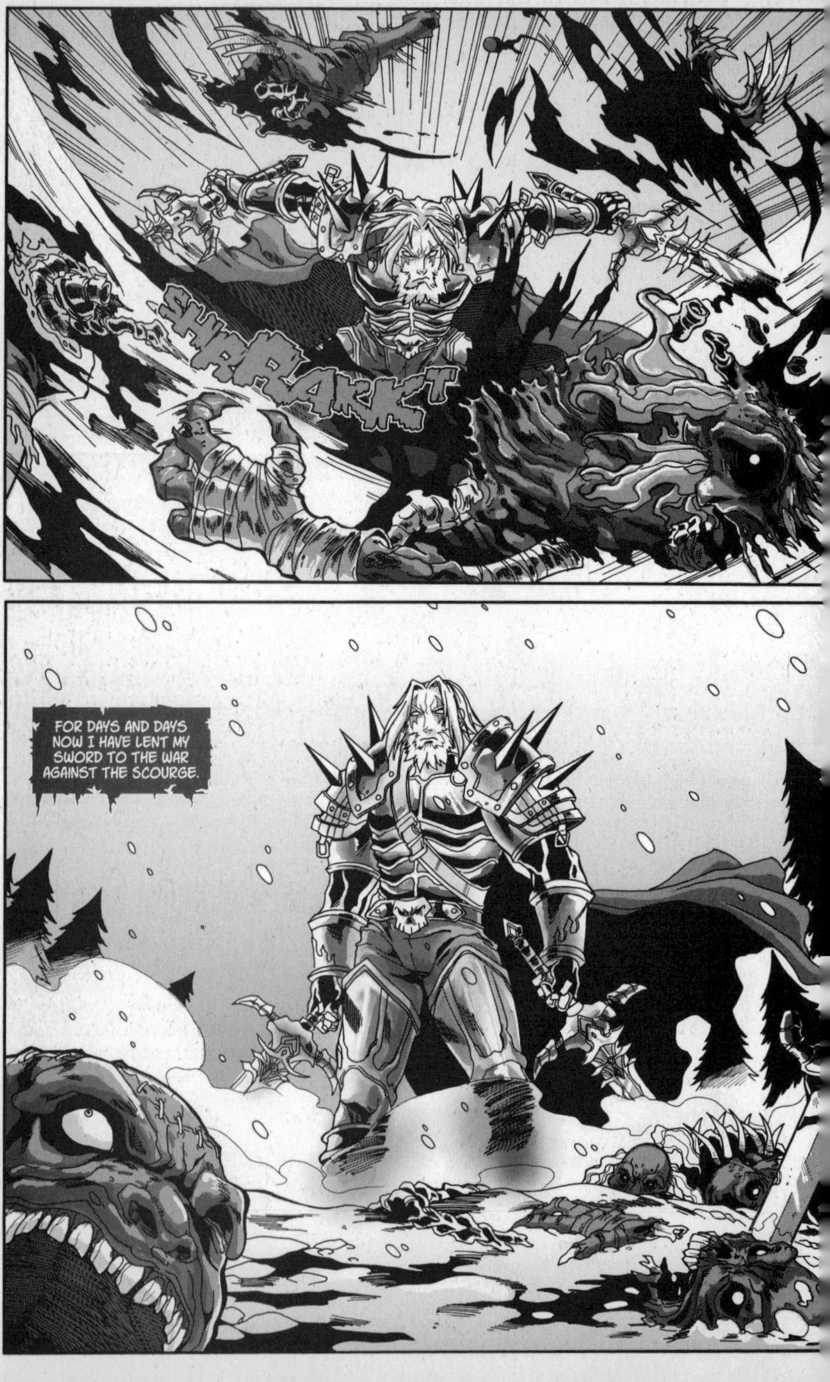
SHRRAKK'T
FOR DAYS AND DAYS NOW I HAVE LENT MY SWORD TO THE WAR AGAINST THE SCOURGE.

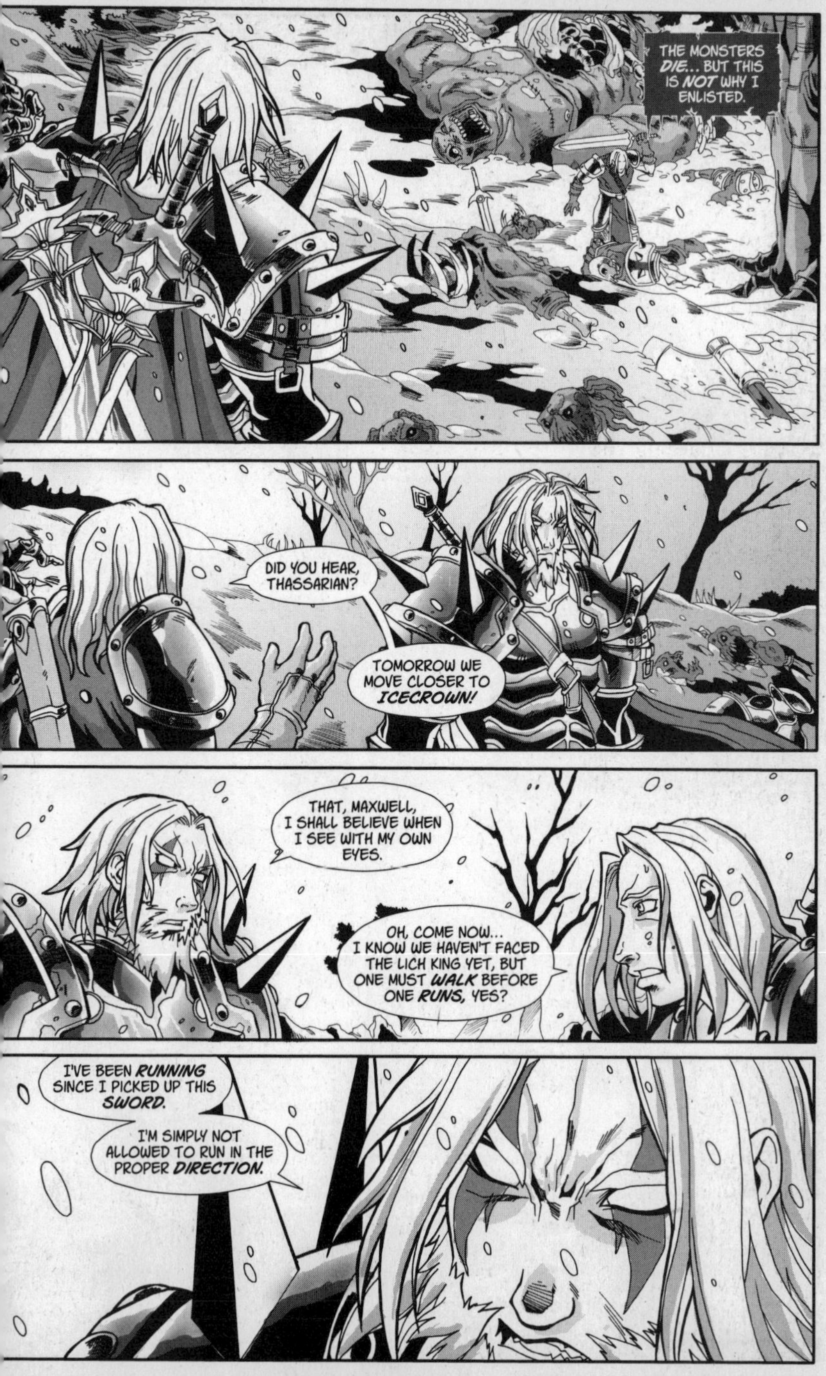
THE MONSTERS DIE... BUT THIS IS NOT WHY I ENLISTED.
DID YOU HEAR, THASSARIAN?
TOMORROW WE MOVE CLOSER TO ICECROWN!
THAT, MAXWELL, I SHALL BELIEVE WHEN I SEE WITH MY OWN EYES.
OH, COME NOW... I KNOW WE HAVEN'T FACED THE LICH KING YET, BUT ONE MUST WALK BEFORE ONE RUNS, YES?
I'VE BEEN RUNNING SINCE I PICKED UP THIS SWORD.
I'M SIMPLY NOT ALLOWED TO RUN IN THE PROPER DIRECTION.

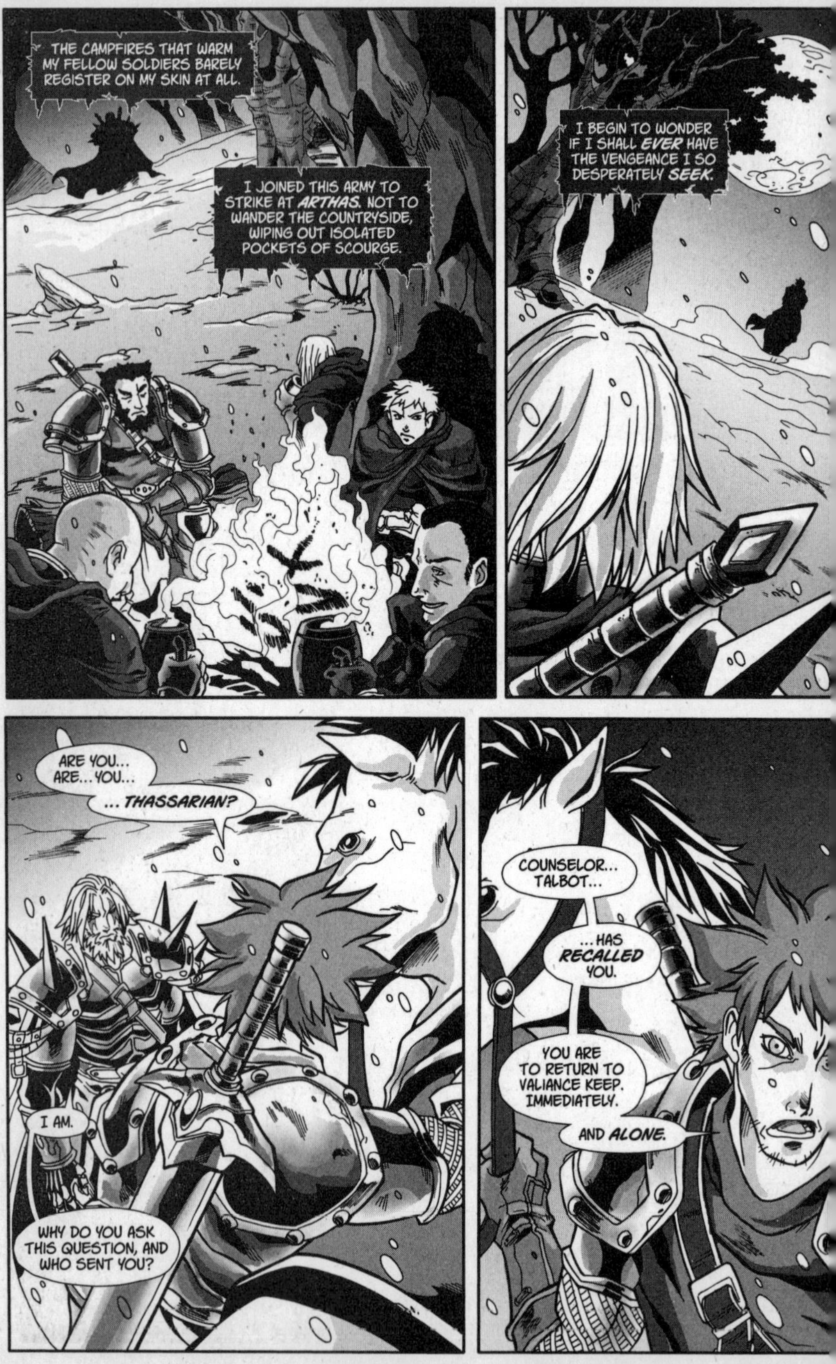
THE CAMPFIRES THAT WARM MY FELLOW SOLDIERS BARELY REGISTER ON MY SKIN AT ALL.
I JOINED THIS ARMY TO STRIKE AT ARTHAS. NOT TO WANDER THE COUNTRYSIDE, WIPING OUT ISOLATED POCKETS OF SCOURGE.
I BEGIN TO WONDER IF I SHALL EVER HAVE THE VENGEANCE I SO DESPERATELY SEEK.
ARE YOU... ARE... YOU...
... THASSARIAN?
I AM.
WHY DO YOU ASK THIS QUESTION, AND WHO SENT YOU?
COUNSELOR... TALBOT...
... HAS RECALLED YOU.
YOU ARE TO RETURN TO VALIANCE KEEP. IMMEDIATELY.
AND ALONE.

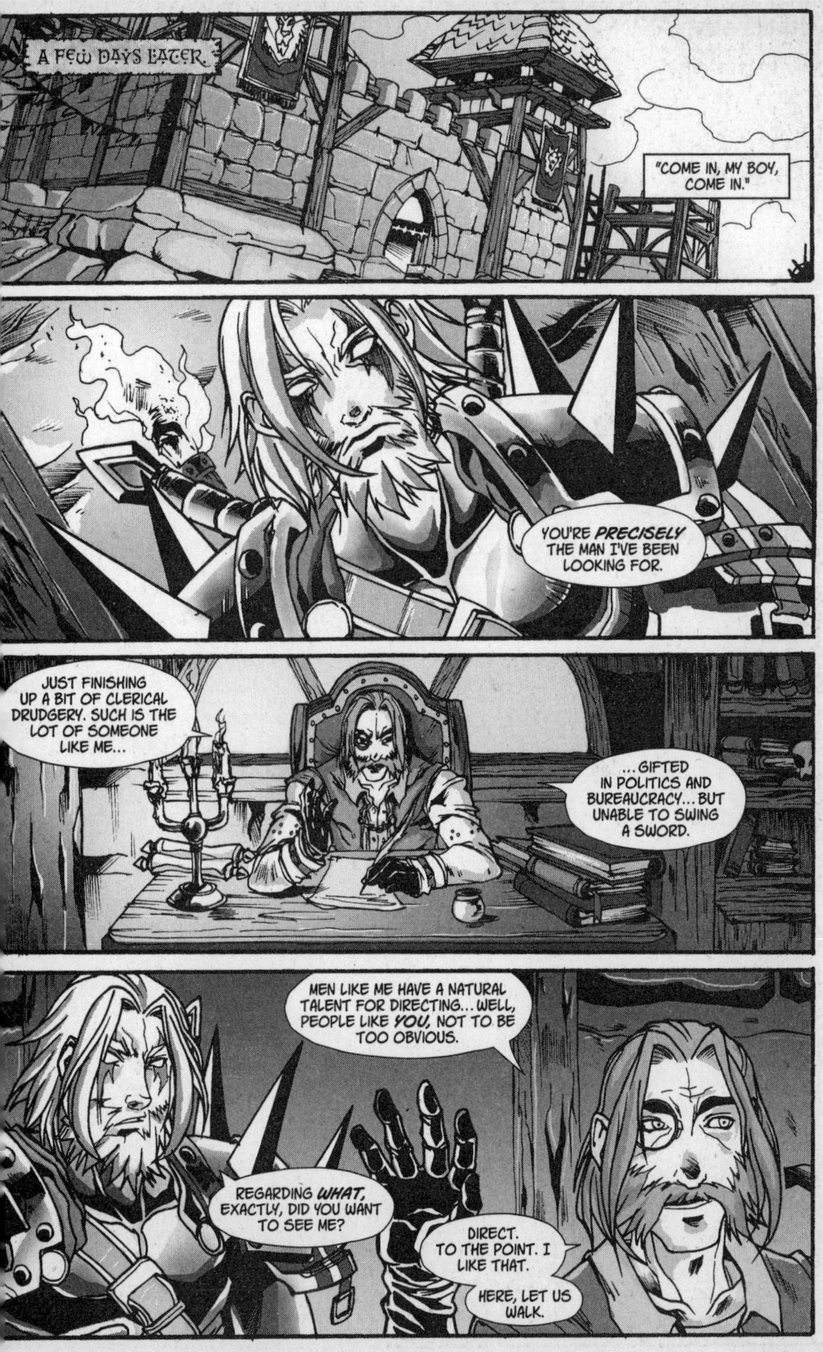
A FEW DAYS LATER.
"COME IN, MY BOY, COME IN."
YOU'RE PRECISELY THE MAN I'VE BEEN LOOKING FOR.
JUST FINISHING UP A BIT OF CLERICAL DRUDGERY. SUCH IS THE LOT OF SOMEONE LIKE ME...
...GIFTED IN POLITICS AND BUREAUCRACY... BUT UNABLE TO SWING A SWORD.
MEN LIKE ME HAVE A NATURAL TALENT FOR DIRECTING... WELL, PEOPLE LIKE YOU, NOT TO BE TOO OBVIOUS.
REGARDING WHAT, EXACTLY, DID YOU WANT TO SEE ME?
DIRECT. TO THE POINT. I LIKE THAT.
HERE, LET US WALK.

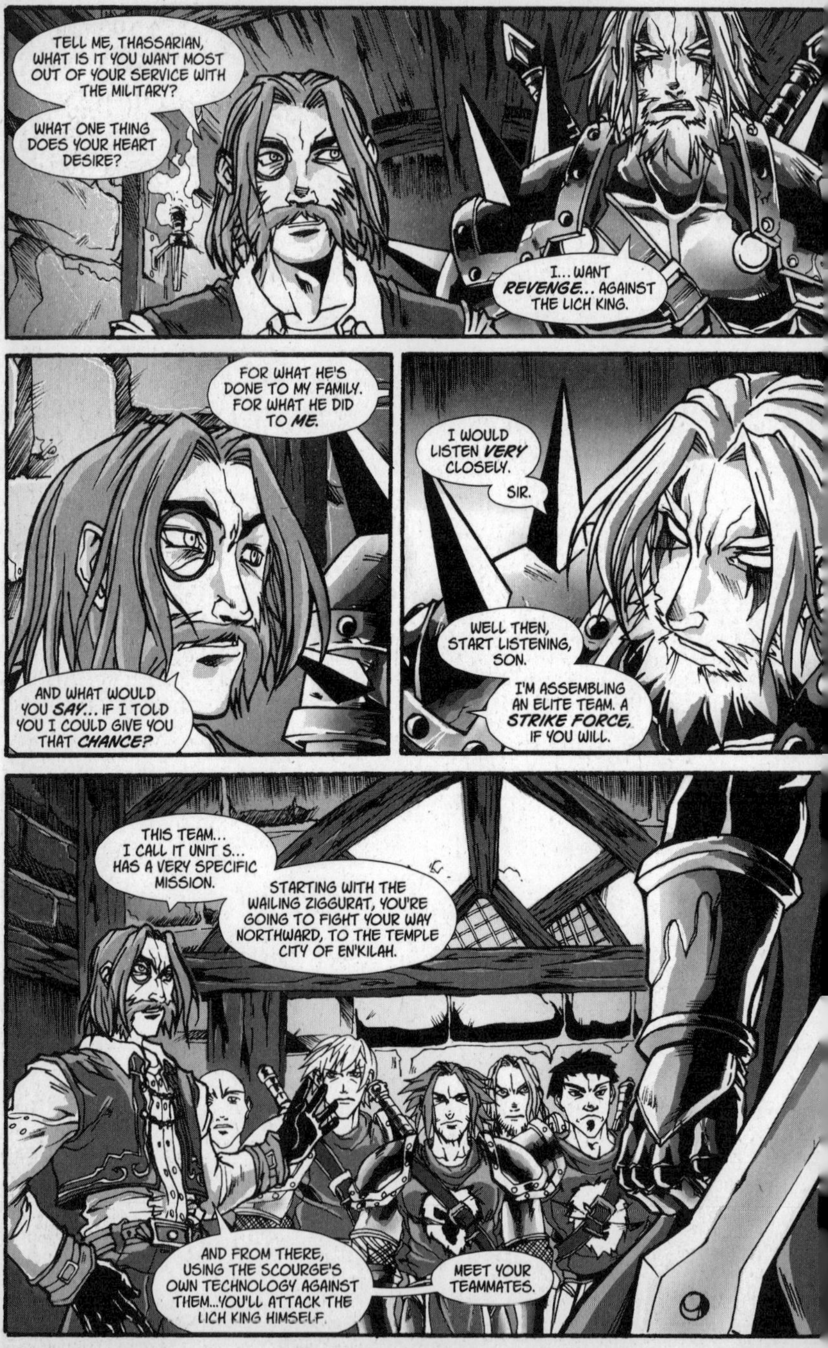
TELL ME, THASSARIAN, WHAT IS IT YOU WANT MOST OUT OF YOUR SERVICE WITH THE MILITARY?
WHAT ONE THING DOES YOUR HEART DESIRE?
I... WANT *REVENGE...* AGAINST THE LICH KING.
FOR WHAT HE'S DONE TO MY FAMILY. FOR WHAT HE DID TO *ME*.
AND WHAT WOULD YOU *SAY...* IF I TOLD YOU I COULD GIVE YOU THAT *CHANCE?*
I WOULD LISTEN *VERY* CLOSELY.
SIR.
WELL THEN, START LISTENING, SON.
I'M ASSEMBLING AN ELITE TEAM. A *STRIKE FORCE,* IF YOU WILL.
THIS TEAM... I CALL IT UNIT S... HAS A VERY SPECIFIC MISSION.
STARTING WITH THE WAILING ZIGGURAT, YOU'RE GOING TO FIGHT YOUR WAY NORTHWARD, TO THE TEMPLE CITY OF EN'KILAH.
AND FROM THERE, USING THE SCOURGE'S OWN TECHNOLOGY AGAINST THEM...YOU'LL ATTACK THE LICH KING HIMSELF.
MEET YOUR TEAMMATES.

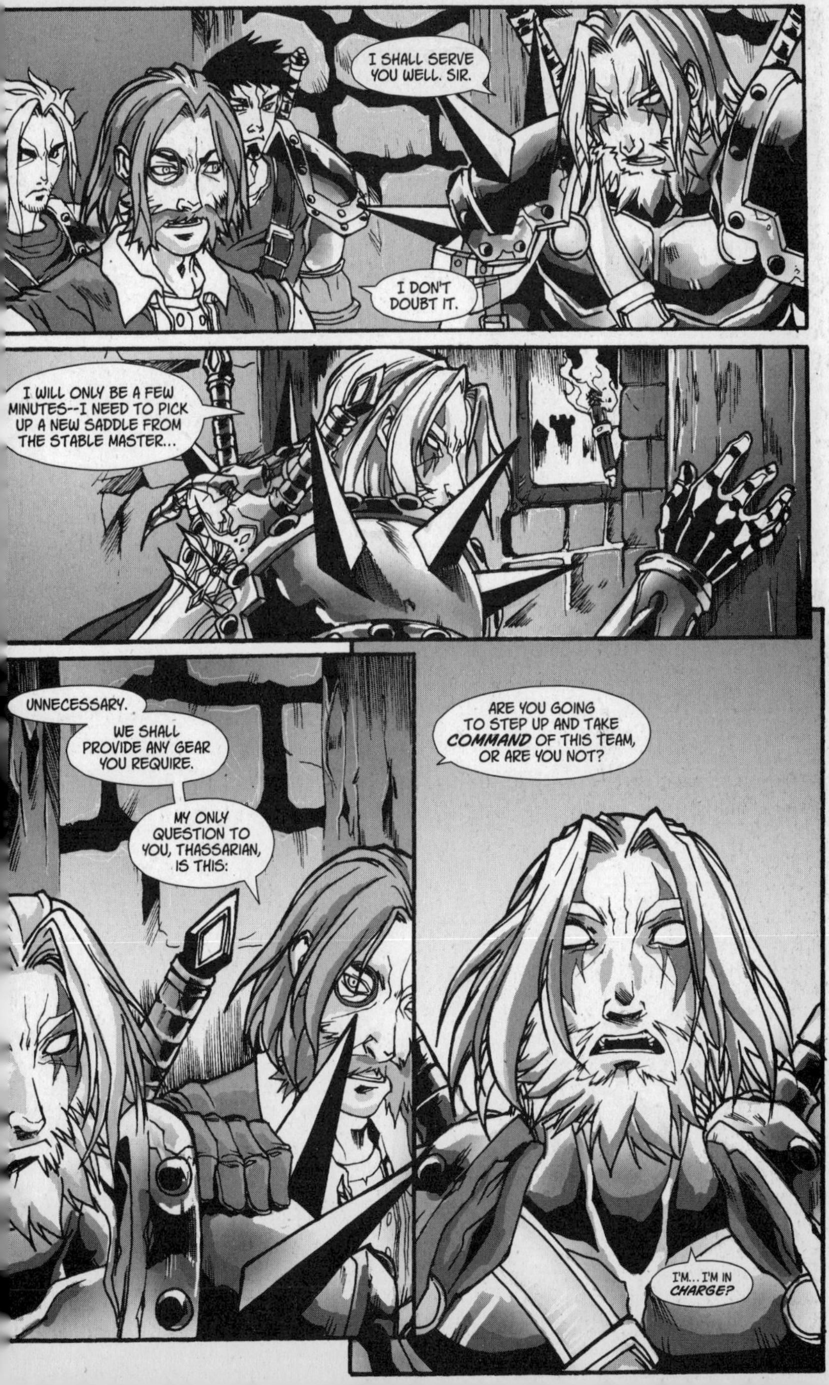
I SHALL SERVE YOU WELL. SIR.
I DON'T DOUBT IT.
I WILL ONLY BE A FEW MINUTES--I NEED TO PICK UP A NEW SADDLE FROM THE STABLE MASTER...
UNNECESSARY.
WE SHALL PROVIDE ANY GEAR YOU REQUIRE.
MY ONLY QUESTION TO YOU, THASSARIAN, IS THIS:
ARE YOU GOING TO STEP UP AND TAKE *COMMAND* OF THIS TEAM, OR ARE YOU NOT?
I'M... I'M IN *CHARGE?*

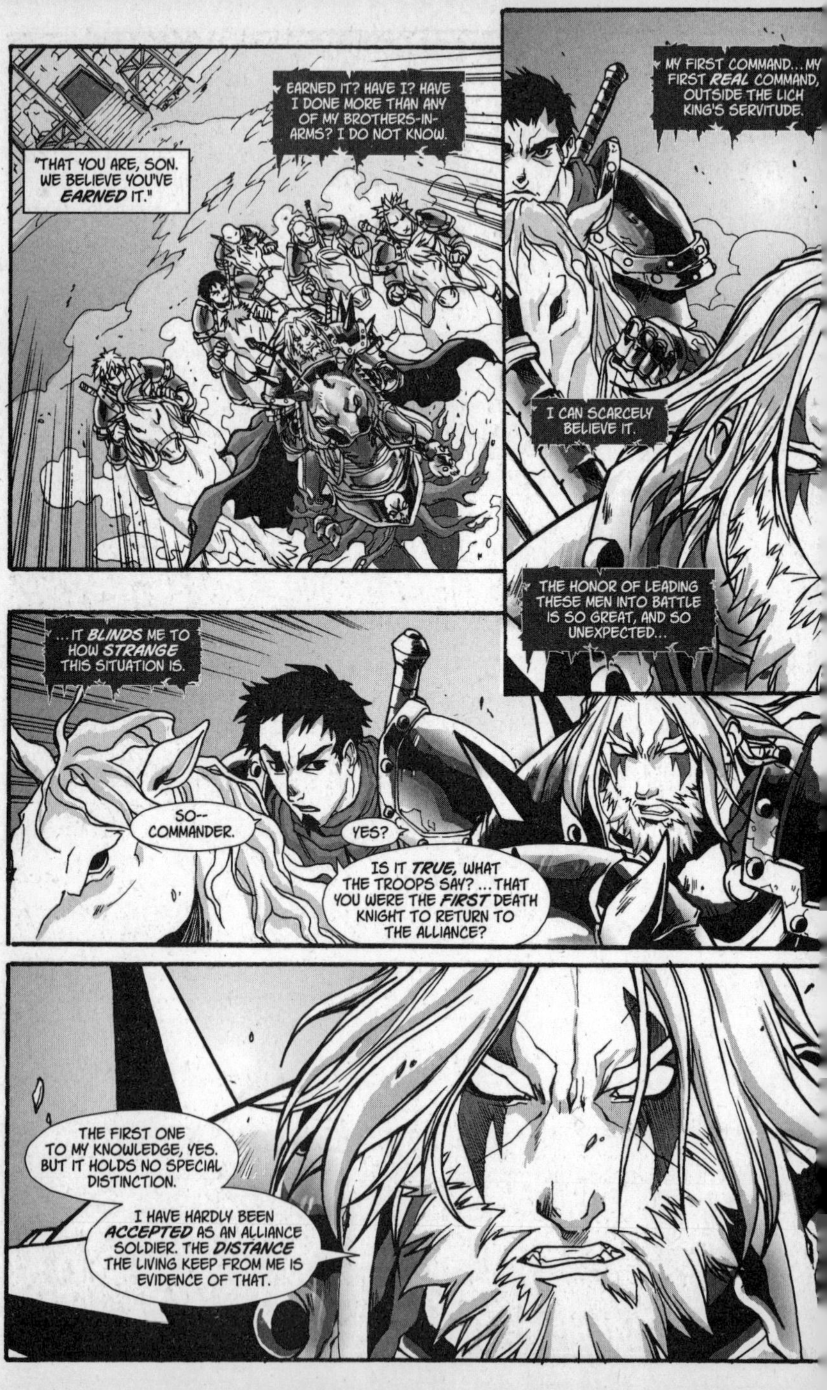
"THAT YOU ARE, SON. WE BELIEVE YOU'VE *EARNED* IT."
EARNED IT? HAVE I? HAVE I DONE MORE THAN ANY OF MY BROTHERS-IN-ARMS? I DO NOT KNOW.
MY FIRST COMMAND... MY FIRST *REAL* COMMAND, OUTSIDE THE LICH KING'S SERVITUDE.
I CAN SCARCELY BELIEVE IT.
THE HONOR OF LEADING THESE MEN INTO BATTLE IS SO GREAT, AND SO UNEXPECTED...
...IT *BLINDS* ME TO HOW *STRANGE* THIS SITUATION IS.
SO-- COMMANDER.
YES?
IS IT *TRUE,* WHAT THE TROOPS SAY? ...THAT YOU WERE THE *FIRST* DEATH KNIGHT TO RETURN TO THE ALLIANCE?
THE FIRST ONE TO MY KNOWLEDGE, YES. BUT IT HOLDS NO SPECIAL DISTINCTION.
I HAVE HARDLY BEEN *ACCEPTED* AS AN ALLIANCE SOLDIER. THE *DISTANCE* THE LIVING KEEP FROM ME IS EVIDENCE OF THAT.

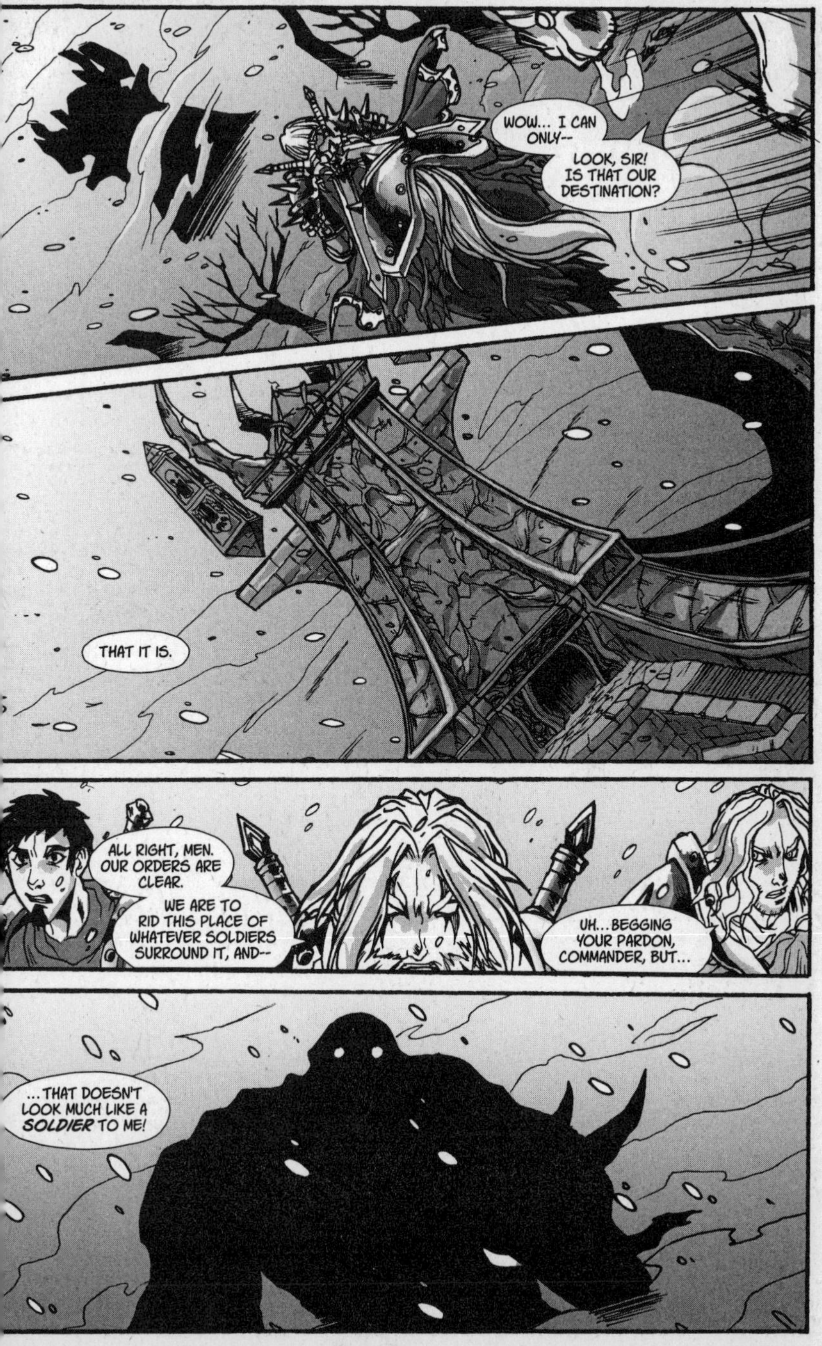
WOW... I CAN ONLY--
LOOK, SIR! IS THAT OUR DESTINATION?
THAT IT IS.
ALL RIGHT, MEN. OUR ORDERS ARE CLEAR.
WE ARE TO RID THIS PLACE OF WHATEVER SOLDIERS SURROUND IT, AND--
UH...BEGGING YOUR PARDON, COMMANDER, BUT...
...THAT DOESN'T LOOK MUCH LIKE A *SOLDIER* TO ME!

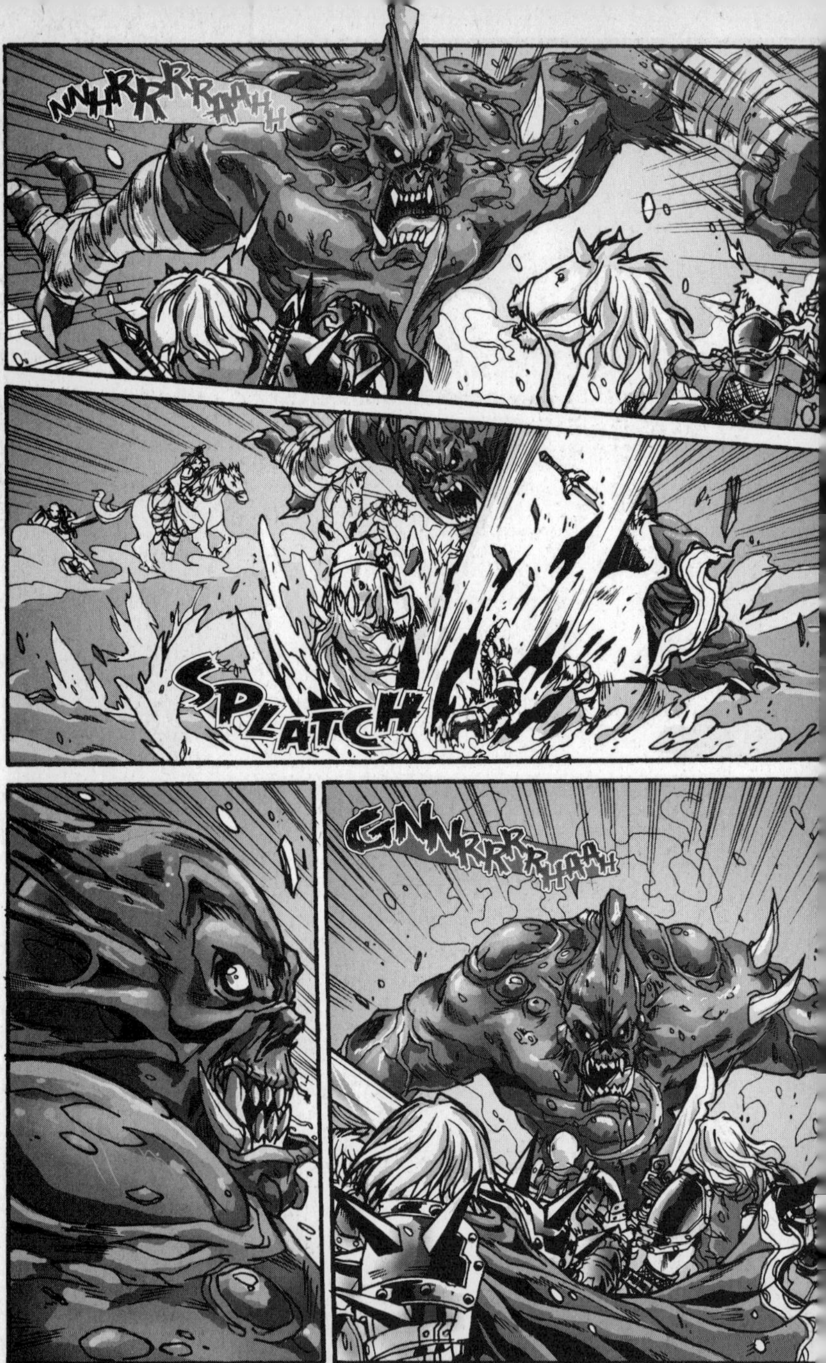
NNHRRRRAAHH
SPLATCH
GNNRRRRHAAH

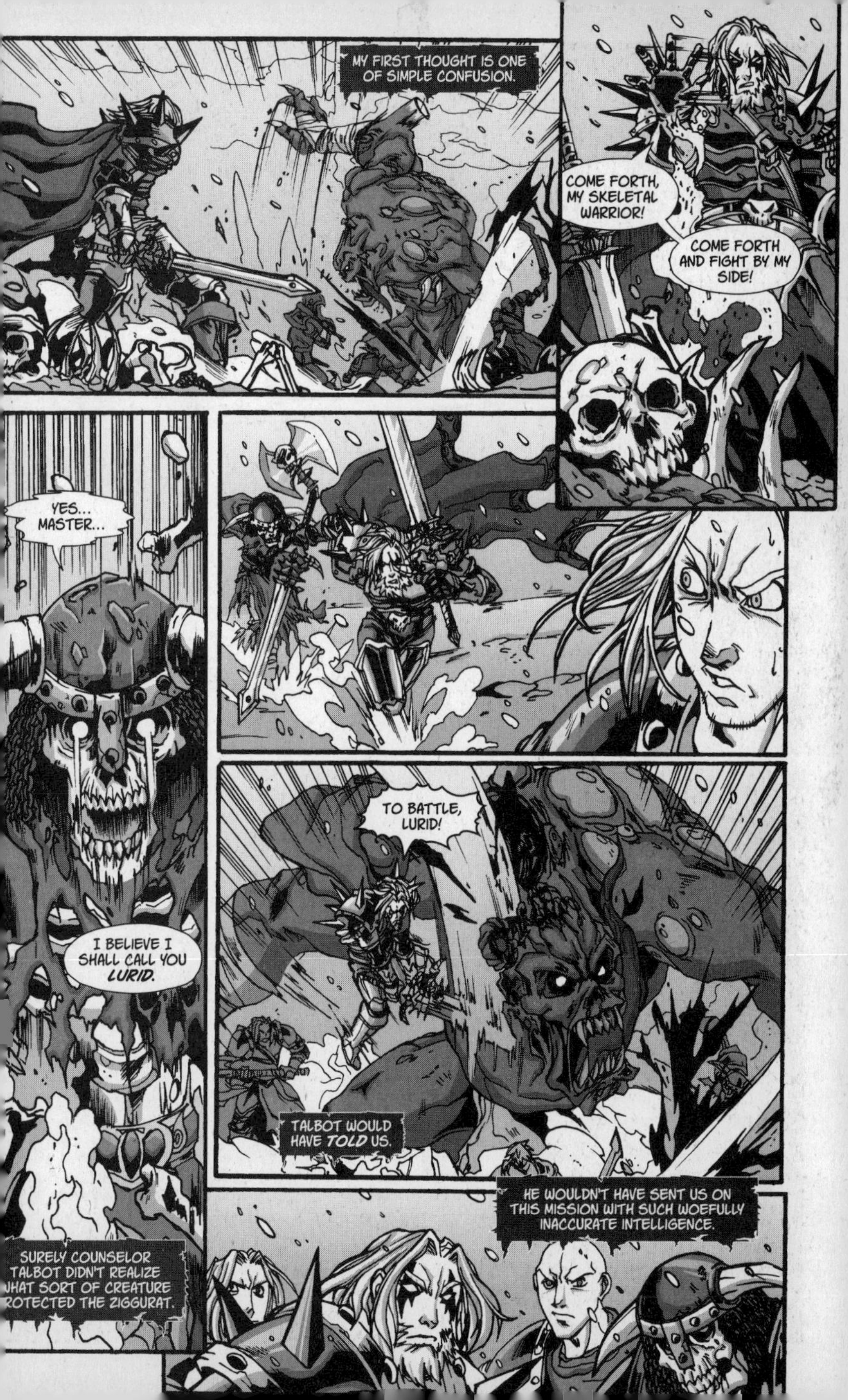
MY FIRST THOUGHT IS ONE OF SIMPLE CONFUSION.
COME FORTH, MY SKELETAL WARRIOR!
COME FORTH AND FIGHT BY MY SIDE!
YES... MASTER...
I BELIEVE I SHALL CALL YOU *LURID*.
SURELY COUNSELOR TALBOT DIDN'T REALIZE WHAT SORT OF CREATURE PROTECTED THE ZIGGURAT.
TO BATTLE, LURID!
TALBOT WOULD HAVE *TOLD* US.
HE WOULDN'T HAVE SENT US ON THIS MISSION WITH SUCH WOEFULLY INACCURATE INTELLIGENCE.

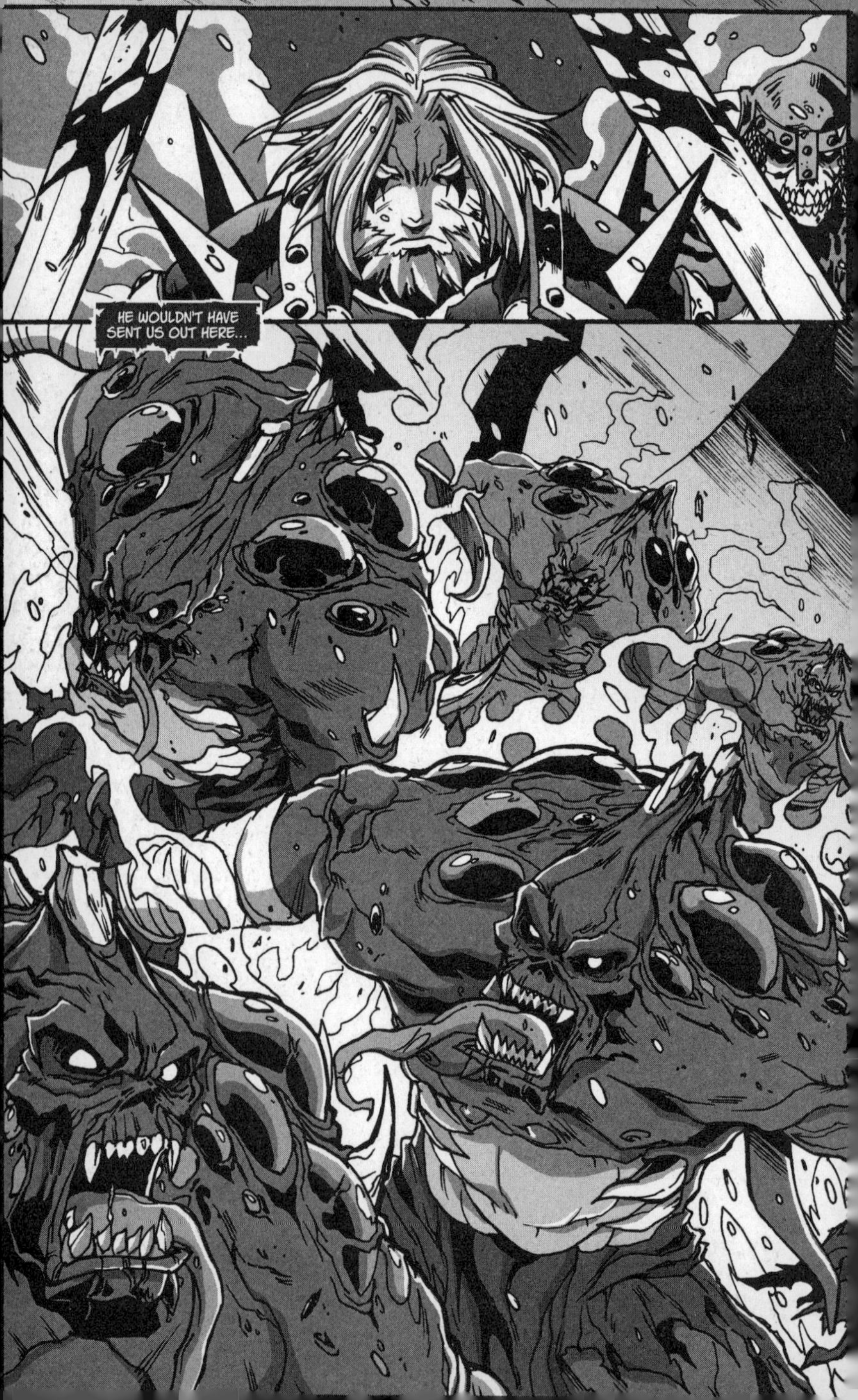
HE WOULDN'T HAVE SENT US OUT HERE...

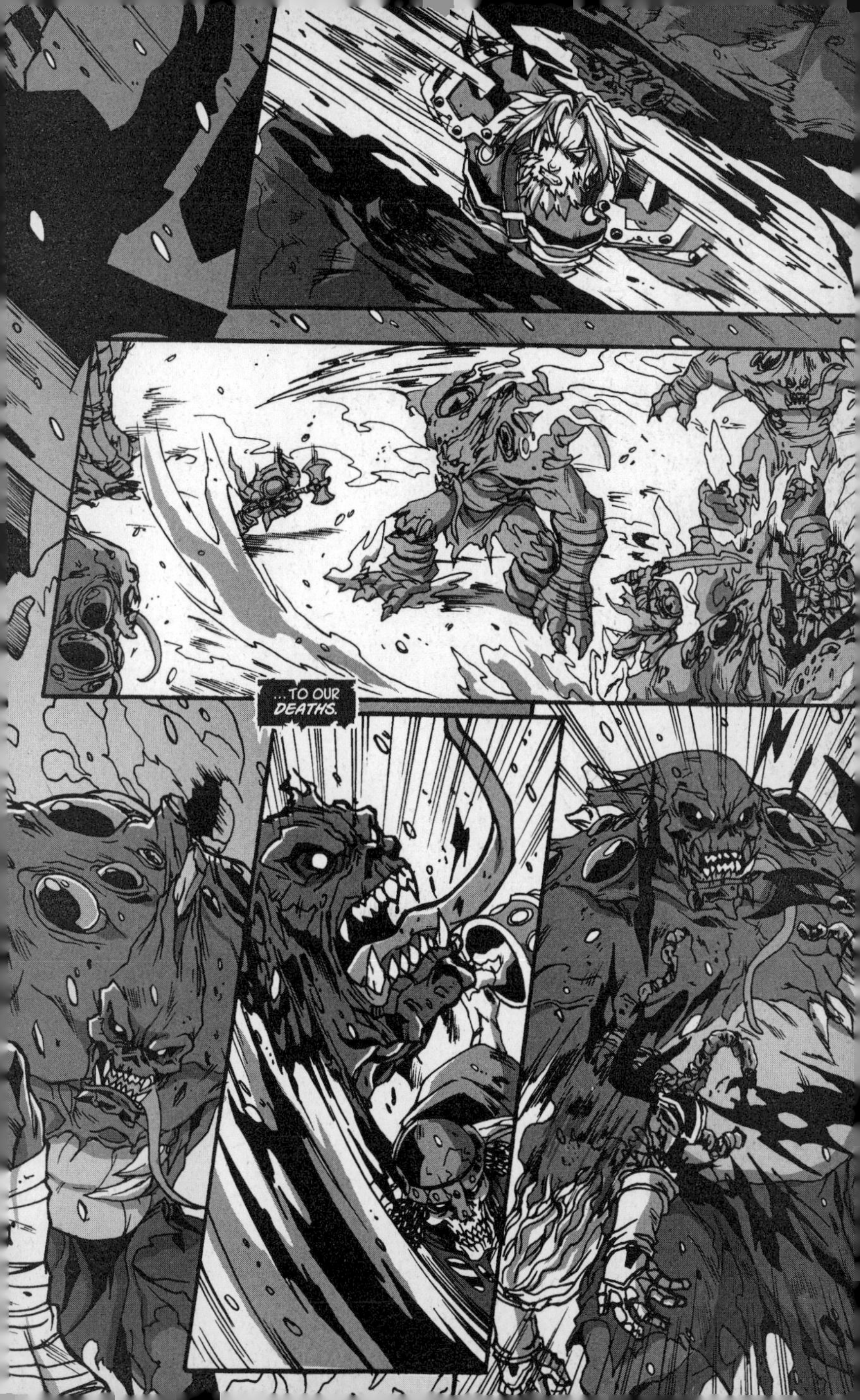
...TO OUR DEATHS.

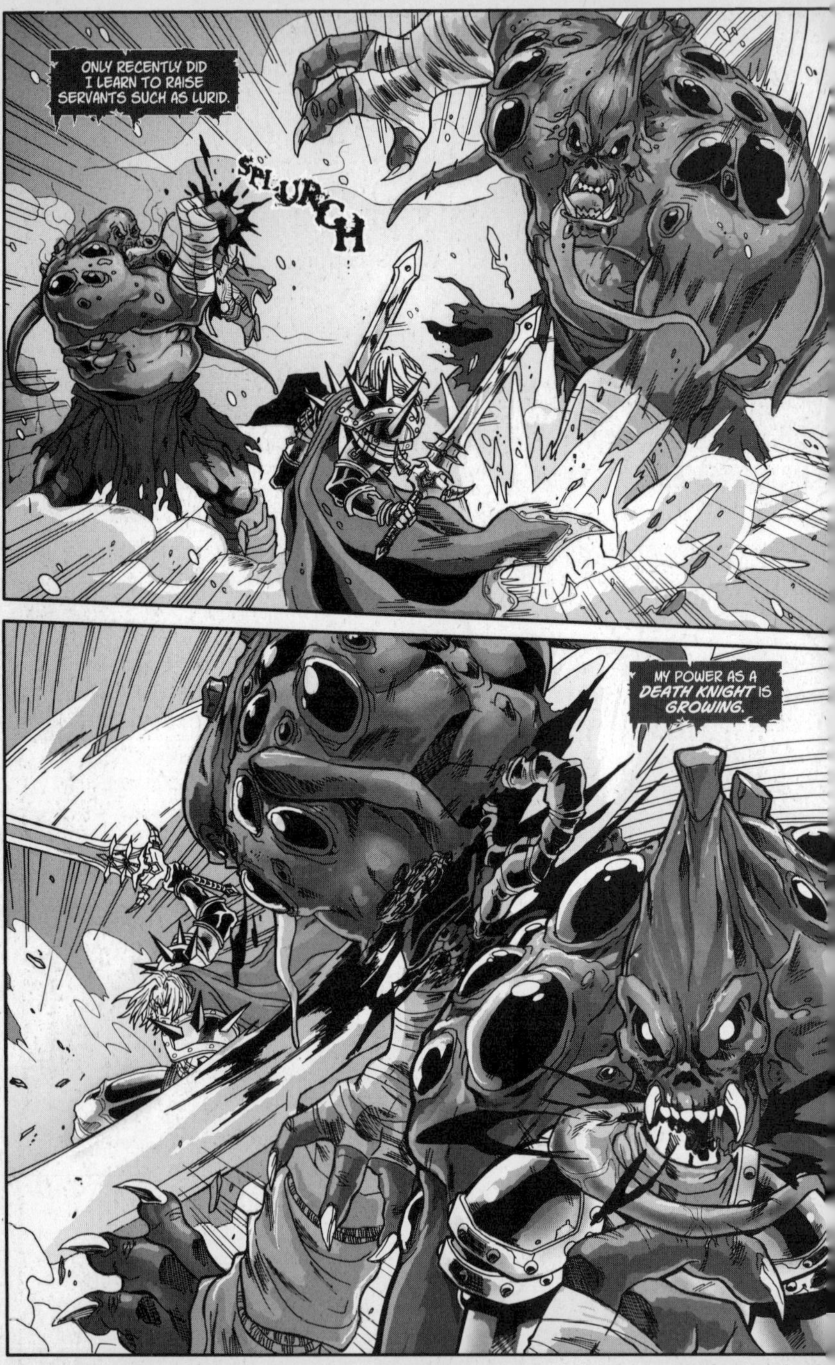
ONLY RECENTLY DID I LEARN TO RAISE SERVANTS SUCH AS LURID.
SPLURCH
MY POWER AS A DEATH KNIGHT IS GROWING.

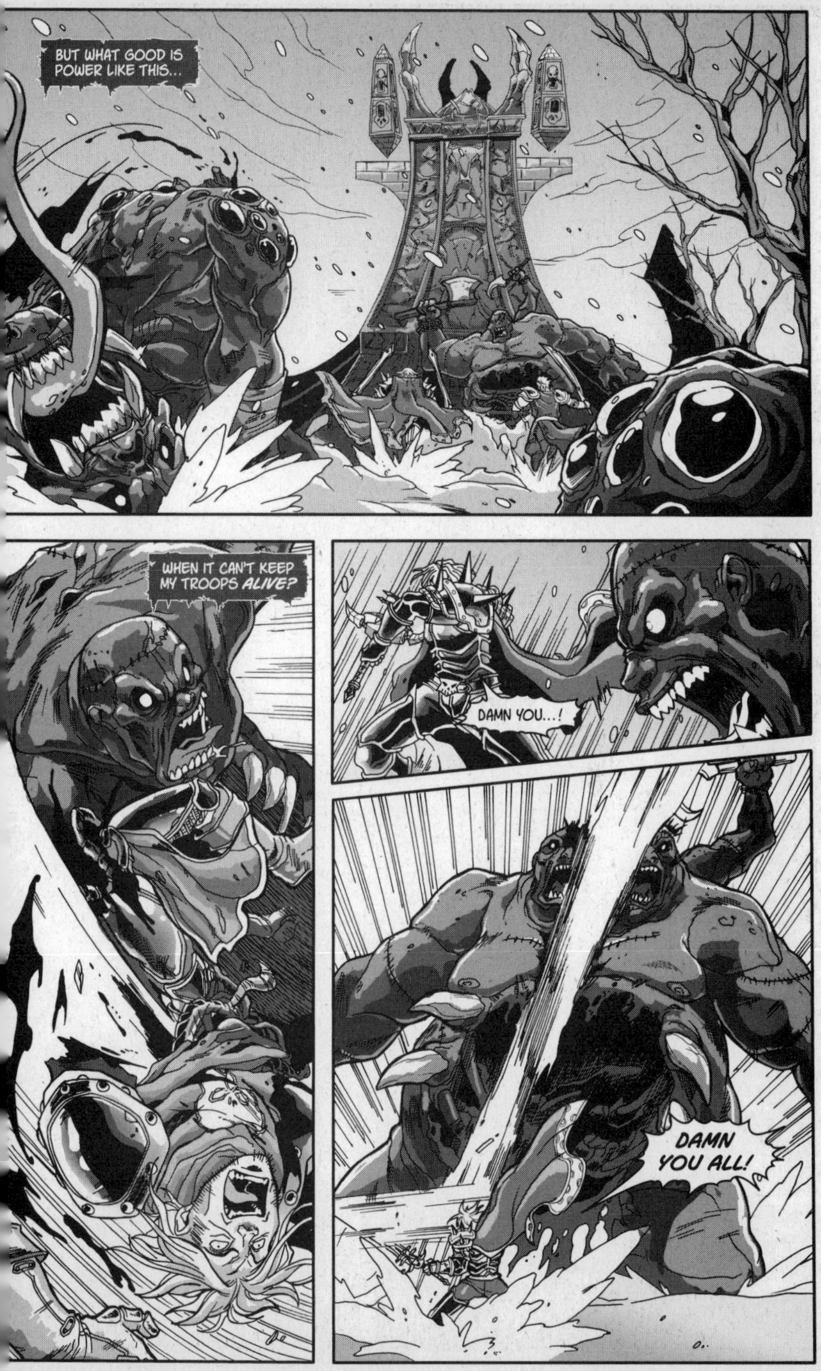
BUT WHAT GOOD IS POWER LIKE THIS...
WHEN IT CAN'T KEEP MY TROOPS *ALIVE?*
DAMN YOU...!
DAMN YOU ALL!

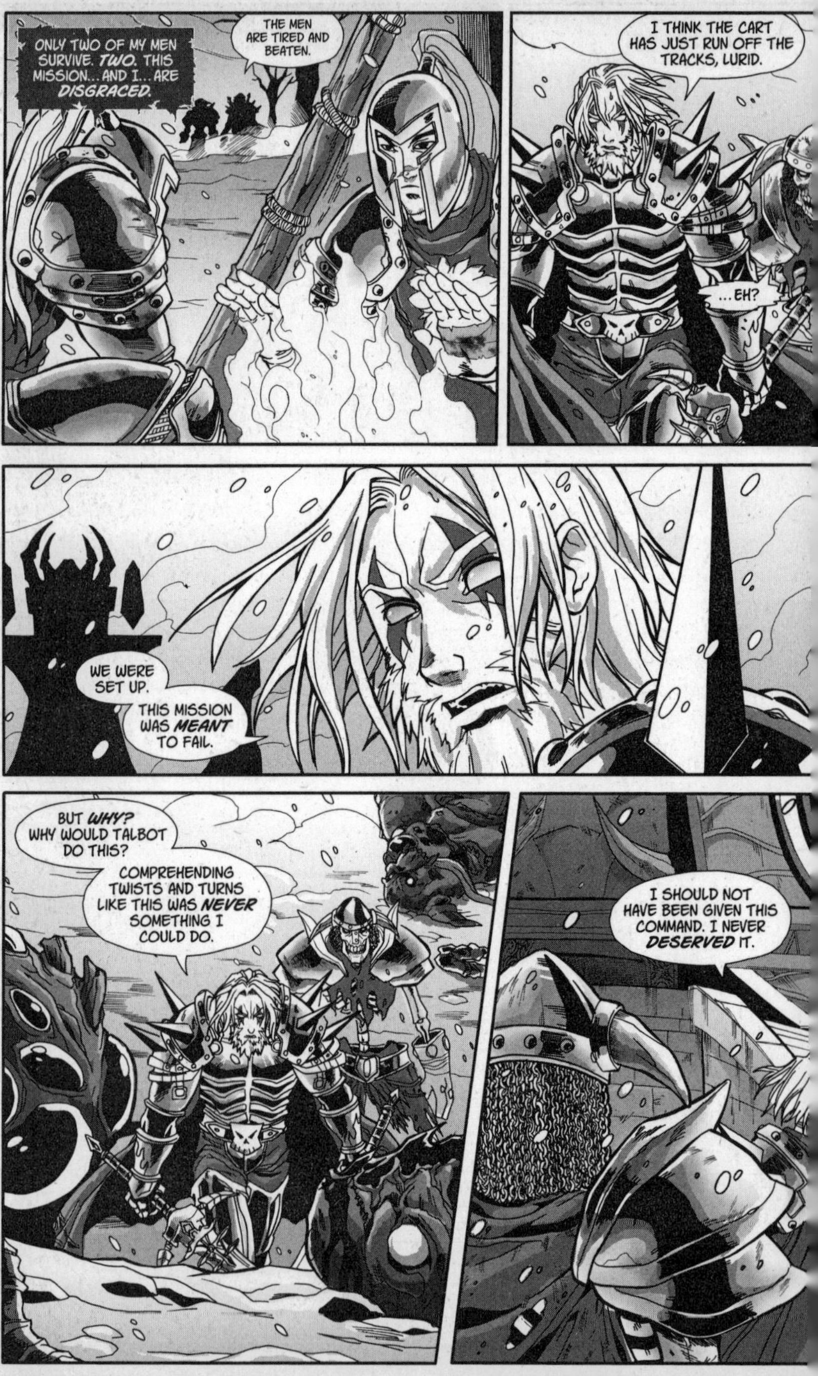
ONLY TWO OF MY MEN SURVIVE. TWO. THIS MISSION... AND I... ARE DISGRACED.
THE MEN ARE TIRED AND BEATEN.
I THINK THE CART HAS JUST RUN OFF THE TRACKS, LURID.
...EH?
WE WERE SET UP.
THIS MISSION WAS MEANT TO FAIL.
BUT WHY? WHY WOULD TALBOT DO THIS?
COMPREHENDING TWISTS AND TURNS LIKE THIS WAS NEVER SOMETHING I COULD DO.
I SHOULD NOT HAVE BEEN GIVEN THIS COMMAND. I NEVER DESERVED IT.

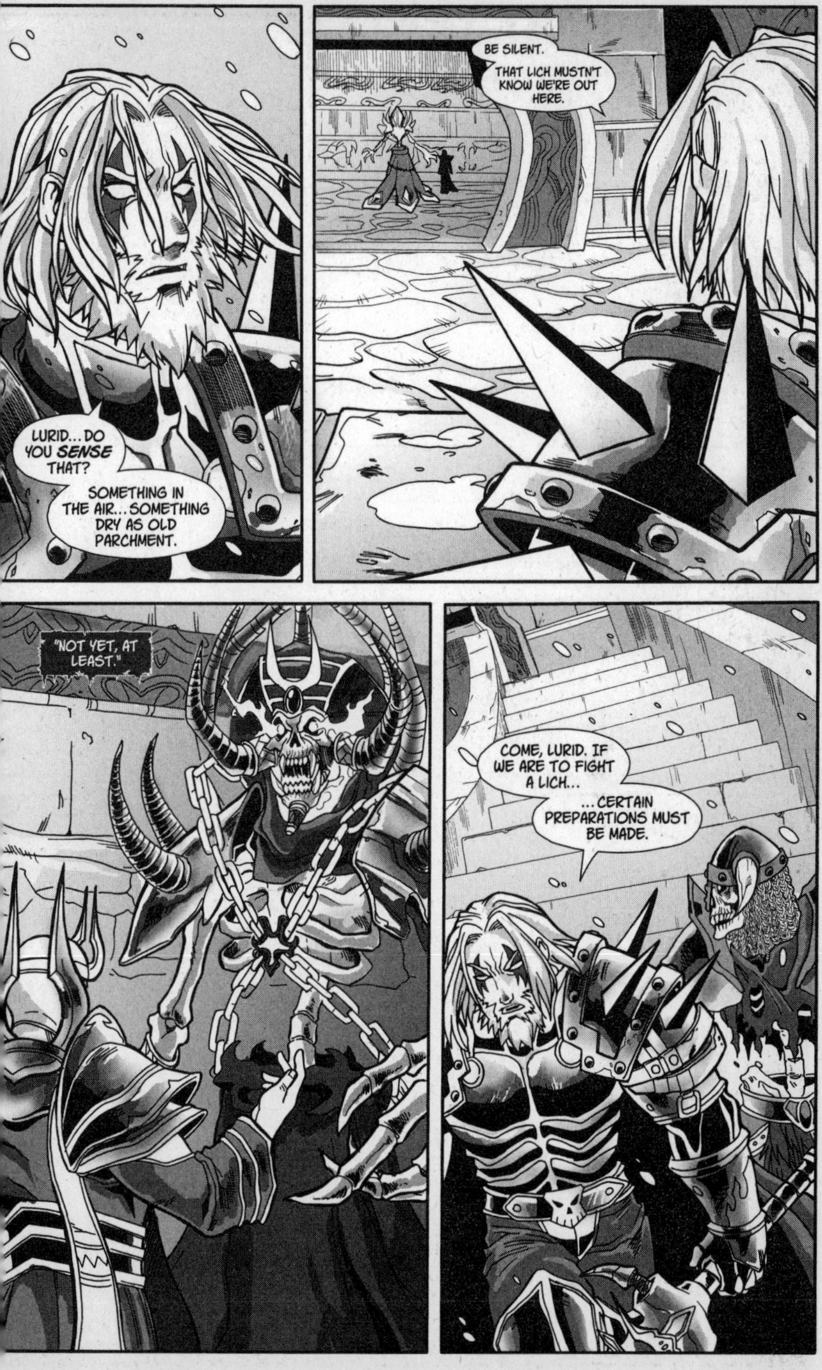
LURID... DO YOU SENSE THAT?
SOMETHING IN THE AIR... SOMETHING DRY AS OLD PARCHMENT.
BE SILENT.
THAT LICH MUSTN'T KNOW WE'RE OUT HERE.
"NOT YET, AT LEAST."
COME, LURID. IF WE ARE TO FIGHT A LICH...
...CERTAIN PREPARATIONS MUST BE MADE.

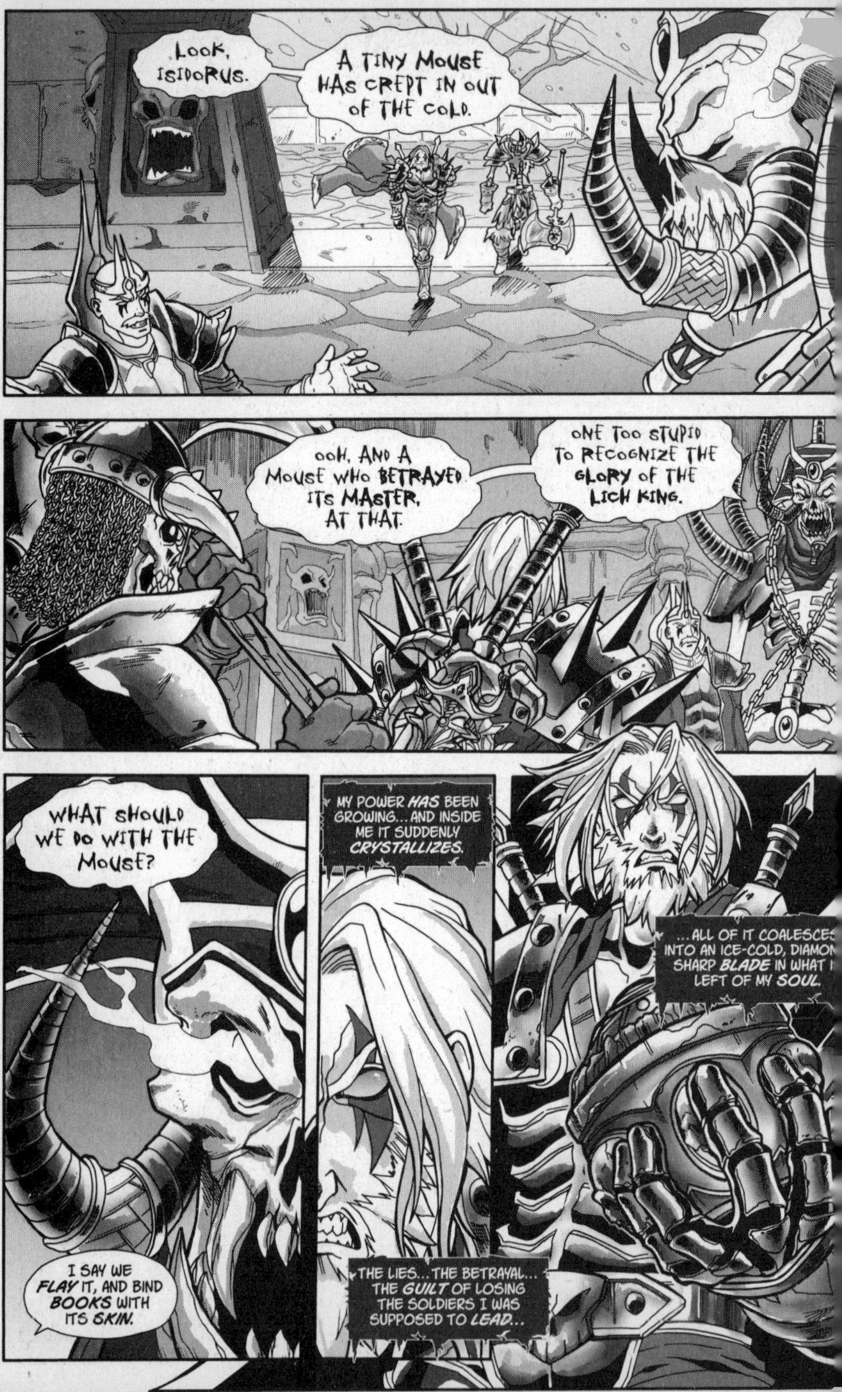
LOOK, ISIDORUS.
A TINY MOUSE HAS CREPT IN OUT OF THE COLD.
OOH, AND A MOUSE WHO BETRAYED ITS MASTER, AT THAT.
ONE TOO STUPID TO RECOGNIZE THE GLORY OF THE LICH KING.
WHAT SHOULD WE DO WITH THE MOUSE?
I SAY WE *FLAY* IT, AND BIND *BOOKS* WITH ITS *SKIN.*
MY POWER *HAS* BEEN GROWING... AND INSIDE ME IT SUDDENLY *CRYSTALLIZES.*
THE LIES... THE BETRAYAL... THE *GUILT* OF LOSING THE SOLDIERS I WAS SUPPOSED TO *LEAD...*
...ALL OF IT COALESCES INTO AN ICE-COLD, DIAMON SHARP *BLADE* IN WHAT LEFT OF MY *SOUL.*

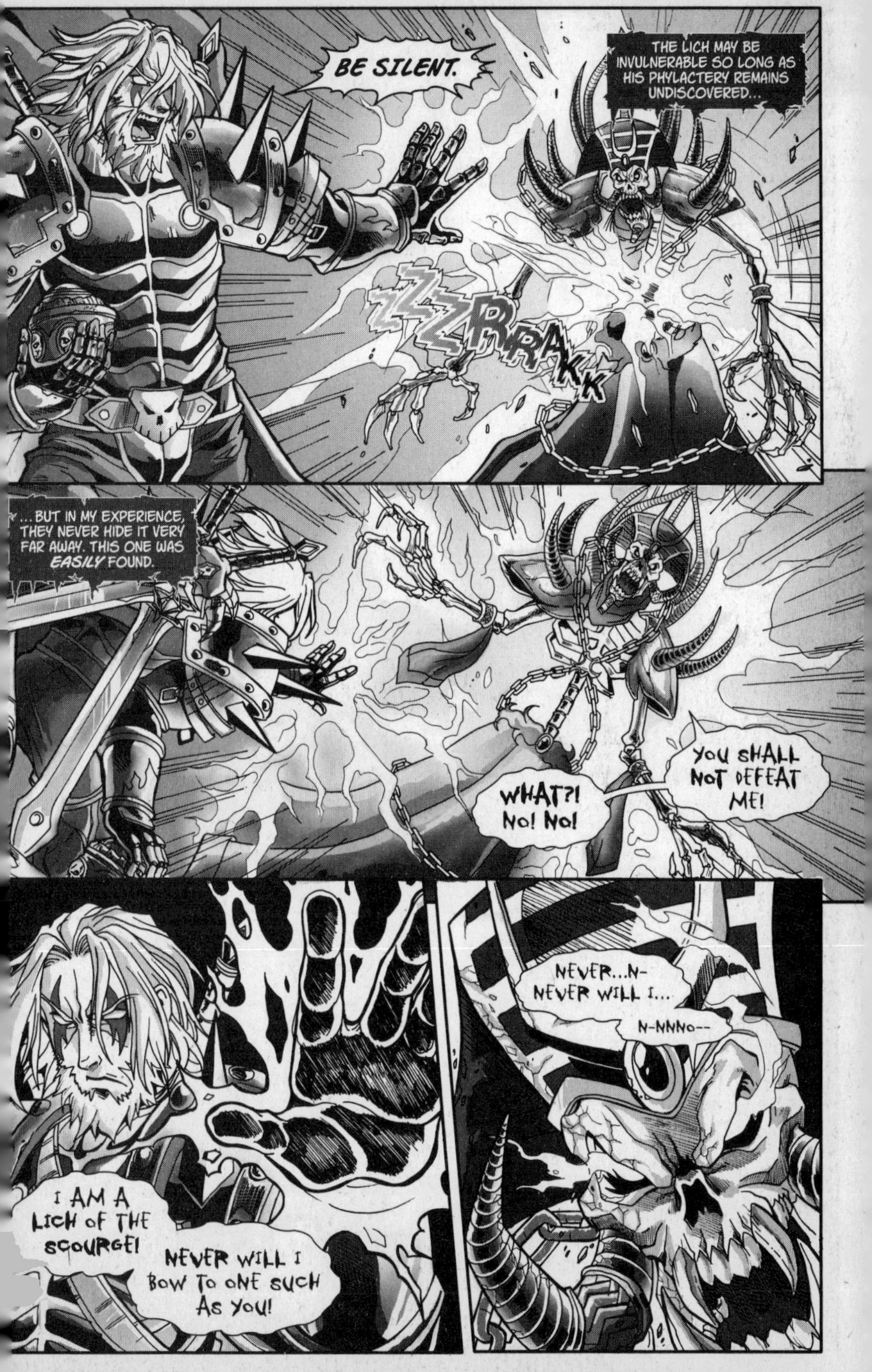
BE SILENT.
THE LICH MAY BE INVULNERABLE SO LONG AS HIS PHYLACTERY REMAINS UNDISCOVERED...
ZZZRRRAKK
...BUT IN MY EXPERIENCE, THEY NEVER HIDE IT VERY FAR AWAY. THIS ONE WAS *EASILY* FOUND.
WHAT?! No! No!
YOU SHALL NOT DEFEAT ME!
I AM A LICH OF THE SCOURGE!
NEVER WILL I BOW TO ONE SUCH AS YOU!
NEVER...N-NEVER WILL I...
N-NNNO--

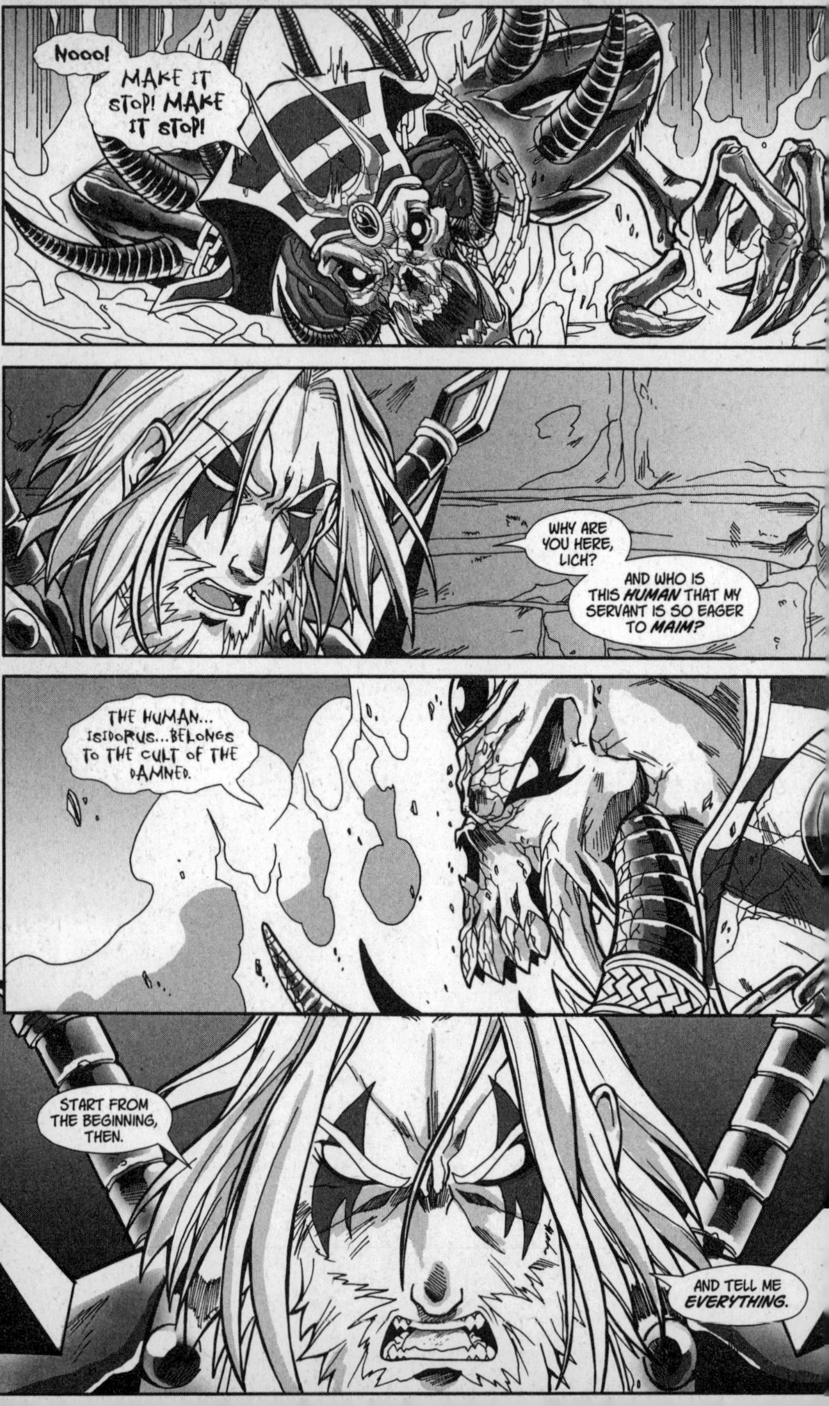
Nooo!
MAKE IT STOP! MAKE IT STOP!
WHY ARE YOU HERE, LICH?
AND WHO IS THIS *HUMAN* THAT MY SERVANT IS SO EAGER TO *MAIM?*
THE HUMAN... ISIDORUS...BELONGS TO THE CULT OF THE DAMNED.
START FROM THE BEGINNING, THEN.
AND TELL ME *EVERYTHING.*

CHAPTER 6

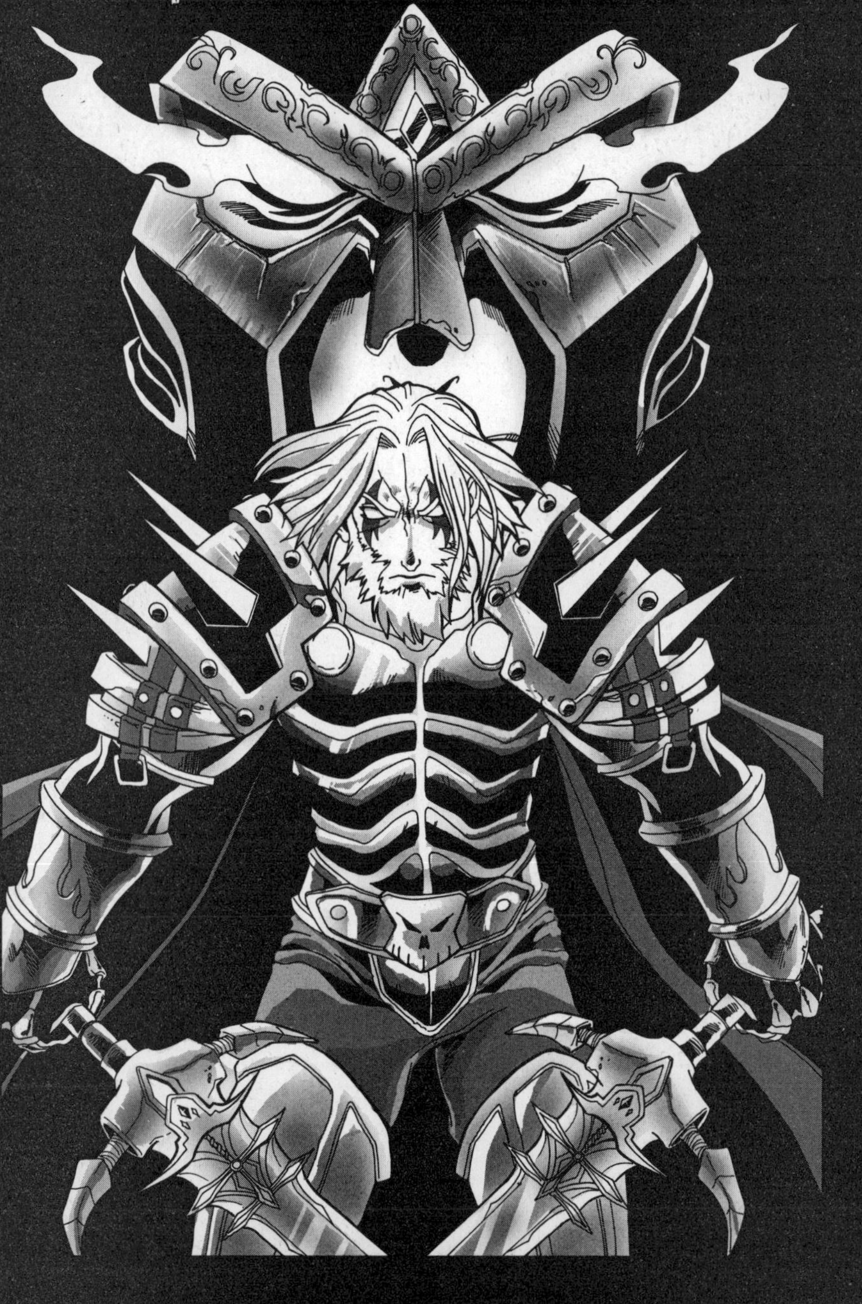

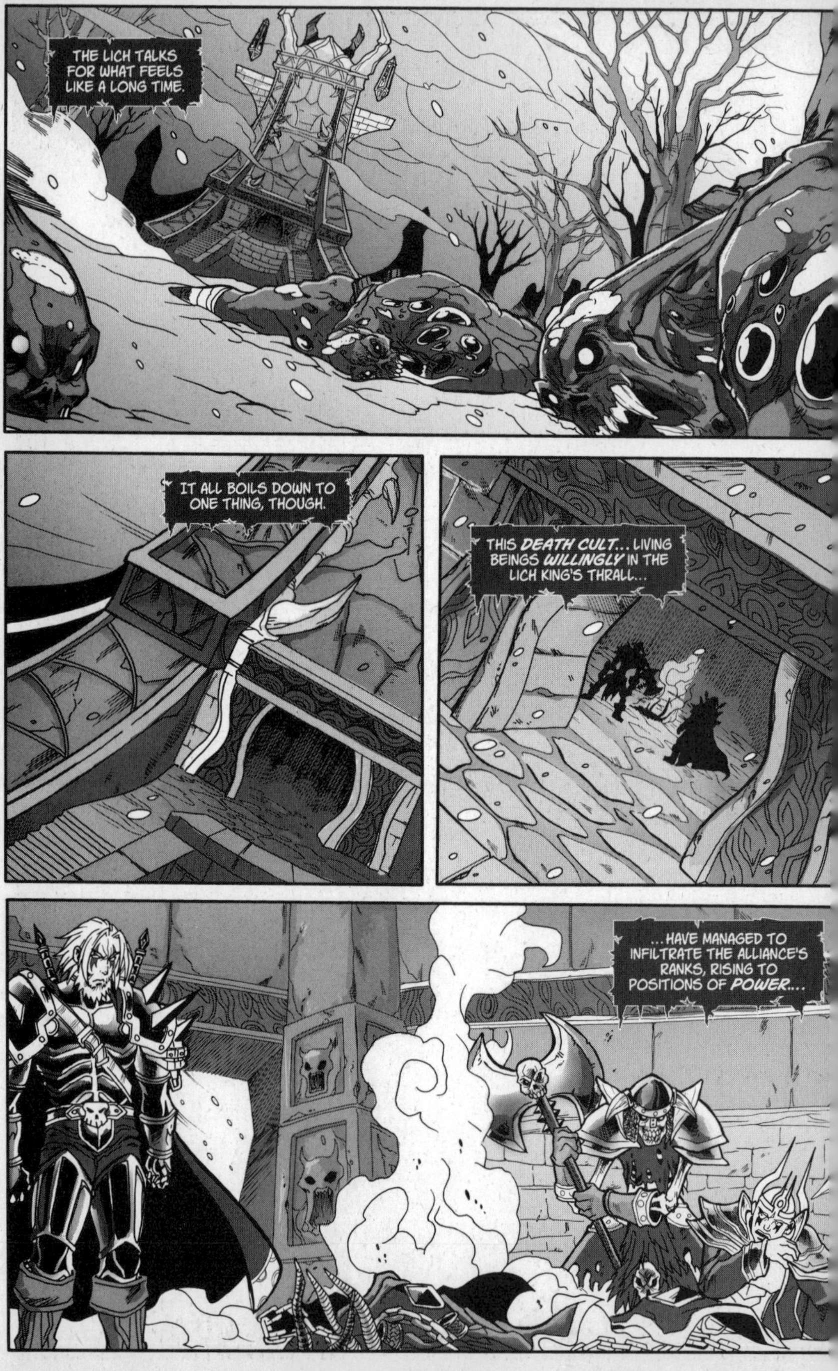
THE LICH TALKS FOR WHAT FEELS LIKE A LONG TIME.
IT ALL BOILS DOWN TO ONE THING, THOUGH.
THIS DEATH CULT... LIVING BEINGS WILLINGLY IN THE LICH KING'S THRALL...
...HAVE MANAGED TO INFILTRATE THE ALLIANCE'S RANKS, RISING TO POSITIONS OF POWER...

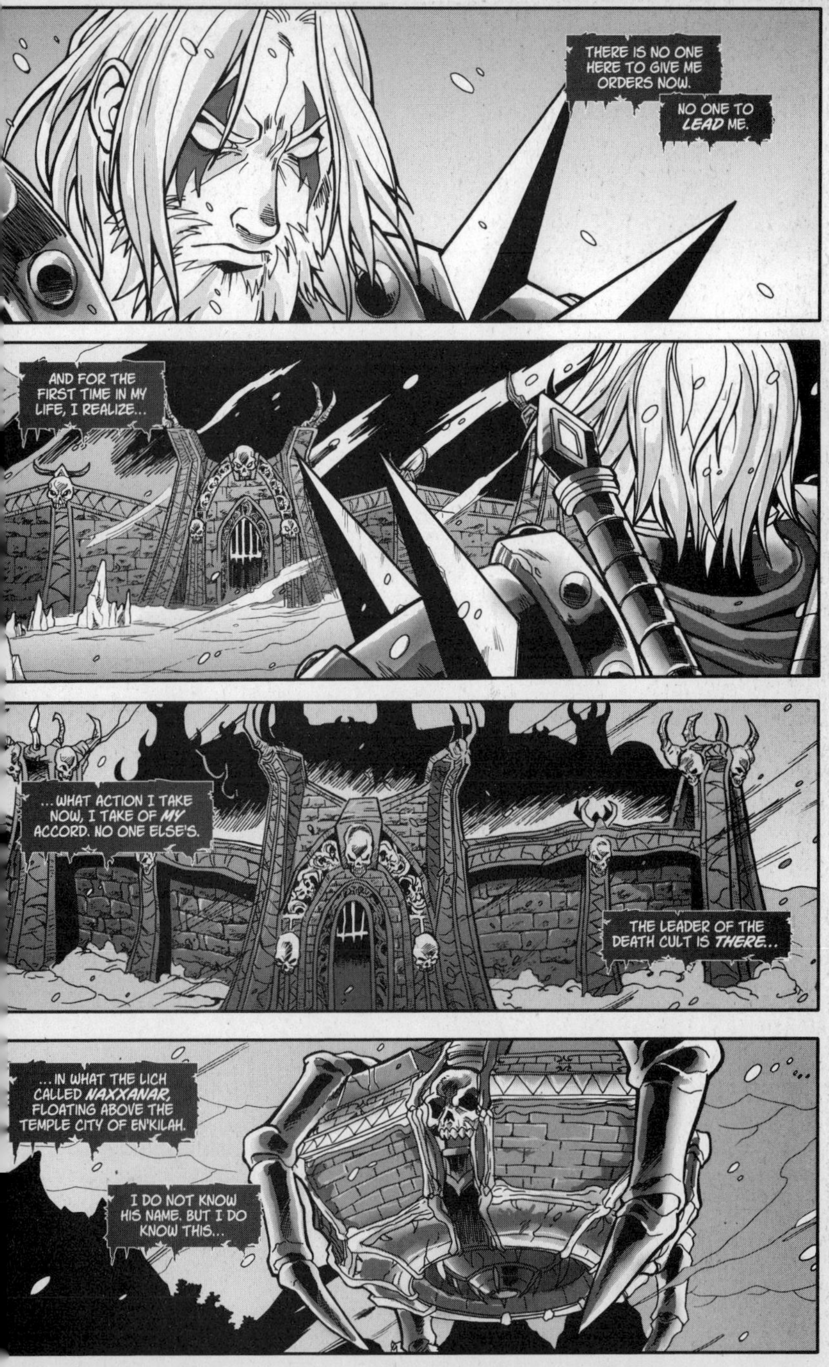
THERE IS NO ONE HERE TO GIVE ME ORDERS NOW.
NO ONE TO *LEAD* ME.
AND FOR THE FIRST TIME IN MY LIFE, I REALIZE...
...WHAT ACTION I TAKE NOW, I TAKE OF *MY* ACCORD. NO ONE ELSE'S.
THE LEADER OF THE DEATH CULT IS *THERE*...
...IN WHAT THE LICH CALLED *NAXXANAR*, FLOATING ABOVE THE TEMPLE CITY OF EN'KILAH.
I DO NOT KNOW HIS NAME. BUT I DO KNOW THIS...

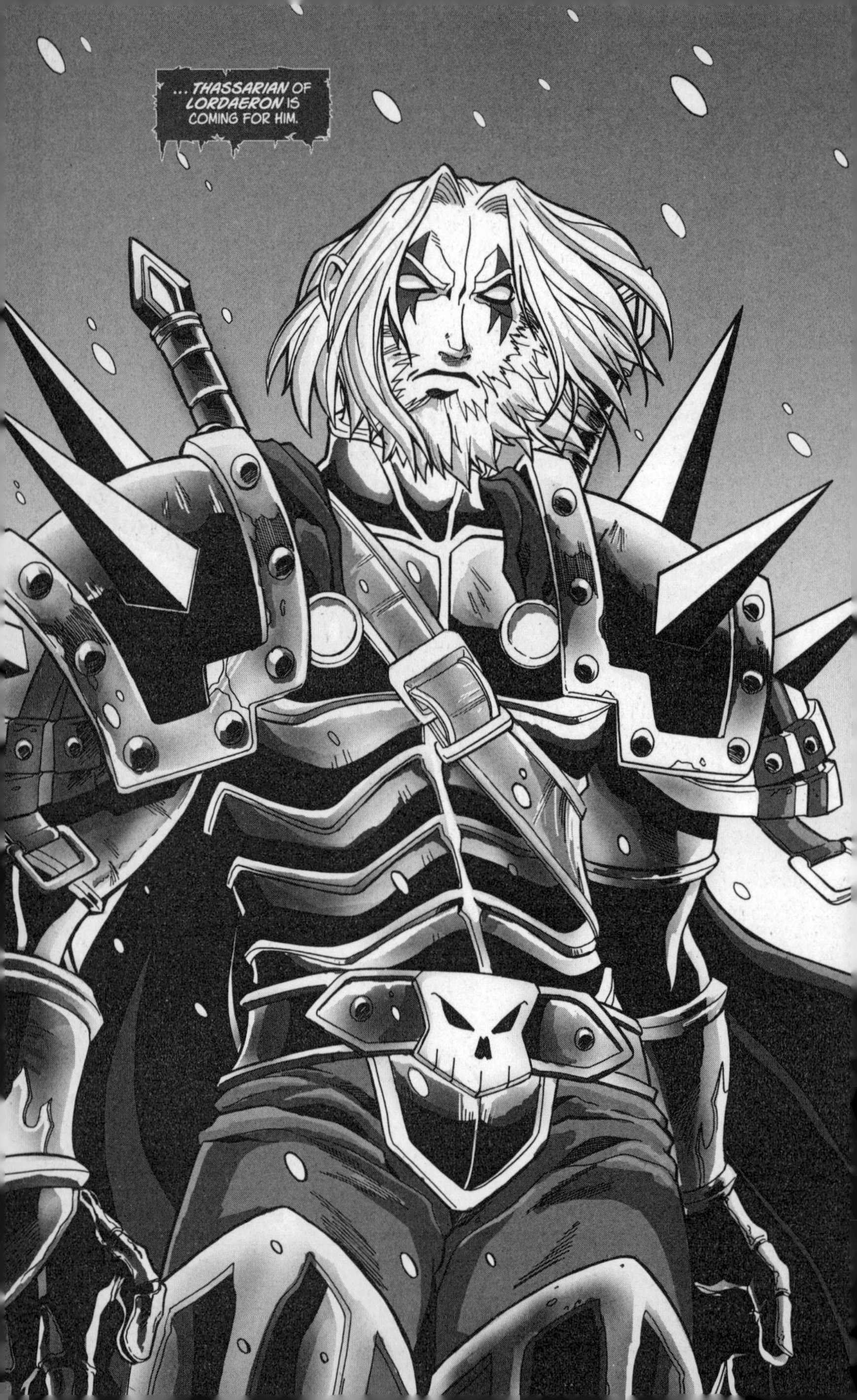
...THASSARIAN OF LORDAERON IS COMING FOR HIM.

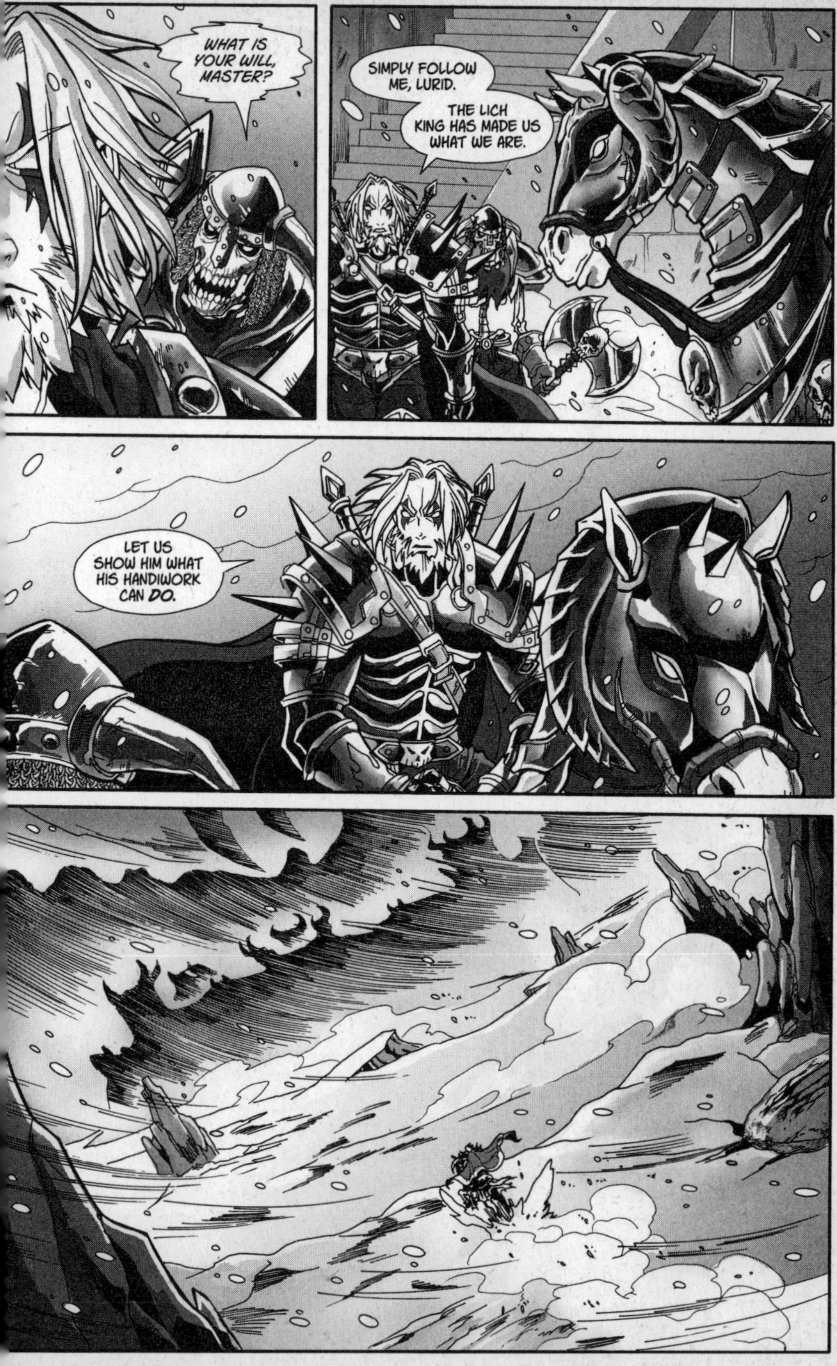
WHAT IS YOUR WILL, MASTER?
SIMPLY FOLLOW ME, LURID.
THE LICH KING HAS MADE US WHAT WE ARE.
LET US SHOW HIM WHAT HIS HANDIWORK CAN DO.

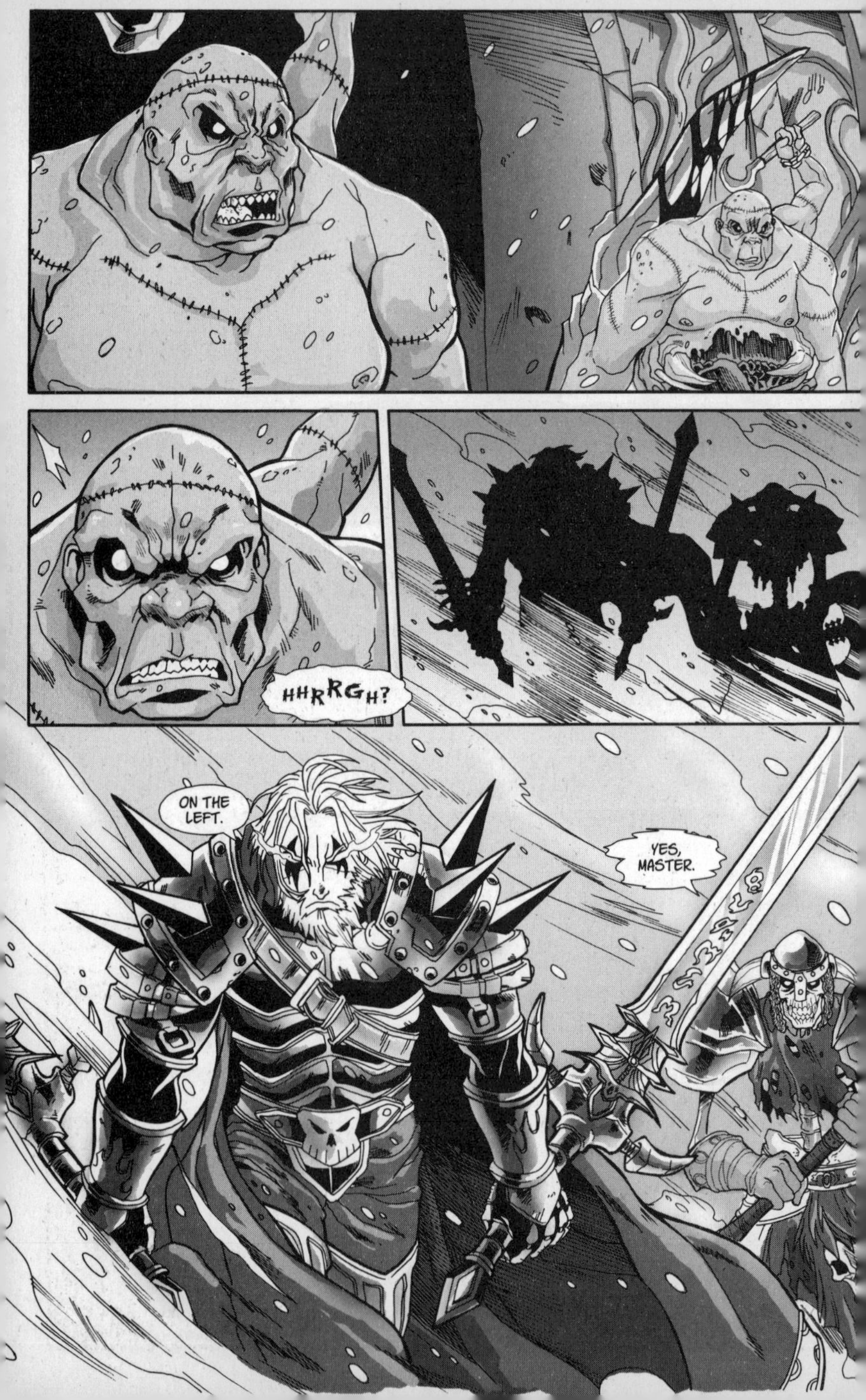
HHRRGH?
ON THE LEFT.
YES, MASTER.

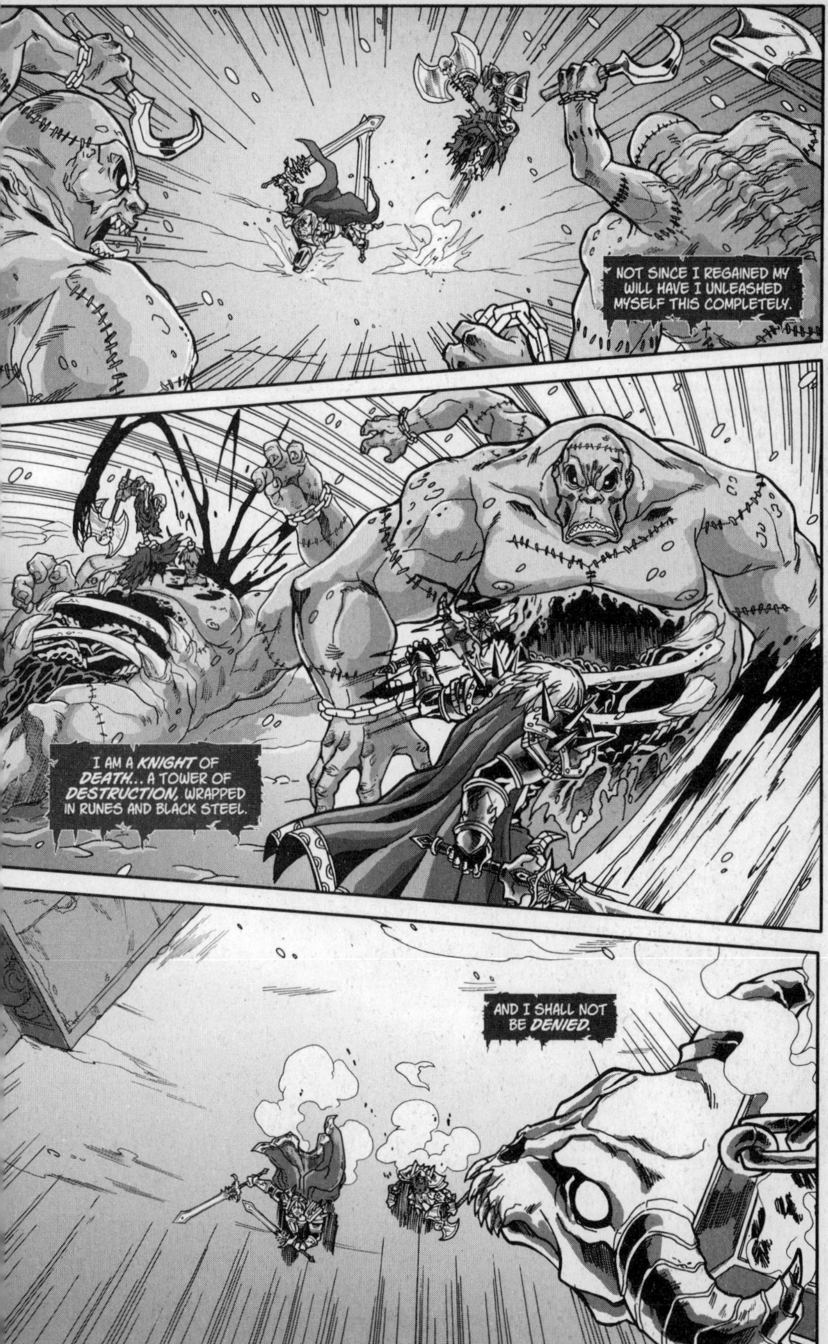
NOT SINCE I REGAINED MY WILL HAVE I UNLEASHED MYSELF THIS COMPLETELY.
I AM A KNIGHT OF DEATH... A TOWER OF DESTRUCTION, WRAPPED IN RUNES AND BLACK STEEL.
AND I SHALL NOT BE DENIED.

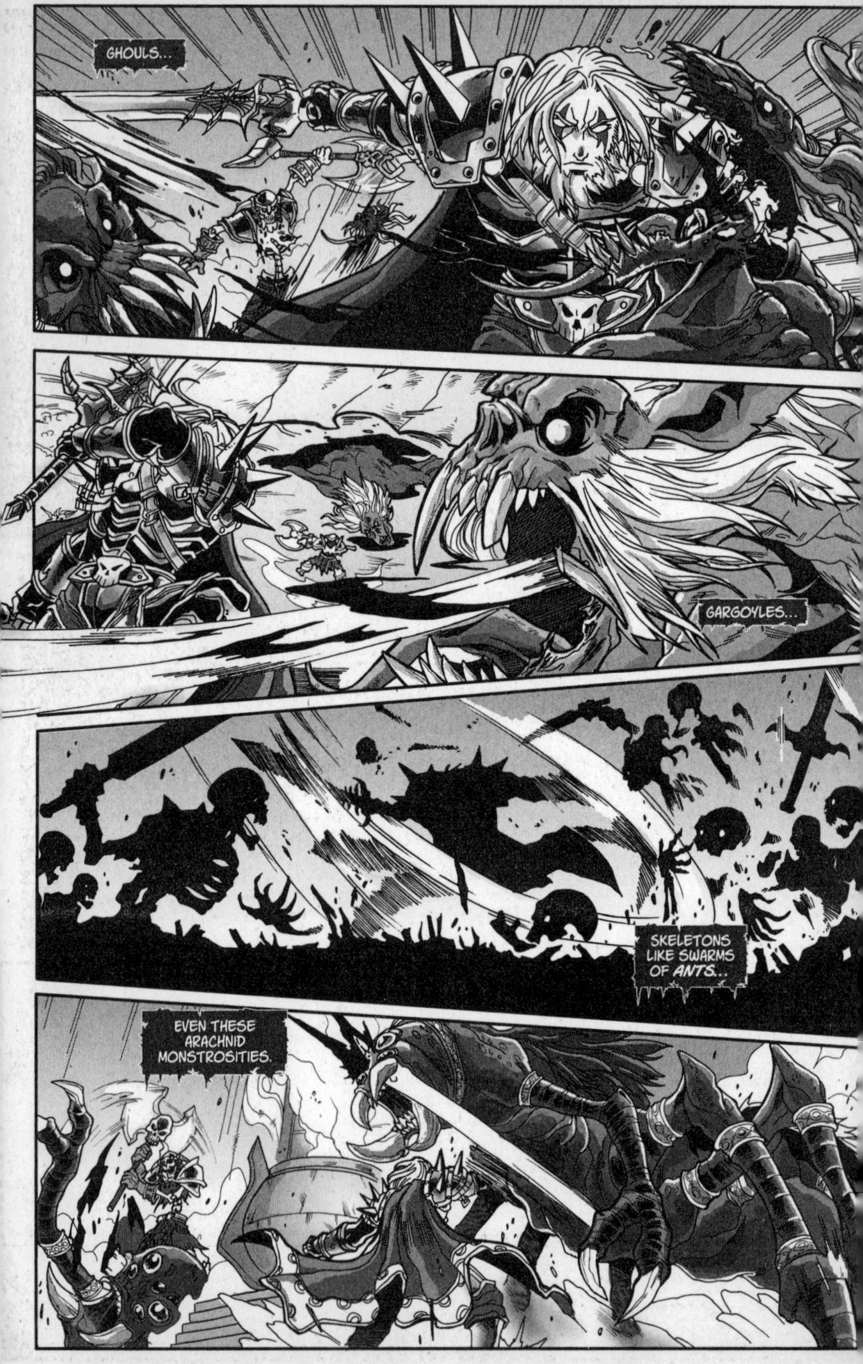
GHOULS...
GARGOYLES...
SKELETONS LIKE SWARMS OF ANTS...
EVEN THESE ARACHNID MONSTROSITIES.

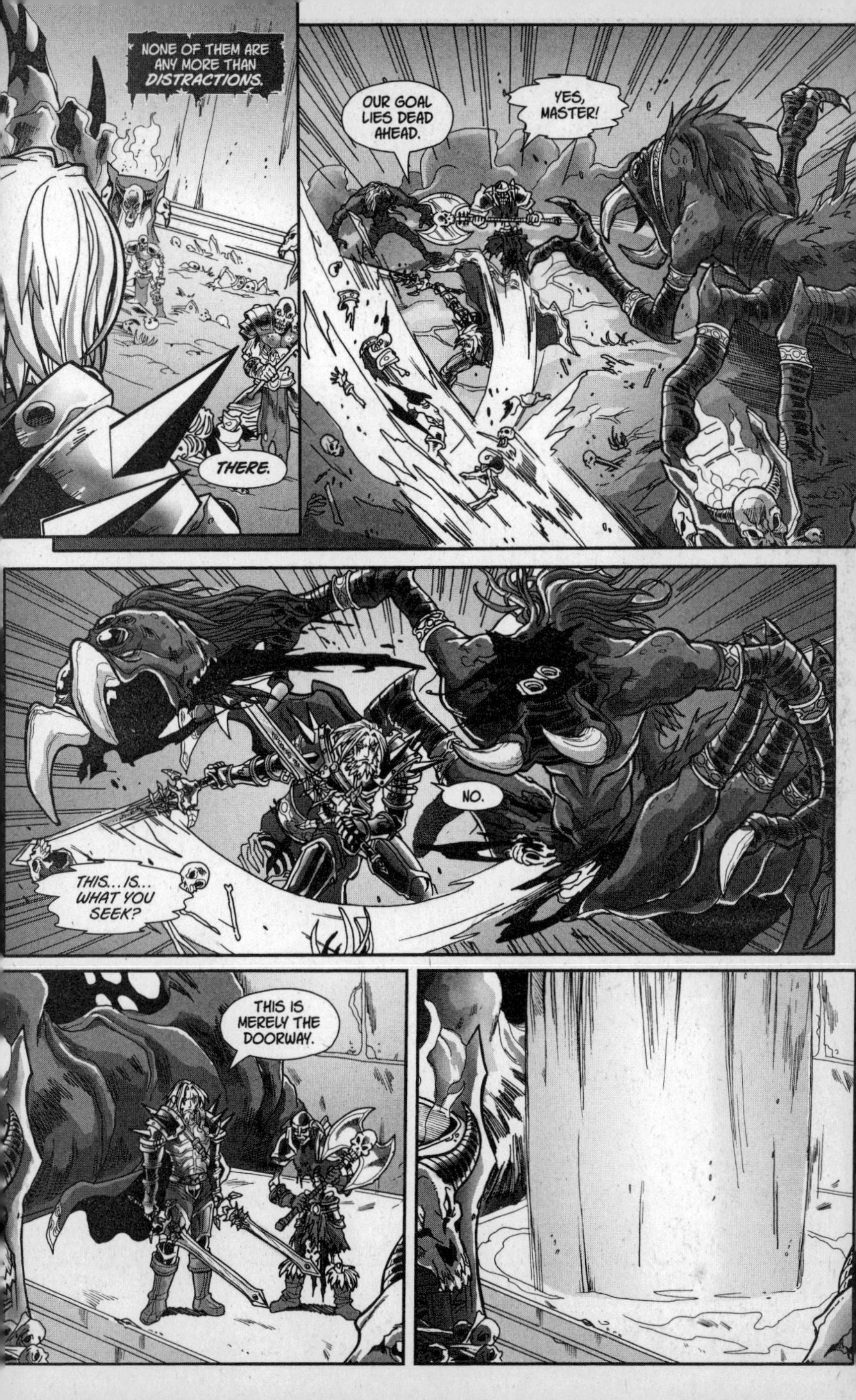
NONE OF THEM ARE ANY MORE THAN DISTRACTIONS.
THERE.
OUR GOAL LIES DEAD AHEAD.
YES, MASTER!
THIS... IS... WHAT YOU SEEK?
NO.
THIS IS MERELY THE DOORWAY.

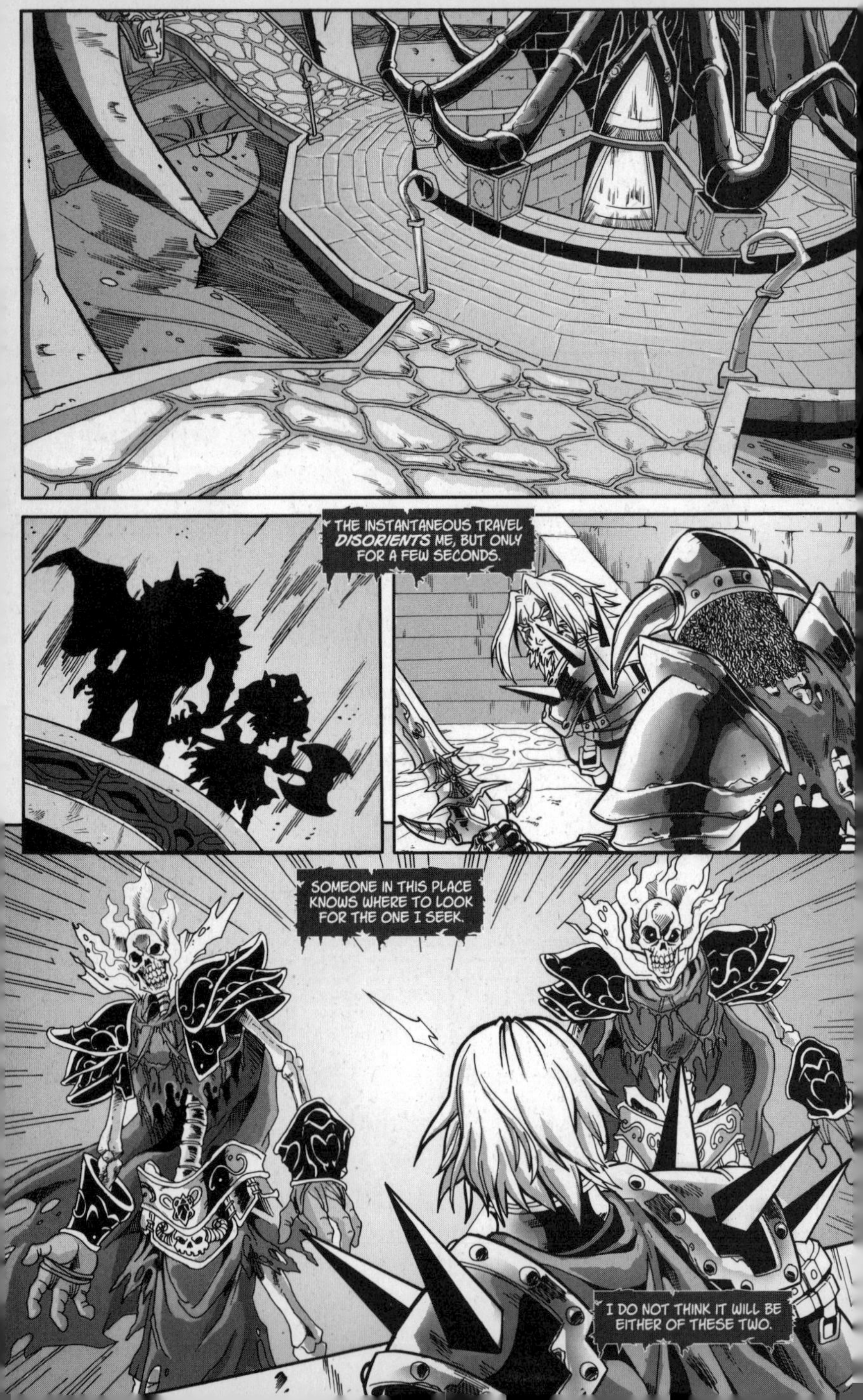
THE INSTANTANEOUS TRAVEL DISORIENTS ME, BUT ONLY FOR A FEW SECONDS.
SOMEONE IN THIS PLACE KNOWS WHERE TO LOOK FOR THE ONE I SEEK.
I DO NOT THINK IT WILL BE EITHER OF THESE TWO.

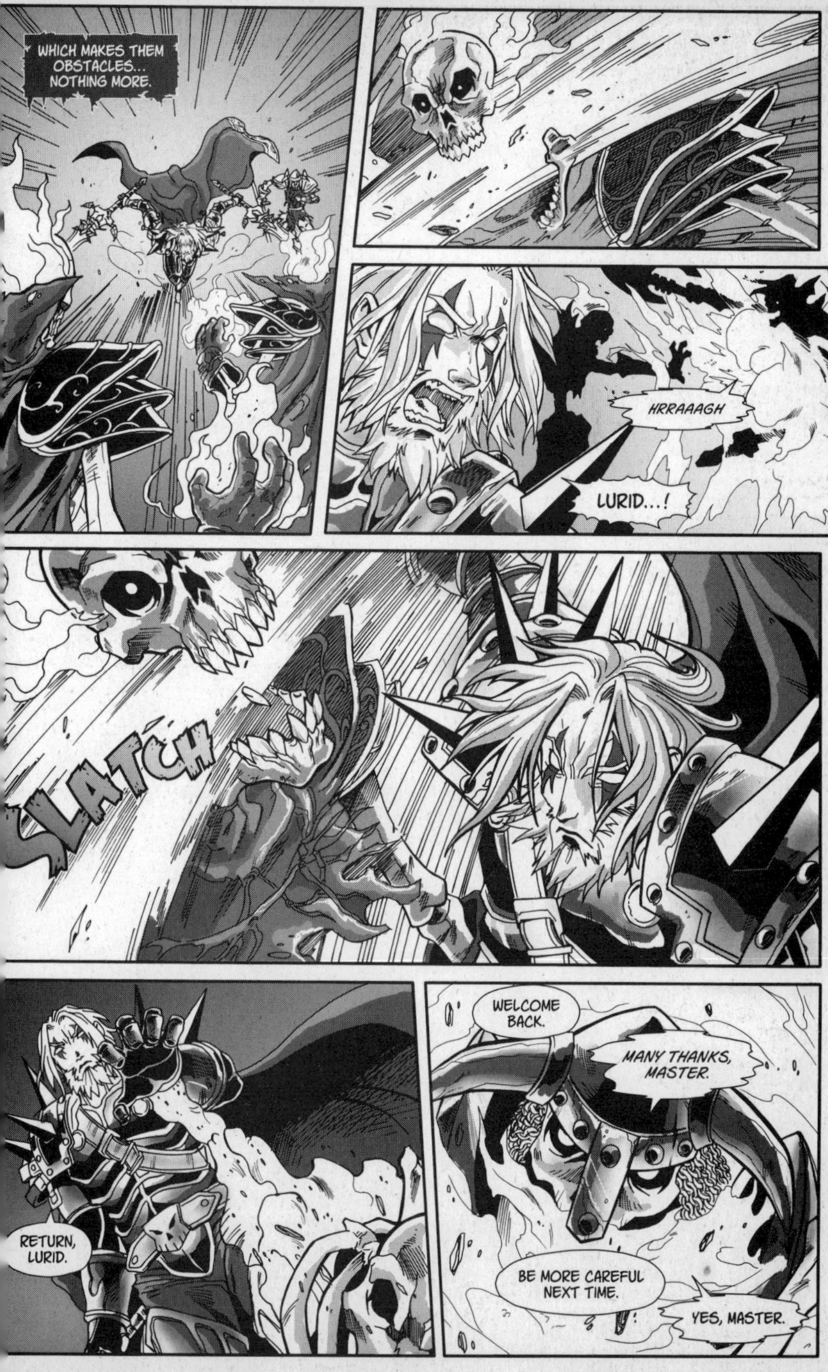
WHICH MAKES THEM OBSTACLES... NOTHING MORE.
HRRAAAGH
LURID...!
SLATCH
RETURN, LURID.
WELCOME BACK.
MANY THANKS, MASTER.
BE MORE CAREFUL NEXT TIME.
YES, MASTER.

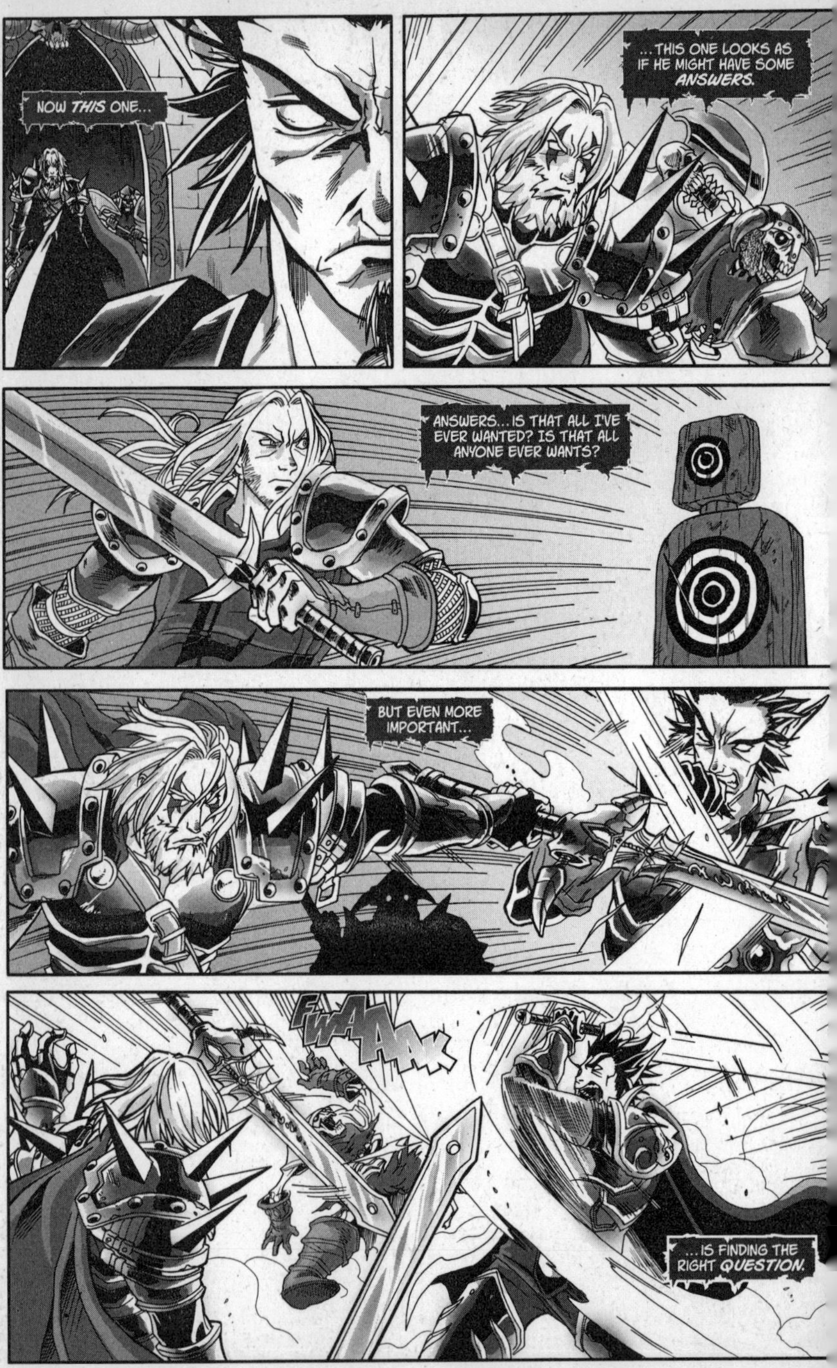
NOW THIS ONE...
...THIS ONE LOOKS AS IF HE MIGHT HAVE SOME ANSWERS.
ANSWERS...IS THAT ALL I'VE EVER WANTED? IS THAT ALL ANYONE EVER WANTS?
BUT EVEN MORE IMPORTANT...
FWAAAAK
...IS FINDING THE RIGHT QUESTION.

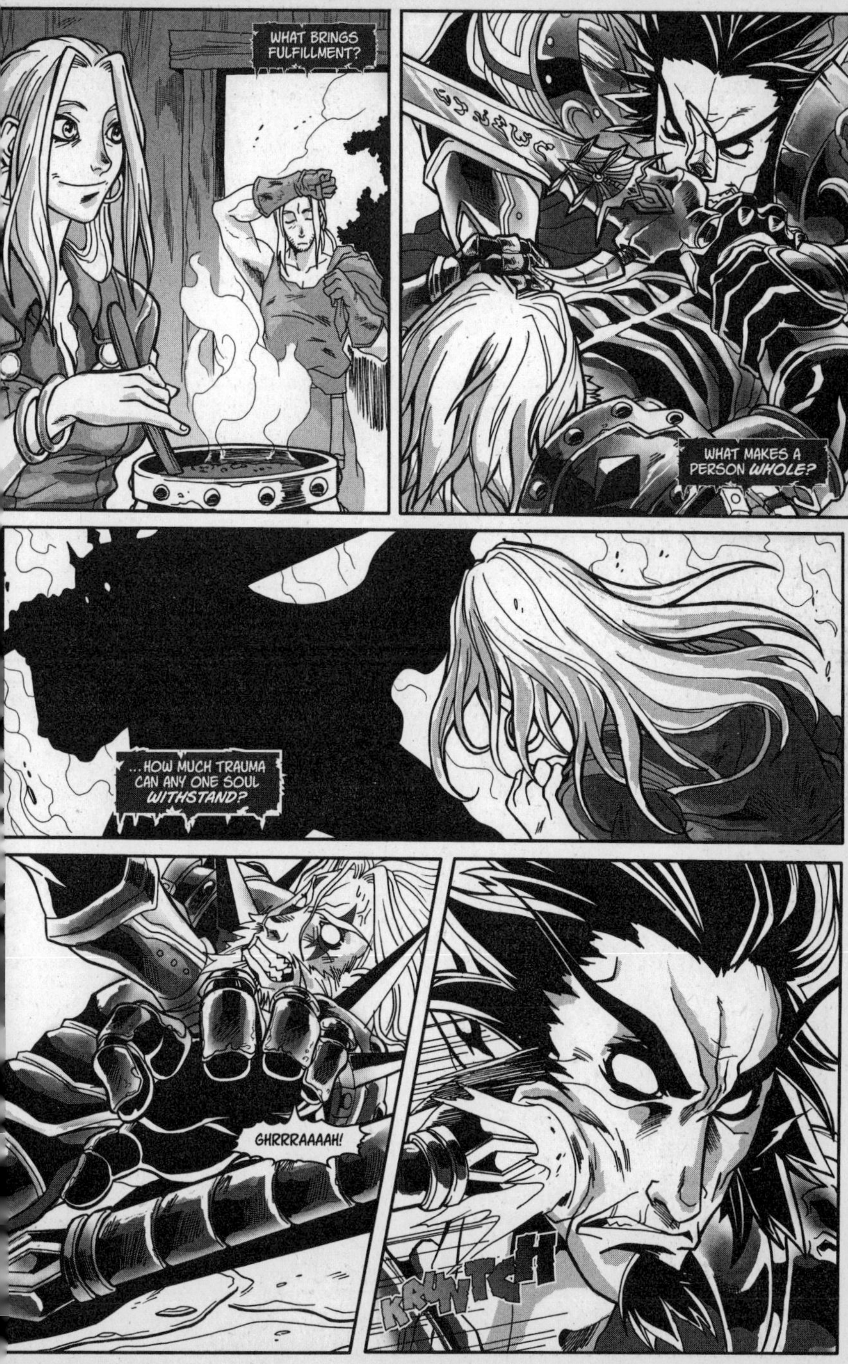
WHAT BRINGS FULFILLMENT?
WHAT MAKES A PERSON WHOLE?
...HOW MUCH TRAUMA CAN ANY ONE SOUL WITHSTAND?
GHRRRAAAAH!
KRUNTCH

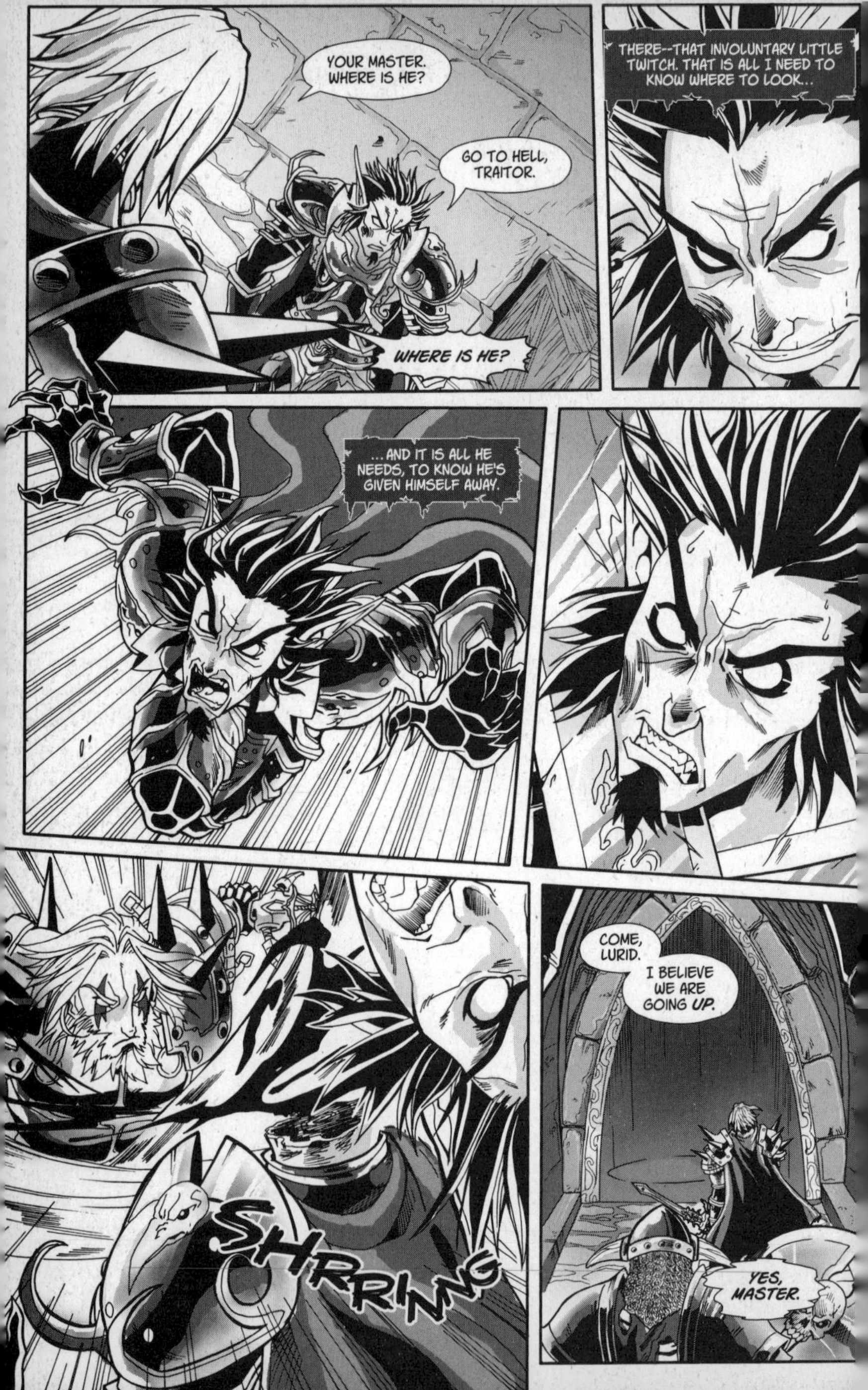
YOUR MASTER. WHERE IS HE?
GO TO HELL, TRAITOR.
WHERE IS HE?
THERE--THAT INVOLUNTARY LITTLE TWITCH. THAT IS ALL I NEED TO KNOW WHERE TO LOOK...
...AND IT IS ALL HE NEEDS, TO KNOW HE'S GIVEN HIMSELF AWAY.
SHRRING
COME, LURID.
I BELIEVE WE ARE GOING UP.
YES, MASTER.

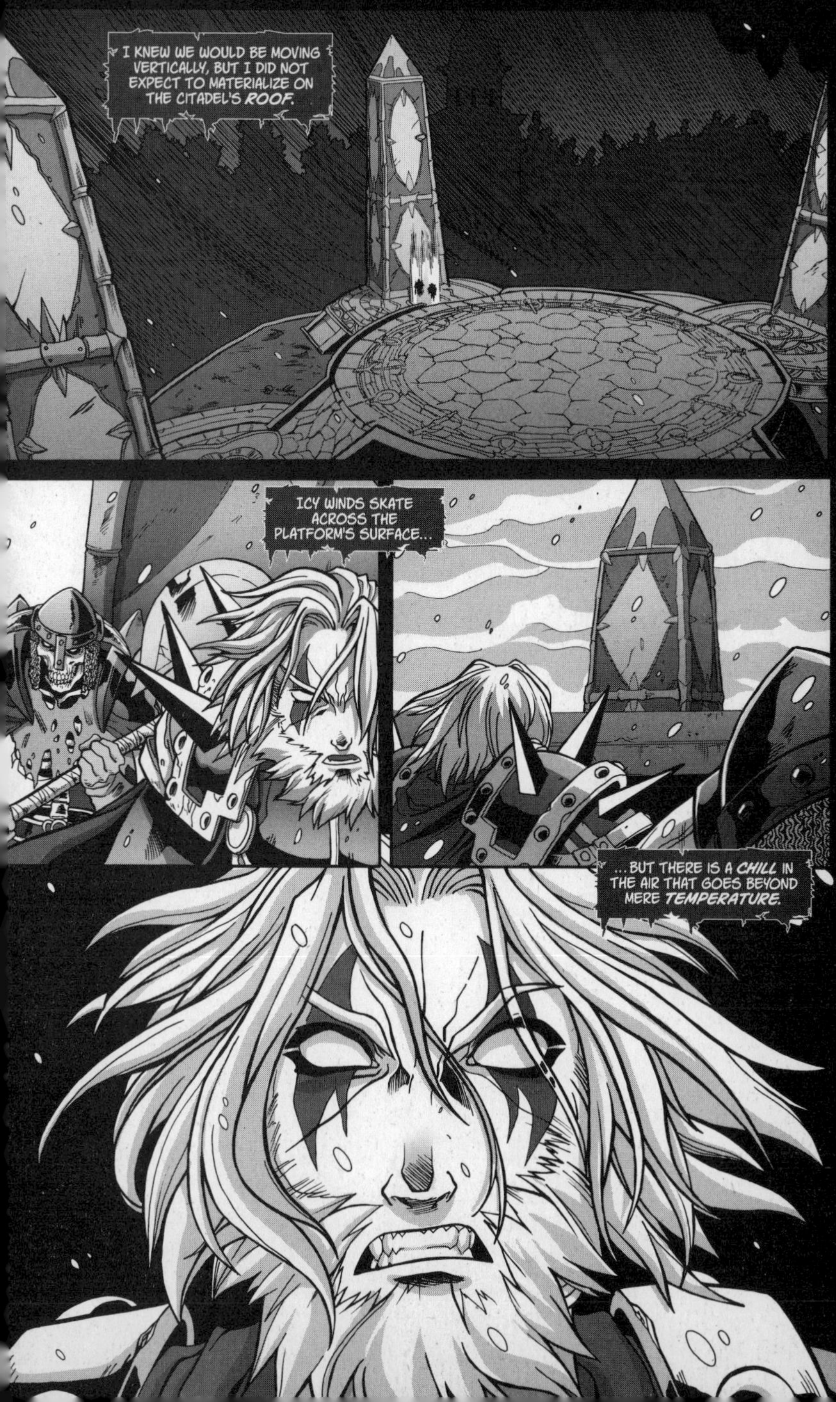
I KNEW WE WOULD BE MOVING VERTICALLY, BUT I DID NOT EXPECT TO MATERIALIZE ON THE CITADEL'S *ROOF.*
ICY WINDS SKATE ACROSS THE PLATFORM'S SURFACE...
...BUT THERE IS A *CHILL* IN THE AIR THAT GOES BEYOND MERE *TEMPERATURE.*

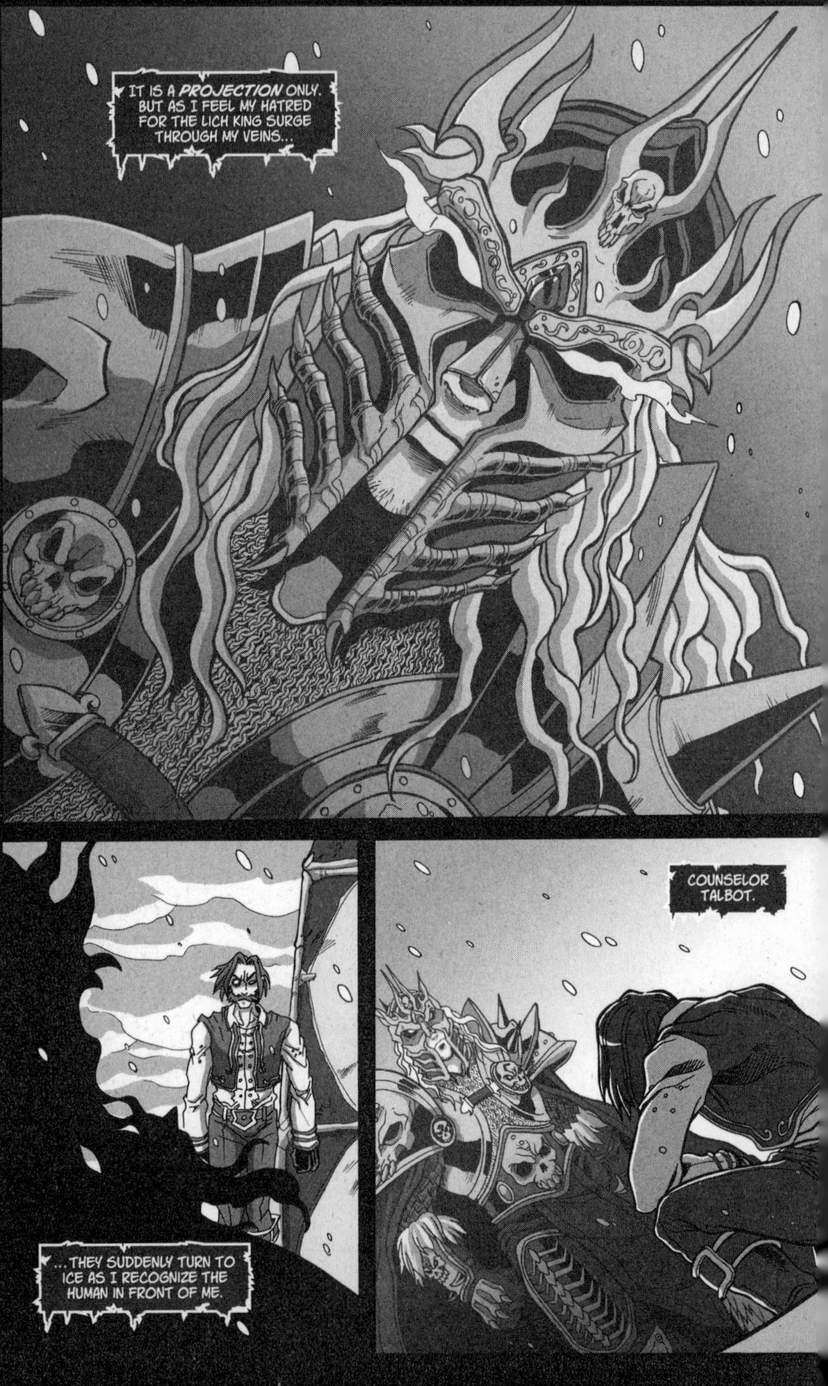
IT IS A PROJECTION ONLY. BUT AS I FEEL MY HATRED FOR THE LICH KING SURGE THROUGH MY VEINS...
...THEY SUDDENLY TURN TO ICE AS I RECOGNIZE THE HUMAN IN FRONT OF ME.
COUNSELOR TALBOT.

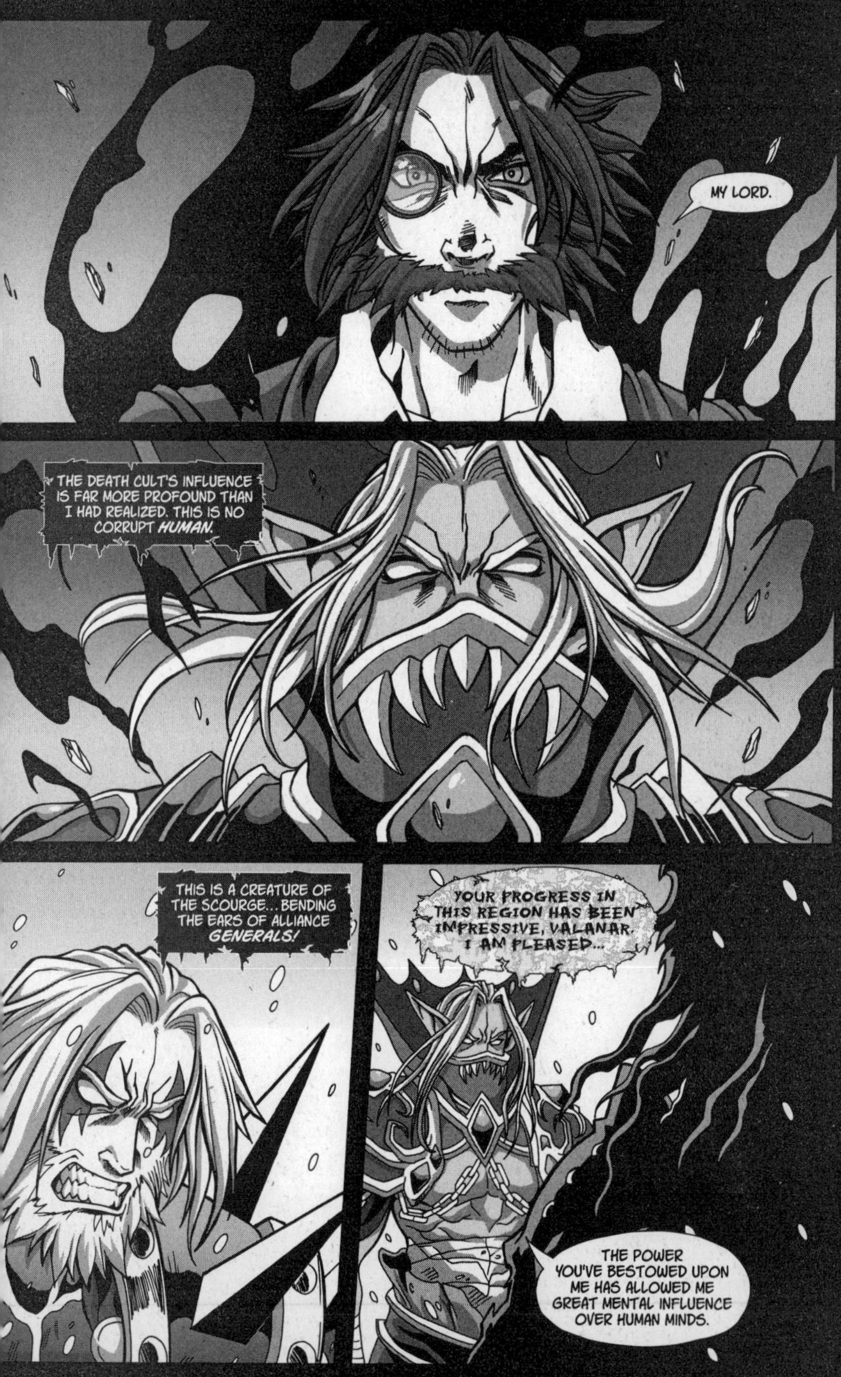
MY LORD.
THE DEATH CULT'S INFLUENCE IS FAR MORE PROFOUND THAN I HAD REALIZED. THIS IS NO CORRUPT *HUMAN*.
THIS IS A CREATURE OF THE SCOURGE...BENDING THE EARS OF ALLIANCE *GENERALS!*
YOUR PROGRESS IN THIS REGION HAS BEEN IMPRESSIVE, VALANAR. I AM PLEASED...
THE POWER YOU'VE BESTOWED UPON ME HAS ALLOWED ME GREAT MENTAL INFLUENCE OVER HUMAN MINDS.

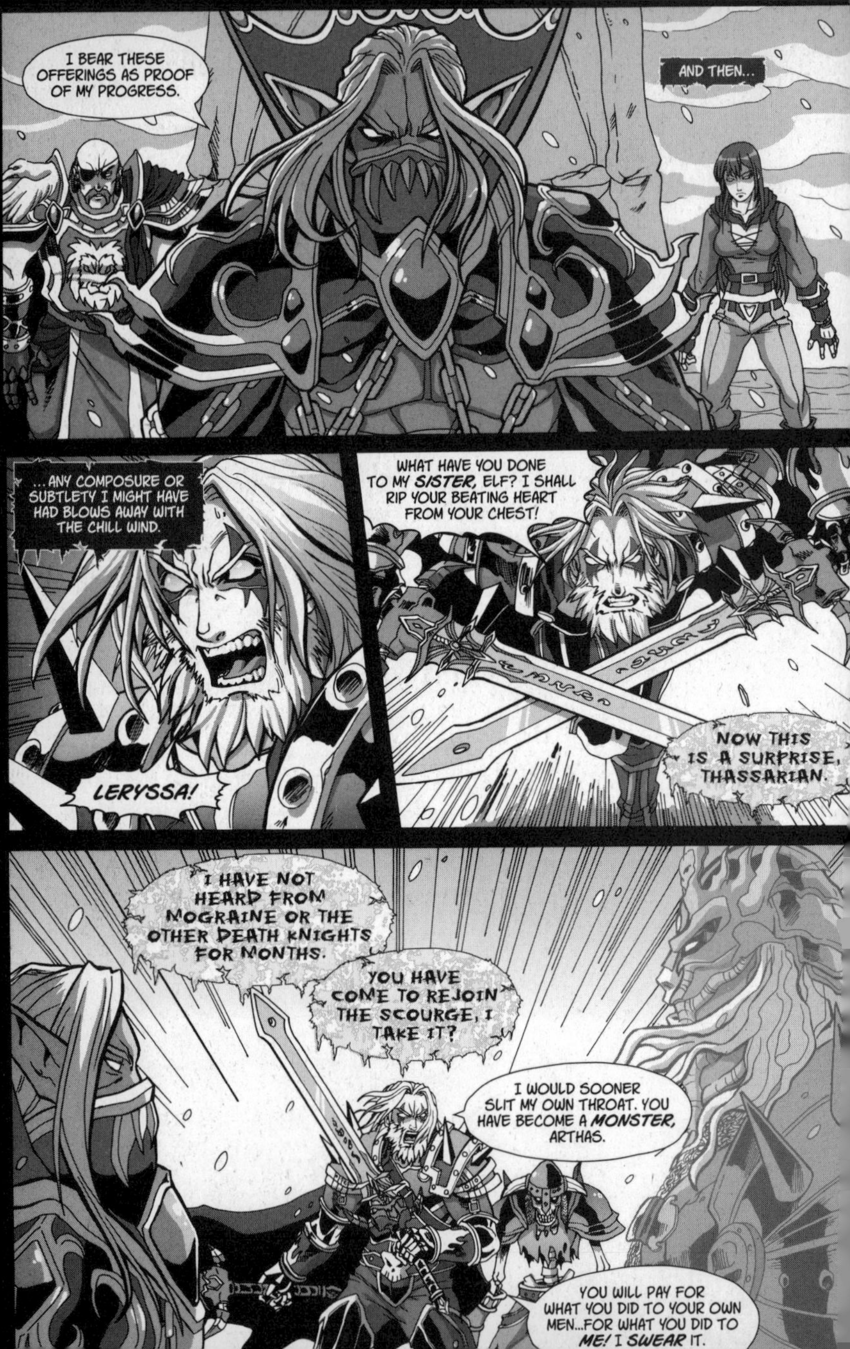
I BEAR THESE OFFERINGS AS PROOF OF MY PROGRESS.
AND THEN...
...ANY COMPOSURE OR SUBTLETY I MIGHT HAVE HAD BLOWS AWAY WITH THE CHILL WIND.
LERYSSA!
WHAT HAVE YOU DONE TO MY *SISTER,* ELF? I SHALL RIP YOUR BEATING HEART FROM YOUR CHEST!
NOW THIS IS A SURPRISE, THASSARIAN.
I HAVE NOT HEARD FROM MOGRAINE OR THE OTHER DEATH KNIGHTS FOR MONTHS.
YOU HAVE COME TO REJOIN THE SCOURGE, I TAKE IT?
I WOULD SOONER SLIT MY OWN THROAT. YOU HAVE BECOME A ***MONSTER,*** ARTHAS.
YOU WILL PAY FOR WHAT YOU DID TO YOUR OWN MEN...FOR WHAT YOU DID TO ***ME!*** I ***SWEAR*** IT.

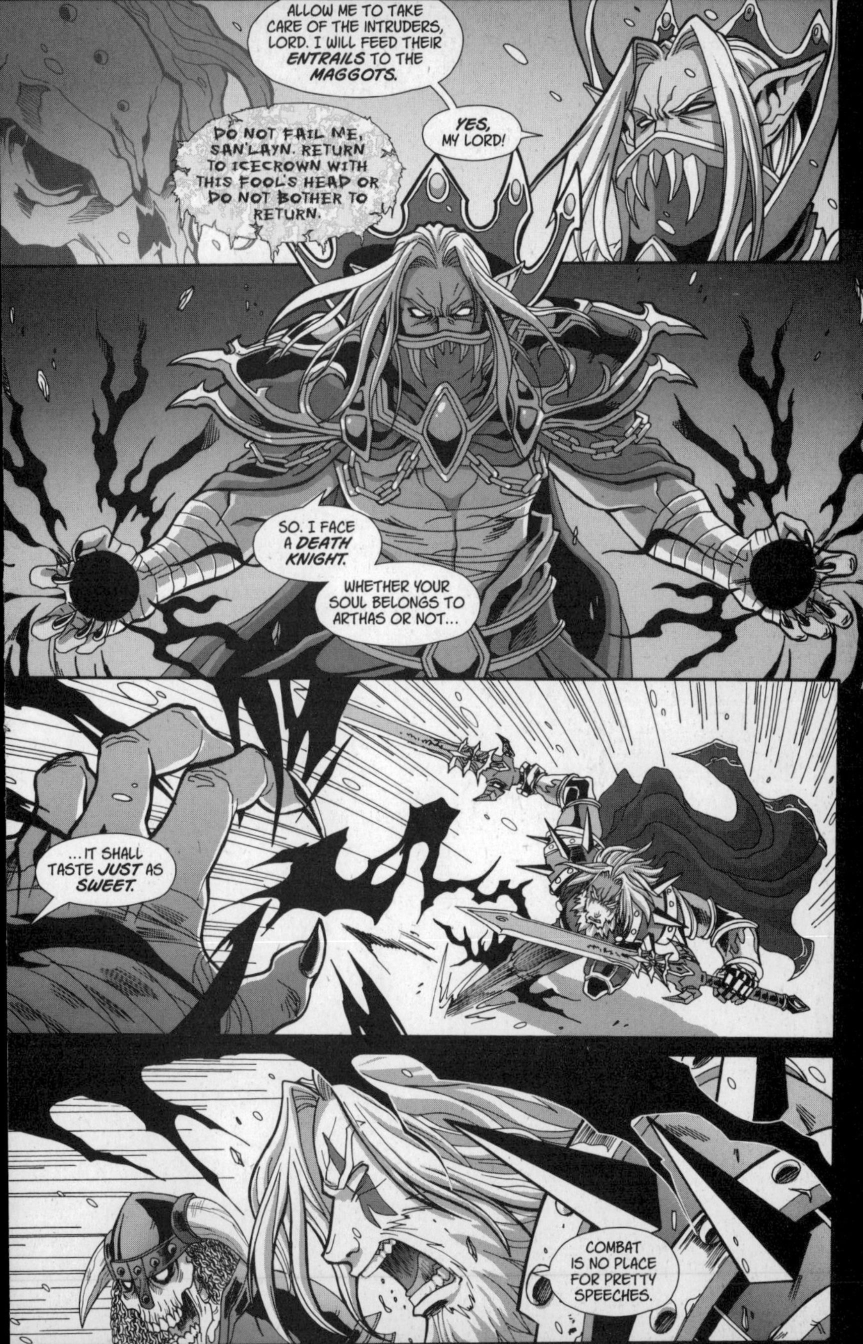
ALLOW ME TO TAKE CARE OF THE INTRUDERS, LORD. I WILL FEED THEIR ENTRAILS TO THE MAGGOTS.
DO NOT FAIL ME, SAN'LAYN. RETURN TO ICECROWN WITH THIS FOOL'S HEAD OR DO NOT BOTHER TO RETURN.
YES, MY LORD!
SO. I FACE A DEATH KNIGHT.
WHETHER YOUR SOUL BELONGS TO ARTHAS OR NOT...
...IT SHALL TASTE JUST AS SWEET.
COMBAT IS NO PLACE FOR PRETTY SPEECHES.

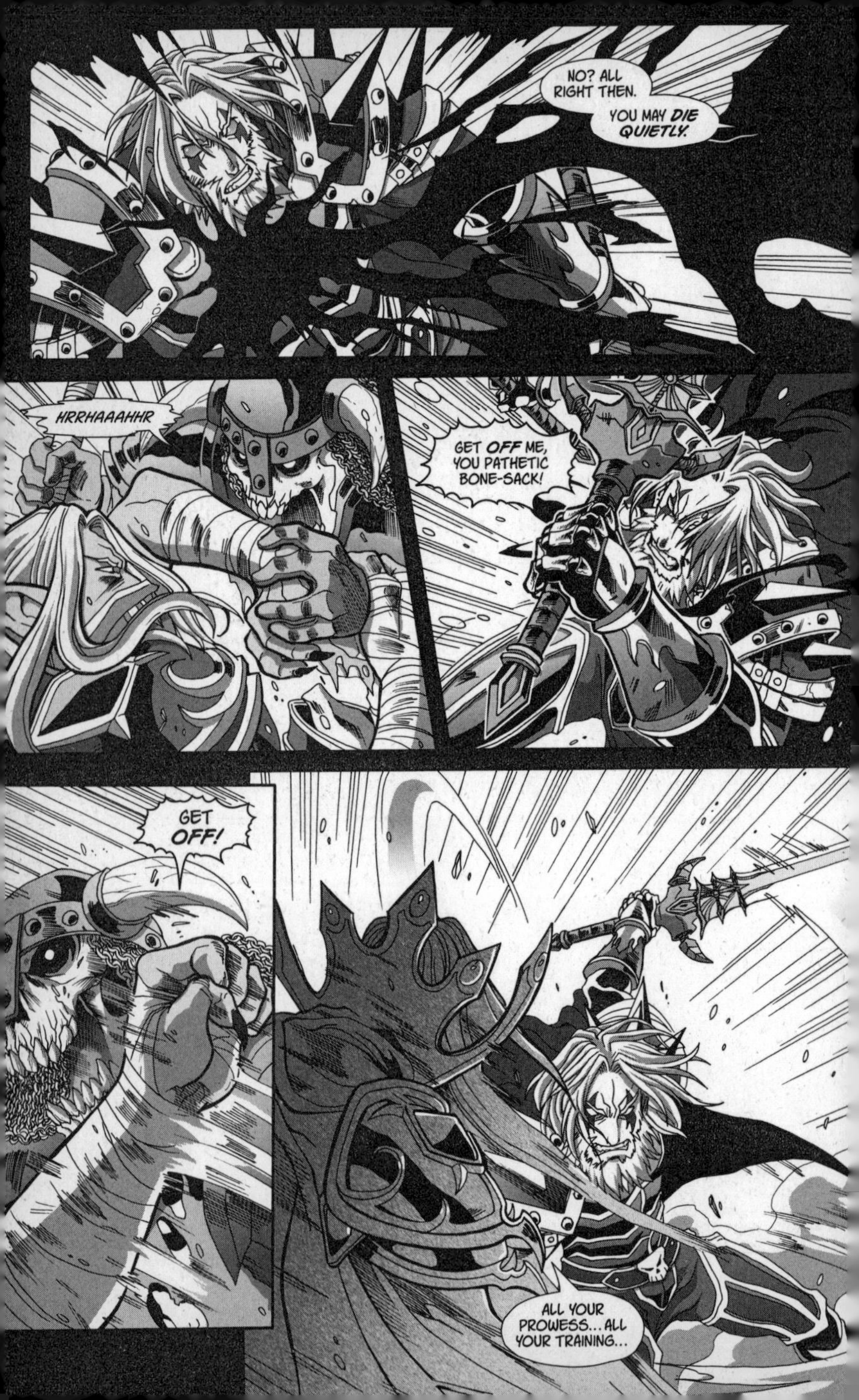
NO? ALL RIGHT THEN.
YOU MAY DIE QUIETLY.
HRRHAAAHHR
GET OFF ME, YOU PATHETIC BONE-SACK!
GET OFF!
ALL YOUR PROWESS... ALL YOUR TRAINING...

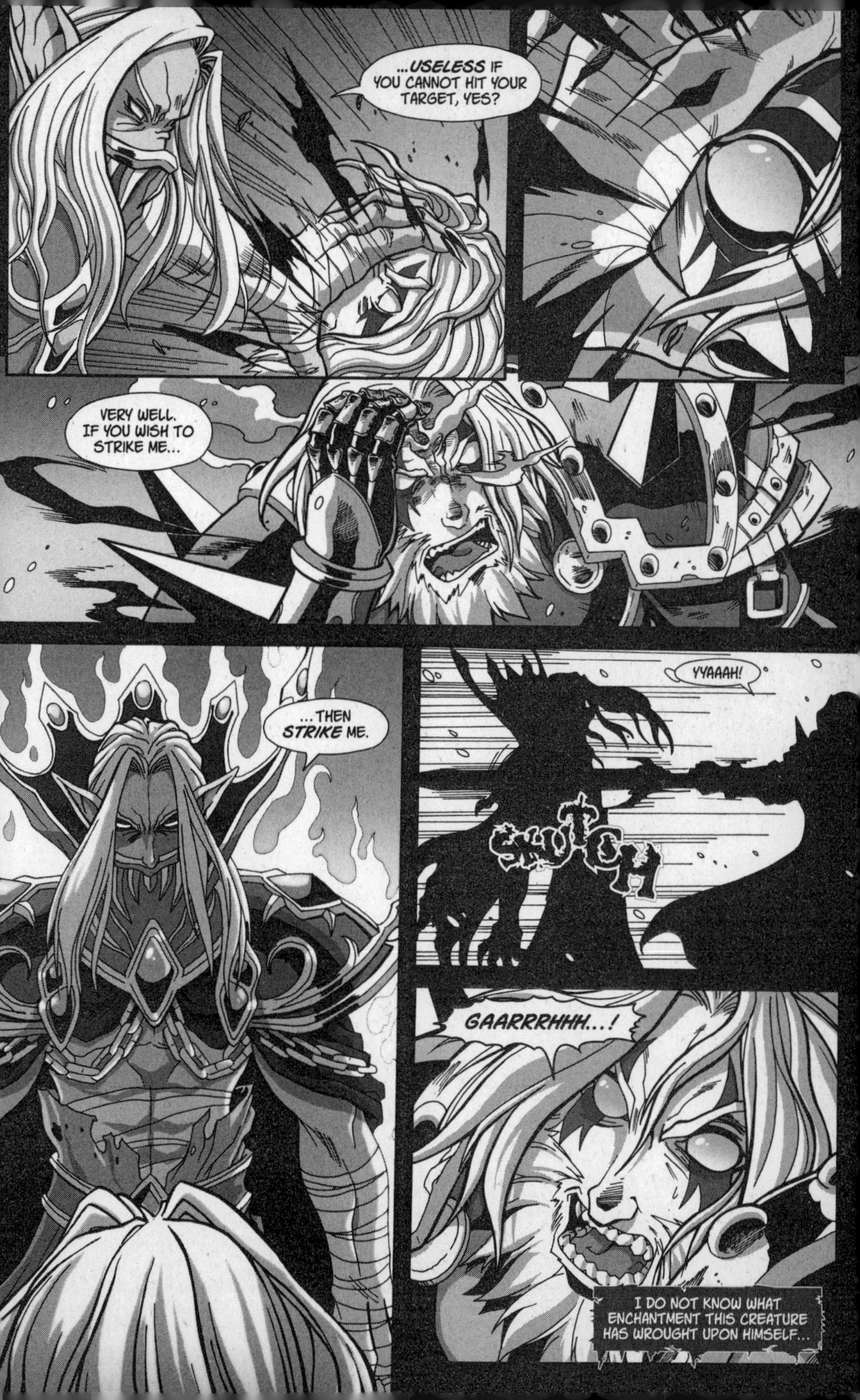
...USELESS IF YOU CANNOT HIT YOUR TARGET, YES?
VERY WELL. IF YOU WISH TO STRIKE ME...
...THEN STRIKE ME.
YYAAAH!
GAARRRHHH...!
I DO NOT KNOW WHAT ENCHANTMENT THIS CREATURE HAS WROUGHT UPON HIMSELF...

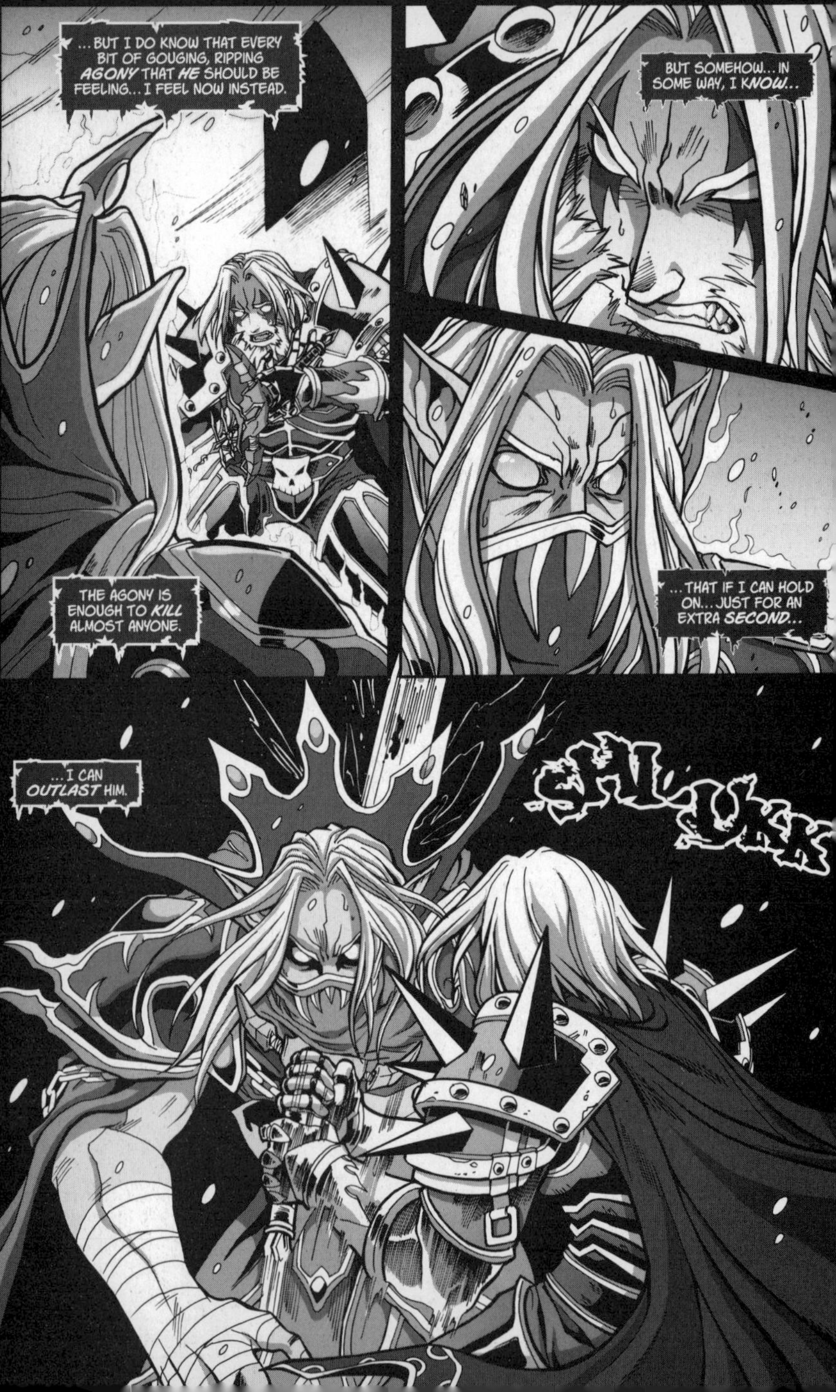
...BUT I DO KNOW THAT EVERY BIT OF GOUGING, RIPPING AGONY THAT HE SHOULD BE FEELING... I FEEL NOW INSTEAD.
THE AGONY IS ENOUGH TO KILL ALMOST ANYONE.
BUT SOMEHOW... IN SOME WAY, I KNOW...
...THAT IF I CAN HOLD ON... JUST FOR AN EXTRA SECOND...
...I CAN OUTLAST HIM.
SHLUKK

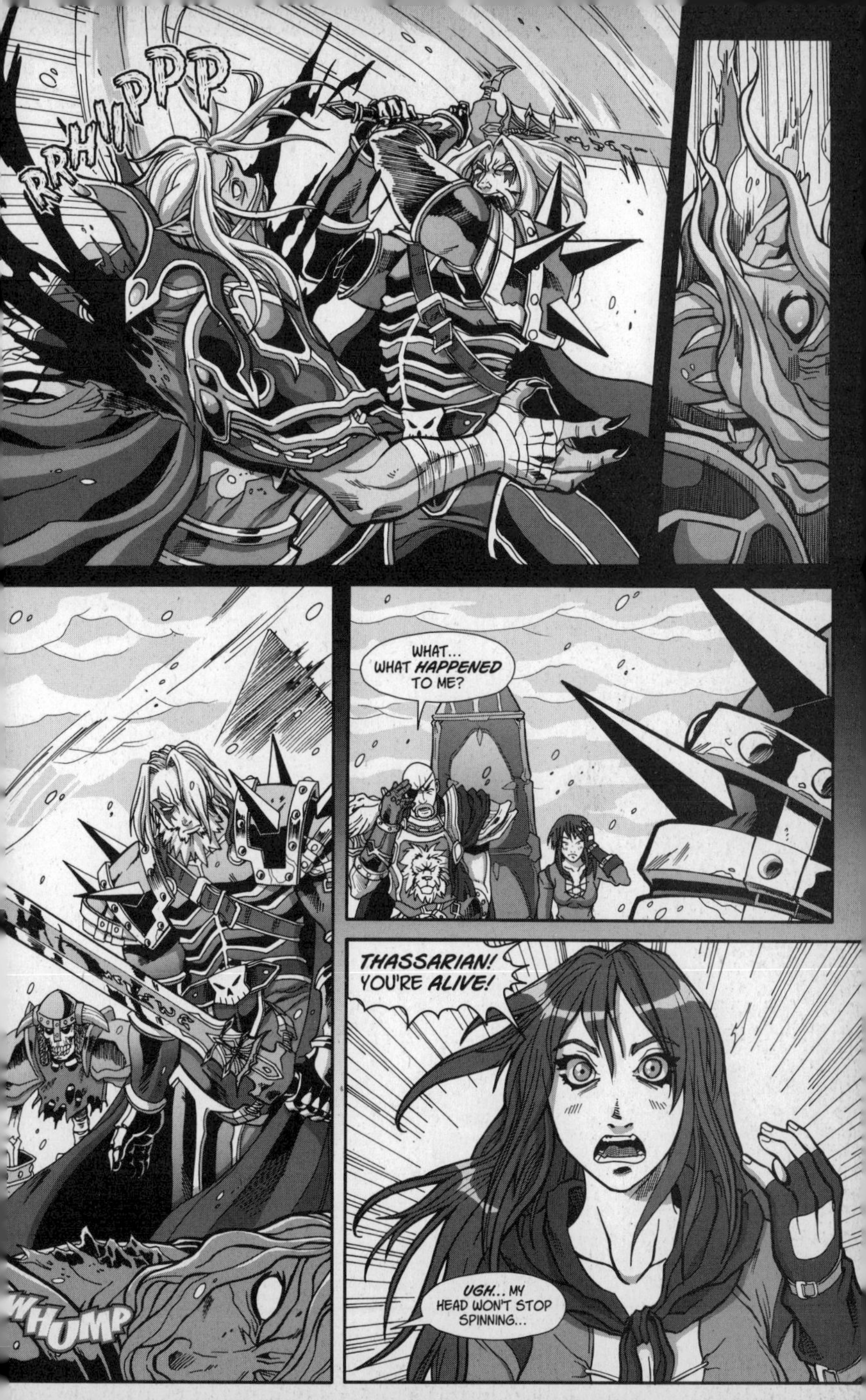
RRHIIPPPP
WHUMP
WHAT... WHAT HAPPENED TO ME?
THASSARIAN! YOU'RE ALIVE!
UGH... MY HEAD WON'T STOP SPINNING...

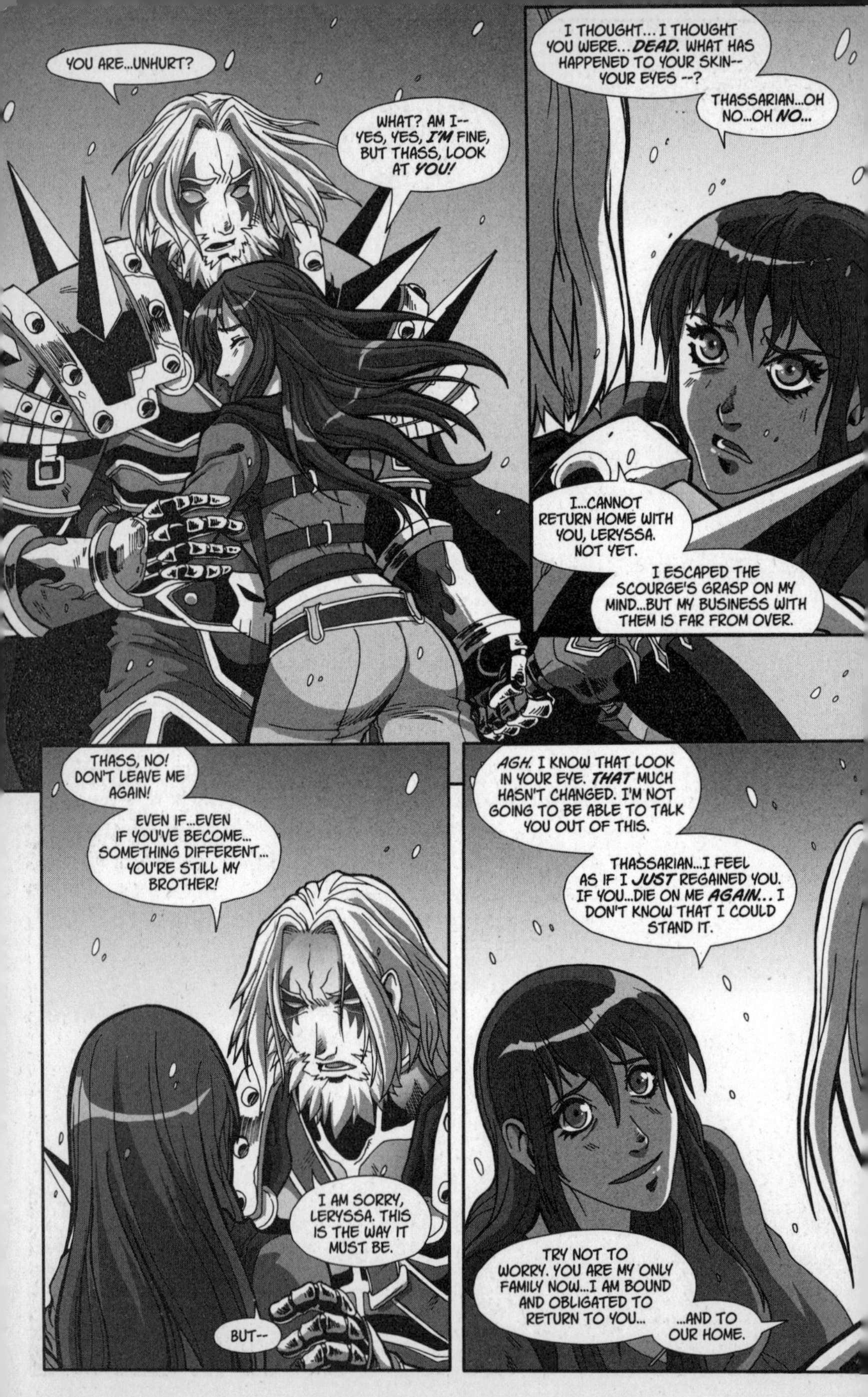
YOU ARE...UNHURT?
WHAT? AM I-- YES, YES, I'M FINE, BUT THASS, LOOK AT YOU!
I THOUGHT... I THOUGHT YOU WERE... DEAD. WHAT HAS HAPPENED TO YOUR SKIN-- YOUR EYES --?
THASSARIAN...OH NO...OH NO...
I...CANNOT RETURN HOME WITH YOU, LERYSSA. NOT YET.
I ESCAPED THE SCOURGE'S GRASP ON MY MIND...BUT MY BUSINESS WITH THEM IS FAR FROM OVER.
THASS, NO! DON'T LEAVE ME AGAIN!
EVEN IF...EVEN IF YOU'VE BECOME... SOMETHING DIFFERENT... YOU'RE STILL MY BROTHER!
I AM SORRY, LERYSSA. THIS IS THE WAY IT MUST BE.
BUT--
AGH. I KNOW THAT LOOK IN YOUR EYE. THAT MUCH HASN'T CHANGED. I'M NOT GOING TO BE ABLE TO TALK YOU OUT OF THIS.
THASSARIAN...I FEEL AS IF I JUST REGAINED YOU. IF YOU...DIE ON ME AGAIN... I DON'T KNOW THAT I COULD STAND IT.
TRY NOT TO WORRY. YOU ARE MY ONLY FAMILY NOW...I AM BOUND AND OBLIGATED TO RETURN TO YOU...
...AND TO OUR HOME.

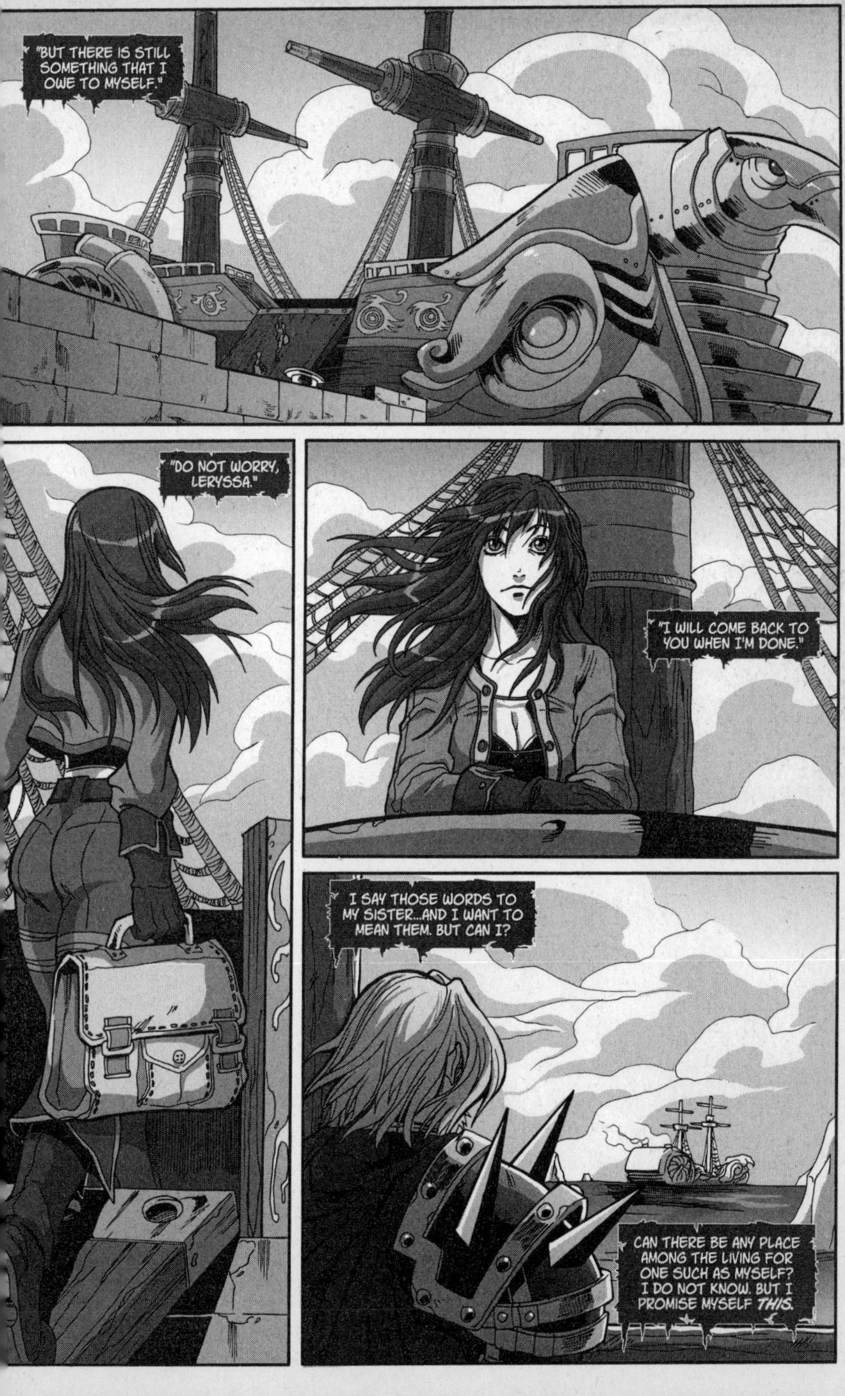
"BUT THERE IS STILL SOMETHING THAT I OWE TO MYSELF."
"DO NOT WORRY, LERYSSA."
"I WILL COME BACK TO YOU WHEN I'M DONE."
I SAY THOSE WORDS TO MY SISTER...AND I WANT TO MEAN THEM. BUT CAN I?
CAN THERE BE ANY PLACE AMONG THE LIVING FOR ONE SUCH AS MYSELF? I DO NOT KNOW. BUT I PROMISE MYSELF *THIS*.

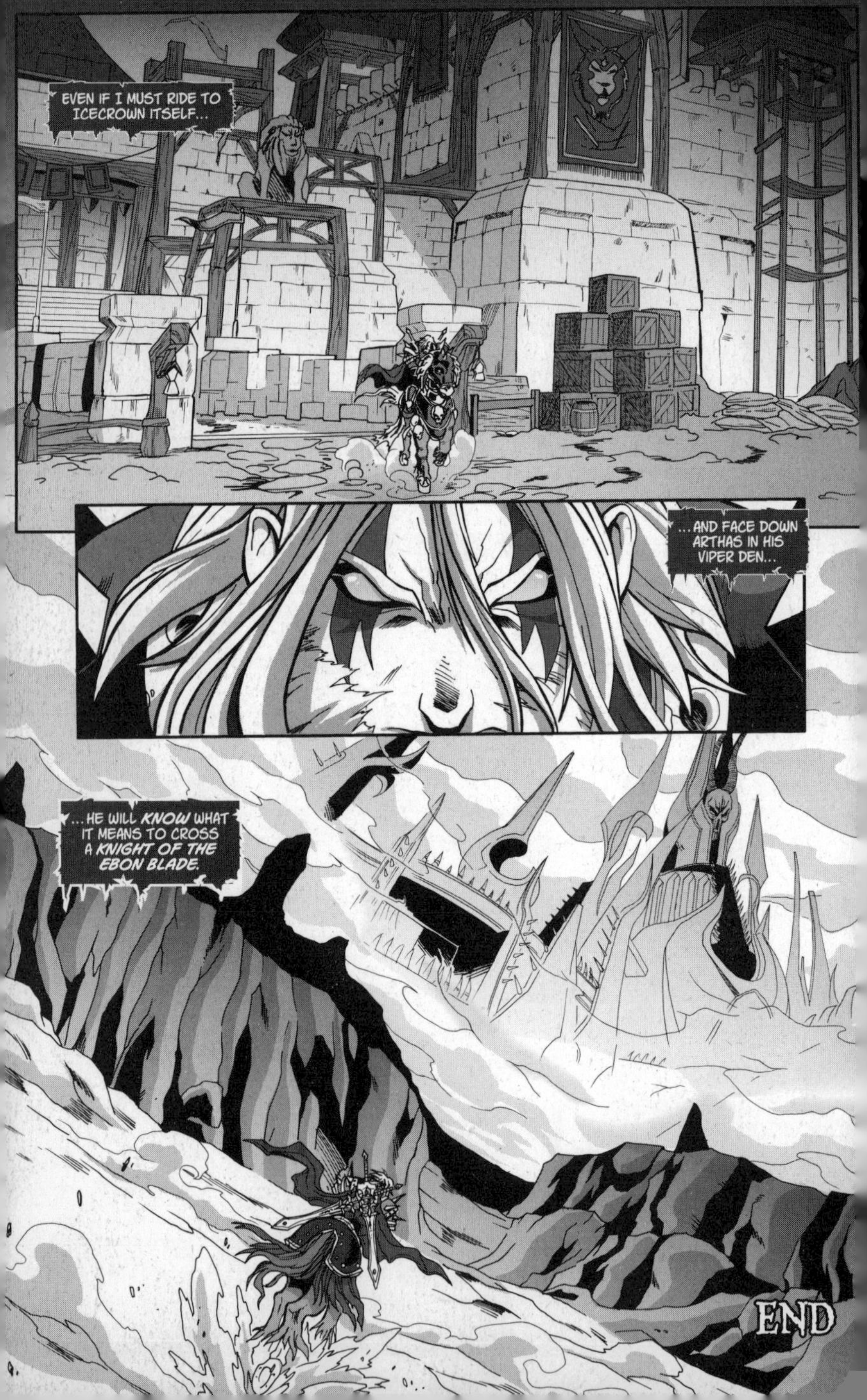
EVEN IF I MUST RIDE TO ICECROWN ITSELF...
...AND FACE DOWN ARTHAS IN HIS VIPER DEN...
...HE WILL *KNOW* WHAT IT MEANS TO CROSS A *KNIGHT OF THE EBON BLADE.*
END

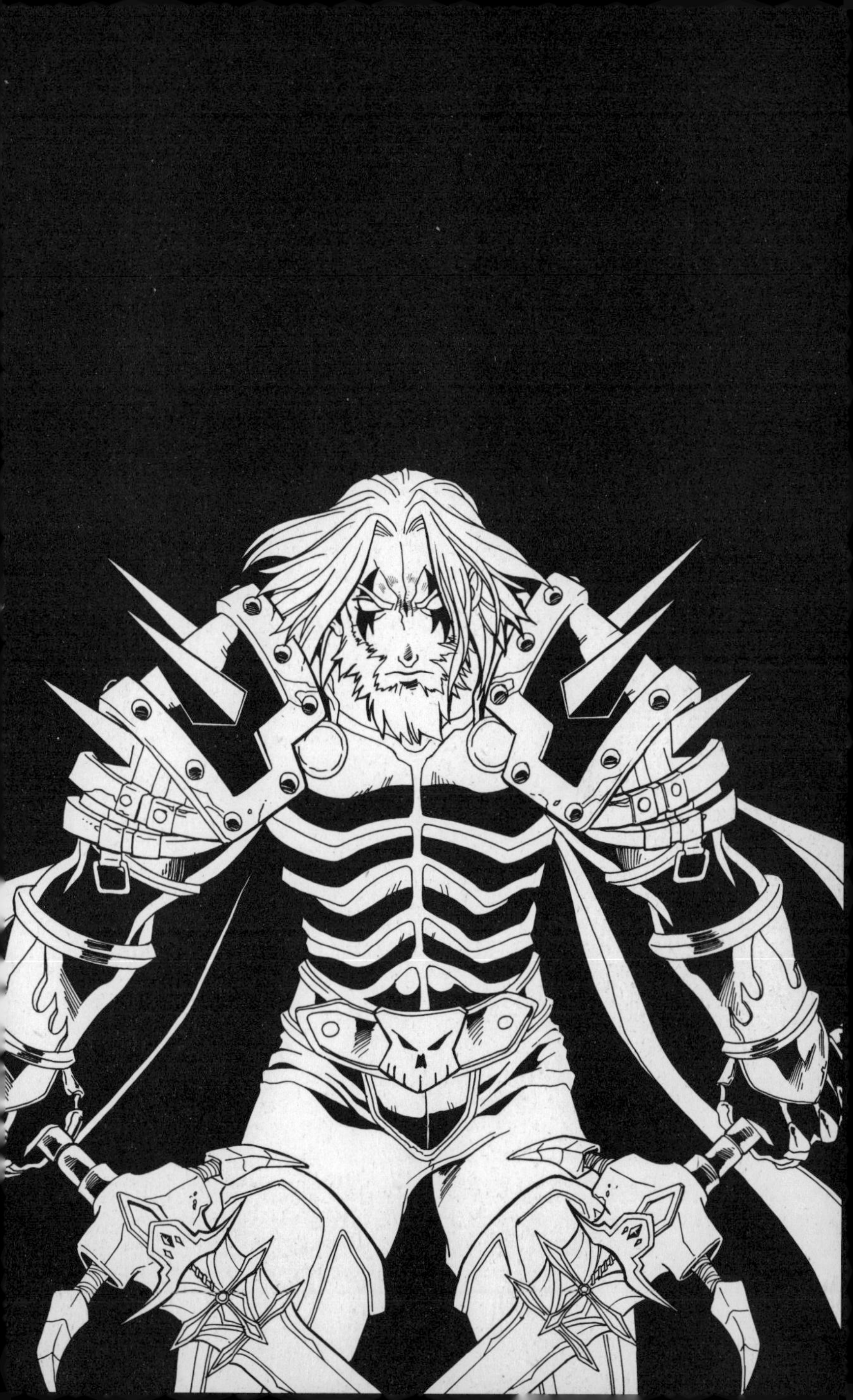

SPECIAL THANKS

On behalf of TOKYOPOP and Blizzard, we hope you enjoyed *Warcraft: Death Knight*. It's our very first class-based *Warcraft* manga, and I hope you found it as thrilling and gut-wrenching as I did. While you're taking a breather from all of the pulse-pounding action of *Warcraft: Death Knight*, brace yourself for even **more** class-based *Warcraft* titles. *Mage* and *Shaman* are currently in production!

Of course, none of this would be possible without the excellent team at Blizzard. They continue to impress me with their devoted stewardship of the *Warcraft* world, their dedication to quality, and their strong story sense. Many thanks to Jason Bischoff, Micky Neilson, Rob Tokar, James Waugh, Samwise Didier, Tommy Newcomer and Chris Metzen. I've reserved a special shout-out to Evelyn Fredericksen. Evelyn is Blizzard's historian and overall lore master. During a recent story session with the Blizzard team, she amazed me with her incredibly vast knowledge of the *Warcraft* world. She's an amazing resource!

I came aboard the *Death Knight* train after it had left the station, but I already knew the story was going to be something special. That's because my old friend Dan Jolley wrote the script. Dan and I have worked on many projects together, including his recent run on *Toy Story* for BOOM! He's an incredibly versatile writer, but I think he outdid himself with *Death Knight*. It has all the hardcore action you expect from a *Warcraft* story, but what really hooked me was Thassarian's tragic journey. Dan, you managed to make me really care about Thassarian!

Rocio Zucchi is the amazing artist who brought Dan's words to life, and I am very grateful for all of her talent and hard work! When the deadline was looming close, Rocio rose to the challenge and delivered! I'd also like to shine the spotlight on Matias Timarchi and his amazing art team at Altercomics Studios. Without their Herculean efforts, Rocio's glorious pencils would not have been inked and toned so wonderfully against a brutal deadline!

I'd like to thank the entire gang at TOKYOPOP. Troy Lewter and Marco Pavia, I appreciate you giving me the keys to the *Warcraft* kingdom. And if anyone knows the *Warcraft* kingdom, it's Michael Paolilli. Sure, Michael letters these books and makes various art fixes, but he's also able to give us fantastic reference material! When asked, Michael signs on to his Warcraft account at work and strolls through Azeroth, taking "pictures" of everything our artists will need to draw these books. Michael, there are people reading this right now who would kill for your job!

Lastly, I want to express my gratitude to all of the fans! Without you, these books wouldn't exist at all. So, do me a favor and buy a **ton** of copies so we can keep making compelling *Warcraft* stories!

- Paul Morrissey
  Editor

CREATOR BIO'S

DAN JOLLEY

Dan Jolley has been writing professionally since age 19, and has written novels, video games, and lots and lots of comic books. Dan authored "How to Win Friends," "Miles to Go" and "Crusader's Blood," short stories for *Warcraft: Legends* Volumes 1-3. More information on Dan can be found at his website, www.danjolley.com. He lives in Georgia.

ROCIO ZUCCHI

Rocio Zucchi was born in Buenos Aires, Argentina, daughter of an Italian mother and an Argentinian father. She began to draw at a very young age. When she was 13, she met Fernando Heinz Furukawa (her fiancé) who helped her develop her artistic abilities. Rocio began her career as a collaborator for local books and magazines (such as *Time:5*, written by Mauro Mantella, featuring art by Fernando H.F., which will soon be published in the US).

Rocio recently contributed art for the *Street Fighter Tribute* and *Darkstalkers Tribute* books from Udon Studios. She also works as a colorist. In addition, she is working on a webcomic series called *Heist* (created by Brendan McGinley with art by Andres Ponce).

Rocio is no stranger to *Warcraft* and TOKYOPOP. She inked the story "Crusaders Blood" from *Warcraft: Legends* vol. 3, and contributed to *Tantric Stripfighter Trina* (published by TOKYOPOP). Rocio is one of the key members of Altercomics Studios, and this is her first major assignment as an artist.

INTERVIEW WITH DAN JOLLEY

We pestered *Warcraft: Legends* and *Death Knight* writer Dan Jolley with a horde of questions. Always the good soldier, Dan gave us some very interesting answers!

Are you a Warcraft fan, and if so, how long have you played the game?

Yeah, I'm a pretty big fan. I don't have as much time to play as, say, your average raiding guild member, but I've been playing for about three years now, and I have two characters up to level 80, along with about a dozen others ranging from 10 to 70.

How did you get involved with the Warcraft manga?

I was already working for TOKYOPOP, writing my original *Alex Unlimited* prose novels and the manga based on Erin Hunter's *Warriors* books, when I heard that they'd signed a deal with Blizzard to do these. So I immediately called up TOKYOPOP editorial and acted obnoxious enough for long enough that they gave me some of the work. :)

What challenges did you face writing the short stories? Which story was you favorite (if you have one)?

Well, Blizzard is very protective of *World of Warcraft*--rightly and understandably so--and the biggest thing I had to do was just to make sure what I was writing fit with their vision of how they want their IP represented. Y'know, inject my own ideas and my own creativity into an already **VERY** well-defined world. But that's what mainstream comic book writers do every day, and I've done a pretty decent amount of work for mainstream publishers, so I felt right at home. I think my favorite story so far is *Crusader's Blood*...just 'cause it's so unrelentingly **BLEAK**. I don't usually turn stuff in that's quite that dark. :)

What were the challenges you faced in writing *Death Knight*?

My short stories all had main characters that I just made up, so I had a certain degree of freedom as to how to handle them and what to do with them. For *Death Knight,* on the other hand, the protagonist is Thassarian, a well-known character who appears in the game. The degree of familiarity players have with him is directly proportional to the amount of attention Blizzard paid to my script...so I had to be **REALLY** careful. It came out beautifully, though, if I do say so myself.

Short story vs. full volume story--how are they alike/different? How different/same are the challenges for each?

They're both pretty similar; I kind of joked in another interview that the only real difference is that the full volume takes longer to write. But I think I'll revise that here, because in a lot of ways a full-volume book is easier to write than a short story. With a short, you really have to get in, achieve an effect, and get out, and sometimes that's tough to do when your space is tightly constrained. The *Warcraft Legends* stories aren't THAT short, though, so it's not too difficult.

Anything else you'd like to say to fans about your DK book?

If you ever get the chance to write dialogue for a cranky, sword-wielding dead guy, I urge you to take it. It's a lot of fun. :)

So what other projects are you working on?

This is one of the most frustrating parts about being a freelance writer. I'm working on five different projects right now, and thanks to some truly frightening non-disclosure agreements, I can't talk openly about **ANY** of them. Let's see...what can I say in a sufficiently cryptic fashion... I'm writing dialogue for two video games based on major motion pictures...I'm scripting some graphic novels based on a well-known animated TV series...and it looks as if I might be writing some mainstream comics based on an IP very familiar to everyone reading this. There! A lot of words that say very little! I think I'm safe.

Now for the most important question in the world: Shark versus Grizzly Bear--who would win in a battle royale?

Grizzly Bear all the way, man! Bears rule!

A SNEAK PEEK AT OUR FORTHCOMING NEW TRILOY...

WARCRAFT®
DRAGONS OF OUTLAND™

Acclaimed writer Richard A. Knaak and superstar artist Jae-Hwan Kim are teaming up once again! TOKYOPOP and Blizzard are proud to announce *Warcraft: Dragons of Outland*--the thrilling continuation of *Warcraft: The Sunwell Trilogy!*

At the end of *Warcraft: The Sunwell Trilogy,* blue dragon Tyrygosa and human paladin Jorad Mace left the Ghostlands... but their story is far from over! The duo are drawn into a dark portal and into Outland...where they encounter a group of dragons unlike any Tyri has ever seen. Observing all of this is Ragnok Bloodreaver, a mysterious death knight with a dark agenda...

I wish I could tell you more, but I am sworn to secrecy! However, I can present a few sketches as a sneak preview! And don't miss our interview with Richard A. Knaak! If you're lucky, he might just reveal a few more juicy story tidbits...

Look for *Warcraft: Dragons of Outland* in **June 2010**. Trust me, it's going to be worth the wait!

-FORGING A COVER-

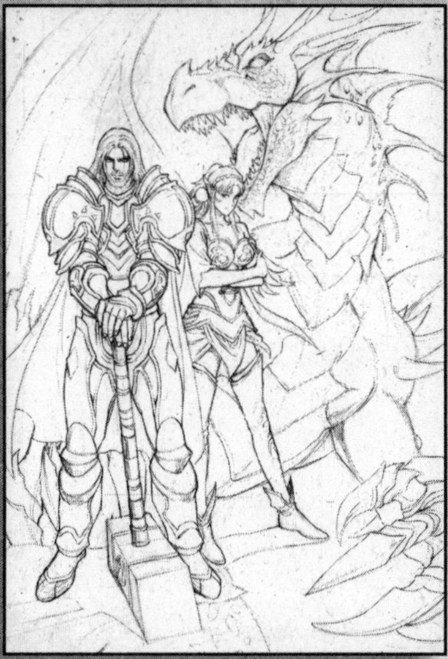

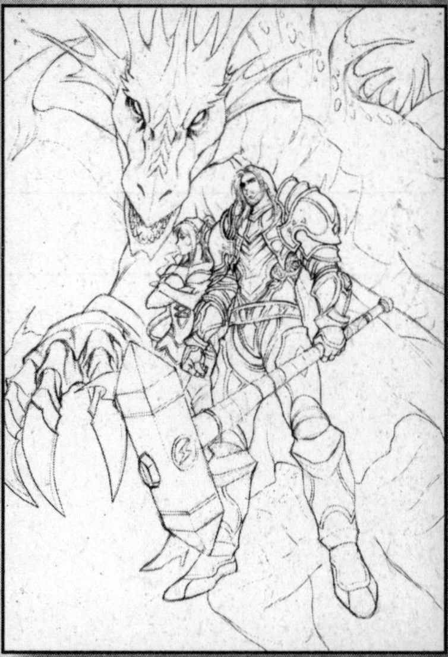

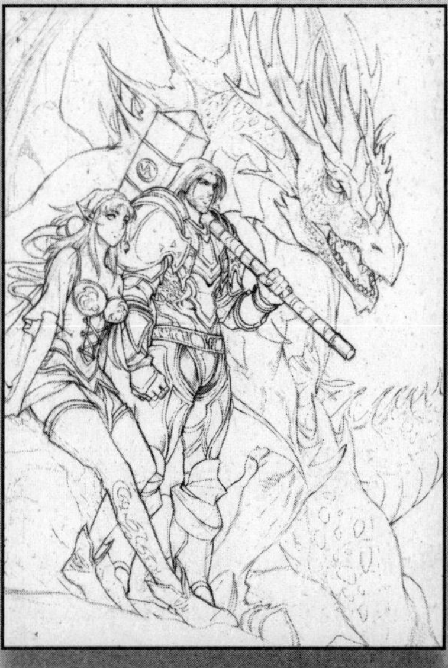

Here are Jae-Hwan's cover concepts. We ultimately picked the bottom one, which has the strongest composition of the three.

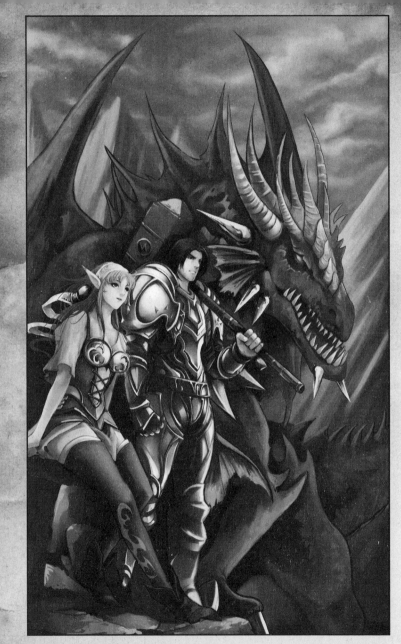

Here's the final version of Jae-Hwan's spectacular cover!
I can't wait until you see it in its full-color glory!

-FORGING A CAST-
TYRI

Here's Jae-Hwan's concept sketch of Tyri in her elf form. Expect plenty more flirting between Tyri and Jorad in *Dragons of Outland...*

JORAD:
OLD SUNWELL ARMOR

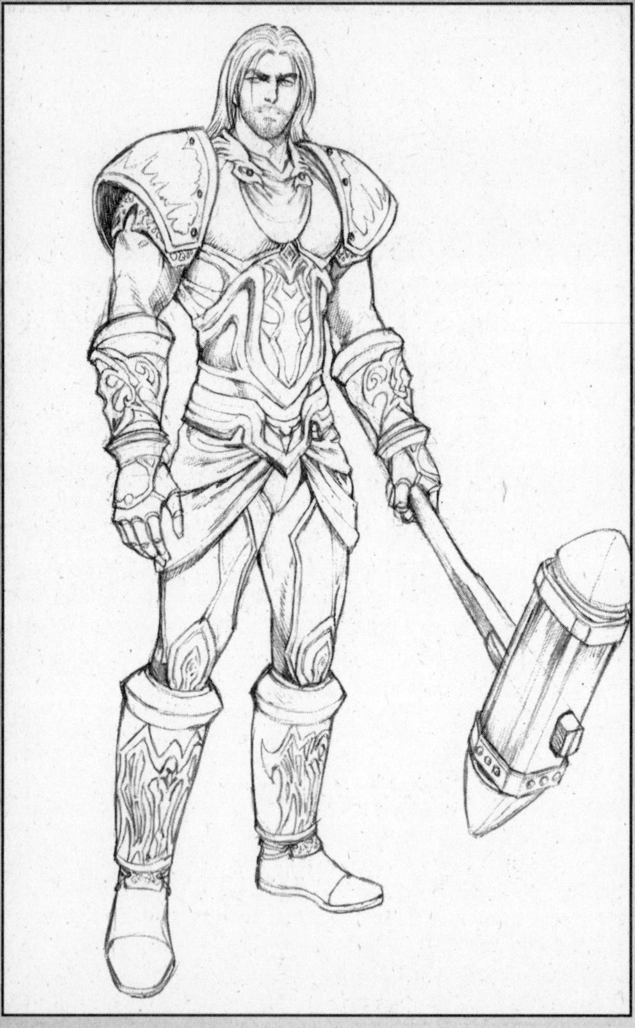

For old time's sake, here's a sketch of Jorad in his Sunwell armor...which gets an awesome upgrade for the new series!

JORAD:
NEW DRAGONS ARMOR

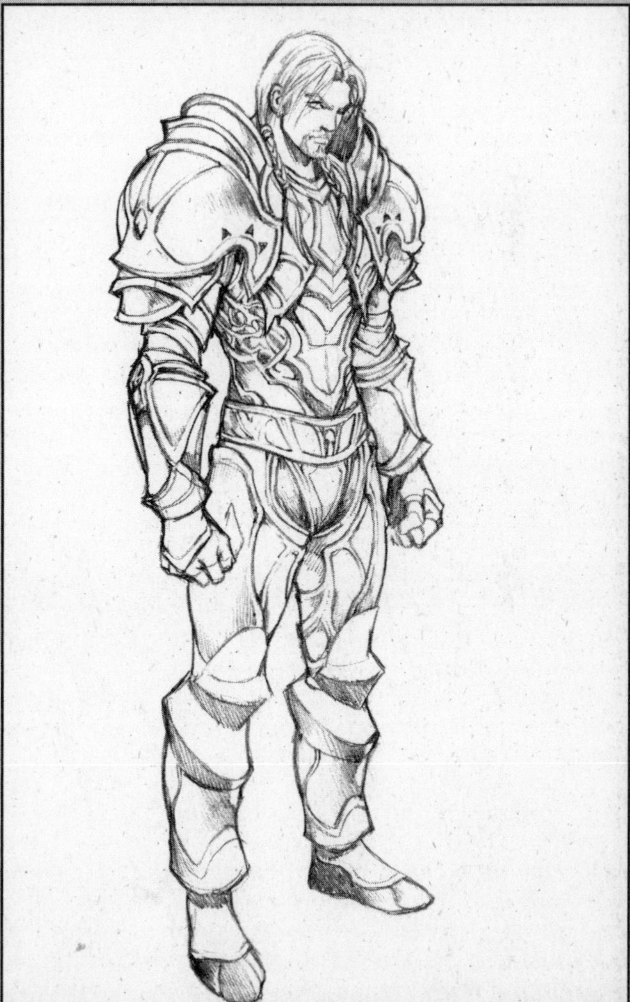

Here's Jorad's new armor that will be featured in *Dragons of Outland.* If you look closely, you can see that Jorad is also sporting some cool braids!

INTERVIEW WITH RICHARD KNAAK

Here's a special treat for all of you *Warcraft* fans! We sat down with writer Richard Knaack and asked him about *Warcraft: Dragons of Outland*--the exciting sequel to *Warcraft: The Sunwell Trilogy!* Enjoy!

Hello, Richard! First of all, many *Warcraft* fans have been extremely enthusiastic about the first manga series you wrote--*The Sunwell Trilogy*. Can you tell us a little bit about that project and how it came together? What were the biggest challenges in writing such an epic story?

I had already worked with TOKYOPOP on the *Ragnarok* series and Pocket on the *Warcraft* novels, so, when the idea of a manga concerning *Warcraft* came up, apparently both TP and Blizzard decided I should be the one to write it. I was honored. The first point they made was that we would be introducing a lot of non-*Warcraft* people to this series, too, so the first volume had to set up matters quite a lot. The script went back and forth with TP and Blizzard and the characters came together nicely. They were especially pleased with Anveena and Kalec, the most pivotal.

In truth, the biggest challenge was fitting the entire story in three volumes. The world was rich enough that we could have done twelve. :)

You also wrote a series of short stories for the *Warcraft: Legends* anthologies. Did you find that writing shorter stories presented a different set of challenges? Did you approach the short stories differently?

The shorter stories were definitely challenging in a different manner. I had to condense much of the background and yet have the story move on. One helpful aspect was that each of my stories for Vol. 1-4 were part of one larger story. That enabled me to build on the previous, rather than start over each time. The story for Vol. 5 offered some challenge in that I had to tie it to my forthcoming novel, *Stormrage*, and yet not give away too much. I think it worked well.

On your *Warcraft* manga, you've had the extreme privilige of working with such an incredible artist as Jae-Hwan Kim. Do you find that you now write with his style in mind? What's it like having Jae-Hwan breathe life into your words? Is there any particular

image or page that took you by surprise or really impressed you?

I tend to think of everything in terms of Jae-Hwan's art now, but, fortunately, that hasn't hindered the other artists I've worked with. Jae-Hwan's art is truly epic and he seems to enjoy the two-page spreads I ask of him. His dragons are fantastic and when he first revealed Trag in the second volume, I was blown away.

Everyone is very excited about the new *Warcraft* trilogy you're creating with Jae-Hwan, which is called *Dragons of Outland*. Can you tell us a little bit about the story and how it ties in with the *Sunwell Trilogy* and the Trag storyline featured in *Warcraft: Legends*?

The trilogy ties in more with Sunwell and will concern the nether dragons--no surprise there based on the title. We will see the return of Jo-rad Mace and Tyri, both of whom had personal troubles. You will get to see some of Outland's fantastic aspects and meet some surprising characters.

What other *Warcraft* projects are you working on?

As mentioned, I am also finishing up *Stormrage* for Pocket. It concerns Malfurion and the Nightmare and ties in significantly with many coming game events. It is due out at the end of February, I believe. *Legends Vol. 5* has an excerpt of it. I am also working on a single volume manga concerning the Mages, which will be out in 2010. Not much I can reveal on that one just yet!

Do you have a website?

Go to *richardaknaak.com* for more on my Blizzard projects, my own *Dragonrealm* series, *Dragonlance*, and others!

WARCRAFT

LEGENDS
VOLUME FIVE

PREVIEW

Hello, dear reader. You've truly reached the final pages of *Warcraft: Death Knight*. You've read the special thanks and the interviews, and you're still looking for a *Warcraft* fix. Well, as a reward for your journey, we're proud to present an exciting excerpt from *Warcraft: Legends Vol. 5!*

FIRST GUARDIAN

Thousands of years ago, when the magical city-state of Dalaran was under siege by demons from the Burning Legion, it was discovered no single mage had a chance against these creatures...so a secret order of magi was created. From acclaimed comic book writer Louise Simonson and sensational artist Seung-Hui Kye comes the never-before-revealed origin story of the first Guardian of Tirisfal.

Warcraft: Legends Vol. 5 is available now!

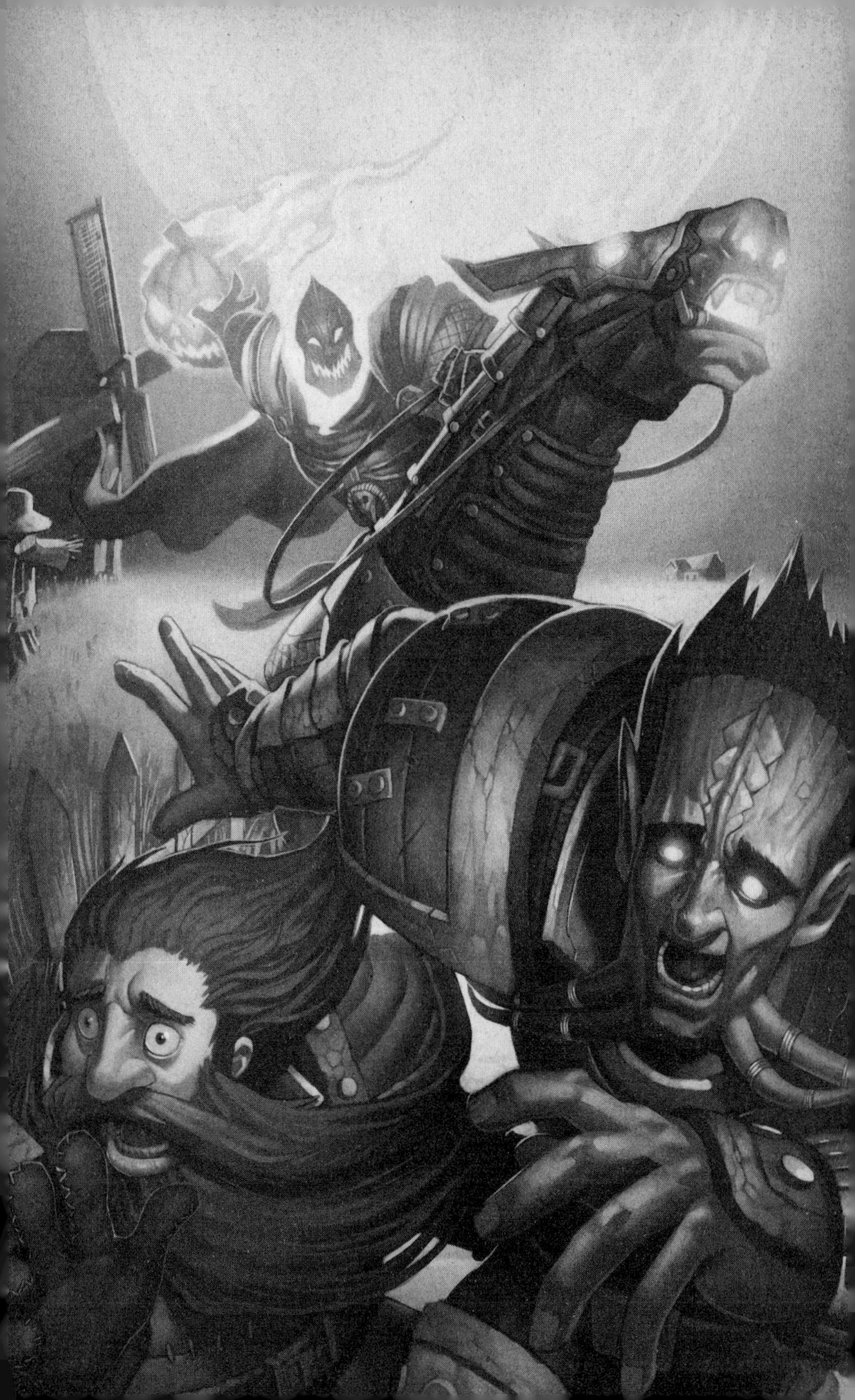

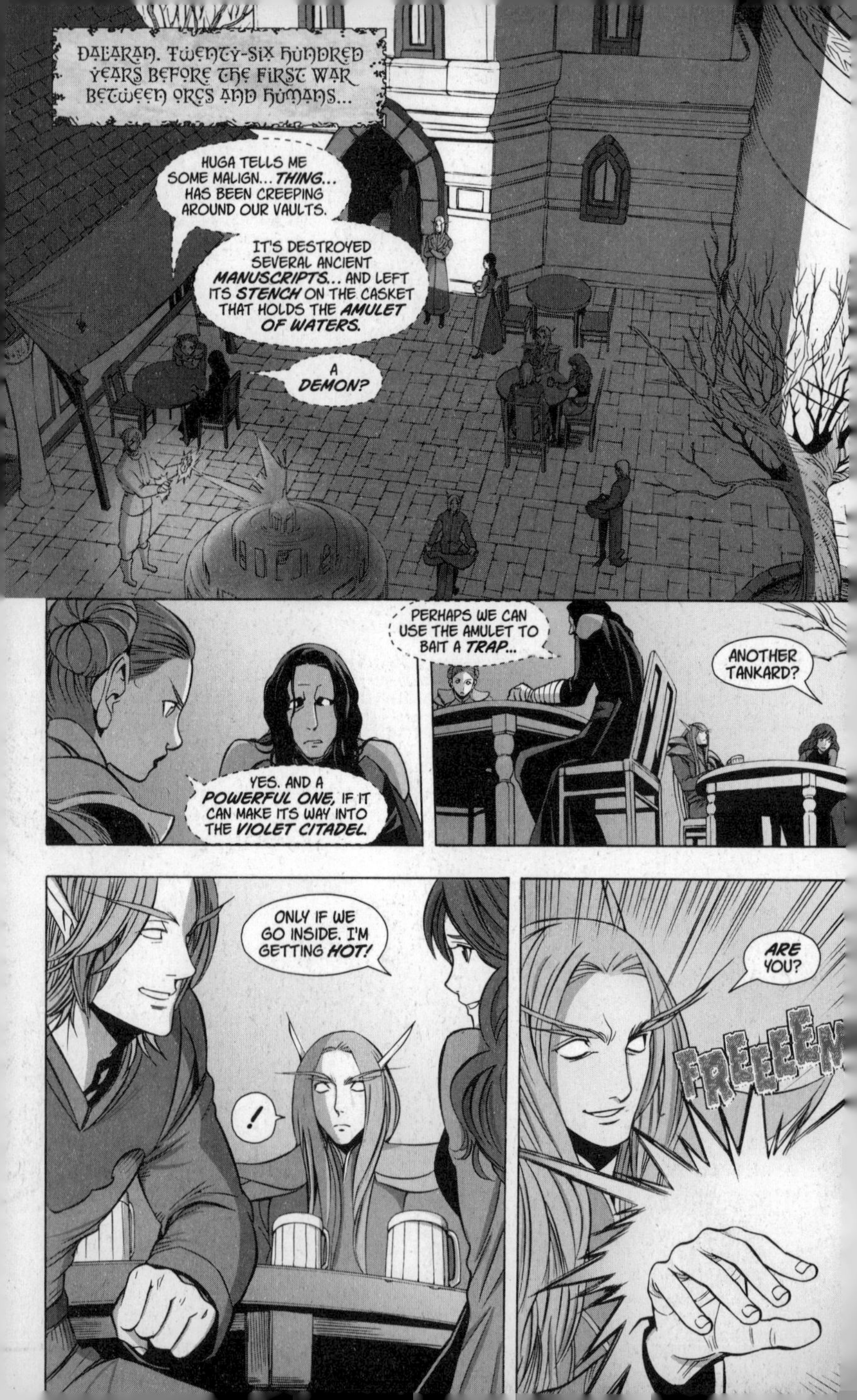
DALARAN. TWENTY-SIX HUNDRED YEARS BEFORE THE FIRST WAR BETWEEN ORCS AND HUMANS...
HUGA TELLS ME SOME MALIGN... THING... HAS BEEN CREEPING AROUND OUR VAULTS.
IT'S DESTROYED SEVERAL ANCIENT MANUSCRIPTS... AND LEFT ITS STENCH ON THE CASKET THAT HOLDS THE AMULET OF WATERS.
A DEMON?
YES. AND A POWERFUL ONE, IF IT CAN MAKE ITS WAY INTO THE VIOLET CITADEL.
PERHAPS WE CAN USE THE AMULET TO BAIT A TRAP...
ANOTHER TANKARD?
ONLY IF WE GO INSIDE. I'M GETTING HOT!
!
ARE YOU?
FREEEEN

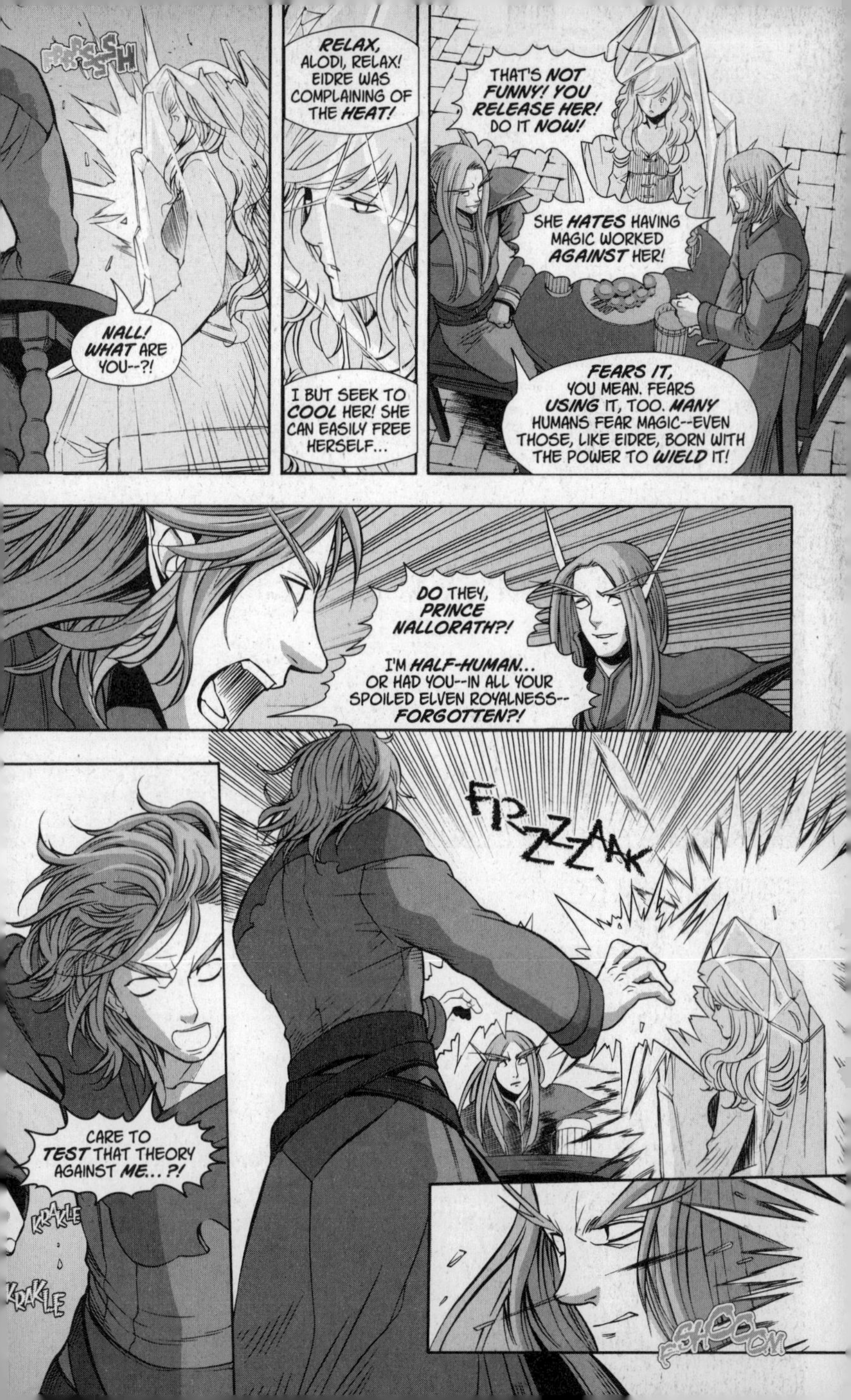
NALL! WHAT ARE YOU--?!
RELAX, ALODI, RELAX! EIDRE WAS COMPLAINING OF THE **HEAT!**
I BUT SEEK TO **COOL** HER! SHE CAN EASILY FREE HERSELF...
THAT'S **NOT FUNNY! YOU RELEASE HER!** DO IT **NOW!**
SHE **HATES** HAVING MAGIC WORKED **AGAINST** HER!
FEARS IT, YOU MEAN. FEARS **USING** IT, TOO. **MANY** HUMANS FEAR MAGIC--EVEN THOSE, LIKE EIDRE, BORN WITH THE POWER TO **WIELD** IT!
DO THEY, **PRINCE NALLORATH?!**
I'M **HALF-HUMAN...** OR HAD YOU--IN ALL YOUR SPOILED ELVEN ROYALNESS-- **FORGOTTEN?!**
CARE TO **TEST** THAT THEORY AGAINST **ME...?!**
KRAKLE
KRAKLE
FRZZZAAK

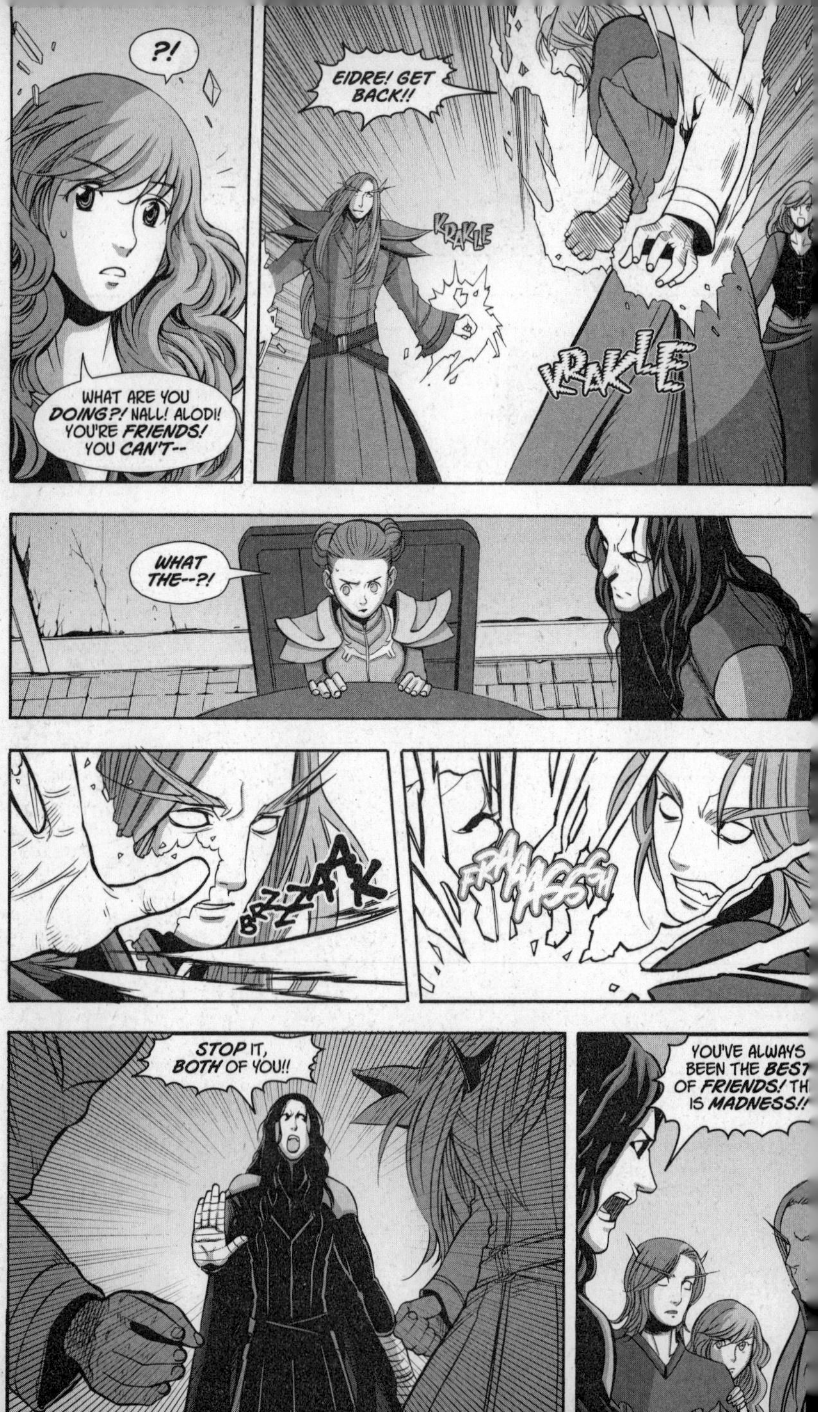
?!
WHAT ARE YOU DOING?! NALL! ALODI! YOU'RE FRIENDS! YOU CAN'T--
EIDRE! GET BACK!!
KRAKLE
KRAKLE
WHAT THE--?!
BRZZAAK
STOP IT, BOTH OF YOU!!
YOU'VE ALWAYS BEEN THE BEST OF FRIENDS! TH IS MADNESS!!

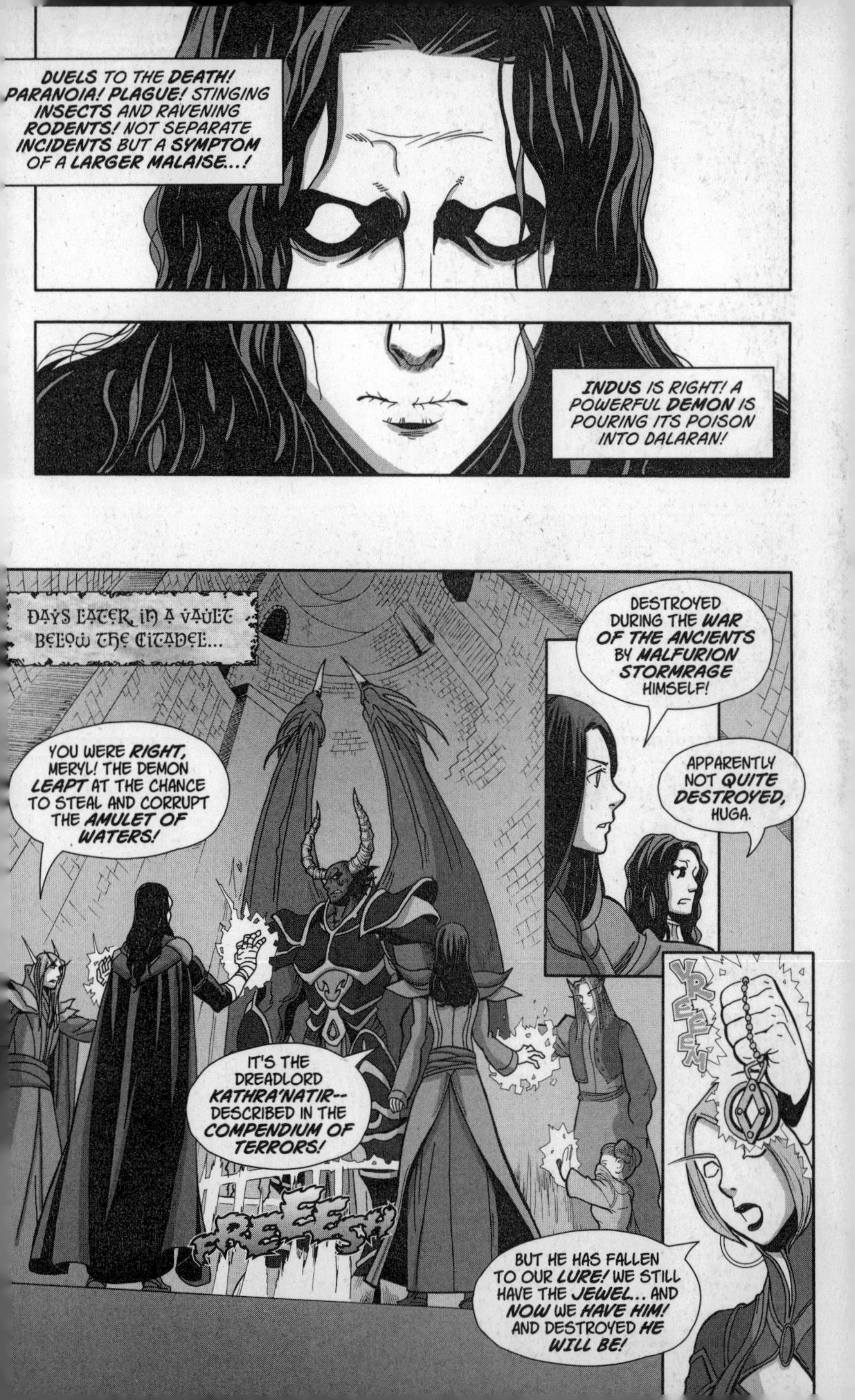

DUELS TO THE DEATH! PARANOIA! PLAGUE! STINGING INSECTS AND RAVENING RODENTS! NOT SEPARATE INCIDENTS BUT A SYMPTOM OF A LARGER MALAISE...!
INDUS IS RIGHT! A POWERFUL DEMON IS POURING ITS POISON INTO DALARAN!
DAYS LATER, IN A VAULT BELOW THE CITADEL...
YOU WERE RIGHT, MERYL! THE DEMON LEAPT AT THE CHANCE TO STEAL AND CORRUPT THE AMULET OF WATERS!
IT'S THE DREADLORD KATHRA'NATIR-- DESCRIBED IN THE COMPENDIUM OF TERRORS!
DESTROYED DURING THE WAR OF THE ANCIENTS BY MALFURION STORMRAGE HIMSELF!
APPARENTLY NOT QUITE DESTROYED, HUGA.
VREEEM
BUT HE HAS FALLEN TO OUR LURE! WE STILL HAVE THE JEWEL... AND NOW WE HAVE HIM! AND DESTROYED HE WILL BE!

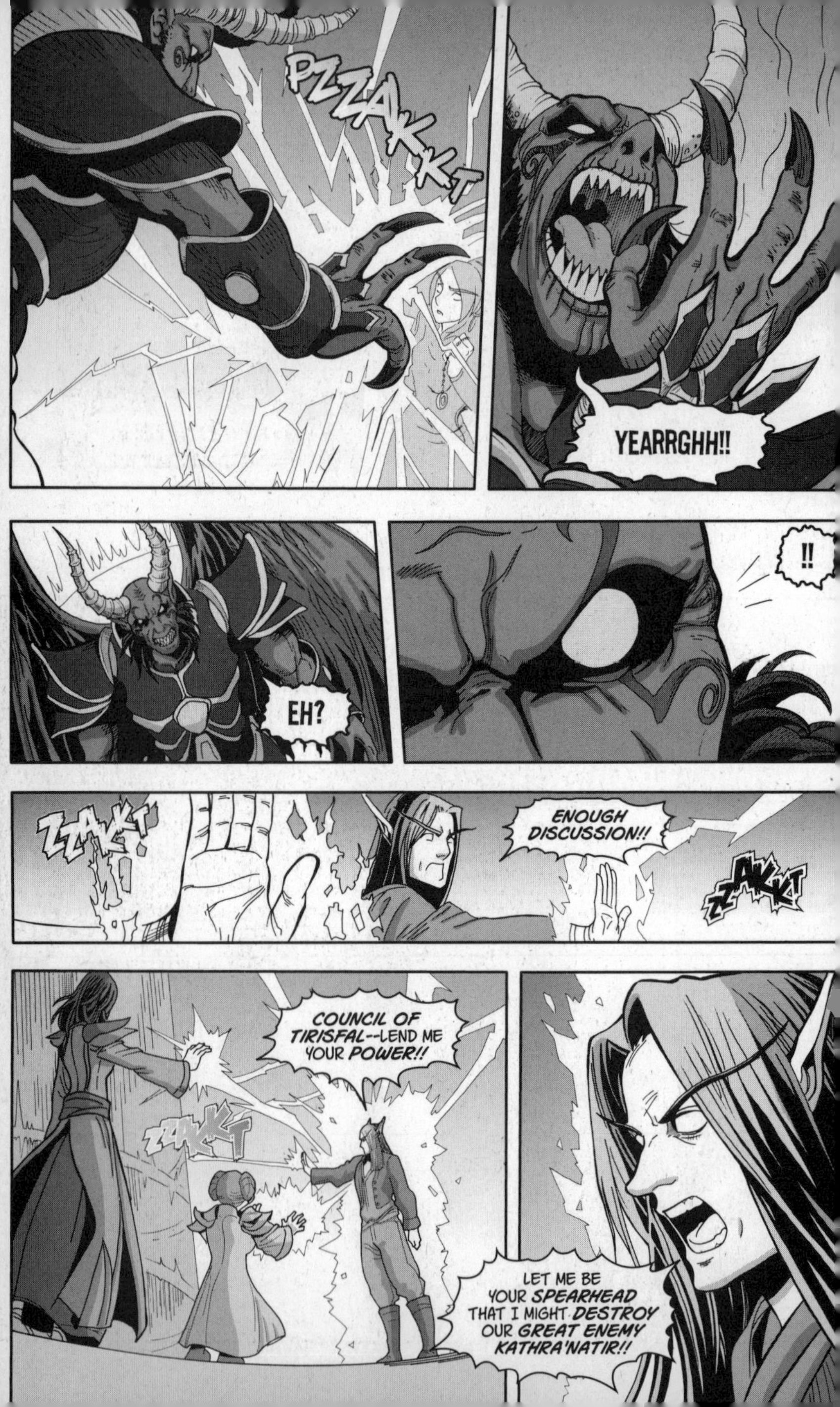
PZZAKKT
YEARRGHH!!
EH?
!!
ZZAKT
ENOUGH DISCUSSION!!
ZZAKKT
COUNCIL OF TIRISFAL--LEND ME YOUR POWER!!
ZZAKKT
LET ME BE YOUR SPEARHEAD THAT I MIGHT DESTROY OUR GREAT ENEMY KATHRA'NATIR!!

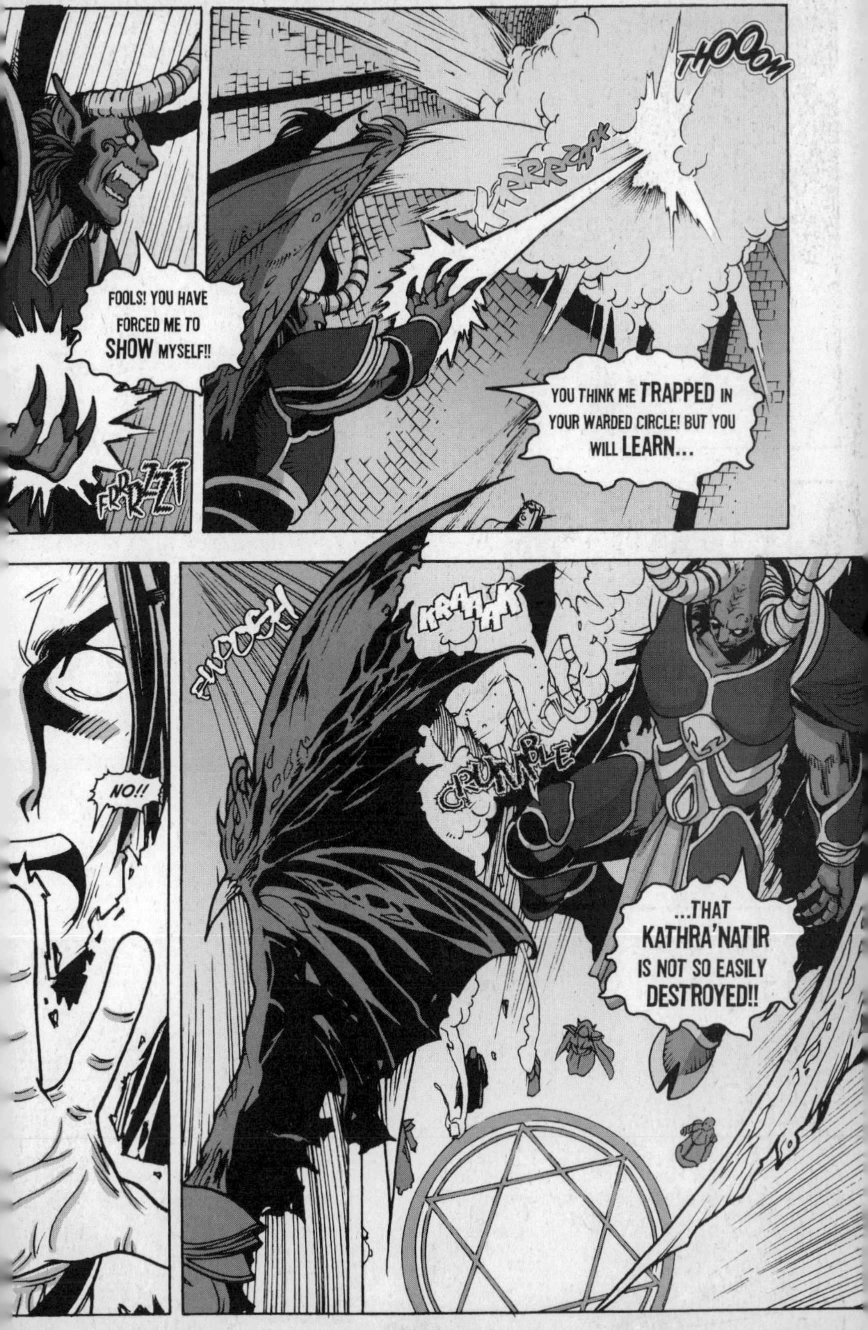
THOOOM
KRRRZAAK
FOOLS! YOU HAVE FORCED ME TO SHOW MYSELF!!
FRRRZZT
YOU THINK ME TRAPPED IN YOUR WARDED CIRCLE! BUT YOU WILL LEARN...
NO!!
FWOOOSH
KRAAAAK
CRUMBLE
...THAT KATHRA'NATIR IS NOT SO EASILY DESTROYED!!

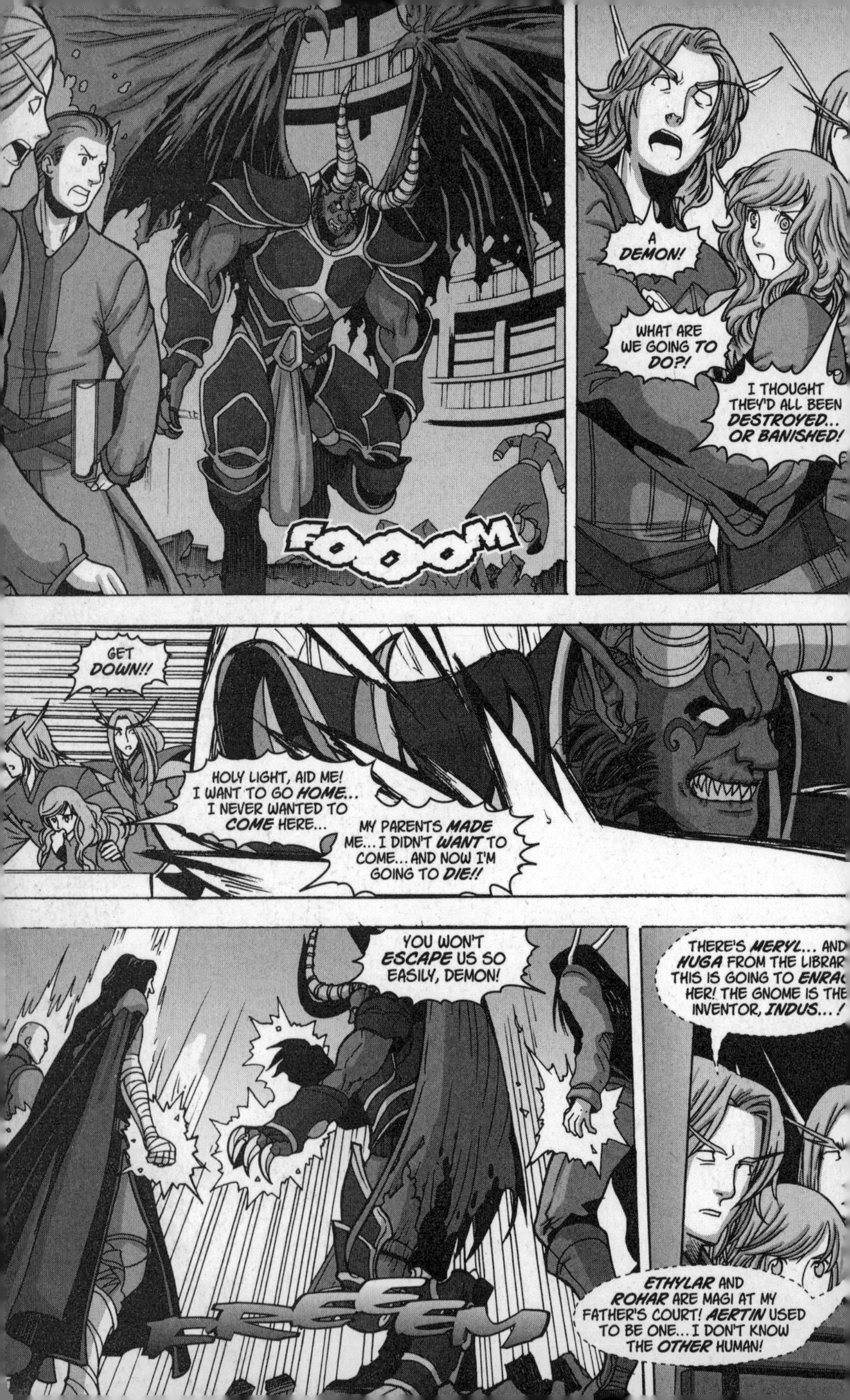
FOOOM
A DEMON!
WHAT ARE WE GOING TO DO?!
I THOUGHT THEY'D ALL BEEN DESTROYED... OR BANISHED!
GET DOWN!!
HOLY LIGHT, AID ME! I WANT TO GO HOME... I NEVER WANTED TO COME HERE...
MY PARENTS MADE ME... I DIDN'T WANT TO COME... AND NOW I'M GOING TO DIE!!
YOU WON'T ESCAPE US SO EASILY, DEMON!
THERE'S MERYL... AND HUGA FROM THE LIBRAR THIS IS GOING TO ENRA HER! THE GNOME IS THE INVENTOR, INDUS...!
ETHYLAR AND ROHAR ARE MAGI AT MY FATHER'S COURT! AERTIN USED TO BE ONE... I DON'T KNOW THE OTHER HUMAN!

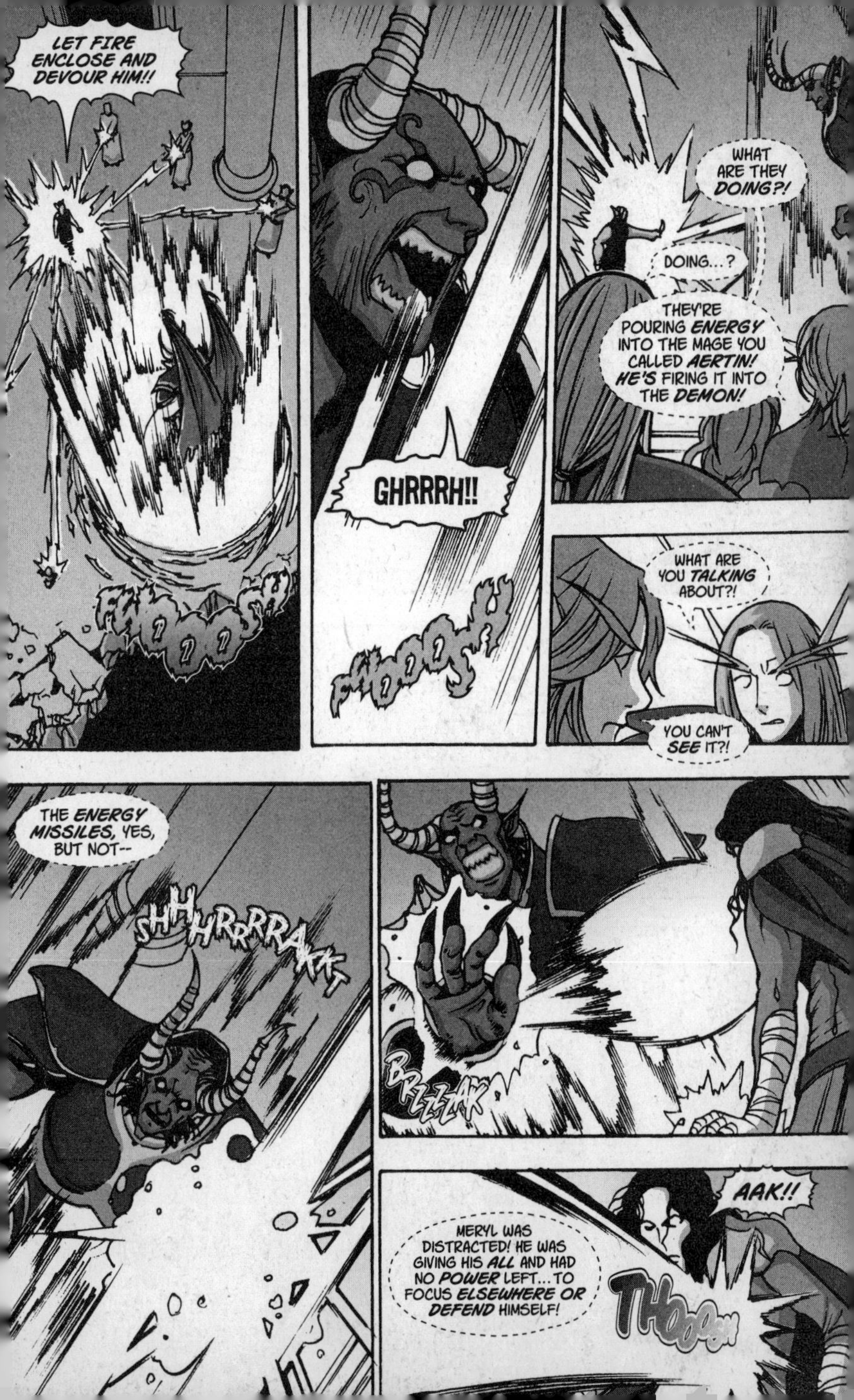
LET FIRE ENCLOSE AND DEVOUR HIM!!
FWOOOSH
GHRRRH!!
FWOOOSH
WHAT ARE THEY DOING?!
DOING...?
THEY'RE POURING ENERGY INTO THE MAGE YOU CALLED AERTIN! HE'S FIRING IT INTO THE DEMON!
WHAT ARE YOU TALKING ABOUT?!
YOU CAN'T SEE IT?!
THE ENERGY MISSILES, YES, BUT NOT--
SHHHRRRRAKKT
BRZZZAK
AAK!!
MERYL WAS DISTRACTED! HE WAS GIVING HIS ALL AND HAD NO POWER LEFT... TO FOCUS ELSEWHERE OR DEFEND HIMSELF!
THOOOSH

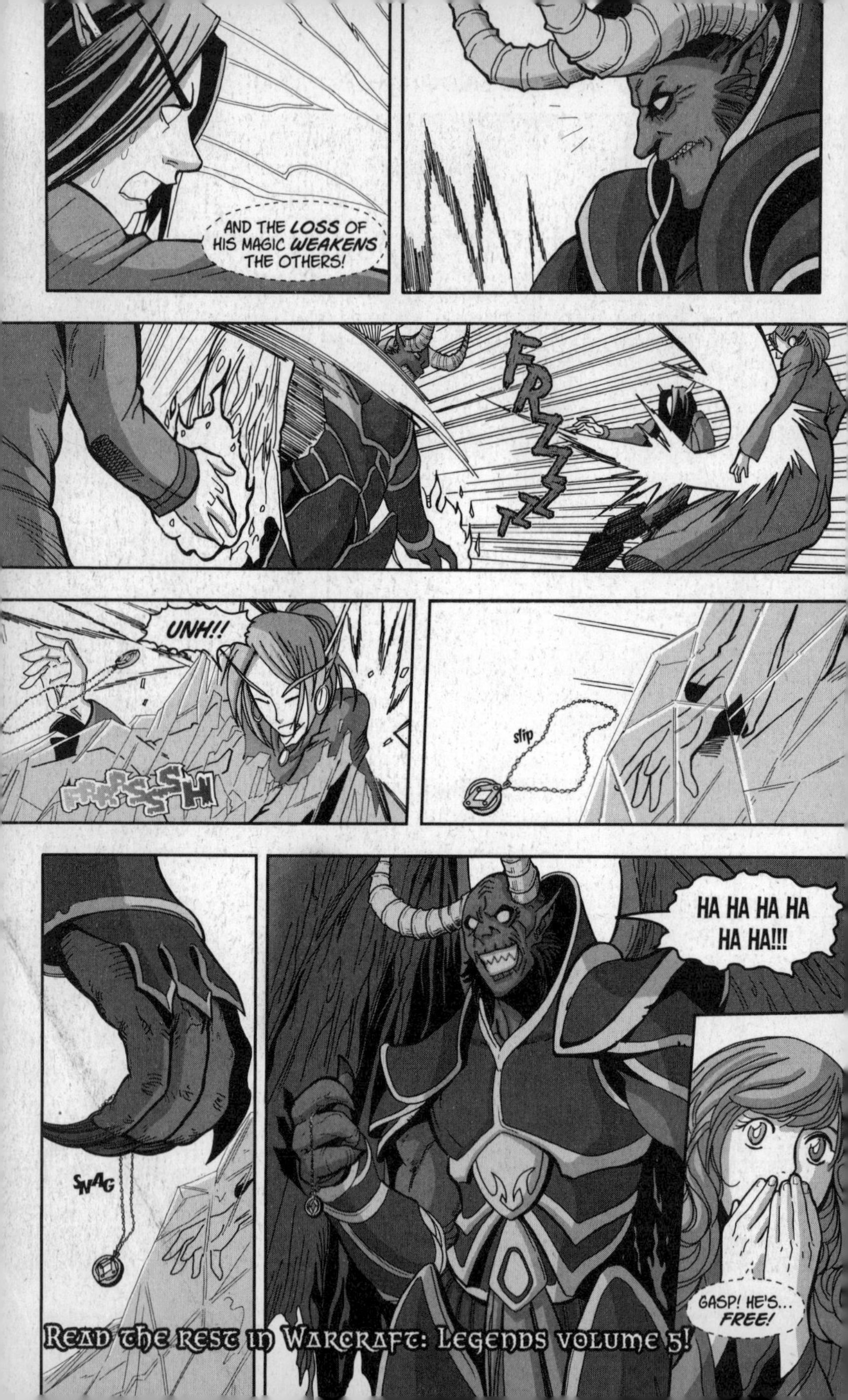
AND THE *LOSS* OF HIS MAGIC *WEAKENS* THE OTHERS!
FRZZZZT
UNH!!
FRRSSSH
slip
SNAG
HA HA HA HA HA HA!!!
GASP! HE'S... *FREE!*
Read the rest in Warcraft: Legends volume 5!

Stop Poking Me!

Lazy Peons

Quest

Orc Hero Required

Lazy Peons enters play exhausted.

Exhaust Lazy Peons to complete this quest.

Reward: Draw a card.

"Stop poking me!"

DARK PORTAL 303/319

Art by: Steve Ellis